The Causes of Peace

WHAT WE KNOW NOW

This book is the result of the 161st Nobel Symposium in 2016.

Published by:

NOBEL SYMPOSIUM
PROCEEDINGS

OSLO, NORWAY

THE CAUSES OF PEACE
What We Know Now

ISBN 978-1-5445-0504-6 *Paperback*
        978-1-5445-0505-3 *Hardcover*
        978-1-5445-0506-0 *ebook*

The Causes of Peace

WHAT WE KNOW NOW

Asle Toje and Bård Nikolas Vik Steen (eds.)

NOBEL SYMPOSIUM PROCEEDINGS, OSLO (PUBL.)

CONTENTS

CONTRIBUTORS   7

INTRODUCTION
Asle Toje and Bård Nikolas Vik Steen   15

Section I: Is the World Getting More Peaceful?   27
1. Systemic Trends in War and Peace
Bear F. Braumoeller   29

2. The Decline of Violent Conflicts: What Do the Data Really Say?
Nassim Nicholas Taleb and Pasquale Cirillo   57

Section II: Hegemony and Peace   87
3. The Quest for Hegemony: A Threat to the Global Order
Richard Ned Lebow and Simon Reich   89

4. Neoclassical Realism, Non-proliferation, and the Limits
of US Hegemony in the Middle East and South Asia
Jeffrey W. Taliaferro   113

Section III: Ideology and Peace   145
5. Ideology and Peace: Historical Perspectives
Niall Ferguson   147

6. The Paradox of American Diplomacy in the Cold War
Fredrik Logevall   173

Section IV: Democratic Peace 197

7. A Somewhat Personal History of the Democratic Peace
   and Its Expansion to the Kantian Peace
   Bruce Russett 199

8. The Democratic-Peace Debate
   Joanne Gowa and Tyler Pratt 221

Section V: Peace through Institutions 249

9. Can Domestic Institutions Destroy the International Order?
   Petr Kratochvíl 251

10. EU Institutions and Peace
    Mai'a K. Davis Cross 277

Section VI: Peace and Development 305

11. Fragile States and International Support
    Paul Collier 307

12. Peace through Security-Development:
    Nebulous Connections, Desirable Confluences?
    Maria Stern and Joakim Öjendal 329

Section VII: Deterrence and Disarmament 363

13. The Causes of Peace: The Role of Deterrence
    Bruno Tertrais 365

14. Disarmament: Cause, Consequence, or Early Warning
    Indicator of Peace?
    Paul F. Diehl 387

Section VIII: The Causes of Peace: The Statistical Evidence 413

15. The Causes of Peace and the Future of Peace
    Kristian Skrede Gleditsch 415

CONTRIBUTORS

Bear F. Braumoeller

Bear F. Braumoeller is professor of political science at The Ohio State University. He previously held faculty positions at Harvard University and the University of Illinois at Urbana-Champaign. He is, or has been, on the editorial boards of five major journals or series, and he is a past councillor of the Peace Science Society. Professor Braumoeller's research is in the areas of international relations, especially international security, and statistical methodology. His substantive research includes a book-length systemic theory of international relations, *The Great Powers and the International System* (2012), and his new book, *Only the Dead: The Persistence of War in the Modern Age*, will be published by Oxford University Press in 2019.

Pasquale Cirillo

Pasquale Cirillo is an associate professor of applied probability at Delft University of Technology (NL). He specializes in risk and extreme value statistics, with applications to the social sciences. He received his Venia Docendi (Habilitation) in applied statistics from the University of Bern (CH) and his PhD in statistics from Bocconi University (IT). As a consultant, he has collaborated with international institutions such as the World Bank. (www.pasqualecirillo.eu)

Paul Collier

Paul Collier is professor of economics and public policy at the Blavatnik

School of Government, and a professorial fellow of St Antony's College, University of Oxford. He was the founding director of the Centre for the Study of African Economies, also at Oxford. From 1998 to 2003 he took public service leave, during which time he was director of the Research Development Department of the World Bank. He also serves on the Economic Advisory Board of the International Finance Corporation and is a director of the International Growth Centre. His research covers the causes and consequences of civil war, the effects of aid, and the problems of democracy in low-income and natural-resources-rich societies. In 2014, Professor Collier received a knighthood for services to promoting research and policy change in Africa.

Mai'a K. Davis Cross

Mai'a K. Davis Cross is the Edward W. Brooke Professor and associate professor of political science and international affairs at Northeastern University. She holds a PhD in politics from Princeton University and a bachelor's degree in government from Harvard University. She is the author of three books, the most recent of which is *The Politics of Crisis in Europe* (Cambridge University Press, 2017).

Paul F. Diehl

Paul F. Diehl is the Ashbel Smith Professor of political science at the University of Texas at Dallas. Previously, he was Henning Larsen Professor of Political Science at the University of Illinois at Urbana-Champaign. He is co-author most recently of *The Puzzle of Peace* (Oxford University Press, 2016) and past president of the International Studies Association and the Peace Science Society (International), respectively.

Niall Ferguson

Niall Ferguson is a senior fellow at the Hoover Institution, Stanford University, a senior fellow of the Center for European Studies at Harvard University, and a visiting professor at Tsinghua University, Beijing. He is the author of fifteen books, including *Empire: The Rise and Demise of the British World Order and the Lessons for Global Power* (2003), *The War of the World: History's Age of Hatred* (2006), *The Ascent of Money: A Financial History of the World* (2008), and *High Financier: The Lives and Time of Siegmund*

Warburg (2010). His most recent publications are *Kissinger, 1923–1968: The Idealist* (2015) and *The Square and the Tower* (2017).

Kristian Skrede Gleditsch

Kristian Skrede Gleditsch is Regius Professor of political science, University of Essex, and research associate, Peace Research Institute Oslo. His research interests include conflict and cooperation, democratization, and mobilization. He is the author, with Lars-Erik Cederman and Halvard Buhaug, of *Inequality, Grievances, and Civil War* (Cambridge University Press, 2013) and *All International Politics Is Local* (University of Michigan Press, 2002).

Joanne Gowa

Joanne Gowa is the William P. Boswell Professor of world politics of peace and war at Princeton University. She is the author of *Closing the Gold Window: Domestic Politics and the End of Bretton Woods*; *Allies, Adversaries, and International Trade*; *Ballots and Bullets: The Elusive Democratic Peace* (Princeton University Press, 2011); and articles about political economy and democracy and disputes. She is a trustee of Tufts University.

Petr Kratochvíl

Petr Kratochvíl is professor of international relations and a senior researcher at the Institute of International Relations, Prague. He is the chairman of the Academic Council of the Diplomatic Academy of the Ministry of Foreign Affairs of the Czech Republic as well as a member of a range of academic and scientific councils. Petr Kratochvíl represents the Institute of International Relations (IIR) in various international associations, such as the Trans European Policy Studies Association and the European Consortium for Political Research. He has published extensively on European integration, EU-Russian relations, institutional reform and EU enlargement, the role of religion in international affairs, and international relations theory.

Richard Ned Lebow

Richard Ned Lebow is professor of international political theory in the War Studies Department of King's College London, Bye-Fellow of Pembroke College, University of Cambridge, and the James O. Freedman Presidential Professor Emeritus of government at Dartmouth College, Hanover, US.

He is a fellow of the British Academy. He has published thirty-four books and more than 300 peer-reviewed articles and chapters. Recent books include *The Rise and Fall of Political Orders* (Cambridge University Press, 2018), *Max Weber and International Relations* (Cambridge University Press, 2017), and *Avoiding War, Making Peace* (Palgrave-Macmillan, 2018).

Fredrik Logevall

Fredrik Logevall is the Laurence D. Belfer Professor of international affairs and history at Harvard University. He is the author or editor of nine books, most recently *Embers of War: The Fall of an Empire and the Making of America's Vietnam* (Random House, 2012), which won the 2013 Pulitzer Prize for History and the 2013 Francis Parkman Prize, awarded by the Society of American Historians to the book that 'exemplifies the union of the historian and the artist'. It also received the 2013 American Library in Paris Book Award and the 2013 Arthur Ross Book Award from the Council on Foreign Relations. Logevall's commentary has been featured on BBC, CBS, CNN, and National Public Radio, and his reviews and essays have appeared in *The New York Times*, *The Washington Post*, the *Los Angeles Times*, *Politico*, and *Foreign Affairs*, among other publications.

Joakim Öjendal

Joakim Öjendal is a professor in peace and development studies at the School of Global Studies, Gothenburg University, Sweden. For more than two decades, he has been doing research on peacebuilding, democratization, and post-conflict reconstruction. Among his resent books are the *Routledge Handbook of Environmental Conflict and Peacebuilding* (Routledge, 2018) and *Politics and Development in a Transboundary Watershed: The Case of the Lower Mekong Basin* (Springer, 2012).

Tyler Pratt

Tyler Pratt is an assistant professor in the Department of Political Science at Yale University. He holds a PhD in politics from Princeton University and a bachelor's degree in international affairs from the University of Georgia. His work has been published in *International Organization*. His research interests include international cooperation, global governance, and network analysis. He previously worked in diplomacy and intelligence.

Simon Reich

Simon Reich is a professor in the Division of Global Affairs and Department of Political Science at Rutgers, Newark. He has authored or edited eleven books, most recently *The End of Grand Strategy: US Maritime Operations in the Twenty-First Century* with Peter Dombrowski (Cornell University Press, 2018). Reich's twelfth book will be a co-edited volume, *Comparative Grand Strategy in the Modern Age* with Thierry Balzacq and Peter Dombrowski (Oxford University Press, 2019). Reich previously served as director of research and analysis at the Royal Institute for International Affairs in London.

Bruce Russett

Bruce Russett gained his PhD from Yale University in 1961 and is Dean Acheson Research Professor of international relations and political science at Yale. He is a fellow of the American Academy of Arts and Sciences and has honorary doctorates from Uppsala University, Sweden (2002), and Williams College, Massachusetts, US (2011). A past president of the International Studies Association and of the Peace Science Society (International), of his twenty-seven books, recent ones include *Grasping the Democratic Peace* (Princeton University Press, 1993); *The Once and Future Security Council* (Palgrave Macmillan, 1997); and, with John Oneal, *Triangulating Peace: Democracy, Interdependence, and International Organizations* (W. W. Norton & Company, 2001), which was awarded the International Studies Association's prize for Best Book of the Decade 2000–2009; and *Hegemony and Democracy* (Routledge, 2011).

Bård Nikolas Vik Steen

Bård Nikolas Vik Steen is the Programme Manager of the Norwegian Nobel Institute. Steen received his education from Durham University and the University of Oslo. His current research interests include nuclear disarmament and the relationship between geopolitics, hegemonic change, and war. His latest publications include *Nuclear Disarmament: A Critical Assessment* (Routledge, 2019), co-edited with Olav Njølstad.

Maria Stern

Maria Stern is professor in peace and development studies at the School of Global Studies, Gothenburg University, Sweden. For more than two decades she has been conducting research on security, development, war, and gender. She has written and co-edited books and special journal issues on the topics of security, methodology, conflict-related sexual violence, militarism, and the security-development nexus. Additionally, she has published widely in leading international academic journals.

Nassim Nicholas Taleb

Nassim Nicholas Taleb spent twenty-one years as a trader and practitioner of mathematical finance and complex derivatives before becoming a researcher in mathematical and practical problems with probability, particularly extreme events. Taleb is the author of a multivolume essay, the *Incerto: The Black Swan* (Penguin, 2008), *Fooled by Randomness* (Penguin, 2007), *Antifragile* (Penguin, 2013), and *Skin in the Game* (Penguin, 2018), covering broad facets of uncertainty. It has more than 110 translations into thirty-six languages. Taleb, in his second career, has produced, as a backup of the *Incerto*, more than seventy scholarly papers in statistical physics, statistics, philosophy, ethics, economics, international affairs, and quantitative finance, all around the notion of risk and probability. He is currently Distinguished Professor of risk engineering at NYU's Tandon School of Engineering and principal of the Real World Risk Institute, LLC. His current focus is on the properties of systems that can handle disorder (antifragile) and a program for statistical inference under fat tails.

Jeffrey W. Taliaferro

Jeffrey W. Taliaferro is associate professor of political science at Tufts University, in Medford, Massachusetts. He is the author of *Balancing Risks: Great Power Intervention in the Periphery* (Cornell University Press, 2004), which won the Robert Jervis-Paul Schroeder Prize in International History and Politics. He is co-author, with Norrin M. Ripsman and Steven E. Lobell, of *Neoclassical Realist Theory of International Politics* (Oxford University Press, 2016) and co-editor, also with Ripsman and Lobell, of *The Challenge of Grand Strategy* (Cambridge University Press, 2012) and of *Neoclassical Realism, the State, and Foreign Policy* (Cambridge University Press, 2009). He is currently writing a book on alliance coercion in US foreign policy.

Bruno Tertrais

Bruno Tertrais has been a senior research fellow at the Fondation pour la Recherche Stratégique since 2001. His areas of expertise include geopolitics and international relations; military and nuclear issues; and security in Europe, the Middle East, and Asia. He was previously special assistant to the director of strategic affairs at the French Ministry of Defense (1993–2001); visiting fellow at the RAND Corporation (1995–1996); and director of the Civilian Affairs Committee at the NATO Parliamentary Assembly (1990–1993). He was a member of the two commissions on the NATO White Paper on Defence and National Security (2007 and 2012). He is an associate editor of *Survival* and a member of the editorial boards of *The Washington Quarterly* and *Strategic & Military Affairs*. In 2010, he received the Vauban Prize for his distinguished career. In 2014, he was awarded the Legion of Honour. A graduate of the Institut d'études politiques de Paris (1984), he holds a master's in public law (1985), a doctorate in political science (1994), as well as a *habilitation à diriger des recherches* (1994).

Asle Toje

Asle Toje is the former research director at the Norwegian Nobel Institute. He has a PhD in International Studies from the University of Cambridge (2006). Among his lastest works are *America, the EU and Strategic Culture* (Routledge, 2008); *The European Union as a Small Power* (Macmillan, 2010); *Neoclassical Realism in Europe* (Manchester University Press 2012); and *Will China's Rise Be Peaceful?: The Rise of a Great Power in Theory, History, Politics, and the Future* (Oxford University Press, 2018). Toje is a serving member of the Norwegian Nobel Committee.

INTRODUCTION

Asle Toje and Bård Nikolas Vik Steen

In a letter dated 7 January 1893, Alfred Nobel wrote to his long-time friend Bertha von Suttner, 'I should like to dispose of a part of my fortune by founding a prize to be granted every five years—say six times, for if in thirty years they have not succeeded in reforming the present system they will infallibly relapse into barbarism.'

'I am not speaking to you of disarmament, which can be achieved only very slowly; I am not even speaking to you of obligatory arbitration between nations. But this result ought to be reached soon—and it can be attained—to which all states shall with solidarity agree to turn against the first aggressor. Then wars will become impossible. The result would be to force even the most quarrelsome state to have recourse to a tribunal or else remain peaceful. If [such an alliance] enlist all states, the peace of the centuries would be assured.'[1]

The idea of collective security was at the heart of the League of Nations system, initiated in 1920. The participants agreed that any breach of the peace was to be declared a concern to all the participating states and would result in a collective response.[2] However, the attempt at a global security system built on collective security failed comprehensively. In 1895, two years after the letter where Alfred Nobel floated the idea of a Nobel Peace Prize, he wrote his testament in Paris. Here Nobel appeared less certain regarding the causes of peace. He stipulated that the prize should be given to '[...]

the person who shall have done the most or the best work for fraternity between nations, for the abolition or reduction of standing armies and for the holding and promotion of peace congresses.'[3]

This roughly coincides with the three causal pathways pursued by contemporary peace scholarship—the societal conditions favourable to peace and the institutions and disarmament that underpin stability and individual efforts to end war. In some ways the trends in peace and conflict studies and the Nobel Peace Prize have progressed abreast over the 118 years that have passed since the prize was first awarded in 1901. The focus on arbitration and the peace congresses of the early 20th century gradually shifted towards greater emphasis on strategic stability and 'keeping the darkness at bay' during the Cold War. The years following the end of the Cold War have seen renewed interest in the causes of peace, buoyed by new political possibilities and an expansion in scholarship on the topic.

The causes of war and peace remain among the most contested questions in the study of not only international politics, but of human affairs in general. Research has been carried out by historians, philosophers, and social scientists that has increased our knowledge, with a baffling array of theories that attempt to explain peace in theory and practice. They span from the relative relevance of domestic and international institutions to human psychology, economic incentives and technology, to the logic of democracy and sovereignty. Perhaps surprisingly, however, these various strains have rarely been brought together in order to attempt to establish an overview of the present 'state of the art'.

While debates rage within research communities, different schools of thought are rarely brought into direct contact with each other. That is a shame; fruitful debates tend to take place between those who agree on the fundamentals. Disagreements over methods, emphasis, empirical material, and even the very concept of peace, have left potentially complimentary research traditions estranged. This book is an attempt to help bridge this gap and establish a shared platform from which the study of peace may progress.

First, however, let us start with the fundamentals: What is peace? The

Swedish term used by Alfred Nobel, *Frid* (peace), has various meanings etymologically, the main one being *Friðr*, meaning 'not war'.[4] This is the most common use of the word, which skirts the many other levels of strife, exploitation, and violence that occur within and among states. Although the concept of peace was at the heart of early enquires into International Relations, during the Cold War it was ousted to the margins of the discipline, which subsequently saw the emergence of the separate sub-discipline of Peace Studies.

The lines of communication between academia and practitioners have often been hampered by a micro-macro divide where case studies are often difficult to translate into more general insights, and vice versa. Research generally gives few straightforward answers to the most acute questions concerning peace and war. The challenge, as AJP Taylor pointed out in reference to the causes of World War I, is that the great armies, the secret diplomacy, and the balance of power were the same as those that had given Europe the long period of peace prior to 1914.[5] The search for a singular theory of peace, therefore, resembles what Alasdair MacIntyre disparagingly referred to as the quest for a 'general theory of holes'.[6]

The theorization of peace has largely been a by-product of the theorization of war. The causes-of-war literature is rich in meta-level concepts seeking to grasp the reasons behind organized armed conflicts. These include focus on structure and agency; opportunity and willingness; grievances and mobilization; resources and interests; capabilities and intentions; depravation and governance; greed and resentment; capabilities and resolve.[7] A main division long persisted between 'old school' and 'new school' approaches. Old school uses interstate approaches—focusing on high politics and formal power. New school approaches often focus on intrastate conflict and the role of non-government actors, as well as the role of irregular forces, sexual violence, economic grievances, and so on.

A characteristic of Peace Studies as an academic sub-discipline is that peace is not just the absence of war—negative peace—but also the establishment of life-affirming values and structures, what is known as 'positive peace'. Scholars such as Johan Galtung see negative peace as a necessary, but not sufficient, condition for positive peace, defined as 'the integration of human society'.[8] In a philosophical sense, this view of peace is what mathematicians call *asymptotic*—something that may be approached, but never fully achieved. Likewise, a lack of positive peace can make the absence of negative peace more likely, but war can also reduce structural grievances. One could, for instance, think of cases where war can strengthen the societal standing of marginalized groups through military service, thereby fostering positive peace.

In sum, attempts to the contrary have, in practice, not delivered in added insights what is lost in clarity and parsimony in the war-peace dichotomy. For that reason we will, unless otherwise stated, rely on the definition of war employed by the Uppsala Conflict Data Program (UCDP), where it is defined as 'a contested incompatibility that concerns government and/or territory over which the use of armed force between the military forces of two parties, of which at least one is the government of a state, has resulted in at least 25 battle-related deaths each year'. Battle-related deaths refer to those deaths caused by the warring parties that can directly be related to combat over the contested incompatibility.[9]

The concept of peace has spawned a large body of literature seeking to delineate the ways to create a more peaceful world, yet there has been a great deal of competition between the adherents of the various approaches. This lack of coherence is even more pronounced when casting even a casual glance over the full body of peace scholarship. Communication among the various academic perspectives has either been disrupted or was never established in the first place. As a result, most scholars pursue a single perspective or, more frequently, drift between various research perspectives, unaware of their history and relationship to other traditions.

Key aspects of the book

Surely, one might ask, there have been endeavours to collect a bird's-eye view of the state of the art? In fact, there are many separate traditions, each with their own overview of what peace and conflict studies looks like. Delving into each goes beyond the scope of any single volume. The goal of our endeavour is therefore not to provide a comprehensive reader of peace and conflict studies. Rather, we take a targeted approach, with eight sections, spanning eight of the most fruitful points of entry into the causes of peace. After a discussion of whether the world is in fact getting more peaceful, we consider the influence of hegemony; ideology; democracy; institutions; development; deterrence; and disarmament, before finally considering the causes of declining political violence from a statistical perspective.

Section I begins with the claim that an 'upward surge of humanity' has made wars less frequent and destructive. Popularised by Steven Pinker and his seminal book *The Better Angels of our Nature*, 'the decline of war thesis' has recently become influential in both academia and in popular culture.[10] That does not mean Pinker is without his detractors. In chapter 1, Bear F. Braumoeller takes a sceptical view and argues that the lack of appropriate statistical tests makes it difficult to distinguish the noise from actual proof of progress. He finds little support for the idea that war has declined after the end of the Cold War and argues instead that variations in the international situation account for fluctuations in conflict frequency.

In chapter 2, Pasquale Cirillo and Nassim Nicholas Taleb support and expand on Braumoeller's conclusions. By setting out a new approach on the basis of 'extra value theory', they provide a methodology robust to the often-imprecise measurements of extreme events. Cirillo and Taleb find scant support for what John Lewis Gaddis famously termed 'the long peace'. Instead, they conclude that the decline of war thesis is the result of methodological inaccuracies, with results fragile to minor errors of measurement.

While confidence in the decline of war thesis has flourished over the past decade, these chapters underscore just how far from settled that argument is. Still, that does nothing to undermine the primary undertaking of this volume: what causes peace? Whether it is simple or nearly impossible, the path to peace will always remain among humanity's greatest concerns. By focusing on the most influential traditions attempting to illuminate the path, we hope to reveal the contours of the state of the art and provide a new baseline from which research may flourish.

Section II starts the search by training the spotlight on one of the grand debates of security studies: that of hegemonic stability—does hegemony make sense and, if so, does it foster peace? For Richard Ned Lebow and Simon Reich, the answer is a resounding 'no' to both questions. Taking issue with the influence of arguments claiming that America's hegemonic role in world politics fosters peace and stability, they argue instead that American hegemony has contributed significantly to global instability. Viewing this state of affairs as not only detrimental to global interests, but to the interests of the United States (US), Lebow and Reich conclude by sketching an alternative path for the future of American foreign policy.

In chapter 4, Jeffrey W. Taliaferro continues the assessment of hegemony by considering the real magnitude of US influence. Noting that US officials view limiting the spread of nuclear weapons as critical to regional stability, he investigates the United States' ability to convince allies to restrain or halt their nuclear weapons programmes. Investigating the Nixon administration's response to the Israeli nuclear programme as well as the Carter and Reagan administration's efforts toward Pakistan, the evidence is found to match neoclassical realist predictions. Taliaferro reveals that the US's influence toward an issue that its leaders considers critical to the preservation of peace is considerably less potent than the hegemonic stability thesis might suggest.

Looking elsewhere for a viable path to peace, Niall Ferguson and Fredrik Logevall discuss one of the most disputed questions within International Relations in Section III: what impact does ideology have on maintaining peace? Ferguson starts the discussion by investigating the collision between idealist proclamations of peace and the attempts of statesmen to deliver upon them. Focusing on the career of Henry Kissinger, he traces the development of a sophisticated doctrine of 'peacemaking' during Kissinger's tenure and considers its connection to the subsequent decline of organized violence. Ferguson defends Kissinger's idealistic pragmatism and illustrates how idealism must combine with realism to yield optimal results. While he does not see solutions in a blind pursuit of peace, nor in realist cynicism without hope or ambition, Ferguson views their combination as ideal for making lasting contributions to global stability.

Fredrik Logevall agrees that strength is best paired with good diplomacy, but takes a somewhat broader approach. Studying the impact of ideas through the lens of American foreign policy during the Cold War, he notes how American deterrence policies are rarely paired with diplomatic action. In his view, an overreliance on tough talk on the American campaign trail has limited the scope for diplomacy, leaving untapped opportunities to further both national security and global peace efforts. Leaders who dare to question a logic where compromise is seen as weakness, have often left office with their presidential legacies improved.

Section IV turns the spotlight to what Jack Levy once characterised as 'the closest thing to an empirical law in international relations'.[11] Bruce Russett, one of the central figures in the development of the democratic peace thesis, opens the discussion in chapter seven, providing an authoritative and personal account of the theory's path from obscurity to universal wisdom as well as its later expansion into the Kantian peace. Having delivered a definitive account of the logic and evidence that shaped so much of his illustrious career, Russett remains confident that 'the democratic peace has been heavily criticized, but not overturned'.

Joanne Gowa and Tyler Pratt confirm that the democratic peace thesis has a unique position in both the academe and the halls of power. However, having noted the scepticism of Erik Gartzke and Steven Pinker, as well as troubling variations in the relevant data, they remain unconvinced that Russet's confidence is warranted. Reanalysing the data while controlling for variations in the international system, they find that the connection between democracy and peace is severely weakened. Showing that dispute rates fluctuate over time, they argue that the changes in conflict propensity are the result of changes in the international system rather than of regime type. The democratic peace having long been recognised as the strongest empirical regularity in international relations—an old debate has been reopened.

Section V shifts focus yet again but stays within the Kantian peace triangle. While the connection between international organisations and peace has been discussed since the days of Immanuel Kant, it has become a constant talking point with the European Union's perpetual challenges and the political chaos following Britain's decision to leave. Continuing this path of inquest in chapter 9, Petr Kratochvil gives an introduction to the state of institutionalist literature and notes the neglected influence of domestic institutions and the domestic roots of international norms. Making a first attempt to revive this 'second image' perspective, Kratochvil reveals how international organisations are influenced by domestic institutions through four mechanisms: re-socialization, reversed nesting, agenda replacement, and institutional isomorphism, casting the pacifying impact of international institutions in a new light and opening a new academic landscape for discussion.

Sympathetic to the idea that the international system is experiencing a 'long peace', Mai'a Davis Cross picks up the institutional mantle in chapter 10 by investigating how and why the institutions of the European Union have contributed to the establishment and maintenance of peace. Drawing a line back to the influence of ideology, she provides an institutionalist argument, claiming that the sharing of ideas has been central to the way in which EU institutions have shaped the peace in Europe. Introducing the major schools of thought as well as recent archival research, Cross attributes significance to the federalist movement, which she views as being both the central driver of European integration and the EU's contribution to peace.

In section VI, attention shifts to consider the vast sums spent to insulate the less fortunate against the horrors of war. Doyen of developmental economics Paul Collier turns his attention to what he views as the most important remaining development challenge—'fragile states'—where limited government capacity renders society vulnerable to collapse and conflict. Collier argues that only states with a non-predatory social order are capable of development. In his view, idealistic western overemphasis on the introduction of multi-party democracy has therefore not only hampered development but has been detrimental to both development and peace. If free elections are held too soon, as in Iraq, Collier argues that the non-predatory order necessary to avoid a return to instability and conflict becomes difficult to achieve. Thus, in clear opposition to recent policy, Collier concludes by urging a more pragmatic approach to development, where the focus on democracy is relaxed.

Maria Stern and Joakim Öjendal consider the impact of development on the preservation of peace by exploring the efficiency of peacebuilding in post-conflict societies. Following a conceptual exploration of peace, development, and security, they consider the problems inherent to peacebuilding. Delivering a powerful critique, Stern and Öjendal show how the peace, development and security nexus has failed to deliver on the promise of post-conflict peacebuilding. They conclude that an over-reliance on this approach becomes too de-contextualized to succeed, and even suggest that the chances of ever delivering on the promise of peacekeeping using the security-development nexus are slim.

Section VII considers two, depending on perspective, complimentary or competing scholarly traditions dealing with the force of arms: deterrence and disarmament as paths to peace. In chapter 13, Bruno Tertrais considers the impact of deterrence on the recent absence of great power warfare. Tertrais recognises both the statistical controversies noted at the beginning of this book and the alternative explanation offered by Pinker, but considers them unsatisfactory explanations for the absence of wars against, and between, states in possession of nuclear weapons. Concerned that the 74-year absence of conflict between the great powers might end without the presence of a nuclear deterrent, Tertrais urges significant caution in attempting disarmament.

Paul F. Diehl flips the coin and tries to disentangle the relationship between peace and nuclear disarmament. Noting the large number of Nobel laureates among disarmament activists, he attempts to determine the direction of causality—does disarmament promote peace or does peace promote disarmament? Do fewer weapons reduce the risk of war, or is the number of weapons reduced as a result of a reduced risk of war? Considering the existing literature and the relatively limited empirical data on disarmament, Diehl finds no solid evidence to suggest that disarmament promotes peace. While careful to note that both the evidence and the existing research suffer from serious flaws, he considers such claims to be the result of 'wishful thinking' and echoes Tertrais's warning that disarmament might not deliver on its peaceful promise.

Section VIII concludes this book by considering arguably the most fraught and contentious question of them all: what makes peace last? In chapter 15, Kristian Skrede Gleditsch argues that much of the evidence points toward greater political accommodation. Gleditsch finds that political inclusion significantly decreases the motivation to use violence while political opportunity improves the number of alternatives to it. He concludes his chapter and this book with a discussion of the prospects of future progress. Given the number of promising pathways discussed in this book, it is only fitting that he is optimistic. Positive trends relating to group-accommodation and political democracy, as well as the lack of a reversal in conflict trends after the Cold War, provide ample reason to believe that the current state of relative tranquility will continue, and even improve.

It is our hope that this book will provide a useful summing up of the research on the patterns of peace and conflict and that our collective effort will be of help to students, scholars, policymakers, and the general public. If, by having succeeded in answering some questions, we have created new ones, that is all the more welcome. Our final—and most important— ambition is to put forth a good read. As editors, our goal with this book is to give readers some pleasant moments while giving them new perspectives and insights on one of the most pressing questions of contemporary international politics. In order to encourage a global readership, we have chosen to self-publish the book, thereby keeping costs to the reader low.

Notes

1. Bertha von Suttner, *Memoirs of Bertha von Suttner: the Records of an Eventful Life* (Boston: Published for the International School of Peace [by] Ginn and Co., 1910), 438–39.

2. League of Nations, *The Covenant of the League of Nations* (Montreal: A.T. Chapman, 1919).

3. Ragnar Sohlman and Guy de Faramond, *L'héritage d'Alfred Nobel: le Testament À L'origine Des Prix* (Paris: M. de Maule, 2008).

4. Harald Bjorvand and Fredrik Otto Lindeman, *Våre Arveord: Etymologisk Ordbok* (Oslo: Novus, 2000), 252.

5. Taylor, A. J. P., *The struggle for mastery in Europe: 1848–1918* (Oxford: Clarendon Press, 2007).

6. Alasdair MacIntyre, '*Is a Science Of Comparative Politics Possible?*' *Against the Self-Images of the Age: Essays on Ideology and Philosophy* (Duckworth, 1971), 260.

7. Thomas Ohlson, 'Understanding the causes of war and peace,' *European Journal of International relations* 14, no. 1 (2008): 135.

8. Johan Galtung, 'An Editorial,' *Journal of Peace Research* 1, no. 1, (1964): 1–4.

9. Gleditsch et al., 'Armed Conflict 1946–2002, A New Dataset,' *Journal of Peace Research* 39, no. 5 (2002): 615–637.

10. Steven Pinker, *The better angels of our nature: a history of violence and humanity* (London: Penguin Books, 2012).

11. Jack Levy and William R. Thompson, *The Causes of War* (Chichester: Wiley Blackwell), 124.

Is the World Getting More Peaceful?

1.

Systemic Trends in War and Peace

Bear F. Braumoeller[1]

Introduction

The decline of war thesis is an argument made by a growing number of social scientists, including Steven Pinker, at Harvard, some of the researchers at Uppsala and the Peace Research Institute Oslo (PRIO), and my own colleague at Ohio State University, John Mueller. These scholars argue that, thanks to things such as the gradual expansion of human empathy and the spread of norms of nonviolence, the frequency and intensity of war are in decline and have been in decline for many decades.

Despite the fact that all of the main authors in this debate marshal data in favour of their arguments, the evidentiary basis for the decline of war thesis remains surprisingly thin. This is in part due to persistent mismatches between the quantities of interest—the rate of conflict initiation and the deadliness of war—and the measures used to capture them. It is also due to the near absence of formal and correct statistical tests.

When I started to use revised measures and tests to explore the argument that the institution of warfare is in decline and has been for some time, I soon came to the conclusion that I didn't believe it. That conclusion prompted me to dig further, to look at different measures, and to learn new statistical methodologies and apply them to the task. Having done so, I still don't believe it. So my first reaction to the invitation to be a part of this symposium was, 'I can't go to a Nobel Symposium and say that peace isn't breaking out!'

After a fair bit of reflection, I decided to come anyway, for two reasons. First, the decline of war thesis has achieved a nearly taken-for-granted status in the mainstream press. A typical review concludes, 'Pinker convincingly demonstrates that there has been a dramatic decline in violence, and he is persuasive about the causes of that decline.'[2] To the extent that this assessment is wrong, the record needs to be set straight. The stakes here are non-trivial: if such assessments make politicians and their publics complacent in the face of rising threats, for example, they could have the perverse effect of making the world less safe if they are incorrect.

My second reason for coming is that, as paradoxical as it may sound at first blush, I don't think that the bad news about war is necessarily bad news about peace. In fact, I think that for much of the last two centuries we have seen both the spread of war and the spread of peace. The decline-of-war scholars may actually be correct when they say that the world is becoming a more peaceful place. However, it has not become less warlike at the same time—in fact, just the opposite.

The Decline of War Thesis

Let me start by discussing the decline of war thesis. I will focus on the three authors whose work is most closely associated with it.

Mueller argues that the institution of war, like the institutions of duelling and slavery before it, is simply going out of style. In *Retreat from Doomsday*, Mueller argued that this change in attitudes was taking place among developed countries. In his follow-up book, *The Remnants of War*, he argued that the normative prohibition against war, which was largely the product of the horrors of World War I, has been spreading from developed countries to the rest of the world ever since.[3] To the obvious question—Why was there a World War II?—Mueller argues that it was 'fabricated almost single-handedly by history's supreme atavism, Adolf Hitler'.

In *Winning the War on War,* Joshua Goldstein argues that the decrease in warfare is quite recent, and he does not argue that it is irreversible.[4] He explicitly does not argue that the evolution of civilization has produced increasingly strong norms of nonviolence. Goldstein does argue, however, that the end of the Cold War helps explain the reduction in violence after 1989, but he points to peacekeeping as the key causal variable: he argues that peacekeeping started having an impact on war in 1945 and accelerated after 1989, mostly due to the effect that peacekeeping has on the durability of post-war settlements.

Pinker, in his best-selling book *The Better Angels of Our Nature*, argues that, in general, there has been a gradual decline in violence over the course of centuries, that both the frequency and intensity of international conflict have decreased since 1945, and that we now live in what is arguably the most peaceful period in history.[5] He argues that three overlapping and somewhat irregular processes have driven this decline: the pacification process (humanity's transition from hunter-gatherer societies to agricultural civilizations), the civilizing process (the gradual strengthening of domestic authority and growth of commerce), and the humanitarian revolution (the expansion of empathy that resulted in the abolition of slavery, duelling, and cruel physical punishment and an increase in pacifism).

While these arguments differ in terms of the reasons that they posit for a decline in warfare, the exact aspects of warfare that they think have declined, and the duration of that decline, it is possible to discern two core claims that make up the decline of war thesis, each of which is emphasized to different degrees by different authors:

1. States use force against one another less often than they did decades or centuries ago.

2. When wars do occur, fewer people die in them than in decades past.

These are fairly straightforward hypotheses. Unfortunately, very few analyses that have been done to date contain a reasonable test of either one of them.

Main Issues with Existing Analyses

Studies of the decline of war thesis exhibit a surprising number of theoretical and empirical pathologies. For the sake of space, I will focus on two of the most serious in the latter category: the use of measures that do not reflect the quantity of theoretical interest and the failure to use formal statistical tests that would separate real changes in that quantity from random variation.

When I started exploring the evidence presented in favour of these arguments, I discovered that these claims were based on surprisingly little data. This may seem like a bold statement, given that all three books contain data analysis of some sort. Pinker's book alone is more than 800 pages long and contains, by my count, 116 distinct figures. Most of these figures, however, contain data that relate to his larger claim that all forms of human violence are in decline: they chart changes in rates of homicide, judicial torture, spousal abuse, and so on—even spanking. The charts that relate to interstate warfare are located at the end of chapter 5 and the beginning of chapter 6.

Of these charts, very few actually show worldwide trends in warfare. Most show trends in warfare either within Europe or among the great powers, which are almost without exception European. Granted, both Pinker and Mueller argue that the process of pacification began in the developed world, but they also argue that the process has spread far enough to the rest of the world that it's had an impact on war in general.

When I looked for data on trends in the rate or frequency of the use of force worldwide, however, I found not a single graph or table in any of the three books, or in the rest of the literature for that matter. The only exception is a 1999 conference paper written by Peter Brecke, who compiled a catalogue of known conflicts with at least twenty-five fatalities, starting from the 1400s to the present day.[6] Pinker reproduces Brecke's Figure 2, which shows a general downward trend in the number of conflicts per year that were initiated in Europe since the 1400s, as Figure 5-17 in his book. It is reproduced here as the bottom graph in Figure 1.2. He does not reproduce Brecke's Figure 1, which shows an even larger *upward* trend in the number of conflicts that were initiated worldwide in the same period (figure 1.1, top).

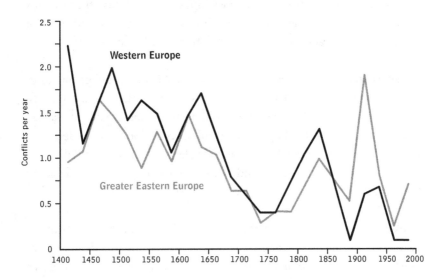

FIGURE 1.1. *Conflicts per year worldwide (top) and in greater Europe (bottom), 1400–2000. Conflicts include interstate and civil wars, genocides, insurrections, and riots. The top figure is from Brecke (1999); the bottom figure is from Pinker (2011), who cites Brecke as the source.*[7,8]

Unfortunately, the list of conflicts is very incomplete, and missing data make it difficult to compare frequencies over time, so to my mind neither figure is really very helpful for our purposes. Regardless, it makes little sense to argue that one is relevant and the other is not.

Even if we had a complete list of conflicts, figure 1.1 would still be misleading because it does not take into account the increase in the number of conflict opportunities that has accompanied the growth of the international system over time. In other words, the *rate* of conflict onset, rather than the raw *frequency*, is the best measure of how often states use force against one another because it accounts for the growth over time in the number of states that *can* use force against one another.

Studies of fatalities, which generally include all conflicts worldwide, also measure the deadliness of war in a misleading way: in battle deaths as a fraction of world population.[9] Why is this measure misleading? Clearly, some adjustment for population size is necessary: a loss of 1,500 soldiers means something very different to the Chinese than it does to the residents of the Bahamas.[10] We measure the deadliness of cancer, or heart disease, or pneumonia as a fraction of world population, so why not wars?

The short answer is that wars are not diseases. Anyone could get pneumonia or cancer; but every person on Earth is *not* potentially at risk of death from a war fought between two small African nations. Deaths in war are not viruses or bacteria: they are the result of conscious human decisions to use force. Therefore, when we analyse decisions, it is essential to use measures that reflect concepts and ideas as people themselves understand them when they are making the decisions that we're trying to analyse.[11]

Take, for example, the Paraguayan War, a contest that pitted Paraguay against Argentina, Brazil, and Uruguay in the 1860s. The body count was nowhere near that of either of the world wars in absolute terms, and as a percentage of the world population, casualties were trivial. However, it remains the bloodiest war in Latin American history. By some estimates, Paraguay lost 70 percent of its adult male population. These deaths were the result of conscious decisions—by the three allies to establish war aims that would have resulted in the partition and absorption of Paraguay; by Argentinean President Bartolomé Mitre to continue to push for those war aims once Paraguay had lost; and of Paraguayan President Francisco Solano López to wage guerrilla warfare in the countryside until his own death brought the war to a close. Those decisions were based not on how many people would die relative to the populations of India and China, but rather on the likely costs to the societies of the combatants themselves. This better measure—battle deaths divided by the pooled population of the combatants, or what the Correlates of War (COW) project dubbed the intensity of war—has been widely used in studies of the lethality of armed conflict.[12]

Both the data on conflict initiation and the data on fatalities suffer from another flaw: disaggregation across time. Instead of the number of conflicts initiated in a given year, for example, we are shown the total number of conflicts in a given year. Instead of the number of battle deaths in a given war, we are shown the number of battle deaths per year. The problem is that the simple duration of a conflict is irrelevant to the question at hand. The Korean War resulted in a little over 900,000 battle deaths over the course of only three years. The Iran–Iraq War resulted in roughly 1.25 million battle deaths over the course of almost eight years. If deaths are measured on an annual basis, this looks like progress. However, the Iran–Iraq War was not less bloody than the Korean War. It just killed people more slowly. The decline of war thesis argues that we are killing fewer people than we used to—*not* that we are killing them more slowly.

The effects of this inferential muddle are especially pernicious in the case of a graph of country-war-years that has appeared multiple times in this literature (figure 1.2). While the threshold for conflict differs,[13] the general trends are remarkably similar.

The main problem in this case is that the 'mountain' of civil conflicts prior to the end of the Cold War represents not an increase in the rate of conflict initiation, but an accumulation of existing conflicts.[14] By the same logic, the apparent decrease in civil war after the Cold War could represent a decrease in duration rather than in the rate of initiation.[15] It's hard to tell, of course, because measuring country-years of war conflates initiation with

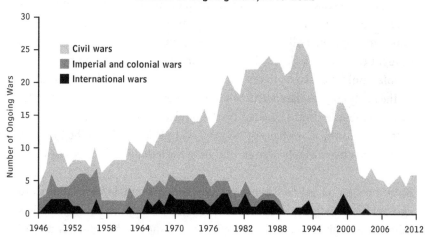

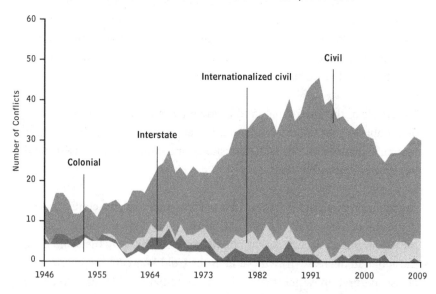

FIGURE 1.2. *Number of violent armed conflicts worldwide, by year.*[16,17]

duration. Duration, strictly speaking, is irrelevant: nothing in the decline of war thesis argues that wars should take less time than they used to— only that they should happen less often and/or kill fewer people.

In order to get a better sense of what the data tell us about changes in the rate of civil war initiation, I consulted a former graduate student of mine, Professor Benjamin Jones, whose dissertation on civil wars used the same dataset as the books by Pinker and Mueller. As part of his research on the dynamics of civil war initiation and termination, Jones distinguished between new and ongoing fighting in both new and recurring civil conflicts since 1950.[18] I've plotted the result in figure 1.3. This figure tells a very different story than the previous ones. While the number of recurring wars slowly increased over time, and in the case of new ongoing wars decreased after 1990, the raw frequency of conflict initiation actually increased a bit following the Cold War.

Of course, this only represents the frequency of civil war onset, not the rate: the number of opportunities for civil war to occur increased as the number of countries in the international system increased.

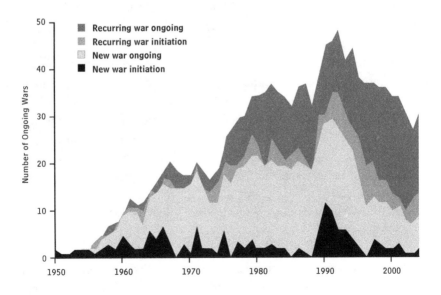

FIGURE 1.3. *Number of civil wars worldwide, by year and type.*

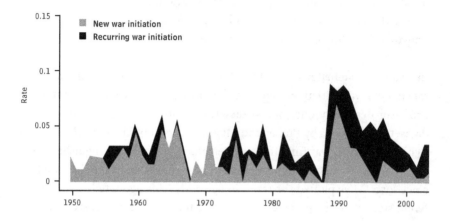

FIGURE 1.4. Rate of civil conflict initiation worldwide, by year and type.

The easiest way to correct that problem is to assume that the number of possible civil wars in the international system at any given point in time is directly proportional to the number of countries in the system at that time and simply divide the number of initiations by the number of countries. Doing so using the UCDP/PRIO Armed Conflict Dataset and eliminating ongoing wars produces the graph in figure 1.4.

Even the most diehard optimist would find it difficult to construe figure 1.4 as good news for the decline of war thesis. For the most part, it's hard to see a pattern at all during the Cold War, and to the extent that one can be discerned we actually see an increase rather than a decrease in the rate of civil conflict initiation after the fall of the Iron Curtain.[19] That said, it's worth noting that, as Professor Kristian Gleditsch pointed out during my presentation of an earlier draft of this chapter, it's probably not wise to make too much of this break one way or the other, as the end of the Cold War also corresponds to a change in the coding procedures used in the UCDP/PRIO data.

A final, very serious objection has to do with statistical inference. Given that political scientists increasingly use statistics to test their arguments, this literature is remarkable for the paucity of formal statistical tests. Their near absence is a problem when it comes to measuring the rate of conflict onset, because without them it's hard to know whether we're looking at a real change or at random fluctuation. It's a much worse problem when it comes to war intensity because war intensity follows a power-law distribution, meaning roughly that there are a lot of very small wars and a small number of very, very big ones. As Nassim Nicholas Taleb has pointed out, distributions like these make it extremely difficult to spot changes over time because our perception of the difference between time periods can be dramatically distorted by very large events. Even standard statistical tests give misleading answers because the small-sample properties of most tests when applied to data like these are unbelievably bad. So unless we use tests that are designed with the challenges of these distributions in mind, we are very, very likely, as Taleb puts it, to be fooled by randomness.[20]

Pinker's discussion of the Long Peace—the seventy-year absence of major war among the great powers in the wake of World War II—offers a very simple example of the value of statistical reasoning. The author himself goes into significant depth in this section on the implications of randomness for historical patterns of conflict. His goal is to demonstrate that the massive bloodlettings of the twentieth century might have been nothing more than 'a run of extremely bad luck', which is a fair point. He does not, however, address the opposite possibility: that the seventy years of peace following WWII could be nothing more than a run of good luck.

Although the inferential issues surrounding the Long Peace can be fairly complex, even very simple statistics should give us pause. If we look at the record of major great-power wars over the past five centuries, we find an average of about two per century prior to the twentieth century. Based on historical precedent, then, let's take the probability of a systemic war breaking out in any given year to be 0.02.[21] We can calculate the probability of seeing a given number of wars over a given period of time by using the binomial distribution—the same distribution used by introductory statistics students to calculate the probability of observing 'heads' in five successive flips of a coin. Here, we can use it to get a sense of just how unlikely a Long Peace of seventy years' duration really is.[22]

Figure 1.5 uses the binomial distribution to compare the probability of observing no wars in the seventy years since WWII with the probabilities of observing one, two, three, or more wars in the same time period, assuming that the probability of systemic war has not deviated from its historical average of two per century. As we can see, if fifty years go by on average between major great-power wars, the passage of seventy years without one should not in and of itself be very surprising.

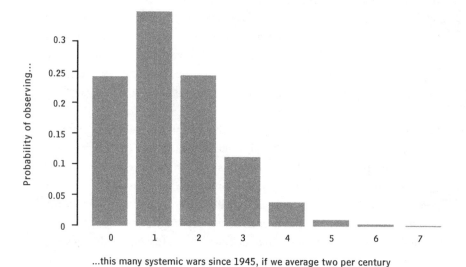

FIGURE 1.5. *The entirely probable Long Peace.*

Analysis: The Rate of the Use of Force

What happens when we rectify these problems? Having completed most of the book manuscript that gave rise to this article,[23] I can say that the short answer is that not much support remains. The patterns that emerge from the data do, however, support some interesting alternative interpretations.

Because the lethality of war has been debated previously and will be discussed elsewhere in this volume,[24] I focus on the other quantity of interest for the decline of war thesis: the rate at which force is used between countries in the international system.

In order to do so, I first examined the frequency with which military force was used by one country against another and reciprocated, as captured by the Correlates of War project's Militarized Interstate Dispute data. I should emphasize that these are officially authorized uses of force, not just border skirmishes: someone in a position of authority on one side or the other has to give the order to use force. This strikes me as the most reasonable point at which to draw the big red line that, according to the decline of war theorists, humanity is increasingly unwilling to cross. By requiring that the use of force be reciprocated, moreover, it ensures that escalation is a realistic possibility.

I then measured the annual rate of the use of force by dividing that frequency by the number of opportunities for conflict, as measured by the number of so-called politically relevant pairs of states in the international system. In the most straightforward definition, a pair of states is politically relevant if the states are contiguous or if at least one of the states is a major power. I used a slightly more complex measure,[25] but the basic idea is very similar, and the choice of which one to use doesn't matter much for the results.

I ran these data through a nonparametric, hierarchical change-point detection algorithm.[26] The algorithm is designed to separate signal (real changes in the rate of the use of force) from noise (random variation). It is very robust, because it doesn't rely on distributional assumptions. Because it is built on permutation tests, it is also very powerful.

The good news is that there was, in fact, a significant drop in the rate of conflict initiation just after the end of the Cold War. That part of the decline of war argument holds up to scrutiny. The bad news is that that's the only good news. There has been no significant decline in the rate of international conflict initiation since the end of the Cold War. What is worse, leaving aside the spikes in conflict initiation that characterized the two world wars, the end of the Cold War represents the first significant decline in the rate of international conflict initiation for nearly 200 years. The period between the Napoleonic Wars and the end of the Cold War is characterized by a steady series of *increases* in the rate of the use of force worldwide.

Figure 1.6 tells the story. In the first third of the century following the Napoleonic Wars the median rate of conflict initiation was zero: the majority of years were characterized by no conflicts at all. In the last two-thirds of that period the median rate of conflict initiation was 7 uses of force per 1,000 relevant dyads per year. During the interwar period the median was 10 uses of force per 1,000 relevant dyads per year. During the Cold War, the median was 15 uses of force per 1,000 relevant dyads per year. After the Cold War, the median rate of conflict drops very significantly, back down to 6 uses of force per 1,000 relevant dyads per year.

So, far from representing progress toward peace, the Cold War was the most violent period on record except for the two world wars. This result is, of course, not remotely consistent with the hypothesis that humanity's steadily growing aversion to war has led to a decline in war over time, even when we take random fluctuations into account.

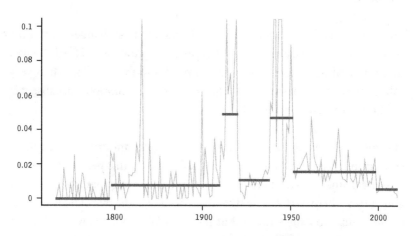

Rate of International Conflict Initiation, 1816-2010

FIGURE 1.6. *Change point analysis of Correlates of War use of force data, 1816–2014, with Y-axis truncated to make trends more visible. The light grey trend line charts the rate at which force was used between countries; the horizontal lines indicate medians. Breaks between the horizontal lines indicate points at which the change in the overall trend is larger than one could reasonably expect by chance.*

It is also somewhat difficult to square with Goldstein's thesis that peace-keeping is a major driver of overall rates of conflict initiation: the Cold War wasn't especially peaceful, and the decrease in conflict after the Cold War is actually so big—a two-thirds reduction!—that I find it difficult to believe that peacekeeping deserves all of the credit.

This conclusion might also, at first blush, seem to be at odds with the finding of Cirillo and Taleb, who conclude that the inter-arrival time of major conflicts does not support the claim that violence has become less frequent.[27] The authors argue, for example, that the absence of a conflict generating more than, say, 20 million casualties in the last twenty years is highly insufficient to state that its occurrence probability has decreased over time, given that the average inter-arrival time is 252 years (73 for res-caled), with a MAD of 267 (86 for rescaled) years. Unfortunately, we still have to wait quite some time to say that we are living in a more peaceful era.

The main difference between the two studies lies in the granularity of the data: Cirillo and Taleb examine very large international wars—those with 500,000 fatalities or more—while I examine reciprocated uses of force. They conclude that there isn't enough evidence to support the thesis that the frequency of major wars has changed. Nothing in this study contra-dicts that conclusion.

I carried out a wide range of checks to assess the robustness of these findings, including the use of different measures, different data, differ-ent levels of the use of force, and different measures of political relevance. None of these analyses revealed a sustained decline in the rate of conflict initiation. Most revealed just the opposite. While space precludes discus-sion of all of these threats to inference, one is worth discussing in detail—the possibility that a lot of older militarized interstate disputes were not recorded and did not show up in the data. To the extent that the data suffer from this sort of bias, the nineteenth century might appear more peaceful than it really was because we don't have a complete record of nineteenth century conflicts.

There are a few reasons to be sceptical of this claim. First, the data only include actual uses of force by one government against another. Lower-level disputes, such as threats and displays of force, are those most likely to be missed in previous centuries. And even a quick glance at the sources used by the COW project[28] for coding militarized interstate disputes reveals an impressively comprehensive array of source materials: far from just relying on the *New York Times* or *The Times* of London, the COW project has delved into an impressive array of histories, biographies, notes, memoranda, military and political encyclopaedias, and foreign-language sources.

It's possible for an armed clash to go unrecorded in any of these sources, of course, but the scholars at the COW project have certainly done due diligence in minimizing that possibility. Given that effort, the burden of proof lies on sceptics to unearth sources and conflicts that they have missed.

Second, the trend in the data is very consistent with the mainstream historical record, which portrays the nineteenth century as a remarkably peaceful one and the Cold War as being very conflictual. The Concert of Europe period from the early to mid-1800s was remarkable for the degree to which the great powers joined together to manage conflict. The latter half of the nineteenth century saw some conflict among great powers over colonies as well as a rash of militarized disputes in Latin America following the dissolution of the Spanish Empire in the Americas. The interwar period witnessed continued conflict in the Far East and ongoing instability in Europe that snowballed in the 1930s. However, the Cold War was the first period in which two superpowers fought proxy wars throughout the globe. The sudden collapse of the Soviet Union transformed the context within which international politics played out and in so doing rendered such conflicts meaningless.[29]

If the thoroughness of the data-gathering effort and the high degree of correspondence with the historical record aren't totally convincing, the question then becomes this: how many militarized disputes would have to have been missed for us to believe that the world is actually getting more peaceful?

A good, rough-and-ready way to answer this question is to add hypothetical conflicts to the most conflictual part of the nineteenth century, the second half, until the change-point algorithm tells us that its rate of conflict is significantly *greater* than that of the Cold War. When I did so, I found that the median rate of conflict would have to be about 2.5 times as high as its historical value before we could reasonably believe that peace broke out during the Cold War. In other words, the COW project would have had to have missed about three uses of force out of every five for this argument to hold water. That's a lot of missing data—so much so that I find it to be an awfully implausible claim. However, since the first half of the nineteenth century is the more peaceful of the two, this is the best-case scenario for anyone who wants to claim that missing data are masking a real decline in the rate of the use of force.

War and Positive Peace

These results set up an interesting question. The central people writing about and researching the decline of war are very smart. Their work is cited often. Their books are actually bought by people who aren't academics, and it might seem implausible that they could have been entirely wrong on such a straightforward question.

In fact, I suspect they're not. I believe that they are mistaken when it comes to trends in warfare, but I also suspect that they made the arguments that they made because they failed to differentiate carefully enough between war and peace. In order to make sense out of that statement, I have to go back to the beginning of the peace science movement and the scholarship of Johan Galtung, the Norwegian sociologist and mathematician who founded PRIO and the *Journal of Peace Research*. In a 1967 manuscript, *Theories of Peace*, Galtung makes an important distinction between what he calls 'negative peace' and 'positive peace'.[30] Negative peace is the absence of organized collective violence. This is the sort of peace that countries such as North and South Korea have experienced following the ceasefire that ended their hostilities in the Korean War: they're not actively killing one another, but that's about the best you can say about the situation.

Positive peace, according to Galtung, is quite different. As he puts it, 'This is peace as a synonym for all other good things in the world community, particularly cooperation and integration between human groups, with less emphasis on the absence of violence. [T]he concept would exclude major violence, but tolerate occasional violence.'

Galtung clearly sees positive peace as being the more profound and meaningful form of peace—a positive and cooperative relationship, rather than the simple absence of a negative one. It's important to note, however, that because peace is not the same thing as the absence of war, the spread of peace—of positive peace, that is—does not necessarily imply the diminution of war.

In fact, as my colleagues Gary Goertz, Paul Diehl, and Alexandru Balas have shown in their 2016 book, *The Puzzle of Peace*, peaceful relationships in the positive-peace sense have been on the rise throughout the Cold War and into the post-Cold War period.[31] By their measure, the relationships of 7.2 percent of all politically relevant states could be characterized by positive peace at the beginning of the Cold War.

By the end of the Cold War, the percentage had more than doubled, to 16.6 percent. After the end of the Cold War, the percentage remains roughly the same, but, of that 16 percent, a majority of states transition from 'warm peace' (the lowest level of positive peace, characterized, among other things, by the absence of war plans against one another and the presence of significant commonalities of interest) to a Deutschian security community, in which we see a degree of integration, coordination, and dependable expectation of peaceful change (figure 1.7).

I think they're largely correct in that assessment.[32] Precisely because peace is not synonymous with the absence of war, it is possible for these two trends—the spread of peace and the spread of war—to coexist. The big question is—how?

This question poses real challenges for existing perspectives on peace. A betterment of human nature or human institutions, or the spread of liberal ideology, might explain the spread of peace but not the spread of war. Arguably, they do a better job of explaining peace within Europe during

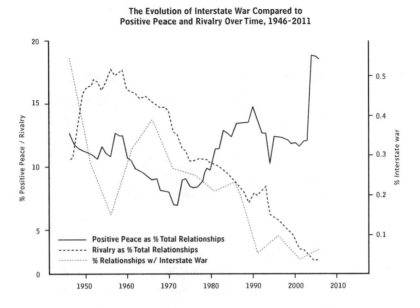

FIGURE 1.7. *Trends in positive peace, rivalry, and interstate war.*[33]

the last seventy years, which is probably the best case that one can make for the decline of war argument.

As historians well know, however, the Western liberal order is hardly unique. Attempts to create international order—by which I mean a set of coercive laws and practices, reflective of an underlying principle of legitimacy and balance of power, to which some set of powerful states submits in exchange for security[34]—date back at least to the Persian Empire under Cyrus the Great.[35] It is inherent in such orders to quell violence among their constituent units—that is, to create negative peace. International orders aimed specifically at the promotion of positive peace are a more recent development, but even at a conservative estimate they've been around for more than 200 years.[36]

To date, however, most studies of the relationship between international order and peace have focused on the prospects for building peace within international orders rather than the potential for conflict across international orders. I now turn to a brief (and, if truth be told, preliminary and rather speculative) discussion of the tension between the two.

International Conflict and International Order?

As the sociologist Charles Tilly famously wrote, 'War made the state and the state made war.'[37] In its most general form, this is an elegant statement of a near-truism: warfare was part of the process of the formation of political order within modern states—an order that was synonymous at least with negative peace and ideally with positive peace. Once those states had formed, however, they used war to survive and thrive in the larger system of states.

My hypothesis is that Tilly's insight applies to international political orders as well and that the creation of international political orders and their relationship to one another is largely responsible for the patterns of violence that we see over the past two centuries. International orders, for the most part, decrease the incidence of violence within their sphere. On the other hand, when competing international orders collide, they encounter a new issue—the nature of the political ordering principles to which states should subscribe—that has the potential to generate conflict where none had previously existed. Conflict over the nature of international order is especially pernicious because principles of legitimacy are generally indivisible: there is no way to divide the pie and arrive at a compromise. For that reason, the most peaceful periods on record are periods in which one international order is largely uncontested.

The Cold War is an outstanding example of this interplay between internal peace and external conflict. The Western liberal international order did not, of course, exist in a vacuum: its formation was greatly aided by the existence and likely expansionist tendencies of another international order, based in Moscow, that saw itself as the inevitable successor to the liberal, capitalist West. As Professor Sir Michael Howard put it in his brilliant little book *The Invention of Peace,* it was 'a confrontation between two sides with incompatible visions of world order, each believing that peace ultimately could be established only by the elimination of the other.'[38] At the same time, and partly as a result, peace spread within the Western camp as the North Atlantic security community formed and solidified. The Soviet Union managed conflict within its own sphere as well: although the result was not quite as peaceful, Goertz and co-authors still cite the Warsaw Pact as an example of positive peace.

Here, then, are the two faces of international order: peace was fostered within international orders, while conflict was fostered across them, each process in some measure abetting the other. Other periods of peace in the nineteenth and twentieth centuries follow a similar logic. The Concert of Europe, formed to preserve a conservative order and prevent liberal uprisings in the wake of the French Revolution, was forged in the aftermath of the Napoleonic Wars. It remained entirely unopposed by any other scheme for producing international order, and while it operated—from 1815 to, most reasonably, 1853—warfare was all but absent from the continent. After World War I, another order was born, a liberal one grounded in the League of Nations (1920–1946), but it was soon opposed by two revisionist international orders arising from Nazi Germany and imperial Japan. The resulting 'broken balance'[39] was characterized by extreme uncertainty and volatility. The post-Cold War world has witnessed a remarkable reduction in conflict, not only because of the existence of the Western liberal order, but because that order has been unopposed in any meaningful way since the late 1980s.

It is tempting to portray this as a narrative that pits the Enlightenment, as the side of peace, against successive resurgences of bellicose counter-Enlightenment thinking. To do so, however, would be gravely ahistorical. The international order constructed by British Foreign Secretary Lord Castlereagh, Austrian conservative statesman Klemens von Metternich, and the other architects of the 1815 Vienna Settlement was anything but liberal. The Concert of Europe owed more to the Irish statesman and political thinker Edmund Burke, the most iconic philosopher in the tradition of modern conservatism, than to the German moral philosopher Immanuel Kant.

Told from this perspective, the story of the decline in warfare following the Cold War takes on an entirely different hue. The hero is not Kant, or an increasingly enlightened human race, but rather Mikhail Gorbachev—a fact recognized, and recognized wisely I think, by the Nobel Institute in 1990.

Conclusion

If this perspective is correct—and I am increasingly convinced that it is—what are the implications for minimizing or eradicating warfare as an instrument of national policy going forward? At the risk of compounding speculation with futurism, I can offer a few tentative thoughts.

First of all, it's not clear that we can count on the Western liberal world order to continue to expand the zone of peace that it created over the course of the last half-century. Indeed, it may be reaching the limits of its own attractiveness to the rest of the world. If the recent surge in the popularity of populist politicians in countries such as Austria, France, Poland, Switzerland, and the US is any indication, it may even be beginning a slow backward slide.[40] It's not clear how long Americans will continue to see value in the present degree of integration, or whether Europeans will want to remain tethered to, in former Nobel Institute director Professor Geir Lundestad's memorable caricature of the European perspective, 'vulgar, gas-guzzling, hormone-eating supporters of the death penalty'.[41] In other words, if this is indeed an American 'empire by invitation', we might be wearing out our welcome. The erosion or dissolution of the Atlantic community could well reverse the impressive trend toward peace that characterized its growth and maturation.

At the same time, as I hope to have made clear, the widespread belief that humanity is on the threshold of perpetual peace and that we need to do little save bask in our own goodness in order to enjoy it is almost certainly unfounded. Moreover, if this belief forms the basis of policy, it might actually be dangerous: if it prompts us to ignore a rising threat or contributes to the sentiment that the growth of international order is superfluous, the belief that mankind is becoming more peaceful could, perversely, make the world a more dangerous place.

That said, I do think the historical record confirms the viability of the idea of an international order in which war plays no part. We've managed to create multiple working prototypes over the past 200 years. Importantly, we've shown that they can be based on very different ideas of political legitimacy. At the same time, the record seems to indicate that international orders based on different principles coexist tenuously at best, catastrophically at worst. Although the Kantian peace is founded on cosmopolitan principles, in practice its core has been Western liberal democracies, with a broad range of shared values, culture, and history. We don't really know whether, or how well, it can be extended to the rest of the world.

All of this leaves us with a set of hard questions, to which the data really cannot speak: What are the limits of a cosmopolitan international order? What degree of order can reasonably be sustained outside of the common ideology and culture of the North Atlantic community? Can we even maintain international order in the long run within the North Atlantic community, in the absence of external threats? If we cannot, to what extent would Europe play an independent role in building order? Would it work to maintain and expand its zone of peace, or would there continue to be a 'consensus–expectations gap'[42] that will undermine Europe's ability to act as a great power? Is the current Western liberal order a help or a hindrance to the project of a more universal order? That is, if the West is satisfied with our current 'two-tiered' international order—crudely, NATO and the EU for us, the UN for everyone else—where is the incentive for the major powers to deepen and strengthen global institutions? If we do face 'the end of American world order,'[43] with multiple regional orders—in the Middle East, Asia, and perhaps in a more independent Europe—evolving to take its place, can we successfully manage their interactions? Or will tensions among them usher in a new era of large-scale warfare? More broadly, will it be possible for institutions to preserve cooperation 'after hegemony' as Keohane argued, or will the existence of a hegemon prove to be a necessary condition for world order?[44] Finally, it seems clear that support for building international order was very strong following the three major great-power wars since the late 1700s.[45] Is the converse also true? Does the drive to maintain international order weaken as the memory of cataclysmic war fades into the past?

As the reader might have guessed, I am pessimistic about the answers to many of these questions. However, if our goal is to reduce war as well as spread peace, we cannot simply rely on human nature. We should instead maintain as our aim, as a recent Nobel laureate put it, 'a gradual evolution of human institutions'[46] that will move us toward a more inclusive international order, built by consensus and in our own self-interest, to protect each of us from all of us.

Notes

1. Department of Political Science, The Ohio State University, Columbus. This chapter is an extended and revised version of a lecture presented at the Nobel Peace Prize Research and Information summer seminar series on May 26, 2016. I am grateful to the Nobel Institute for hosting me during the preparation of that lecture and to the audience for exceptionally useful feedback.

2. Peter Singer, 'Is Violence History?' New York Times, October 9, 2011, https://www.nytimes.com/2011/10/09/books/review/the-better-angels-of-our-nature-by-steven-pinker-book-review.html?mtrref=www.google.com&gwh=1881DFBF47B76D192FFD9FE4C7974441&gwt=pay.

3. John E. Mueller, *Retreat from Doomsday: The Obsolescence of Major War* (New York: Basic Books, 1989); and John E. Mueller, *The Remnants of War* (Ithaca, NY: Cornell University Press, 2007).

4. Joshua S. Goldstein, *Winning the War on War: The Decline of Armed Conflict Worldwide* (New York: Dutton Adult, 2011).

5. Steven Pinker, *The Better Angels of Our Nature: Why Violence Has Declined* (New York: Viking Adult, 2011).

6. Peter Brecke, 'Violent Conflicts 1400 A.D. to the Present in Different Regions of the World.' Paper prepared for the 1999 Meeting of the Peace Science Society (International) on October 8–10, 1999, Ann Arbor, Michigan. Archived at http://web.archive.org/web/20121023154335/http://www.inta.gatech.edu/peter/PSS99_paper.html.

7. Peter Brecke, 'Violent Conflicts 1400 A.D. to the Present in Different Regions of the World.' Paper prepared for the 1999 Meeting of the Peace Science Society (International) on October 8–10, 1999, Ann Arbor, Michigan.

8. Steven Pinker, *The Better Angels of Our Nature: Why Violence Has Declined* (New York: Viking Adult, 2011).

9. Here, see also Bethany Lacina, Nils Petter Gleditsch, and Bruce Russett, 'The Declining Risk of Death in Battle,' *International Studies Quarterly* 50, no. 3 (2006): 673–80; and Bethany Lacina and Nils Petter Gleditsch, 'The Waning of War Is Real: A Response to Gohdes and Price,' *Journal of Conflict Resolution* 57, no. 6 (2012): 1109–27.

10. In fact, it would represent the complete destruction of the armed forces of the Bahamas.

11. Eric Uslaner, 'The Pitfalls of Per Capita,' *American Journal of Political Science* 20, no. 1 (1976): 125–33.

12. See e.g., Melvin Small and J. David Singer, *Resort to Arms: International and Civil Wars, 1816–1980* (Beverly Hills: Sage Publications, 1982); D.C. Roberts and D.L. Turcotte, 'Fractality and Self-Organized Criticality of Wars,' *Fractals* 6, no. 4 (1998): 351–57; M.E.J. Newman, 'Power Laws, Pareto Distributions and Zipf's Law,' *Contemporary Physics* 46, no. 5 (2005): 323–51; and Aaron Clauset, Cosma Rohilla Shalizi, and M.E.J. Newman, 'Power-Law Distributions in Empirical Data,' *SIAM Review* 51, no. 4 (2009): 661–703.

13. Pinker includes both minor armed conflicts (between 25 and 999 battle-related deaths in a given year) and wars (1,000 or more battle-related deaths), while Mueller focuses on the latter.

14. See James D. Fearon and David Laitin, 'Ethnicity, Insurgency, and Civil War,' *American Political Science Review* 97, no. 1 (2003): 75–90, at 77; and Håvard Hegre, 'The Duration and Termination of Civil War,' *Journal of Peace Research* 41, no. 3 (2004): 243–52, at 243–44'.

15. See Stathis N. Kalyvas and Laia Balcells, 'International System and Technologies of Rebellion: How the End of the Cold War Shaped Internal Conflict,' *American Political Science Review* 104, no. 3 (2010): 415–29, for an argument to this effect.

16. Steven Pinker, *The Better Angels of Our Nature: Why Violence Has Declined* (New York: Viking Adult, 2011).

17. John E. Mueller, "Did History End? Assessing the Fukuyama Thesis." *Political Science Quarterly* 129, no. 1 (2014): 35–54.

18. See Benjamin Thomas Jones, 'The Past Is Ever-Present: Civil War as a Dynamic Process' (PhD thesis, The Ohio State University, 2013). I haven't done the same for other kinds of wars, mostly because the trends in civil conflict dominate these graphs.

19. Getting ahead of myself slightly, the change-point algorithm that I describe below confirms that the increase is significantly greater than what one would expect to see by chance.

20. Nassim Nicholas Taleb, *Fooled by Randomness: The Hidden Role of Chance in Life and in the Markets*, 2nd ed., updated ed. (New York: Random House, 2005). I have been able to find only one analysis of the deadliness of war that involves a useful test of change over time (Lars-Erik Cederman, T. Camber Warren, and Didier Sornette, 'Testing Clausewitz: Nationalism, Mass Mobilization, and the Severity of War,' *International Organization* 65, no. 4 [2011]: 605–38). That article shows an increase in the deadliness of war at about the time that Napoleon revolutionized warfare by introducing the *levee en masse*. It finds no significant decline in war severity after that point. Bethany Lacina, Nils Petter Gleditsch, and Bruce Russett, 'The Declining Risk of Death in Battle,' *International Studies Quarterly* 50, no. 3 (2006): 673–80 does include a regression analysis of battle deaths per capita worldwide on time; I have already pointed out issues with the per-capita-worldwide measure, and Nassim Nicholas Taleb, 'The "Long Peace" Is a Statistical Illusion,' (2012) (Online manuscript,

https://web.archive.org/web/20121207093344/http://www.fooledbyrandomness.com /longpeace.pdf) critiques the use of standard statistical tools like regression in the context of thick-tailed distributions like war deaths. Pasquale Cirillo and Nassim Nicholas Taleb, 'On the Statistical Properties and Tail Risk of Violent Conflicts', *Physica A: Statistical Mechanics and Its Applications* 452 (2016): 29–45, which introduces a new methodology for analysing empirical power-law relationships with infinite means in situations in which the data are bounded, uses large-scale international warfare as an example. Although the paper does not offer a formal test of change in the power-law exponent over time, the authors argue based on their results that the observed change following World War II is very plausibly the result of chance.

21. For great-power wars over this period, see Jack S. Levy, *War in the Modern Great Power System, 1495–1975* (Lexington: University Press of Kentucky, 1983) and Joshua S. Goldstein, *Long Cycles: Prosperity and War in the Modern Age* (New Haven: Yale University Press, 1988). It's possible to use different time periods, of course: to assume that the probability of a systemic war breaking out in a given five-year period is 0.1, or that the probability in a given day is 0.000054757. Doing so makes little difference.

22. The probability of seeing k 'successes' (wars) in n 'trials' (years) given an underlying probability of success p is given by the probability mass function of a binomial distribution.

23. Bear F. Braumoeller, *Only the Dead: The Persistence of War in the Modern Age* (New York: Oxford University Press, 2019).

24. Pasquale Cirillo and Nassim Nicholas Taleb, 'The Decline of Violent Conflicts: What Do the Data Really Say?' in *The Causes of Peace* (Oslo, Norway: The Norwegian Nobel Institute, 2019), 44–76.

25. The general idea behind the measure is that political relevance should be estimated rather than assumed. See Bear F. Braumoeller and Austin Carson, 'Political Irrelevance, Democracy, and the Limits of Militarized Conflict', *Journal of Conflict Resolution* 55, no. 2 (2011): 292–320, for details. The Braumoeller-Carson measure of political relevance can be generated quite easily using variables from the Correlates of War dataset. To do so, I used their formula and estimated coefficients: $\Lambda(4.801 + 4.50$ contiguity $1.051 \log(\text{distance}) + 2.901$ major power$)$, where Λ denotes a standard logistic curve with equation $f(x) = 1/(1 + e^{-x})$ and contiguity, distance, and major power status are defined as in Maoz, Zeev and Bruce Russett, 'Normative and Structural Causes of Democratic Peace, 1946–1986', *American Political Science Review* 87 no. 3 (1993): 624–38.

26. More specifically, I've chosen an algorithm that does a hierarchical divisive estimation of change points using a permutation test, one that is contained in the ecp package in the R statistical language; for details, see Nicholas A. James and David S. Matteson, 'Ecp: An R Package for Non-parametric Multiple Change Point Analysis of Multivariate Data', *Journal of Statistical Software* 62, no. 7 (2014): 1–25, in which the

authors demonstrate the strong consistency of the change point estimates given independent observations. The permutation test allows for a powerful test with minimal distributional assumptions.

27. Cirillo and Taleb, 'The Decline of Violent Conflicts,' fn. 15.

28. See http://cow.dss.ucdavis.edu/data-sets/MIDs.

29. For general diplomatic histories, the indispensable starting point is Paul Schroeder's 1994 book *The Transformation of European Politics* (Clarendon Press), which chronicles the underappreciated transition from balance-of-power politics to collective international governance following the Napoleonic Wars. The old Harper & Row series entitled The Rise of Modern Europe, comprising twenty volumes by prominent historians and spanning seven centuries, is a treasure if it can be found in the dusty shelves of a used bookstore. René Albrecht-Carrié's 1973 *Diplomatic History of Europe Since the Congress of Vienna* (HarperCollins), a standard for many years, is a bit long in the tooth, as is A.J.P. Taylor's *Struggle for Mastery in Europe* (Oxford University Press, 2001), though both are still useful. F.R. Bridge and Roger Bullen's 2004 *The Great Powers and the European States System 1814–1914* (Routledge) remains a remarkably accessible history of the long nineteenth century as a whole. Gordon Craig and Alexander George's 1983 *Force and Statecraft* (Oxford University Press), a too-rare collaboration between an historian and a political scientist, is a succinct and thoughtful gem of a book: the chapter on the nineteenth century especially stands out. John Lewis Gaddis's 2007 *The Cold War: A New History* (Penguin) is a reasonably comprehensive history, written for a general audience. Geoffrey Blainey's 2006 *A Short History of the Twentieth Century* (Ivan R. Dee) is lucid and brisk, while Martin Gilbert's *A History of the Twentieth Century* (Harper Perennial, 2002) is more comprehensive.

30. Johan Galtung, 'Theories of Peace: A Synthetic Approach to Peace Thinking,' (Oslo: International Peace Research Institute, 1967), https://www.transcend.org/files /Galtung_Book_unpub_Theories_of_Peace_-_A_Synthetic_Approach_to_Peace _Thinking_1967.pdf.

31. Gary Goertz, Paul F. Diehl, and Alexandru Balas, *The Puzzle of Peace: The Evolution of Peace in the International System* (New York: Oxford University Press, 2016).

32. The trend in warfare from 1950 to 2010 that they chart seems roughly consistent with my own findings of a significant drop around 1990 but no obvious trend before or after, though I have not yet undertaken a thorough examination of the similarities and differences in coding rules.

33. Goertz, Diehl, and Balas, *The Puzzle of Peace*.

34. This definition is my own, though it's a bit of an amalgam. The requirement that laws and practices be coercive is from Immanuel Kant, *To Perpetual Peace: A Philosophical Sketch* (Indianapolis, IN: Hackett, 2003); the commingling of power and legitimacy is a major theme in Henry Kissinger, *World Order* (New York: Penguin, 2014); and the idea that the resulting hierarchy represents a 'functional bargain' came together as I was reading Janice Bially Mattern and Ayşe Zarakol, 'Hierarchies in World Politics,'

International Organization 70 (2016): 623–654. I should note that, in some cases, this bargain itself is coercive in nature.

35. See e.g., Samuel E. Finer, *The History of Government from the Earliest Times* (Oxford: Oxford University Press, 1997); and Kissinger, *World Order*.

36. Michael Howard, *The Invention of Peace: Reflections on War and International Order* (New Haven: Yale University Press, 2000).

37. Charles Tilly, 'Reflections on the History of European State-Making', in *The Formation of National States in Western Europe*, ed. Charles Tilly (Princeton: Princeton University Press, 1975), 3–83.

38. Michael Howard, *The Invention of Peace: Reflections on War and International Order* (New Haven: Yale University Press, 2000), 76.

39. Jeffrey W. Taliaferro, *The Challenge of Grand Strategy: The Great Powers and the Broken Balance between the World Wars* (Cambridge: Cambridge University Press, 2012).

40. On the West's rightward slide, see Gregor Pearce, Adam Aisch, and Bryant Rousseau, 'How Far Is Europe Swinging to the Right?' *New York Times*, May 22, 2016; and Jochen Bittner, 'Is This the West's Weimar Moment?' *New York Times*, May 31, 2016, A23; on NATO's struggle to remain credible, see Steven Erlanger, 'Tested by Russia, NATO Struggles to Stay Credible,' *New York Times*, June 1, 2016, A4.

41. Geir Lundestad, *The United States and Western Europe Since 1945: From 'Empire' by Invitation to Transatlantic Drift* (Oxford; New York: Oxford University Press, 2003). Lundestad could easily have added 'deniers of anthropogenic climate change.'

42. Asle Toje, *The European Union as a Small Power: After the Post-Cold War* (New York: Palgrave Macmillan, 2010).

43. Amitav Acharya, 'Global International Relations (IR) and Regional Worlds: A New Agenda for International Studies,' *International Studies Quarterly* 58, no. 4 (2014): 647–59.

44. Robert O. Keohane, *After Hegemony: Cooperation and Discord in the World Political Economy* (Princeton, NJ: Princeton University Press, 2010).

45. See e.g., G. John Ikenberry, *After Victory: Institutions, Strategic Restraint, and the Rebuilding of Order after Major Wars* (Princeton, NJ: Princeton University Press, 2001), and G. John Ikenberry, ed., *Power, Order, and Change in World Politics* (Cambridge; New York: Cambridge University Press, 2014).

46. Barack H. Obama, 'A Just and Lasting Peace,' Nobel Peace Prize Lecture, Oslo, Norway, December 10, 2009. The phrase is from President John F. Kennedy's Spring Commencement address at American University, June 10, 1963. President Kennedy argued that peace must be 'based not on a sudden revolution in human nature but on a gradual evolution in human institutions—on a series of concrete actions and effective agreements which are in the interest of all concerned. . . World peace, like community peace, does not require that each man love his neighbour—it requires only that they live together in mutual tolerance, submitting their disputes to a just and peaceful settlement.'

2.

The Decline of Violent Conflicts: What Do the Data Really Say?

Nassim Nicholas Taleb and Pasquale Cirillo

Introduction

The first theory of Long Peace appeared in 1858, when H.T. Buckle[1] wrote:

> That this barbarous pursuit is, in the progress of society, steadily declining, must be evident, even to the most hasty reader of European history. If we compare one country with another, we shall find that for a very long period wars have been becoming less frequent; and now so clearly is the movement marked, that, until the late commencement of hostilities, we had remained at peace for nearly forty years: a circumstance unparalleled ... The question arises, as to what share our moral feelings have had in bringing about this great improvement.

Buckle was perhaps right—with minor hiccups—for another five decades, but moral feelings or not, as we all know, the century following Buckle's prose turned out to be the most murderous in human history. The first obvious problem is that Buckle made a severely flawed risk assessment. The second is that he felt obligated to mount a narrative entailing moral feelings for what he perceived were the changes in the environment.[2]

In 2004, Ben Bernanke, then a member of the board of the US Federal Reserve System proclaimed that economic life was undergoing a 'great moderation', on the basis of an unprecedented stability of economic variables.[3] Like Buckle, he was sure to have found empirical reasons for that. His view became the norm until the dramatic financial crisis of 2007, when, once again, the world experienced a similar revision of belief.

In this chapter we show how not to make the same mistakes when speaking about wars and armed conflicts; how not to be fooled by historical data, transforming wishful thinking into theories. It is organized as follows: First, we present the problems associated with historical analyses of violence. Second, we discuss the relative quantitative approaches since the first works by L.F. Richardson[4] and present the statistical flaws and methodological errors in some widely held theories, such as those collected by Steven Pinker,[5] in his best-selling *The Better Angels of our Nature*. Third, we discuss our approach. Fourth, we provide a slightly more technical backup. Fifth, we give our verdict, which the reader will find complementary to and consistent with Braumoeller (in this volume). But the central contribution of the chapter is to provide a methodology to deal with extreme events such as war based on extra value theory and to produce analyses that are robust to the imprecision of war estimates.

Some Problems in Quantitative Historiography

Studying the history of violence to detect trends and changes over a time period is a non-trivial task for a scientist constrained by rigor. We list here five problems that are not only specific to violence, but that may also be universal to any form of quantitative and statistical historiography. All problems will be analysed in more detail in the rest of the chapter.

Problem 1: Fat Tails

First, we are dealing with a fat-tailed phenomenon. We define violence seen quantitatively as either fatalities over a specific time period or fatalities per specific event, and both are fat-tailed variables. What characterizes fat-tailed variables? These have their properties (e.g., the average) dominated by extreme events, those 'in the tails'. The most popularly known version is the Pareto 80/20 rule (80 percent of the people in Italy, Pareto noticed, owned 20 percent of the land, and vice versa).

These tools are not just changing the colour of the dress, but they require a new statistical framework and a different way of thinking, going from the tail to the body (standing the usual statistical logic, which consists of going from the body to the tail, on its head)—and the great majority of researchers who are trained in statistics are not familiar with the branches of the discipline and theorems needed for fat tails.[6] To add to the problem, our examination shows that war turned out to be the mother of fat tails, far worse than the popular Pareto 80/20 rule: there are few phenomena such as fluid turbulence or thermal spikes on the surface of the sun that can rival the fat-tailedness of violence. Further, historical data are temporal (spread out over time) and statistical analyses of time series (such as financial data) require far more sophistication than simple statistical tests found in empirical scientific papers. For instance, one cannot blindly use the same methods to compute the statistical properties of city size and the time series of war—since, in the latter case, the observed properties depend on our survival (say a 1960 nuclear war would have prevented us from having this discussion), hence restrictions apply to what can or cannot be inferred—there is a difference between ensemble probability and time probability, though not always, and the effect of the bias needs to be established.

Problem 2: Boundedness

Not only are we dealing with extreme fat tails, but the effect is bounded quantitatively, with an almost precisely known upper limit—no war can kill more than the population of the planet. This brings in an additional mathematical complication, since all techniques for fat tails require an infinite support for the variable. The boundedness requires some formulaic adjustment to the statistics of violence—which, as we show in some detail, has had so far a mathematically and statistically naive literature. However, it is not all bad news, since there will be a statistical mean, which, carefully interpreted, can help in the analysis—while naive statistical analysis produces an infinite or undefined mean.

Problem 3: Reliability of Historical Data

The analysis needs to incorporate the unreliability of historical data—there is no way to go back and fact-check the casualties in the Peloponnesian War, and we rarely have more than one side to the story. Estimates of war casualties are often anecdotal, spreading via citations, and based on vague computations, almost impossible to verify using period sources. Even more, recent events, such as the Algerian War of the 1950–60s have two polarized sides to the story; in some cases, such as the Armenian-Syriac genocide of 1915–1917, the numbers do not converge and have actually been diverging over the course of a century. This unreliability requires taking into account another layer of uncertainty. In addition, the analysis must consider that many wars went unreported—we just do not know how many, and such a number is itself a random variable. There exists even a third layer of uncertainty: the number of gaps between wars can be treated as a random variable, and its effect must be taken into consideration in the interpretation of the results.

Problem 4: The Definition of an Event

One hurdle can be the precise definition of an event, which appears to be a function of the sophistication of the historian and his or her closeness to one side involved in the event. We mentioned earlier the underlying statistical variable defined as fatalities per specific event, but the very definition of an event matters—and the analysis should not be fragile to the specification. For instance, Pinker treats as a single event the Mongol invasions, which actually occurred over a time span of more than a century and a quarter. This swelled the numbers per event over the Middle Ages and contributed to the illusion that violence has dropped since, given that subsequent events had shorter durations. It is not surprising that important sources like the *Encyclopaedia of War*[7] actually list numerous (between twelve and fifty-five) conflicts in place of the so-called Mongol invasions.[8]

Not only are named conflicts—part of what Richardson called 'deadly quarrels'—an arbitrary designation that, often, does not make sense statistically, but a conflict can have two or more names, two or more conflicts can have the same name, and we found no satisfactory clear-cut hierarchy between war and conflict. Our solution is (1) to treat events as the shorter of event or its disaggregation into units with a maximum duration of twenty-five years each, which corresponds to a generation, and (2) to perform a study of statistical robustness to assess whether other time windows and geographic redefinitions produce different results.

Likewise, the data makes it hard to assess whether the numbers include people who died of the side effects of wars—for example, it makes a difference whether the victims of famine from the siege of Jerusalem are included or not in the historical figures.

Problem 5: Units for the Analysis

Should one consider, in a trend analysis, raw or relative numbers, that is the actual number of people killed or their ratio to the total population? Given that the population of the earth has been increasing over time, a constant rate of violence would give the illusion of an increase in casualties. To deal with the first problem (fat tails) we made use of extreme value theory. For problem 2 we had to develop a technique to allow boundedness in the analysis and to publish it as a standalone.[9] To deal with problems 3 through 5 we relied on various methods from the branch of robust statistics.[10]

Fat Tails and Theories of Violence

The first main attempt to model violence using power laws was done in 1948 by the polymath Lewis Fry Richardson who visually fit a power law to war data between 1820 and 1945. Richardson himself came from discoveries of self-similarity and scaling in nature,[11] particularly coastlines and some turbulent phenomena.

Intuitively, we can explain power laws as follows:

the ratio $\dfrac{\#events\ killing\ more\ than\ 100k}{\#events\ killing\ more\ than\ 50k}$

is approximately equal to $\dfrac{\#events\ killing\ more\ than\ 200k}{\#events\ killing\ more\ than\ 100k}$.

This scalability is crucial, as it makes the law both intuitive and tractable. More precisely, there is an exponent in the tails, such that, for a large deviation K,

Probability of exceeding a value K = proportional to $K^{-\alpha}$,

where alpha is the tail exponent and the major determinant to the shape of the distribution. The lower the alpha, the fatter the tails. A helpful property of alpha is that it is *robust to mistakes in the data*: as we will see, data imprecisions do not affect its estimation. Please note that the proportionality holds in the tails, that is, for K very large, but not necessarily for smaller values.

Many research papers later confirmed the power law nature of casualties' data[12] (although Cirillo[13] recently showed that many phenomena identified as power laws are something else, though still heavy-tailed because of their high variance). Some scholars, such as Cederman,[14] have tried to develop models justifying such a behaviour, for example, agent-based constructions and cellular automata. However, it is not our goal to discuss these models, but rather to focus on statistical evidence and inference.

Fat Tails, Long Peace, and the Foundational Principles of Statistical Inference

Pinker started the promotion of an idea that violence has dropped, invoking the various moral values causing what he calls 'the obsolescence of major wars.' Similarly to Buckle, he writes,[15] 'The most promising explanation, I believe, is that the components of the human mind that inhibit violence—what Abraham Lincoln called "the better angels of our nature"—have become increasingly engaged.'

It is important to discuss Pinker's view, because it has been cited as so-called evidence for the drop in violence across political science. Pinker deals with the phenomenon of violence and its manifestations at different scales, from homicides and rapes to riots and wars, from death penalty and torture issues to civil rights violations and denial.

To explain and sustain his vision about the general decline in violence, Pinker develops the metaphor of a constant battle, within humanity, among some 'inner demons', such as revenge, sadism, and ideology, and some 'better angels', such as empathy, self-control, and reason (even if it is not completely clear, at least to us, what it is that Pinker calls reason). Demons are mainly expressions of atavic feelings and compulsions, going back to the original beast in us. Angels are a result of civil evolution and reason development. Since civilization seems to be an unstoppable process, angels are therefore bound to win the battle.

Using a sort of meta-analysis, relying on others' results, Pinker collects a number of figures to support the idea of a decline in violence in the history of humanity.

He devotes two full chapters to armed conflicts, in all their possible expressions: the fifth, 'The Long Peace', and the sixth, 'The New Peace'. In the specific case of wars, he relies on previous analyses[16]. However, in our view, the way in which he reads and interprets the results of scholars such as Richardson reveals an attempt at bending empirical evidence to his own theory—for example, when he deals with the Poisson nature of the *number* of armed conflicts over time. As we also discovered in our data analysis, consistent with Richardson, there is a lack of sufficient evidence to reject the null hypothesis of a homogenous Poisson process[17], which denies the presence of any trend in the belligerence of humanity. Nevertheless, Pinker refers to some yet-unspecified mathematical model that could also support such a decline in violence, what he calls a 'non-stationary' process, even if the data looks the way it looks. It is on the basis of this and other apodictic statements that Pinker builds his narrative about violence.

In addition, Pinker builds a theory that is not at all statistically robust to problems 3 and 4 in the previous section—such as changes in the An Lushan estimates[18] or the granularity of the Mongolian named conflict[19]. However, at its core, Pinker's severe mistake is one of standard naive empiricism—basically mistaking data (actually, absence of data) for evidence and building his theory of why violence has dropped without even ascertaining whether violence did indeed drop. This is not to say that Pinker's socio-psychological theories can't be right: they are just not sufficiently connected to data to start remotely looking like science. Fundamentally, statistics is about ensuring that people do not build scientific theories out of hot air—that is, without significant departure from random. Otherwise, there is a danger that the researcher is fooled by randomness, and we have a very clear idea of what departure from random means.

For fat-tailed variables, the conventional mechanism of the law of large numbers (on which statistical inference commonly reposes) is considerably slower, and significance requires more data and longer periods to observe convergence, and thus meaningful results. As Taleb shows in *Silent Risk*, one may need up to 10 billion observations to reliably observe the mean of a phenomenon subject to the Pareto 80/20 principle.

Ironically, there are claims that this can be done on little data: inference is asymmetric under fat-tailed domains. We require more data to assert that there are no black swans than to assert that there are black swans, hence we would need much more data to claim a drop in violence than to claim a rise in it.

Finally, statements that are not deemed statistically significant—and shown to be so—should never be used to construct scientific theories. Descriptive statistics, though deemed unscientific and anecdotal, can be useful for exploratory discussions, but not with fat-tailed processes when the random variable entails exposures rather than binary outcomes. These foundational principles are often missed because, typically, social scientists' statistical training is limited to mechanistic tools from thin-tailed domains. In physics, one can often claim evidence from small datasets, bypassing standard statistical methodologies, simply because the variance for these variables is low (or the process has a strong theory verified on a high signal-to-noise ratio). The higher the variance, the more data one needs to make statistical claims. For fat tails, the variance is typically high and underestimated in past data.

The second, more serious error Pinker made in his conclusion is to believe that tail events and the mean are somehow different animals, not realizing that the mean includes these tail events. Further, for fat-tailed variables, the mean is almost entirely determined by extremes. If you are uncertain about the tails, then you are uncertain about the mean. It is thus incoherent to say that violence has dropped but maybe not the risk of tail events; it would be like saying that someone is extremely virtuous except during the school shooting episode when he killed thirty students, or that nuclear weapons are very safe, as they only kill a small percentage of the time.

Our Methodology

The data we have used come from two main sources, the *Encyclopaedia of Wars*[6] and the accurate Necrometrics website by Matthew White,[20] but some extra texts where used for verification purposes.

The first observation in our collection is Boudicca's Revolt of 60–61 CE, while the last one is the still-open international armed conflict against the Islamic State of Iraq and the Levant. In total we have 565 observations.

In principle, we selected all armed conflicts with more than 3,000 absolute casualties in the period from 1 to 2015 CE, counting both soldiers and civilians. There are a few exceptions in our dataset that cannot be considered standard armed conflicts, according to the common definition of Wallensteen and Sollenberg.[21] These are some of the bloodiest dictatorships in history, such as Joseph Stalin's regime in the Soviet Union. This choice has been made to be consistent with other works about war victims and violence.[22,23]

A natural question is why we have chosen to impose a 3,000-casualties threshold when collecting the observations about armed conflicts. We have four main reasons:

- We do not need smaller casualties to get the properties, as smaller casualties do not affect the average. Richardson himself noted, 'Anyone who tries to make a list of "all the wars" encounters the difficulty that there are so many small incidents, that some rule has to be made to exclude them.' The higher the threshold, the fewer the observations and the lower the noise and imprecision.

- The main object of our concern is tail risk, that is, the risk of major destructive conflicts. The statistical techniques we use to study this type of extreme event require the imposition of thresholds for all the approximations to hold.

- Conflicts with many victims are more likely to be registered and studied by historians. It would be impossible to have reliable information about 'small' battles with tens of victims. Empirically, 3,000 victims proved to be a good selection threshold for other aspects of the analysis.

- A 3,000-casualties threshold gives us a better confidence about the estimated number of casualties, thanks to the possibly larger number of sources to compare. However, the risk of over-exaggeration, especially for the large conflicts of antiquity is something we had to take into consideration.

In order to be consistent with the sociological literature on armed conflicts, we have used different types of data in our analyses:

- *Actual data*, that is, data as collected by historians. Statistically speaking, these are the raw data.

- *Rescaled data*, that is, casualties expressed in terms of today's world population, in order to have comparability in terms of relative impact of wars. Rescaled data are obtained by dividing the number of casualties in a given year by the world population in that year, and then multiplying everything by today's world population. When rescaling data, we have used the population estimates of Klein and van Drecht[24] and the UN.[25,26]

- *Transformed-rescaled data*, that is, data obtained via the so-called dual transformation, whose aim is to deal with the boundedness/unboundedness of the support of the distribution of war casualties. This transformation is more technical, but, as we briefly explain in the section about methods, it is meant to correct for an interpretation error about the apparent infinite-mean nature of war casualties data.

Interestingly, our results hold, notwithstanding the definition of data. Numerical estimates may vary, but the qualitative interpretation stays the same.

Data problems: First of all, it is important to notice that our data, especially for what concerns antiquity, is likely to suffer from selection/historiographical bias. It was in fact not possible to collect observations about conflicts taking place in the Americas and Australia before their discovery by European conquerors. Naturally, this lack of evidence does not mean that nothing happened in those areas in the past.

Similarly, because of problems with sources, we probably miss some conflicts of antiquity in Europe or, say, in China in the sixteenth century. However, we can assume that the majority of these conflicts are not in the very tail of the distribution of casualties, say in the top 10 or 20 percent. It is in fact not really plausible that historians have not reported a conflict of 1 million casualties (or more) so that such an event is not present in our sources.

Dealing with historical data, some dating back to the first century CE, also requires some attention, because of the problems of inconsistency and lack of uniformity in the attribution of casualties by historians. It can be difficult, if not impossible, to distinguish casualties from direct violence from those arising from such side effects as contagious diseases and hunger.

We mentioned earlier that reports were highly source dependent and impossible to fact-check. Some data, such as the An Lushan rebellion in China, estimated by Pinker to have killed 36 million people (around 430 million by today's population) are highly dubious[27]—and help perpetuate the impression that the world is less violent. It may have been 13 million, and the numbers were the result of the census and dispersion of officials in the revenue department.[28]

Data aggregation is another issue. We said that conflicts such as the so-called Mongol invasions are nothing more than artificial designations, which need to be treated carefully as synthetic observations. These events are in fact artificial containers created by historians to aggregate those battles sharing important historical, geographical, and political characteristics, but that never really existed as a single event. For historical/historiographical reasons, these events tend to be more present in antiquity and the Middle Ages, thus possibly causing a naive overestimation of the severity of conflicts in the past. Even among these aggregations there are major differences: WWI and WWII naturally also involved several tens of battles in very different locations, but these battles took place in a much shorter time period, with no major time separation among them.

Curing the data problems: All these data problems can be dealt with by considering each single observation in our collection as an imprecise estimate, in the definition of Viertl.[29] Our technique for robustness is as follows. Using Monte Carlo methods, and assuming that the real number of casualties in a conflict is uniformly distributed between the minimum and the maximum estimate in the available historical records, the tail exponent ξ, the quantity that governs the tail of our war casualties distribution, is not affected, apart from the negligible differences in the smaller decimals. We did another battery of tests for other variables. (See figures 2.1 and 2.2 for an idea of how we conducted the tests.)

From a statistical point of view, the methods we use to study tail risk are robust. In simple words, this means that our results—and the relative interpretations—are immune to small changes in the data. Even more, our results cannot be reversed on the basis of a few observations added, removed, or corrected. A thorough analysis of robustness shows that our estimates are preserved and would replicate even if we missed one-third of the data.

To conclude this section about data problems, we think it is important to stress that our dataset, despite its evident temporal connotation, does not form a proper time series. It is in fact trivial to notice that the different conflicts of humanity do not share the same set of causes. Battles belonging to different centuries and continents are not only independent, but also surely have different origins. In statistical words, we cannot assume the existence of a unique *conflict generator process*, as if conflicts were coming from the same source.

For this reason, we believe that performing time-series analysis on this kind of data is useless, if not dangerous, given that one could extrapolate misleading trends, as done, for example, by Pinker. How could the An Lushan rebellion (755 CE) be dependent on the Siege of Constantinople by

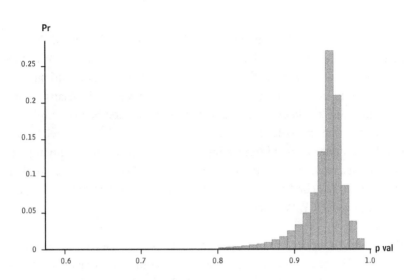

FIGURE 2.1. *How we test our robustness to the reliability of historical reports.*
We create 100,000 different histories as uniform random numbers between high and
low estimates from the datasets (which under aggregation appear Gaussian) and check
if re-combinations lead to different results (we used the p-value, actually 1-p-value,
for the scale parameter not because we rely on p-values but because p-values are
extremely sensitive to changes in data). Some histories include Pinker's exaggerated
numbers for the An Lushan rebellion, others don't.

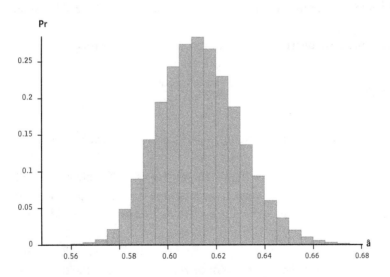

FIGURE 2.2. *The tail exponent from maximum likelihood, not EVT,*
is invariant to errors in the reporting of conflicts.

the Arabs (717 CE) or have an impact on the Viking raids in Ireland? Notice that we are not saying that all conflicts are independent: during WWII, the attack on Pearl Harbor and the Battle of France were not independent, notwithstanding the spatio-temporal divide, and that's why historians merge them into one single event, as we have already noticed before. While we can accept that, historically, most of the causes of WWII are related to WWI, it is better to avoid translating this dependence when studying the number of casualties: it would be quite absurd to believe that the number of victims in 1944 had anything to do with the death toll in 1917. How could the magnitude of WWII depend on WWI?

Since we are interested in estimating the tail risk of violent conflict, that is, the risk of large destructive wars and armed conflicts, we use tools from extreme value theory (EVT) to understand the behaviour of the right tail of the distribution of war casualties. EVT is a branch of statistics dealing with extreme and rare events, in the form of maxima and minima.[30,31,32]

Within the broad field of EVT, we mainly use the so-called generalized Pareto (GP) approximation,[33,34] according to which all the exceedances above a high threshold, if this threshold is correctly chosen, tend to follow a GP distribution, a skewed distribution, which can be characterized by fat tails.

The cumulative distribution function of a GP random variable is

$$GPD(z;\xi,\sigma,u) = \begin{cases} 1 - \left(1 + \xi\frac{z-u}{\sigma}\right)^{-\frac{1}{\xi}} & \xi \neq 0 \\ 1 - e^{-\frac{z-u}{\sigma}} & \xi = 0 \end{cases},$$

where $z \geq u$ for $\xi \geq 0$, and $u \leq z \leq u - \sigma / \xi$ for $\xi < 0$, with $u, \xi \in \mathbb{R}$ and $\sigma > 0$.

The parameter ξ is the most important one for us, as it controls for the fatness of the right tail. The larger ξ, the fatter the tail. For $\xi > 0.5$, the GP distribution has no variance. For $\xi > 1$, even the mean is not defined.

For what concerns war casualties, we find that the Paretian tail is actually so fat that, from a theoretical point of view, the mean of the distribution is not finite (see figure 2.3). In simple terms, this means that the tail risk is so large that one single event, one single war, could destroy the whole of humanity (7.3 billion people). In reality, things are a little bit more complicated, because data can be misleading, even when approaching a problem using the correct methodology (EVT, when studying tails). While we show that the tail risk of violent conflict is actually large—much larger than what one could simply infer using standard descriptive and inferential statistics (not appropriate in this case), we also point out that it cannot be infinite, as data tend to suggest naively using EVT. In fact, no single conflict can kill more than the entire population of the world.

This implies the presence of an upper bound that we can use to correct our estimates. The dual distribution approach,[35] based on a special log transformation of data, is the way in which we deal with apparently infinite mean phenomena like war casualties.

Once again, it is worth underlining that all the statistical methods we use are robust, that is to say, they tend to be immune to even non-trivial changes in the data (a third of reported events in our data could change significantly, and still our results are preserved).

The Distribution of War Casualties: Basic Facts

When looking at the distribution of war casualties, the first thing we notice is that it is highly skewed with a very fat right tail. Figure 2.3 contains a simple histogram using actual data: while most armed conflicts generate a few thousands victims,[36] on the left-hand side of the picture, a few conflicts cause millions of casualties, with WWII totalling between 48.5 and 85 million victims, depending on the source (in the graph we show the median: 73 million).

The average number of casualties in our sample is 1,067,568. The in-sample standard deviation is 5,738,541. However, since the standard deviation is not a reliable measure under fat tails, given that the theoretical variance may not exist, (see endnotes 32 and 35) we also provide the mean absolute deviation, or MAD:[37] 1,747,869. This number shows the extreme volatility of war casualties, something compatible with a fat-tailed phenomenon.

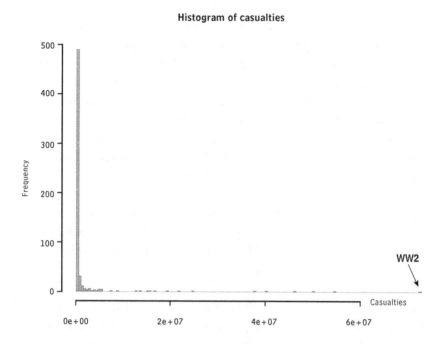

FIGURE 2.3. Histogram of war casualties using raw data.

Other useful statistics are the median (40,000), the first quartile (13,538), and the third quartile (182,000): 75 percent of all armed conflicts generate less than 182,000 casualties, and still the sample mean is almost six times larger!

Figures 2.4 and 2.5 show the number, and the relative magnitude with respect to world population, of war casualties over time, when using two different definitions of data: actual and rescaled observations.

It is interesting to notice how the choice of the type of data may lead to different interpretations of trends and patterns. From rescaled data, one could, for example, superficially infer a decrease in the number of casualties over time. It is in fact obvious that rescaling data will tend to inflate past observations, as already noticed by Epstein,[38] who also objects that rescaling may generate paradoxical situations. Citing him, 'why should we be content with only a relative decrease? By this logic, when we reach a

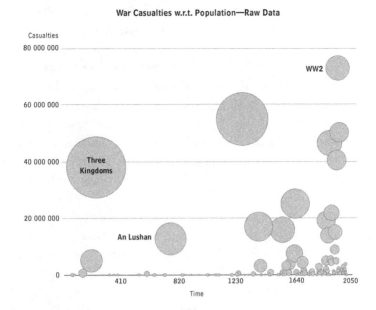

FIGURE 2.4. *War casualties over time with respect to world population using actual data.*

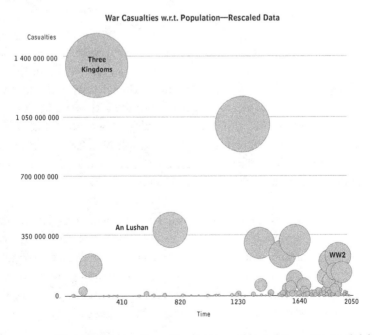

FIGURE 2.5. *War casualties over time with respect to world population using rescaled data.*

world population of nine billion in 2050, Pinker will conceivably be satisfied if a mere two million people are killed in war that year.'

As to the number of armed conflicts, both figures 2.5 and 2.7 seem to suggest an increase of belligerence over time, since most events are concentrated in the last 500 years or so. This is very likely just an illusion, probably due to a reporting bias for the conflicts of antiquity and early Middle Ages. It is certainly easier to obtain decent information about more recent conflicts, and that is why we have many rather precise observations in the last decades and centuries, with respect to what happened in the third century CE.

To correctly study the tail risk of armed conflicts, we need to understand whether our data really exhibit a Paretian right tail, as suggested by figure 2.4. The answer is affirmative. For example, in figure 2.6, we see that, on a log-log scale, the distribution of war casualties shows clear linear behaviour in the right tail. Figure 2.6 is a Zipf plot, and it represents a heuristic tool to look for Paretianity in data by using a property of the survival function of a Pareto-distributed random variable. Many other plots can naturally be used to verify the presence of a fat right tail, such as Maximum-to-Sum and mean excess plots.

Figure 2.6 not only confirms the idea of a Paretian right tail, but it also suggests that the whole distribution of war casualties may be in the domain of attraction of a fat-tailed distribution. The linearity of the survival function starts indeed from the very left-hand side of the plot. In addition, figure 2.6 shows how the right tail tends to close down a little bit. This is a phenomenon commonly known as finite sample bias. It is in fact highly improbable to be able to observe a sufficient number of maxima in the data so that the tail decreases linearly until the end.

Table 2.1 contains some information about the occurrence of armed conflicts over time. For example, if we look at events generating at least 500,000 victims, we discover that, when using raw data, we have to wait an average of twenty-four years to observe such events. The corresponding mean absolute deviation is thirty-three years. If, on the contrary, we use rescaled data, the average inter-arrival time is ten years, with a MAD of 12.

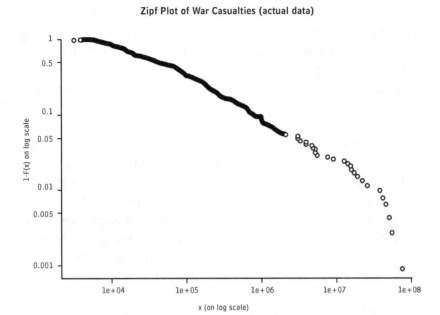

FIGURE 2.6. *Zipf plot (log-log plot of the survival function) of war casualties using actual data.*

Threshold	Average Raw	MAD Raw	Average Rescaled	MAD Rescaled
500,000	24	33	10	12
1,000,000	34	48	13	16
2,000,000	57	73	20	24
5,000,000	93	117	34	43
10,000,000	136	139	52	61
20,000,000	252	267	73	86
50,000,000	372	362	104	114

TABLE 2.1. *Average inter-arrival times and their mean absolute deviation, in integer years, for different casualty thresholds.*

If we increase the threshold[39] and consider conflicts with at least 5 million casualties, we need to wait ninety-three or thirty-four years, depending on the data definition. Intuitively, the bloodier the conflict, the longer the inter-arrival time. For a conflict with at least 50 million victims, an extreme and hopefully rare event, the average inter-arrival time is 372 years, using raw data, with a MAD of 362.

All this tells us that the absence of a conflict generating more than, say, 20 million casualties in the last twenty years is highly insufficient to state that its occurrence probability has decreased over time, given that the average inter-arrival time is 252 years (73 for rescaled), with a MAD of 267 (86 for rescaled) years! Unfortunately, we still have to wait quite some time to say that we are living in a more peaceful era; the actual data we have are neither in favour nor against a structural change in violence when we deal with war casualties. Very simply—we cannot say.

As already stated, using extreme value theory, and in particular the generalized Pareto approximation, we can extrapolate information about the tail risk of armed conflicts.

The estimation of the parameters of a GPD can be performed in different ways; with our data, the best results are obtained using maximum likelihood.[40]

Table 2.2 contains our estimates for the generalized Pareto approximation for the distribution of war casualties, using both actual and rescaled data. For both definitions, we can see that the thresholds above which the GPD approximation holds are definitely larger than the original 3,000 casualties we have imposed in collecting the data. However, in both cases, almost 60 percent of all the observation lies above the two thresholds. Since we are interested in the risk of very large conflicts, dealing with the top 60 percent of all conflicts is definitely more than sufficient for our purposes.[41]

The most interesting result of table 2.2 is the qualitative information we can extrapolate from ξ (decimals are much less relevant). For both actual and rescaled data, we clearly see that $\xi > 1$. This indicates the presence of an infinite mean phenomenon—that is, a phenomenon whose realizations can be so large and erratic that the mean is not a reliable quantity. If the mean of the GPD is not finite, then the mean of the whole distribution of war casualties must be infinite. In fact, since the tail mean is a component of the whole distribution mean, if the former is not finite, the same holds for the latter.

Data	u (threshold)	ξ	Σ
Raw	25,000	1.4985	90620
Rescaled	145,000	1.5868	497436

TABLE 2.2. *Maximum likelihood estimates for the parameters of the GPD approximation of the right tail of the distribution of war casualties. All estimates are significant with a type I error of 5 percent.*

As said, these results are robust to missing or misspecified data. As shown in Cirillo and Taleb,[42] using tools like bootstrap, up to 20 percent of the observations (in the tail or not) could change without affecting the results of the analysis.

If the mean of the distribution of war casualties is not finite, then it means that the tail risk of armed conflicts is not finite. In other words, we could experience at any second a single event annihilating humanity. A nuclear holocaust, or even worse. But can this really be the case?

When dealing with tails, extreme value theory is the right approach. It would be wrong and highly misleading to approach tails using other techniques, mainly relying on normality. However, when using EVT, it is extremely important to take into consideration the real nature of data. Can a conflict kill more than the entire world population? The answer is clearly no. Therefore, this fact needs to be taken into account if we do not want to be fooled by data. The distribution of war casualties is necessarily bounded: we surely cannot kill a negative amount of people, but, on the other side, we cannot kill more than the entire world population (at present, 7.3 billion people, according to the UN). From a statistical point of view, boundedness has one important implication: all the moments of the distribution need to be finite, thus including the mean and the variance. These are the shadow moments, that is to say, moments that cannot be correctly inferred from data, unless we take into consideration the existence of an upper bound, and we correct for it.

Using the so-called dual distribution,[43] a particular log transformation of the original data, to map them on the bounded support, one can obtain the actual moments of the distribution of war casualties. These moments are naturally finite, but they tend to be much larger than those one could estimate from data using their simple empirical counterparts (which are therefore not reliable). For example, using rescaled data, we discover that the tail mean of war casualties above the 1 million threshold is 6.21 million, against a corresponding sample mean of 3.95 million (1.57 times larger). For a threshold of 50 million victims, the sample mean is 28.22 million, while the true (shadow) mean is 67.17 (2.38 times larger).

When dealing with tail risk, another set of important statistics is represented by quantiles. A quantile is the value above which a certain percentage of observations lie. The top 5 percent quantile is the value above which we can find 5 percent of all the observations. Table 2.3 contains the top quantiles of the distribution of war casualties, using the dual distribution approach on both actual and rescaled data. The results are frightening: there is a 5 percent probability, using actual data, of observing a conflict generating at least 2,380,000 casualties; and a 1 percent probability of conflicts with at least 26.8 million victims. Even worse, our data also support a 0.1 percent probability of a war killing something like 800 million people, more than 10 percent of the whole world population. These figures are even scarier when we use rescaled data.

Percentage above	Raw Data $\times 10^7$	Rescaled Data $\times 10^7$
5.0%	2,380,000	15,400,000
1.0%	26,800,000	198,200,000
0.1%	801,100,000	4,751,500,000

TABLE 2.3. *Top quantiles for the distribution of war casualties, as obtained via the dual distribution.*

Conclusion: Is There Any Trend?

The short answer is no. Our data does not support the presence of any particular trend in the number of armed conflicts over time. Humanity seems to be as belligerent as always. No increase nor decrease. Naturally, we are speaking about the type of conflicts for which we have performed our analysis, that is to say the largest and most destructive ones. We cannot say anything about small fights with a few casualties, since they do not belong to our dataset—however, it is crucial that, as a central property of the fat-tailedness of the process, a decline in homicide does not affect the total properties of violence and anyone's risk of death. As we said, the mean is tail-driven.

To the best of our knowledge, no available dataset contains enough information to make credible statements about statistically significant trends in the number of conflicts over time, unless we really think it is reasonable to extrapolate long-term trends on the basis of sixty years of observations, such as those after WWII. Given the inter-arrival times we have observed above, it would be quite naive to act that way.

If we focus our attention on our dataset, and in particular on the observations belonging to the last 600 years (from 1500 CE on), for which missing observations should be fewer and reporting errors smaller, our analyses suggest that the number of large conflicts over time follows a homogeneous Poisson process.[44] In a similar process, the number of observations over time, once we fix a given time interval (say fifty years), follows a Poisson distribution. The number of expected data points only depends on the length of the time interval we choose. For intervals of the same size, the expected number of observations is the same, because the intensity of the process does not vary over time. In simple terms, this finding supports the idea that wars are randomly distributed accidents over time, not following any particular trend, as pointed out by Richardson.

Interestingly, similar conclusions can also be derived by a simple descriptive analysis of data, something that should make our results accessible also to non-statisticians.

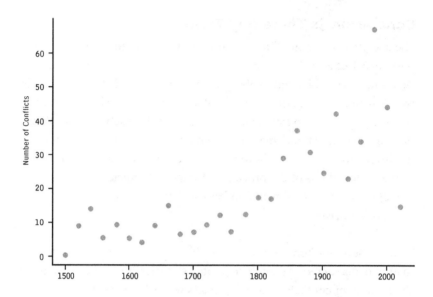

FIGURE 2.7. *Average number of casualties in the period from 1500 to 2015, using a non-overlapping moving window of twenty years. Dark dots: rescaled data. Light dots: actual data.*

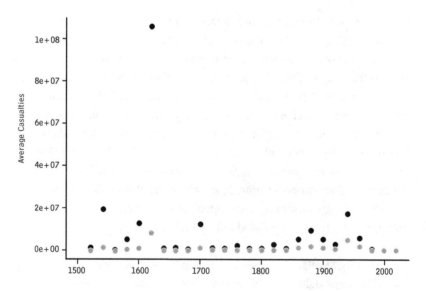

FIGURE 2.8. *Number of conflicts between 1500 and 2015, using a non-overlapping twenty-year moving window. The number of conflicts is clearly increasing over time, together with their volatility.*

In figures 2.7 and 2.8, we show the average number of casualties and the number of conflicts in the period from 1500 to 2015, using a non-overlapping moving window of twenty years. This means that both the average casualties and the number of conflicts are computed for the periods 1501 to 1520 (there is no observation in 1500), 1521 to 1540, 1541 to 1560, and so on.

In figure 2.7, the darker dots represent rescaled data, while the lighter ones are the actual observations. It is quite evident that, for what concerns the average number of casualties, no clear trend is observable.

In figure 2.8, we show the number of armed conflicts in the same moving windows as per figure 2.7. In this case, the number of conflicts seems to be increasing over time, even if the volatility itself appears to be higher. This is an interesting phenomenon from a statistical point of view, as it makes the simple inference based on a few years of data (namely the last sixty years, as in the Long Peace theory) not at all reliable. While we are aware that this behaviour could be due to a historiographical reporting bias, according to which more recent conflicts are more likely to be recorded in data, we would like to stress how, in any case, no Long Peace is observed. In particular, the last 200 years prove to be quite belligerent and stable.

One final comment on the finer-grained period since WWII. Figure 2.9 illustrates the mistake made in theorizing about what has happened since 1945, aside from the fact that we are picking a spike and that a drop is natural after every spike. The way to properly look at the issue is to consider the entire history of wars, simulating from the process, and checking how many periods do not look like the stretch since 1945—by generating simulated regression coefficients. Alas, we are about 0.37 standard deviations away from absence of trend. Note that we are ignoring the survivor bias.

The fact that the shadow mean, or maximum likelihood mean, is in excess of the sample mean across potential values of the parameters (figures 2.10 and 2.11) is not trivial. It means that even a real statistically significant drop in violence would not alter by much the gravity of the situation: the world is even more dangerous than it looks.

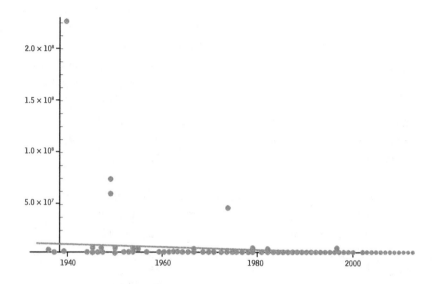

FIGURE 2.9. Violence drop since 1945. Divergence from the process to call it a trend is patently not statistically significant, .37 percent of a standard deviation away. No scientist builds a theory from 0.37 standard deviations.

As observed in the introduction, our work is consistent with (and complements) the findings of Braumoeller (chapter 1 of this volume). Moreover, as the reader will notice, our chapter adds some arguments to the democratic peace debate entailing Russett (chapter 7 of this volume) and Gowa and Pratt (chapter 8 of this volume). In particular, our findings suggest that, at present, even if there has been a rise in democracy at the macro level (something we do not deny), no evidence of decline of wars and general violence can be substantiated with data. It is always tempting to assume that the rise in institutions has contributed to changes in the structure of the world—just as many arguments have been made that the creation of the Federal Reserve and other financial institutions has contributed to stability. In finance, this argument turned out to be wrong: extreme events have been at least as severe (and, if anything, have risen) in spite of the development of such institutions. It may well be the same with violence and, as scientists, we should be aware of that. Hopefully, the future will prove us wrong.

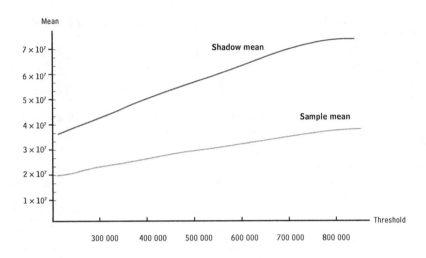

FIGURE 2.10. *Shadow mean at different thresholds.*

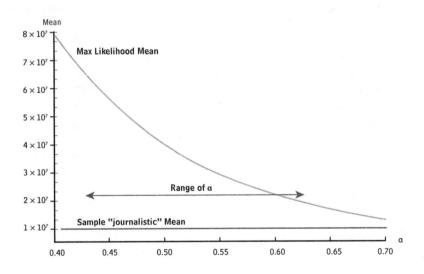

FIGURE 2.11. *Sample mean (journalistic) and maximum likelihood mean at different values of the tail exponent. We notice that a drop in the tail exponent causes an asymmetric effect, hence uncertainty and lack of precision about the tail means worse mean.*

84

Notes

1. H.T. Buckle, *History of Civilization in England*. Vol. 1 (London: John W. Parker and Son, 1858).

2. Note that Buckle was placing himself in the flourishing tradition of scientific social science of Auguste Comte.

3. Nassim Nicholas Taleb, *The Black Swan: The Impact of the Highly Improbable* (London: Random House and Penguin, 2007).

4. Lewis Fry Richardson, 'Variation of the Frequency of Fatal Quarrels with Magnitude,' *Journal of the American Statistical Association* 43, no. 244 (1948): 523–46.

5. Steven Pinker, *The Better Angels of Our Nature: Why Violence Has Declined* (New York: Viking Press, 2011).

6. Nassim Nicholas Taleb, *Silent Risk* (Descartes, 2018), www.fooledbyrandomness.com /FatTails.html.

7. Charles Phillips and Alan Axelrod, *Encyclopedia of Wars*, 3 vols. (New York: Infobase, 2004).

8. Paradoxically, speaking about Mongol invasions as a whole would correspond to some Mongolian-centric historian writing about European wars, possibly bundling all events from the Franco–Prussian War to WWII.

9. Nassim Nicholas Taleb and Pasquale Cirillo, 'On the Shadow Moments of Apparently Infinite-Mean Phenomena,' *Unifying Themes in Complex Systems IX: Proceedings of the Ninth International Conference on Complex Systems*, 2016, 155–164.

10. Ricardo Maronna, Douglas Martin, and Victor Yohai, *Robust Statistics: Theory and Methods* (New York: Wiley, 2006).

11. Benoit Mandelbrot, *The Fractal Geometry of Nature* (New York: Times Books, 1982).

12. For a review: Aaron Clauset, 'Trends and Fluctuations in the Severity of Interstate Wars,' *Science Advances* 4 (2018), 10.1126/sciadv.aao3580; and Pasquale Cirillo and Nassim Nicholas Taleb, 'On the Statistical Properties and Tail Risk of Violent Conflicts,' *Physica A: Statistical Mechanics and Its Applications* 452 (2016): 29–45.

13. Pasquale Cirillo, 'Are Your Data Really Pareto Distributed?' *Physica A: Statistical Mechanics and Its Applications* 392, no. 23 (2013): 5947–62.

14. Lars-Erik Cederman, 'Modeling the Size of Wars: From Billiard Balls to Sandpiles,' *The American Political Science Review* 97, no. 1 (2003): 135–50.

15. Steven Pinker, 'Taming the Beast within Us,' *Nature* 478 (2011): 309–11.

16. Lewis Fry Richardson, *Statistics of Deadly Quarrels* (Chicago: Quadrangle Books, 1960).

17. A Poisson process is a particular stochastic process according to which the number of events over a given time interval follows a Poisson distribution. In a homogeneous Poisson process, the intensity of the process does not change over time, and the expected number of events is a function of the length of the time interval under consideration.

18. BBC, 'The An Lushan Rebellion,' *In Our Times* (London: BBC, 2012), accessed November 5, 2018, https://www.bbc.co.uk/programmes/b01by8ms.

19. Pasquale Cirillo and Nassim N. Taleb, 'On the statistical properties and tail risk of violent conflicts,' *Physica A: Statistical Mechanics and its Applications*, Vol. 452 (2016):29-45.

20. Matthew White, 'Necrometrics: Death Tolls across History,' accessed April 14, 2017, http://www.necrometrics.com/index.htm.

21. Peter Wallensteen and Margareta Sollenberg, 'Armed Conflict 1989-2000,' *Journal of Peace Research* 38, no. 5 (2001): 629-44.

22. John E. Mueller, *Retreat from Doomsday: The Obsolescence of Major War* (New York: Basic Books, 1989).

23. Taylor Seybolt, Jay Aronson, and Baruch Fischhoff, eds., *Counting Civilian Casualties: An Introduction to Recording and Estimating Nonmilitary Deaths in Conflict* (Oxford: Oxford University Press, 2013).

24. Kees Klein Goldewijk and G. van Drecht, 'HYDE 3: Current and Historical Population and Land Cover,' in *Integrated Modelling of Global Environmental Change: An overview of IMAGE 2.4*, eds. A.F. Bouwman, T. Kram, Kees Klein Goldewijk (The Hague: Netherlands Environmental Assessment Agency, 2006), 93-112.

25. United Nations Department of Economic and Social Affairs, *The World at Six Billion* (New York: UN Press, 1999).

26. United Nations Department of Economic and Social Affairs, *2015 Revision of World Population Prospects* (New York: UN Press, 2015).

27. John Durand, 'The Population Statistics of China, AD 2-1953,' *Population Studies* 13, no. 3 (1960): 209-23.

28. Charles Fitzgerald, *China: A Short Cultural History* (London: Cresset Press, 1935).

29. R. Viertl, *Statistical Methods for Non-precise Data* (Boca Raton, FL: CRC Press, 1995).

30. Emil Gumbel, *Statistics of Extremes* (Cambridge: Cambridge University Press, 1958).

31. Laurens de Haan and Ana Ferreira, *Extreme Value Theory: An Introduction* (Berlin: Springer Verlag, 2006).

32. Paul Embrechts, Claudia Klueppelberg, and Thomas Mikosch, *Modelling Extremal Events* (Berlin: Springer Verlag, 1997).

33. James Pickands, 'Statistical Inference Using Extreme Order Statistics,' *The Annals of Statistics* 1, no. 1 (1975): 119-31.

34. A.A. Balkema A.A. and L. de Haan, 'Residual Life Time at Great Age,' *The Annals of Probability* 2, no. 5 (1974): 792-804.

35. Pasquale Cirillo and Nassim Nicholas Taleb, 'Expected Shortfall Estimation for Apparently Infinite-Mean Models of Operational Risk,' *Quantitative Finance* 16, no. 10 (2016): 1485-94.

36. Please notice that we are not giving any ethical judgment. When we say 'a few victims' we think of them as statistical data, numbers. We all agree that, from an ethical point of view, one victim is already too much.

37. The MAD is the mean of all the absolute deviations of each data point from the sample mean. Formally: $MAD(x) = E|X - E[X]|$, where E stands for mathematical expectation.

38. Robert Epstein, 'Book Review: *The Better Angels of Our Nature: Why Violence Has Declined,*' *Scientific American*, October 7, 2011.

39. The thresholds in table 2.1 are just arbitrary and meant to give useful information in a compact table. Other thresholds can be chosen, but one general monotone behaviour can be observed, in accordance with intuition: the higher the threshold, the longer the average inter-arrival time.

40. Michael Falk, Jürg Hüsler, and Rolf-Dieter Reiss, *Laws of Small Numbers: Extremes and Rare Events* (Berlin: Birkhäuser, 2004).

41. In most applications of EVT, only the top 5 percent (or less) of the observations lie above the given threshold. Our 60 percent is definitely very large, confirming the idea of a whole distribution in the domain of attraction of a fat-tailed distribution, like the Fréchet (see Embrechts et al., 1997, note 36 above).

42. Pasquale Cirillo and Nassim N. Taleb, 'On the statistical properties and tail risk of violent conflicts,' *Physica A: Statistical Mechanics and its Applications*, Vol. 452 (2016):29-45.

43. Ibid.

44. Pasquale Cirillo and Nassim N. Taleb, 'The Decline of Violent Conflicts: What Do the Data Really Say?,' *SSRN Electronic Journal*, November 27, 2016.

SECTION II

Hegemony and Peace

3.

The Quest for Hegemony: A Threat to the Global Order

Richard Ned Lebow and Simon Reich

Introduction

American realists, liberals, journalists, and policymakers speak of American hegemony as if it were an established role, although a threatened one, given the rise of China.[1] They describe hegemony as essential to international political and economic stability, and a role that only America can perform. There is no evidence that the US is a hegemon or has provided the benefits that American international relations (IR) theorists attribute to a hegemon. If these benefits are provided, it is the result of the collective efforts of numerous states, by no means all of them great powers. American assertions of hegemony are viewed with jaundiced, if not hostile, eyes by other states. Hegemony is a fiction, propagated by the Americans to gain special privileges, justify an interventionist foreign policy, support the defence industry, and buttress national self-esteem. In practice, the quest for hegemony is a threat, not a prop to global order.

In the 1960s, Hans Morgenthau repeatedly criticized IR theory for failing to speak truth to power. In his view, the close links among universities, foundations, and government made it relatively easy to co-opt the discipline's principal spokesmen and to substantially reward those who said and wrote what those in power wanted to hear.[2] There is a more benign explanation for this phenomenon: scholars are products of the same culture as policymakers and are likely to share worldviews. For this latter reason, we believe, many American IR theorists, as well as foreign policy and national security analysts, have a normative commitment to American world leadership. Theorists have developed the concept of hegemony to justify and advance this project. It rests on a particular understanding of power and its superordinate importance in world politics.

What Is Hegemony?

The definition and consequence of hegemony is debated among liberals and realists. Michael Doyle understands it 'to mean controlling leadership of the international system as a whole.'[3] Michael Mastanduno contends that hegemony exists when one political unit has the 'power to shape the rules of international politics according to its own interests.'[4] Stuart Kaufman, Richard Little, and William Wohlforth describe hierarchy, which they all but equate with hegemony, as the political-military 'domination' of a single unit 'over most of the international system.'[5] John Ikenberry and Charles Kupchan insist that such influence ultimately rests on material power: 'it is most effectively exercised when a hegemon is able to establish a set of norms that others willingly embrace.'[6]

As understood by American IR scholars, hegemony is international leadership provided by a state whose power is grossly disproportionate to that of other actors in the system. Realists and liberals alike maintain that the US has been a hegemon since 1945, although only a partial hegemon during the long Cold War because of the opposition of the powerful Soviet Union and its allies. At the end of that conflict and the subsequent collapse of the Soviet Union, the US, in their view, became closer to a global hegemon, and some claim that bipolarity gave way to unipolarity.

Many realists contend that America's unrivalled military power enables it to impose its leadership, which they openly acknowledge as a form of domination, Brooks and Wohlforth assert.[7] The US accounts for well over 40 percent of the world's military spending, it is the source of one-quarter of the world's economic activity, its share of the world's gross domestic product (GDP) is larger than that of the EU and three times that of China, and some 65 percent of the world's currency reserve is held in US dollars.[8]

This understanding of hegemony describes it as the relatively straightforward outcome of the material dominance of one state.[9]

An alternative, more sophisticated formulation conceives of hegemony as the result of legitimacy as well as power.[10] Drawing on the Marxist philosopher Antonio Gramsci, Roger Simon describes hegemony as a relation 'not of domination by means of force, but of consent by means of political and ideological leadership'.[11] Theorists differ about whether consent is a function of self-interest—it is better to bandwagon than oppose the dominant power—or legitimacy—the hegemon protects and advances shared norms, values, and policies.[12]

Neorealists John Mearsheimer and Christopher Layne emphasize material interests because they see power at the core of all international relations.[13] The ideational explanation appeals to constructivists who distinguish influence from power. Scholars who stress the normative aspects of hegemony note that great-power and hegemonic status rest on the recognition of rights and duties and are therefore quasi-judicial categories. In practice, powerful states, such as Russia, that have not met their responsibilities in the eyes of other actors are denied the standing and respect conferred by great-power status.[14]

Liberals tend to conceive of hegemony as a mix of power and norms. Robert Keohane observes that hegemony rests on the twin premises 'that order in world politics is typically created by a single hegemonic power' and 'that the maintenance of order requires stability'.[15] He argues that it is more fruitful to think of it as leadership by a single state, although not necessarily by military means.[16] Drawing on their economic might and so-called soft power, hegemons construct regimes that facilitate cooperation.[17] Keohane's conception of hegemony emphasizes norms, rules, and decision-making processes over coercion and bribery, but leaves unclear how institutions, norms, and their procedures are related to or dependent on economic or military power.

John Ikenberry suggests that, for five decades, the American-led liberal, rule-based hegemonic order 'has been remarkably successful.' The US has championed multilateralism, built global institutions, and provided services, security, and open markets as 'the owner and operator of the liberal capitalist political system'.[18] Hegemony has 'provided a stable foundation for decades of Western and global growth and advancement'.[19] By this means, the US was able to orchestrate a relatively benign leadership, distinct from an 'imperial hegemonic order'. It helped to foster Western prosperity, democracy elsewhere, and a peaceful end to the Cold War. This is 'a remarkable achievement'.[20]

According to Ikenberry, the current crisis is one 'of authority *within* the old hegemonic organization of liberal order, *not* a crisis in the deep principles of the order itself. It is a crisis of governance.' The 'character of rule in world politics has been thrown into question' and the liberal international order remains resilient.[21] As an organizational logic of world politics, it is, however, a victim of its own success. A new bargain needs to be struck between the US and emergent actors. It will still rest on a unipolar distribution of power, and with it 'constituencies that support a continued—if renegotiated—American hegemonic role' within a liberal hegemonic order. Ikenberry believes that the US will have to surrender some rights and privileges and strike the kind of deal that will allow it to remain a 'liberal leviathan'. Under such a new arrangement, the US would still qualify as a hegemon.[22]

Another prominent liberal, Joseph Nye, Jr. deliberately and explicitly shies away from terms such as 'unipolarity' and 'hegemon' in his more recent work. He nevertheless de facto defines American military power in those terms. He warns that 'mistaken beliefs in decline—at home and abroad—can lead to dangerous mistakes in policy'. He is relatively optimistic about American retrenchment and capacity for renewal. Nye acknowledges the potential of a Chinese threat, domestic economic decline, and a decline in the dollar through rising debt, but insists, 'Despite these problems and uncertainties, it seems probable that with the right policies, the US economy can continue to produce hard power for the country.'[23]

In contrast to many realists, Joseph Nye, Jr. recognizes that power does not in itself determine outcomes; policy choices and implementation also matter. He distinguishes modes of power: economic versus military and soft versus hard. He, nevertheless, remains resolute in his belief of the central-ity of American values and power to the global order. He warns that 'The coming decades are not likely to see a post-American world, but the United States will need a smart strategy that combines hard- and soft-power re-sources.' Toward this end, Nye advocates, as he has for some time, a liberal approach emphasizing multilateralism, bargaining, and the promotion of American values through globalization.[24]

Realists and liberals maintain a state-centric view of the world and evalu-ate states in terms of their relative power. They concur in understanding any change from hegemony to multipolarity as the result of the decline of the US and the rise of other countries. These alarms have a familiar ring. In the 1970s, realists and liberals worried that hegemony was fast disap-pearing in light of America's seeming economic decline and the rise of Japan and Germany. Some even worried about war with Japan![25] Today, the threat is China, which pessimistic realists expect to challenge the US for world leadership within a decade or two.[26] Many realists and liberals portray the US as a declining power.[27] This fear found an official voice in President Obama's 2010 *National Security Strategy*.[28] The differences among realists as to whether the US is a secure or declining hegemon reflect dif-ferences in judgments about power and its relative distribution. They in-dicate just how subjective any such estimates inevitably are. For liberals, who tend to stress so-called soft as well as hard power, this discrepancy is more understandable.[29]

Realists and liberals share a common normative agenda: the preserva-tion of American hegemony. Michael Mandelbaum, a well-known realist, warns of the 'chaos' that would result in the absence of US hegemony. Like Mearsheimer, he worries that US decline and Chinese ascendancy would result in a hegemonic war.[30] Liberals are just as committed as realists to preserving what they believe to be America's pre-eminent position in the global system, conceiving of the US as 'exceptional and indispensable' to the system's stability.[31] They disagree among themselves about the proper mix and relative importance of power projection, economic dominance, in-stitutions, and cultural influence as appropriate means toward this end but still find enough in common to collaborate on major books and articles.[32]

In one recent major article, Brooks, Ikenberry, and Wohlforth, two liberals and a realist, assert that American hegemonic leadership is benign because it provides political and economic benefits for the US and its partners that outweigh its costs. These include the 'reduction of transaction costs, establishment of credible commitments, facilitation of collective action, creation of focal points [and] monitoring'.[33] Hegemony thus produces many public goods, most notably system stability, although the US, they concede, benefits disproportionately from its pre-eminence.

Hegemony Interrogated

Our criticism of the hegemonic discourse is twofold. We maintain the claim of hegemony is empirically false. By definition, it requires both economic and military dominance and leadership. The American partial hegemony of the immediate post-war period eroded quickly. It was based on the extraordinary and short-lived economic and military power of the US in comparison to the rest of the non-Communist world. In 1944, the US GDP peaked at 35 percent of the world total, a figure that had dropped to 25 by 1960 and 20 percent by 1980.[34] Western Europe and Japan not only rebuilt their economies but also regained much of their self-confidence; both developments reduced the need and appeal of American leadership. The Korean War stalemate in the early 1950s demonstrated the limits of this supposed hegemony, as did the failure of intervention in Indochina in the 1960s and 1970s and the delinking of the dollar from the gold standard in 1971. In the 1980s, the US systematically reneged on its own liberal trading rules by introducing a variety of tariffs and quotas instead of bearing the costs of economic adjustments.[35] More recently, imperial overstretch was evident in the interventions in Afghanistan and Iraq. In each instance, America's capacity was found wanting, and its strategic objectives were frustrated. The supposed 'unipolar moment' of US power in the early 1990s was accompanied by an unprecedented number of intrastate wars, with the US unable to impose solutions consistent with hegemony.[36]

Hegemony rests on legitimacy as well as power, and here, too, the US position has seriously eroded. Public opinion in Europe was extremely sympathetic to the US after 9/11, then reversed itself and came to consider the US a greater threat to world peace than North Korea.[37] In Britain, those with favourable opinions of the US dropped from 83 percent in 2000 to 56 percent in 2006. In other countries, the US suffered an even steeper decline.[38] This evaluation had not changed much by 2007, when an opinion poll carried out for the BBC World Service in twenty-seven countries found that 51 percent of respondents regarded the US negatively, a figure surpassed only by their negative evaluations of Iran and Israel—54 and 56 percent, respectively. By comparison, North Korea was regarded negatively by only 48 percent of respondents.[39] Since the onset of the Iraq War, the US has undergone a shift in its profile from a status quo to a revisionist power.[40]

The election of President Obama had a positive effect on these ratings, but the US still trailed other advanced industrial states in popularity. Among Western countries, no country generated as many negative responses as the US (34 percent) in terms of global influence.[41] The 'Obama bump did not last, global opinion about his policies declining significantly by the spring of 2012'.[42] The American IR literature either ignores or minimizes the significance of these events or seeks to explain them away as somehow aberrant to a general trend that has allegedly sustained American power and its acceptance by others.

The second element of our critique concerns the inconsistency and even contradictions of the hegemonic literature. Realists and liberals have long associated the distribution of power with the distribution of functions in the global system. However, they have never developed an adequate metric for measuring power that accounts for the enormous variations in their assessments and forecasts. Such a metric is impossible to formulate because power is a composite of so many different factors, among them territory, population, geographic location, economic development, robustness of the economy, level of technology, military strength, system of government, and quality of leadership. Most of these categories, in turn, are composites, as are the factors that compose them. Consider military power. Among other things, it is based on modern weaponry, skilled personnel, good strategic plans and leadership, and appropriate deployments. Weaponry varies in its capability, maintenance, and relevance to strategic and tactical challenges. Each of these criteria can only be assessed relatively and in context. The more we look into the question of power, the murkier the concept becomes.

Liberals and realists contend that hegemony is legitimate in the eyes of other important actors who welcome American leadership and enforcement as beneficial to global stability and their national interests. The only foreign support for these claims comes from conservative politicians and authoritarian leaders, the latter direct beneficiaries of US military and economic backing. There has been a noticeable decline in pleas for US leadership since the end of the Cold War and, as noted earlier, a corresponding increase in opposition to US military and economic initiatives. Since the Iraq War, the US has undergone a shift in its profile from a status quo to a revisionist power. Germany, Canada, and Japan now top the list of respected countries, followed by France, Britain, China, and India. Even pariah countries such as North Korea score better than the US on some surveys. More recent surveys reflect a sustained theme: the US is rarely perceived as acting in the interests of the international community, and whatever legitimacy its leadership once had has significantly eroded.[43]

Order and Disorder

Charles Kindleberger envisaged hegemony as conferring three benefits on the international community. The first is normative and consists of leadership. This is the capacity to shape the policy agenda of global institutions or ad hoc coalitions.[44] It requires knowledge and manipulation of appropriate discourses.[45] It also requires insight into how other actors define their interests, what they identify as problems, and what responses they consider appropriate. Power is important but must be understood as embedded in institutional and normative structures. Normative influence is heavily dependent on political skill, and all the more so in a world in which so many, if not most, important initiatives are multilateral.

The second benefit of hegemony is economic management. This function is primarily *custodial* and entails management of risk through market signalling (information passed, intentionally or not, among market participants) and intergovernmental negotiations in a variety of venues. The intent, according to Kindleberger, is to stabilize and undergird the functions of the global economic system.[46] Many American IR theorists nevertheless ignore the evidence that America has either willingly contravened, or is increasingly incapable of performing, these functions. While overlooking the declining performance of the US as a manager of the global system, these theorists' understanding of a hegemon has nevertheless expanded to include additional functions: the provision of liberal, multilateral trading rules, the sponsorship of international institutions, and the promotion of liberal democratic values.[47]

The third benefit of hegemony is enforcement of global initiatives, what we call sponsorship. It ultimately depends on capabilities, which may be military, economic, or knowledge based. Sponsorship reflects what IR theorists consider essential to the creation and maintenance of international institutions and of the enforcement of global regulations or norms. Effective sponsorship requires dialogue, negotiation, and the use of regional or global institutions as venues. Above all, it requires agreed goals and procedures to confer legitimacy on any initiative and achieve a division of responsibilities. Sponsorship is not the same as leadership. It is neither unilateralism nor 'a first among equals' in a traditional multilateral forum or alliance. Rather, it entails a capacity to listen, and then a selective willingness to use a variety of capabilities to implement consensual goals that are consistent with self-interest.

Jeffrey Taliaferro notes in his chapter all three functions of hegemony require contingent forms of influence rather than the blunt exercise of power. Their application is becoming increasingly diffused among states rather than concentrated in the hands of a hegemon. These functions are performed by multiple states, sometimes in collaboration with non-state actors. Global governance practices are sharply at odds with the formulations of realists and liberals alike. Western Europeans have made consistent efforts to extend their normative influence by promoting agendas well beyond those with which they are traditionally associated. These include environmental and human rights initiatives, but also security issues and corporate regulation. Asian states, most notably China, have increasingly assumed a custodial role, albeit embryonic at this point, quite at odds with the neo-mercantilist or rising military power depiction of realists.

The first function, agenda setting, describes the capacity to initiate, legitimate, and advocate policy issues. These issues cut across the spectrum of social, economic, political, and security concerns. They are characteristically associated with progressive agendas, such as environmentalism, human rights, social or economic justice, or civilian protection. They appeal to broad conceptions of justice, because in today's world, this is a precondition for successful adoption. Agenda setting seeks to have these issues debated within regional or global organizations or broadly representative multilateral forums. It relies heavily on persuasion, generally in an institutional context, and arguably constitutes the most important form of leadership, as it does in domestic politics.[48]

Most liberals, by contrast, downplay the role of agency in multilateral policymaking. They describe international regimes as sets of implicit or explicit principles, norms, rules, and decision-making procedures around which actors' expectations converge, without ever describing how and why expectations converge beyond the leadership a hegemon is expected to provide. That leadership is attributed to the hegemon's material capacities to underwrite the cost of the regime.[49] Material capabilities do not ineluctably promote successful leadership. One need only contrast the US and Soviet experience with their respective European partners during the Cold War. NATO worked much more by consensus and the Warsaw Pact by dictation, with profound consequences for the behaviour and survival of both alliance systems. The difference was not due to material capabilities—both superpowers towered above their respective partners in this respect—but to their leadership styles and abilities.

To be effective, agenda setting requires the adoption of proposed measures in the context of multilateral venues that are designed for negotiation. Persuasion relies as much on the legitimacy of the proposal as on the sticks and carrots of material power.

The problem of civilian protection offers a telling example of how agenda setting works. Norway, not a great power, played an important role in the promotion of the concept of civilian protection. In the 1990s, the Norwegian government awarded funds to the PRIO to think through the concept and what would be required to implement it.[50] In the UN, Norway worked with middle powers such as Canada to promote human security. The Norwegians focused much of their efforts on promoting the responsibility to protect (R2P) doctrine in collaboration with other states and NGOs, including the Brussels-based International Crisis Group. R2P seeks to invert the traditional realist focus on sovereignty and the rights of states by stressing their responsibility to protect civilians or be subject to the prospect of multilateral intervention.[51] By 2001, the R2P initiative had gained significant momentum and won the unstinting support of then UN Secretary General, Kofi Annan. Annan had earlier expressed the sentiment that 'even national sovereignty can be set aside if it stands in the way of the Security Council's overriding duty to preserve international peace and security'.[52]

Over the next two years, Norway and a coalition of smaller powers worked to widen their basis of support by enlisting key states from the global south. By 2005, the language of the R2P doctrine was embraced by the UN as consistent with chapters VI and VIII of the UN Charter. At that time, more than 150 world leaders adopted R2P, legitimating the use of force through multilateral intervention initiatives sanctioned by the UN Security Council.[53] The Obama administration formally adopted R2P's principles as part of US policy in its *National Security Strategy*, issued in 2010.[54] R2P had become operational: it found instantiation in UN resolutions about Kenya's 2008 post-election violence and then in Darfur before being embraced in Libya.[55]

The second benefit is custodianship. Kindleberger famously identified the set of economic tasks a hegemon (although not a term he actually used in that context) must perform in this connection in acting as a lender of last resort.[56] Liberals and some realists insist that only a hegemon can maintain stable patterns of exchange within a pre-existing but evolving global economic structure.[57] Because the US has played this role in the post-war world, liberals assert, the rules of exchange and finance have remained consistent, based on principles of the free exchange of goods and services. The result has been unprecedented and widely distributed economic growth.

This is a questionable claim. The US has often transgressed the principles liberals describe as essential by adopting protectionist measures in the name of fair trade. The US shook the foundations of the global economic order by unilaterally ending the convertibility of the dollar, when it closed the gold window in 1973. It exploited its position by borrowing vast sums of money and at times running high rates of inflation that it would not have been possible for any other country to do without encountering sanctions.[58] It engendered the 2008 Great Recession through lax financial regulation. The image of American hegemony as marked by a broader, enlightened conception of self-interest and of being indispensable to growth and stability, is not only self-serving but also inaccurate.

Liberals have characterized the US as a benign actor; during the Great Depression and its aftermath, it was needed as a stabilizer to provide a series of public goods. Susan Strange offers a markedly different interpretation of the post-war period, one in which purposive American efforts at financial deregulation have undermined its capacity for global economic management.[59] She characterizes American policies as motivated by a long-term systematic effort to accrue benefits and offload costs. Arguably, the US has succeeded. In the Vietnam era, it exported its relatively large deficits and enjoined its major trading partners to hold dollar debt through a series of sticks and carrots that included delinking the dollar to gold. In the last decade, the US generated unprecedented public and private debt, a phenomenon that accelerated in the aftermath of the 2008 global financial crisis until the two forms of debt began moving in opposite directions by 2010 as public bailouts and programs essentially reduced private debt. Both during the Vietnam era and the Great Recession, Washington's exploitation of its position destabilized existing patterns of global finance.[60] Chinese and Japanese investors have—and still do—subsidize American consumers. The US has been a regular exploiter, rather than provider, of public goods.

Washington pumped huge sums of money into the system after WWII to help others rebuild their economies and to create markets for US goods. In later decades, it borrowed money in lieu of balancing its trade deficit or raising taxes, and thus failed to play the role of lender of last resort. The US reliance on Keynesian deficit-spending policies, combined with large public debts well before the 2008 crisis, made the US massively indebted to countries like Japan and China. They hold large dollar currency reserves as a result of favourable export balances.

American borrowing took the form of the issuance of US Treasury bills. By March of 2011, the US Treasury Department estimated that China's holding of US Treasury bills had reached $1.16 trillion, making it the largest foreign lender. Japan's holdings amounted to $882.3 billion by the end of 2010. The total foreign holdings of US Treasury debt stood at $4.44 trillion and the entire national debt had reached $14.3 billion.[61] The pace of borrowing has accelerated in the last few years without much evidence of it being invested in infrastructure or other forms of investment. By the beginning of 2013, debt levels had grown significantly; foreign holdings of US Treasury debt ballooned to more than $5.5 trillion and the national debt reached almost $16.5 trillion.[62] The US relies on China's willingness to hold on to these Treasury bills and maintain the value of the dollar and, by doing so, the US avoids defaulting on payment of its public debt. Only the US could carry such debt without having to embark on stringent budget cuts imposed by multilateral organizations such as the International Monetary Fund, other national governments, or private bankers. American behaviour has become increasingly feckless and destabilizing, and far from propping up the financial system as lender of last resort, the US has emerged as its primary borrower and an increasingly irresponsible one.

American attempts at global economic coordination in the closing year of the George W. Bush administration and the first term of the Obama administration were rebuffed by its closest allies: the UK, Germany, and France. They are among the Group of Eight (G8) countries that comprise the world's traditionally largest economies. Today, the US thus neither leads nor lends. If we assess the US role by the economic management functions thought critical by liberals, it is not a hegemon. For the time being, the global economic system functions, for better and worse, without a hegemon. Key management functions—providing market liquidity, reinforcing open trading patterns and market and currency stability, and reinforcing patterns of economic development—take place without a hegemon. Divorced from the concept of hegemony, these functions are best described as custodianship.

Two economic developments in the last several decades are particularly pertinent to our argument. First is the growth of the global marketplace and, with it, the decline of national models of capitalism, especially in the West. Deregulation, privatization, and liberalization, inspired by the recipe that became known as the Washington Consensus, made economies more permeable and harder to guide by governments than had been the case between 1945 and the 1980s.[63] Second is the faltering of older multilateral financial institutions such as the World Bank and the IMF, as they became less capable of coping with the intensified market gyrations, although this trend was attenuated by European intervention (as discussed in chapter 3). Having been the catalyst for both developments, the US is increasingly unable to guide or control markets. Institutions designed to coordinate policy, such as the Group of Seven (G7), have proved no more effective. The expansion of that club to twenty states has made interstate collaboration on a global scale that much more difficult. These developments have increased the risk of moral hazard; banks, corporations, and even countries (e.g., Cyprus, Greece, Ireland, Portugal, and Italy) are regarded as too big to allow to fail.[64] The 1997 Asian financial crisis and the 2008 global economic crisis suggest that Susan Strange's fear of casino capitalism is becoming increasingly a reality.

These developments are further evidence that the US does not act responsibly or perform the economic functions attributed to a hegemon.[65] China, often in partnership with other Asian states, is beginning to assume some of these functions.[66] Beijing has made no attempt to assume economic dominance or create multilateral institutions based on its priorities or values.[67] China's clear strategic goal is to buttress the global economy, which serves its interests and enhances its influence. China's limited role is nonetheless essential to the effective functioning of a stable financial system.

The third benefit of hegemony is sponsorship. It encompasses enforcement of rules, norms, agreements, and decision-making processes as well as the maintenance of security to enhance trade and finance.[68] Liberals and realists consistently maintain that only hegemons can provide such enforcement because of their preponderance of material power. They assume that American hegemony is legitimate in the eyes of other important actors who welcome its leadership and enforcement as beneficial to global stability and their national interests. When empirical support is mustered for these claims, the foreign voices invariably cited are conservative politicians in allied states or authoritarian leaders who benefit personally from US backing. During the Cold War, German conservatives welcomed US leadership as a means of offsetting Soviet power and of constraining social democratic opponents. The leaders of South Korea, Taiwan, South Vietnam, the Philippines, Iran, Egypt, and various Latin American states were, to varying degrees, dependent on US military and foreign aid and happy to say in public what Washington wanted to hear to keep these dollars flowing. Their opponents regarded US influence as regressive, as it supported regimes opposed to democracy and human rights.

There has been a noticeable decline in pleas for US leadership since the end of the Cold War and, as noted earlier, a corresponding increase in opposition to US military and economic initiatives. Since the Iraq War, the US has undergone a shift in its profile from a status quo to a revisionist power.[69] A BBC World Service poll conducted in early 2007 indicated a significant increase in the standing of countries associated with alternate visions of the international system. When asked what countries exerted a positive influence in the world, Canada and Japan topped the list at 54 percent, followed by France (50), Britain (45), China (42), and India (37).[70] More recent surveys reveal that the US is not perceived as acting in the interests of the international community. Whatever legitimacy its leadership once had has significantly eroded, as the public around the world are particularly worried about the way in which the US uses its military power.[71]

Leadership and legitimacy are closely connected, and enforcement clearly depends on the latter. In situations where US efforts at enforcement have been seen as legitimate (e.g., Korea, the First Gulf War, and Libya), international support has been forthcoming, and with it, backing by relevant regional and international organizations, notably the UN Security Council. Key to the legitimacy of enforcement has been a common perception of threat, but also a commitment on Washington's part to limit its military action in pursuit of a consensus. It often requires collaborative decisions concerning processes of implementation as well. The Truman administration won support for the liberation of South Korea, but not the invasion of the North, and President George H.W. Bush for the liberation of Kuwait, but not the overthrow of Saddam Hussein. When Bush insisted on the invasion of Iraq with the goal of removing Saddam, he was unable to gain support from NATO or the UN. When the administration went to war in the absence of international institutional support, it had to cobble together a coalition based largely on bribes and threats. Its subsequent decline in standing was precipitous, and this began before the insurgency in Iraq.

Conclusion

The theoretical and policy lessons of these experiences are straightforward. Material power is a necessary but insufficient condition for enforcement. The latter depends on legitimacy, an important component of influence. In its absence, even successful enforcement—as defined by Washington— will not be perceived as such by other states, and will possibly be seen as aggrandizement, as the Iraq invasion was seen by public opinion in France, Germany, Canada, and Japan. Such perceptions undermine legitimacy and make future enforcement more difficult.

Sponsorship can involve the threat or use of force, and here the US tries hard to live up to theoretical expectations. It has unparalleled military expertise and capacity and has been involved in more wars, for more years, than any other state in the post-war period.[72] Liberals tend to downplay or ignore the military element of hegemony, focusing more on economic incentives and soft power. Violence in their writings fades into the background under a wealth of incentives and rules. Even Ikenberry claims that the US, while it provides security, nevertheless exercises remarkable self-restraint and refrains from overt aggression.[73] The historical record suggests otherwise.

Enforcement of security is foundational to the concept of sponsorship. It entails a willingness to enforce global security and its rules and norms, or at least underwrite the costs of doing so. It nevertheless also requires the greatest powers to refrain from acting unilaterally and pre-emptively. Sponsorship strategies must be responsive to collectively perceived needs and implemented with the backing and, preferably, active collaboration of a wide coalition of other actors. It requires the use of material power in the context of broader decision-making and consensus.

Why should any state act as a sponsor? A great power may do so for reasons that have nothing to do with hegemony. It may be a state in decline, hoping to regain status by enforcing generally accepted norms. It may be a powerful state aspiring to enhance its legitimacy or prestige and, with it, the willingness of others to accept its leadership on other issues. A great power may do so, or join with others toward this end, because its leaders simply see their state as better off in sustaining the current arrangements. Perhaps they even worry that chaos is otherwise a real possibility. In effect, sponsorship and enforcement can be motivated by self-interest and a commitment to regional or global norms.[74]

Self-interest is one of the more imprecise terms in the political lexicon and is often invoked by realists to explain any policy *ex post facto*. Realists have equated it with security, and liberals have equated it with wealth, while constructivists attempt to reconstruct the different understandings of actors. We side with constructivists in believing that actor goals vary in their importance, framing, and pursuit. We must refrain from imposing our formulations on leaders or their states, but rather struggle to understand how they frame and apply the concept of interest. History indicates that there are often wide variations within the same policymaking elite. People are loath to make hard choices from among their goals, and policymakers are no different; they can construct their interests in ways that appear contradictory, even irrational, to outsiders.

The functions of agenda setting, custodianship, and sponsorship overlap. All confer advantages to states that perform them and to the community at large. They require consultation, bargaining, and consensus, but also reflect competition and jockeying for influence among powerful states. We suggest neither that there is, nor that there should be, a division of labour in the global system. Decisions to perform these functions are driven by cultural conceptions, domestic politics, and consideration of national self-interest. Within limits, powerful actors generally attempt to exert what degrees of influence they can. This will depend in part on the nature of their resources, but also on the priorities they establish and their legitimacy in the eyes of other actors. They are also affected by domestic and international constraints and opportunities.

The policies of European states, the EU, and China reveal the extent to which these functions are becoming distributed globally, entailing states using different combinations of material and social power, and creating new possibilities of order and disruption. This process is due in the first instance to the failure of the US to perform in a responsible way, a choice that cannot simply be attributed to loss of power. It also reflects the growing power of other political units and their interest in playing a more important role in world affairs, but also their recognition that almost all of their national goals, including well-being, depend on an ordered international system.

Ultimately, hegemony is difficult to reconcile with democracy. Leading intellectuals and political leaders have frequently proclaimed that democracy and pluralism in government and decentralization in economics are not only more effective means of governing than hierarchy and centralization but are important ends in their own right. The commitment to democracy and pluralism is equally applicable to international relations. This makes it enigmatic and indefensible for scholars and policymakers to embrace hegemony and the undemocratic hierarchies it aspires to impose and maintain.

Many American IR theorists and foreign policy and national security analysts have a normative commitment to American world leadership. They developed the concept of hegemony to justify and advance this project and incorporated it into the very heart of their research programs. International relations scholars must cut themselves loose from this concept if they want to address the realities of the post-Cold War world.

Notes

1. This chapter draws on Simon Reich and Richard Ned Lebow, *Good-Bye Hegemony! Power and Influence in the Global System* (Princeton: Princeton University Press, 2014).

2. Hans J. Morgenthau, *Scientific Man vs. Power Politics* (Chicago: University of Chicago Press, 1946) and *Truth and Power: Essays of a Decade, 1960–1970* (New York: Praeger, 1970), 14–15; Robert J. Myers, 'Hans J. Morgenthau: On Speaking Truth to Powers,' *Society* 29, no. 2 (1992): 65–71.

3. Michael W. Doyle, *Empires* (Ithaca, NY: Cornell University Press, 1986), 40.

4. Michael Mastanduno, 'Hegemonic Order, September 11, and the Consequences of the Bush Revolution,' *International Relations of the Asia Pacific*, 5 (2005): 177–96.

5. Stuart J. Kaufman, Richard Little, and William C. Wohlforth, *The Balance of Power in World History* (New York: Palgrave-Macmillan, 2007), 7.

6. John G. Ikenberry and Charles A. Kupchan, 'Socialization and Hegemonic Power,' *International Organization* 44, no. 3 (Summer 1990): 283–315.

7. Stephen G. Brooks and William C. Wohlforth, *World Out of Balance: International Relations and the Challenge of American Primacy* (Princeton, NJ: Princeton University Press, 2008); Robert Jervis, 'The Remaking of a Unipolar World,' *Washington Quarterly* 29, no. 3 (2006): 7–19.

8. Carla Norrlof, *America's Global Advantage: US Hegemony and International Cooperation* (Cambridge: Cambridge University Press, 2010), 19–21.

9. Christopher M. Dent, 'Regional Leadership in East Asia: Towards New Analytical Approaches,' in *China, Japan and Regional Leadership in East Asia*, ed. Christopher M. Dent (Cheltenham: Edward Elgard, 2008); Brooks and Wohlforth, *World Out of Balance*, 28. For critiques, Lavina R. Lee, *Hegemony an International Legitimacy: Norms, Power and Followership in the Wars in Iraq* (London: Routledge, 2010); Ian Clark, *Hegemony in International Society* (Oxford: Oxford University Press, 2011).

10. Roger Simon, *Gramsci's Political Thought: An Introduction* (London: Lawrence and Wishart, 1982); Mark Haugard, 'Power an Hegemony in Social Theory,' in *Hegemony and Power: Consensus and Coercion in Contemporary Politics*, eds. Mark Haugard and Howard H. Lentner (Lanham, MD: Lexington, 2006), 50; Richard Ned Lebow, *The Tragic Vision of Politics: Ethics, Interests and Orders* (Cambridge: Cambridge University Press, 2003), 283–84; Clark, *Hegemony in International Society*, 18–23.

11. Simon, *Gramsci's Political Thought*, 21.

12. Lebow, *Tragic Vision of Politics*, 283–84; Ian Hurd, 'Making and Breaking Norms: American Revisionism and Crises of Legitimacy,' *International Politics* 44, nos. 2/3 (2007): 194–213; Clark, *Hegemony in International Society*, 23–28.

13. John G. Mearsheimer, *The Tragedy of Great Power Politics* (New York: Norton, 2001), 40; Christopher Layne, *The Peace of Illusions: American Grand Strategy from 1940 to the Present* (Ithaca, NY: Cornell University Press, 2006), 11–12.

14. Lebow, *Tragic Vision of Politics*, 283–84; Gerry Simpson, *Great Powers and Outlaw States: Unequal Sovereigns in the International Legal Order* (Cambridge: Cambridge University Press, 2004); Ian Hurd, 'Making and Breaking Norms'; Andrew Hurrell, *On Global Order: Power, Values, and the Constitution of International Society* (Oxford: Oxford University Press, 2007); Clark, *Hegemony in International Society*, 23–28.

15. Robert O. Keohane, *After Hegemony: Cooperation and Discord in the Modern World* (Princeton, NJ: Princeton University Press, 1984), 31; David A. Lake, 'Leadership, Hegemony, and the International Economy: Naked Emperor or Tattered Monarch with Potential?' *International Studies Quarterly* 37, no. 4 (1993): 459–89, especially 480.

16. Keohane, *After Hegemony*, 39–40.

17. Ibid., 136.

18. G. John Ikenberry, *After Victory: Institutions, Strategic Restraint, and the Rebuilding of Order after Major War* (Princeton, NJ: Princeton University Press, 2001).

19. G. John Ikenberry, *The Liberal Leviathan* (Princeton, NJ: Princeton University Press, 2011), 2.

20. Ibid, 3.

21. Ibid, 8.

22. Ibid, 2–10.

23. Joseph S. Nye, 'The Future of American Power: Dominance and Decline in Perspective,' *Foreign Affairs* 89, no. 6 (2010): 2–12.

24. Ibid.

25. George Friedman, *The Coming War with Japan* (New York: St-Martin Press, 1991).

26. Christopher Layne, 'The Waning of U.S. Hegemony—Myth or Reality? A Review Essay,' *International Security* 34, no. 1 (2009):147–72, especially 148; Aaron L. Freidberg, 'The Future of U.S.-China Relations: Is Conflict Inevitable?' *International Security* 30, no. 2 (2005): 7–45; Mearsheimer, *The Tragedy of Great Power Politics*, 400; Michael H. Hunt, *The American Ascendancy: How the United States Gained and Wielded Global Dominance* (Chapel Hill, NC: University of North Carolina Press, 2007), 322; Michael Cox, 'Is the United States in Decline—Again? An Essay,' *International Affairs* 83, no. 4 (2007), 261–76; Fareed Zakaria, *The Post-American World* (London: Allen Lane, 2008).

27. Hunt, *American Ascendancy*, 322; Cox, 'Is the United States in Decline—Again?'; Fareed Zakaria, *The Post-American World* (New York: Norton, 2008).

28. United States National Security Council, *US National Security Strategy 2010* (Washington, 2010), 43, accessed 25 February 2013, http://www.whitehouse.gov/nscnss /2010.

29. Hunt, *American Ascendancy*, 322; Inderjeet Parmar and Michael Cox, eds., *Soft Power and US Foreign Policy: Theoretical, Historical and Contemporary Perspectives* (Abingdon: Routledge, 2010).

30. Michael Mandelbaum, *The Frugal Superpower: America's Global Leadership in a Cash-Strapped Era* (Philadelphia: Public Affairs, 2010), 3–8; Roger C. Altman and Richard N. Haass, 'American Profligacy and American Power,' *Foreign Affairs* 89, no. 6 (2010): 25–34.

31. Michael Dobbs and John M. Goshko, 'Albright's Personal Odyssey Shaped Foreign Policy Beliefs,' *Washington Post*, 6 December 1996, A25; Madeleine K. Albright, interview by Matt Lauer, *Today*, NBC, 19 February 1998; Daniel Deudney and G. John

Ikenberry, *Democratic Internationalism: An American Grand Strategy for a Post-Exceptionalist Era* (New York: Council on Foreign Relations, 2012), 1.

32. G. John Ikenberry, Michael Mastanduno, and William Wohlforth, eds., *Unipolarity and International Relations Theory* (New York: Cambridge University Press, 2011); G. John Ikenberry and Joseph Grieco, *State Power and World Markets: The International Political Economy* (New York: Norton, 2003); G. John Ikenberry and Michael Mastanduno, eds., *International Relations Theory and the Asia-Pacific* (New York: Columbia University Press, 2003); G. John Ikenberry, David A. Lake, and Michael Mastanduno, eds., *The State and American Foreign Economic Policy* (Ithaca, NY: Cornell University Press, 1988); G. John Ikenberry and Charles A. Kupchan, 'Socialization and Hegemonic Power,' *International Organization* 44, no. 3 (Summer 1990): 283–315; Stephen G. Brooks, G. John Ikenberry, and William C. Wohlforth, 'Don't Come Home, America: The Case against Retrenchment,' *International Security* 37, no. 3 (Winter 2012/13): 7–51.

33. Brooks, Ikenberry, and Wohlforth, 'Don't Come Home, America.'

34. Angus Maddison, *Monitoring the World Economy, 1820–1992* (Paris: Organization for Economic Cooperation and Development, 1995). Even Robert Gilpin, renowned proponent of hegemonic stability theory, acknowledges the fact that the US's global dominance was fleeting. See Robert Gilpin, *War and Change in World Politics* (New York: Cambridge University Press, 1987), 173–75.

35. On this point see, for example, Charles P. Kindleberger, 'Dominance and Leadership in the International Economy: Exploitation, Public Goods, and Free Rides,' *International Studies Quarterly* 25, no. 2 (1981): 242, 248; Simon Reich, *Restraining Trade to Invoke Investment: MITI and the Japanese Auto Producers: Case Studies in International Negotiation* (Washington, DC: Institute for the Study of Diplomacy, 2002).

36. Human Security Report Project, *The Decline in Global Violence: Evidence, Explanation, and Contestation* (Vancouver: Simon Fraser University, 2013).

37. Steve Schifferes, 'U.S. Names Coalition of the Willing,' *BBC News*, 18 March 2003, http://news.bbc.co.uk/2/hi/americas/2862343.stm; *Time Europe*, 2 June 2003, http://www.time.com/time/europe/gdml/peace2003.html (broken link).

38. Pew Global Attitudes Project, 'America's Image Slips, but Allies Share U.S. Concerns over Iran, Hamas,' 13 June 2006, http://www.pewglobal.org/2006/06/13/americas-image-slips-but-allies-share-us-concerns-over-iran-hamas/.

39. BBC World Service Poll, 'Israel and Iran Share Most Negative Ratings in Global Poll,' 6 March 2007, http://news.bbc.co.uk/2/shared/bsp/hi/pdfs/06_03_07_perceptions.pdf.

40. Christian Reus-Smit, 'Unipolarity and Legitimacy' (unpublished manuscript).

41. Program on International Policy Attitudes (PIPA), *Global Views of United States Improve While Other Countries Decline*, 10 April 2010, http://www.worldpublicopinion.org/pipa/articles/views_on_countriesregions_bt/660.php.

42. Pew Global Attitudes Project, 'Global Opinion of Obama Slips, International Policies Faulted,' 13 June 2012, http://www.pewglobal.org/2012/06/13/global-opinion-of-obama-slips-international-policies-faulted/.

43. Pew Survey, 'Obama More Popular Abroad Than at Home, Global Image of U.S. Continues to Benefit,' 17 June 2011, http://www.pewglobal.org/2010/06/17/obama-more-popular-abroad-than-at-home/.

44. Michael Barnett and Raymond Duvall, 'Power in International Politics,' *International Organization* 59, no. 1 (2005): 39–75; Ian Manners, 'Normative Power Europe: A Contradiction in Terms?' *Journal of Common Market Studies* 40, no. 2 (2002): 235–58, especially 239.

45. Barnett and Duvall, 'Power in International Politics,' 56–57.

46. In more formal terms, these economic functions consist of maintaining an open market for distress goods, providing countercyclical lending, policing a stable system of exchange rates, ensuring the coordination of macroeconomic policies, and acting as a lender of last resort. Charles P. Kindleberger, *The World in Depression, 1929–1939* (Berkeley: University of California Press, 1973), 305.

47. G. John Ikenberry, 'Grand Strategy as Liberal Order Building' (unpublished chapter prepared for conference on 'After the Bush Doctrine: National Security Strategy for a New Administration,' University of Virginia, 7–8 June 2007), 3.

48. John W. Kingdon, *Agendas, Alternatives, and Public Policies* (Boston: Little, Brown, 1984).

49. Stephen D. Krasner, 'Structural Causes and Regime Consequences: Regimes as Intervening Variables,' in *International Regimes*, Stephen D. Krasner, ed. (Ithaca, NY: Cornell University Press, 1983), 2.

50. Steven Radelet, 'A Primer on Foreign Aid' (working chapter no. 92, Center for Global Development, July 2006), 5.

51. Simon Reich, 'The Evolution of a Doctrine: The Curious Case of Kofi Annan, George Bush and the Doctrines of Preventative and Preemptive Intervention' in *Hitting First: Preventive Force in U.S. Security Strategy*, William Keller and Gordon Mitchell, eds. (Pittsburgh: University of Pittsburgh Press, 2006), 45–69.

52. 'Secretary-General Reflects on "Intervention" in Thirty-Fifth Annual Ditchley Foundation Lecture,' UN Press Release SG/SM/6613, 26 June 1998, http://www.un.org/News/Press/docs/1998/19980626.sgsm6613.html; Gareth Evans and Mohamed Sahnoun, *The Responsibility to Protect: A Report by the International Commission of Intervention and State Sovereignty* (Ottawa: International Development Research Center, December 2001), http://www.dfait-maeci.gc.ca/iciss-ciise/pdf/Commission-Report.pdf; Simon Reich, 'Power, Institutions and Moral Entrepreneurs' (ZEF discussion papers no. 65, Center for Development Research, Bonn, March 2003), http://www.zef.de/publications.htm; Bruce W. Jentleson, 'Coercive Prevention: Normative, Political and Policy Dilemmas,' *Peaceworks* 35 (Washington, DC: United States Institute of Peace, October 2000): 20.

53. United Nations General Assembly, '2005 World Summit Outcome,' Articles 138 and 139, A/60/L.1, 15 September 2005.

54. *National Security Strategy*, 2010, 48, and also cited on the website of the International Coalition for the Responsibility to Protect, 28 May 2010, http://www

.responsibilitytoprotect.org/index.php/component/content/article/35-r2pcs-topics/2785 -white-house-releases-may-2010-national-security-strategy-with-reference-to-rtop.

55. UN Security Council, 'Security Council Approves "No-Fly Zone" over Libya, Authorizing "All Necessary Measures" to Protect Civilians, by Vote of 10 in Favour with 5 Abstentions,' 17 March, 2011, http://www.un.org/News/Press/docs/2011/sc10200.doc .htm - Resolution; Gareth Evans and Mohamed Sahnoun, *The Responsibility to Protect: A Report by the International Commission of Intervention and State Sovereignty* (2001); Mark Leon Goldberg, 'A "Responsibility to Protect" in Libya,' 23 February 2011, http//:www.undispatch.com:a-responsibility-to-protect-in-libya; Irwin Cotler and Jared Genser, 'Libya and the Responsibility to Protect,' *New York Times*, 29 February 2011, http://www.nytimes.com/2011/03/01/opinion/01iht-edcotler01.html. For an analysis of the American perspective see Bruce W. Jentleson, 'The Obama Administration and R2P: Progress, Problems and Prospects,' *Global Responsibility to Protect* 4, no. 4 (Winter 2012–13).

56. Charles P. Kindleberger, *The World in Depression, 1929–1939* (Berkeley: University of California Press, 1973), 305.

57. Gilpin, *War and Change in World Politics*, 173–75; Ikenberry, *Liberal Leviathan*, 18–22.

58. Joanne Gowa, *Closing the Gold Window: Domestic Politics and the End of Bretton Woods* (Ithaca, NY: Cornell University Press, 1983); Fred Block, *The Origins of International Economic Disorder: A Study of United States International Monetary Policy From World War II to the Present* (Berkeley: University of California Press, 1977), 182–98.

59. Susan Strange, *Casino Capitalism* (Oxford: Blackwell, 1986) and *Mad Money: When Markets Outgrow Governments* (Ann Arbor, MI: University of Michigan Press, 1998).

60. Block, *The Origins of International Economic Disorder*, 182–98.

61. Michael Shedlock, 'China Holdings of US Treasuries Revised Up 30%; An Unsustainable Model,' Mish's Global Economic Trend Analysis, 1 March 2011, http://www.safehaven.com/article/20135/ china-holdings-of-us-treasuries-revised-up-30-an-unsustainable-model.

62. 'Major Foreign Holders of US Treasury Securities,' US Department of the Treasury, accessed 27 January 2013, http://www.treasury.gov/resource-center/data-chart-center /tic/Documents/mfh.txt, and 'US National Debt Clock,' accessed 27 January 2013, US Department of the Treasury, http://www.brillig.com/debt_clock/.

63. Robert H. Wade, 'US Hegemony and the World Bank,' *Review of International Political Economy* 9, no. 2 (2002): 215–43.

64. Richard Swedberg, 'Capitalism and Ethics: How Conflicts of Interest-Legislation Can Be Used to Handle Moral Dilemmas in the Economy,' *International Social Science Journal* 57, no. 185 (2005): 481–92; Paul Blustein, *The Chastening: Inside the Crisis that Rocked the Global Financial System and Humbled the IMF* (New York: Public Affairs, 2001); J. Bradford DeLong and Barry Eichengreen, 'Between Meltdown and Moral Hazard: The International Monetary and Financial Policies of the Clinton

Administration,' National Bureau of Economic Research (working chapter 8443, August 2001).

65. Carla Norrlof, *America's Global Advantage: US Hegemony and International Coopera-tion* (Cambridge, UK: Cambridge University Press, 2010), 5–6.

66. Norrlof, *America's Global Advantage*, 2–8.

67. Kevin Yao, 'China economy to underpin global demand in 2013—CIC,' 26 January 2013, http://uk.reuters.com/article/2013/01/26/uk-china-economy-growth -idUKBRE90P04T20130126.

68. Reich, *Global Norms*, 62–63.

69. Reus-Smit, 'Unipolarity and Legitimacy.'

70. BBC World Service Poll, 'Israel and Iran Share Most Negative Ratings in Global Poll,' *BBC News*, 6 March 2007, http://news.bbc.co.uk/2/shared/bsp/hi/pdfs/06_03_07 _perceptions.pdf.

71. Pew Survey, 'Obama More Popular'; Pew Research Global Attitudes Project, 'Global Opinion.'

72. Human Security Centre, 'Part I: The Changing Face of Global Violence,' *The Human Security Report 2005* (2005), especially 28.

73. Ikenberry, *After Victory*, 248, 257–73.

74. Gilpin, *War and Change in World Politics,* 96–105; Michael Doyle, 'Liberalism and World Politics,' *American Political Science Review* 80, no. 4, (1986): 1151–69.

4.

Neoclassical Realism, Non-proliferation, and the Limits of US Hegemony in the Middle East and South Asia

Jeffrey W. Taliaferro

Introduction

Here we address some very strategic questions around the United States' non-proliferation policy and the country's relationships with friends and foe. When has the US employed coercive strategies, such as intrusive inspections of nuclear facilities or the threat or imposition of economic sanctions, toward a strategically vulnerable ally in an effort to restrain or even halt that ally's nuclear ambitions? When is the US more likely to offer a strategically vulnerable ally tangible inducements such as arms transfers and explicit security guarantees to accomplish the same non-proliferation objectives? When is the United States likely to acquiesce in an ally's development of nuclear capabilities?

These questions arise in part because US hegemony underpins the global nuclear non-proliferation regime. Much of that regime originated in the 1960s and the 1970s, although unilateral efforts by the US to control the spread of fissile materials and nuclear technology date back to the Baruch Plan, conceived after the US, Great Britain, and Canada called for an international organization to regulate atomic energy in 1945. Indeed, historian Francis J. Gavin contends that nuclear non-proliferation, the containment of great-power adversaries, and the promotion of economic openness have been the three key pillars of US grand strategy for the past seventy years: all three are means to preserve the US's preponderant share of material capabilities and hegemonic role in the post-World War II international system.[1]

Below, I question whether the US has consistently upheld all three pillars. Sometimes the pursuit of containment and non-proliferation came into conflict. On occasion, US policymakers were so concerned about containing the growth of the Soviet Union's influence in certain regions that halting the nuclear weapons of vulnerable US allies took a back seat to the more immediate goal of containment.

The term 'hegemony' connotes both a state's preponderance of material power—both economic and military capabilities—and its leadership role in the international system. The concept of hegemony has its antecedents in Thucydides's analysis of the Athenian–Spartan rivalry in the decades preceding the Peloponnesian War.[2] More relevant to this section of the compendium, however, are various international relations theories that posit a relationship between hegemony and international stability or peace. Liberals and realists in the power preponderance tradition agree that the existence of a hegemon can facilitate the provision of public goods in the areas of security and international political economy. They typically identify Great Britain and the US as the successive hegemons over the past 200 years.

Given space constraints, I cannot fully engage the arguments that Simon Reich and Richard Ned Lebow make in their chapter: the claim that the US is a hegemon is empirically false; that the supposed era of US hegemony ended with the economic recoveries of Western Europe and Japan in the 1960s; and that ill-conceived military interventions, most recently in Iraq and Afghanistan, have eroded American legitimacy and thus US hegemony.[3] Instead, I make two brief observations. First, fears about US relative decline were greatly exaggerated during the Cold War. It was the Soviet Union that confronted deep relative decline by the mid-1980s and ultimately collapsed in 1990–1991. Similarly, predictions today about US relative decline and the imminent transition from a unipolar international system to a bipolar or multipolar system are premature. Instead, by most empirical measures, the capabilities gap between the US and the rest of the world has only grown since 1990.[4]

Second, although the US was not a global hegemon during the Cold War, it did play a hegemonic role over the so-called Free World—the Western Hemisphere, Western Europe, the Middle East (especially the Persian Gulf), and the islands off the East Asian mainland—for four decades. Liberal institutionalists, such as Robert O. Keohane and G. John Ikenberry, and power preponderance realists, such as Robert Gilpin, Stephen D. Krasner, Stephen D. Brooks, and William C. Wohlforth, agree that in the aftermath of World War II, the US created and maintained a network of international institutions, standing alliances, and forward military bases that both provided public goods—namely, economic openness and military security—and enabled Washington to exercise some measure of control over regional powers and weaker states.[5] The main points of disagreement between liberal institutionalists and power preponderance realists is not over the existence of US hegemony, but instead over questions involving the relative importance of material capabilities, international institutions, and legitimacy in sustaining that hegemony and the extent to which the US is now or has ever been constrained by the various institutional frameworks it created.

In recent years, historians and political scientists have drawn upon newly declassified documents to explain how the US sought to thwart the nuclear ambitions of various allies, including the Federal Republic of Germany (FRG), the Republic of Korea (ROK), Taiwan, Israel, South Africa, and Pakistan, among others.[6] There has also been renewed attention among political scientists to the broader dynamics of alliance management and intra-alliance coercion.[7] Intra-alliance coercion entails the use of conditional threats and promises by the stronger alliance member for the express purpose of inducing a change in the cost–benefit calculations and the observable behaviour of the weaker alliance partner. Officials in Washington have employed a variety of such strategies to dissuade other states from acquiring nuclear capabilities, including implicit and explicit threats of abandonment; conventional weapons sales; economic aid packages; economic sanctions; export controls on fissile materials, intellectual property, and dual-use technologies; interdiction of illicit cargos; intelligence sharing; sabotage; and, occasionally, even the consideration of preventive military force.[8]

What is arguably lacking, however, is a theory that can address one of the questions posed above. For example, the US coerced Taiwan and South Korea to abandon their respective nuclear weapons programs in the 1970s.[9] However, US presidents negotiated secret non-proliferation deals with their Israeli and Pakistani counterparts.[10] In the Middle East in the late 1960s and in South Asia in the 1980s, averting the growth of Soviet influence became the overriding objective of presidents and their advisers. The non-proliferation deals struck with Israel and later Pakistan were means toward that end.

In this chapter, I present a neoclassical realist theory of intra-alliance coercion. The theory posits the non-proliferation strategies the US undertakes as a function of both systemic (or international) variables and domestic politics. Presidents and their national security teams initially make calculations about the type of strategic environment of US faces in a particular geographic region and the clarity of the threats and opportunities to US interests in that region. Yet the strategies the administration ultimately pursues toward a nuclear-aspiring ally will also be shaped by US domestic politics, specifically the domestic mobilization hurdles the administration must overcome. Presidents and their administrations are likely to pursue strong coercive strategies to forestall an ally's development of a nuclear capability when they perceive the US to be facing a restrictive strategic environment in the region where that ally is located and when they perceive a high degree of clarity about threats or opportunities for US interests in that region. Here, the domestic mobilization hurdles the administration will need to overcome in order to pursue hard-line strategies toward that ally will likely be low. Conversely, presidents and their administrations will be more inclined to pursue accommodative strategies in response to any ally's nuclear abilities when they perceive the US as facing a less restrictive strategic environment in the region and when they perceive less clarity about the types of threats and opportunities to US interests in that region. Here, domestic mobilization hurdles the administration would have to overcome in order to pursue a coercive strategy toward an ally would be higher.

The next section of this chapter examines the relationship between US hegemony and nuclear non-proliferation. Hegemonic theory and nuclear domino theory suggest that the US, as the hegemon of the so-called Free World during the Cold War and as the global hegemon for the past quarter century, would actively oppose the diffusion of nuclear weapons capabilities to *nth* states in order to minimize the twin risks of containment failure and access denial in particular regions. I contend that hegemonic and nuclear domino theories by themselves, however, do not explain variation in the types of coercive or accommodative non-proliferation strategies the US presidential administration pursued toward certain vulnerable bilateral allies or quasi-allies in the periphery.

The following section outlines a neoclassical realist theory, which I contend might account for that variation. To illustrate the hypotheses, I reference US non-proliferation strategies toward Israel (1960–1969) and Pakistan (1975–1988)—two cases where US presidents negotiated ultimately secret deals regarding nuclear testing, public declarations of nuclear status, and technology transfers. Given space constraints, I cannot present full narrative case studies to test alternative hypotheses using process tracing and the congruence procedure. The conclusion discusses the broader implications for our understanding of US hegemony, nuclear proliferation, and the causes of peace in the twenty-first century.

US Hegemony, Nuclear Dominos, and Regional Stability

Two strands of structural realism—power equilibrium theories and power preponderance theories—provide competing baselines or sets of predictions for how the US would respond to the proliferation of nuclear weapons to adversaries and allies. Both proceed from the expectation that international bargaining outcomes will tend to mirror the relative distribution of material capabilities between the actors.

Power Equilibrium Theories and Proliferation Optimism

Power equilibrium theories (also called balancing theories) call into question why the US would strongly oppose the diffusion of nuclear capabilities to its own allies. The American political scientist Kenneth N. Waltz argues that neither the US nor the Soviet Union should be entrapped by their respective allies, since the addition or the defection of weaker states could not shift the overall distribution of power within a bipolar international system.[11] Moreover, Waltz argues that nuclear weapons had a stabilizing effect on superpower competition by rendering each one's homeland effectively unconquerable and that, over time, both superpowers learned to tread cautiously in brandishing nuclear threats. There is every reason to believe that second- and third-generation nuclear states would learn the same lessons.[12] Likewise, realist political scientist John J. Mearsheimer argues that the US, as the only great power in the Western Hemisphere, would strive to thwart rival great powers from achieving hegemony in their respective parts of the globe, but doing so in a way to minimize the expected costs to itself. Washington policymakers should try to shift the cost of containing would-be hegemons in Eurasia to more proximate states whenever possible.[13] The US can best preserve its security by pursuing a strategy of restraint or offshore balancing toward great-power rivals in Eurasia.[14]

Since even a rudimentary nuclear capability might serve as a strategic deterrent, the power equilibrium or balancing theories might expect the US to have been indifferent to, or perhaps even mildly supportive of, its allies' efforts to cross the nuclear threshold. Nuclear-armed, or at least nuclear-threshold, frontline allies might have deterred possible attacks by the Soviet Union and other proximate adversaries at a far lower cost to the American taxpayer than the maintenance of overseas bases and the forward deployment of conventional and strategic (nuclear) forces. As Gavin notes, however, if the US's overriding grand strategic objective during the Cold War had been merely to contain the Soviet Union and freeze the post-1945 territorial status quo in Europe and East Asia, then the efforts by successive US administrations to inhibit the spread of nuclear weapons to strategically vulnerable allies is puzzling.[15] Instead, the US has actively tried to thwart nuclear proliferation by adversaries such as China, Iraq, Iran, Libya, and

North Korea, as well as by allies such as West Germany, Israel, South Africa, Taiwan, South Korea, and Pakistan.

The Hegemonic Theories and the Risks of Containment Failure and Access Denial

A second strand of structural realism, hegemonic or power preponderance theories, offers a different baseline exception for how the US would respond to nuclear proliferation by adversaries and allies. Unlike the equilibrium or balance-of-power theories, hegemonic theories begin with the supposition that the US should strive to maintain the preponderant power position it has enjoyed since World War II. To achieve this objective, Washington would not only need to maintain conventional military forces capable of dominating what MIT Professor Barry Posen terms the 'global commons' (the high seas, airspace above 15,000 feet, and outer space), but also a network of standing military alliances and forward basing arrangements intended to simultaneously contain great-power adversaries and exercise a certain amount of restraint over local allies.[16] The US currently maintains defence ties, of one form or another, with some sixty other countries, ranging from multilateral defence pacts, such as the North Atlantic Treaty Organization (NATO); to bilateral security treaties, such as those with Japan, South Korea, and the Philippines; to bilateral security obligations governed by peace treaties, legislation, memoranda of understanding, and executive agreements, such as those with Israel, Egypt, Saudi Arabia, the Persian Gulf emirates, and Taiwan.[17] If the US could best advance its security through a strategy of deep engagement (or primacy) in geographic regions outside the Western Hemisphere, then it would behove US policymakers to try to inhibit, or at least control, the diffusion of nuclear weapons to those regions in order to minimize the risks of access denial or containment failure.[18]

Access denial, according to Evan Braden Montgomery, director of research and studies at the Centre for Strategic and Budgetary Assessments, refers to the risk of a local actor withholding critical resources or restricting the access of the hegemon or other outside powers to a region. A local actor might do this by 'withholding indigenous resources or restricting the presence of outside powers within its neighbourhood, in particular by refusing to export commodities, impeding passage through the area, charging higher rents to host foreign troops, or even evicting those forces and barring their return.'[19] Containment failure, according to Montgomery, refers to the risk of a rival great power conquering a geographic region in whole or in part.[20] I broaden the definition of containment failure to include scenarios in which a rival great power increases its economic, political, and/or military penetration of a geographic region through alliance formation, arms sales, foreign direct investment, and development assistance to local states. In other words, containment failure doesn't need to be synonymous with a heightened risk of an outside great power's military forces occupying all or part of a region; it is sufficient for that outside power to increase its political or military penetration of that region.

Nuclear Domino Dynamics

Nicholas Miller, assistant professor at Dartmouth, coined the term 'nuclear domino theory' in reference to a set of beliefs and propositions held by policymakers, across several presidential administrations, about the adverse consequences of nuclear proliferation for international stability and the United States' national security.[21] Nuclear domino theory (or rather US policymakers' belief in it) can be considered a corollary of hegemonic theories. Nuclear domino effects—reactive nuclear proliferation—increases the risk of regional arms races and may prompt states to initiate preventive military actions against nuclear-aspiring neighbours. Nuclear states, or even nuclear threshold states in particular geographic regions, would be less reliant on the US for protection against regional adversaries or outside powers than are non-nuclear states.[22] Reactive proliferation by allies increases the risk of containment failure. During the Cold War, the Soviet Union could respond to the nuclear activities of US allies in a region by increasing arms transfers to its own allies or forward deploying Soviet conventional forces. Reactive proliferation by allies would also undermine the credibility of US non-proliferation strategies worldwide. This last concern became increasingly salient after the Nuclear Non-Proliferation Treaty (NPT) went into effect in 1971 and became the centrepiece of the US's sponsored nuclear non-proliferation regime.[23]

Reactive proliferation also increases the risk of access denial. This could happen through one of three pathways. First, an adversary's development of even a rudimentary nuclear capability and delivery system might increase its ability to threaten US allies in the region and inhibit the US from defending those allies. Second, reactive proliferation by a US ally may increase the risk of access denial by sparking the types of arms races, arms transfers from outside powers, and extensions of security commitments by outside powers described above. Third, a nuclear weapons capability may embolden some states to engage in limited aggression or crisis initiation.[24]

Hegemonic theory and nuclear domino theory might explain why US policymakers did not actively thwart the British and the French nuclear weapons programs in the 1950s and early 1960s. Indeed, the US actively assisted the British nuclear program in the 1950s.[25] Of course, the French and the British nuclear programs developed during a period when the US commitment to maintaining a permanent military presence in Western Europe was unclear. Senior US officials, including President Dwight D. Eisenhower and Secretary of State John Foster Dulles, did not favour the permanent stationing of American troops in Western Europe, but instead saw this as a temporary measure until the European states recovered sufficiently from World War II to defend themselves against the Soviet Union.[26] Nonetheless, Washington exercised a measure of control through the tight integration of US and British nuclear forces and through France's membership in NATO, even after the latter's withdrawal from the alliance's integrated military command in 1964.

Hegemonic and nuclear domino theories might also explain the US's opposition to West Germany's nuclear ambitions, given the FRG's frontline position in Central Europe and fears that an indigenous German nuclear program would provoke the Soviet Union. The Kennedy and Johnson administrations employed a variety of coercive strategies, including the threat of military abandonment, to dissuade the governments of FRG chancellors Konrad Adenauer and Ludwig Erhard from developing an independent nuclear deterrent in the 1960s.[27] Hegemonic theory and nuclear domino theory, however, are arguably less able to explain variation in the US's responses to the nuclear programs of other allies, especially certain strategically vulnerable allies outside of Europe.

A Neoclassical Realist Theory

In order to explain variation in the types of inducements or coercive strategies the US pursued toward certain allies outside of Europe, I outline a neoclassical realist theory. One key tenant of neoclassical realism is that a state's external behaviour is determined first and foremost by its position in the international system, namely its relative share of military capabilities. International pressures, however, can only influence foreign policies and longer-term grand strategic adjustment through the medium of the state's top officials—the members of its foreign policy executive (FPE). The theory outlined below posits two explanatory variables: the nature of the strategic environment the US faces in a particular geographic region and the degree of systemic clarity as perceived by the president and other senior policymakers. The domestic mobilization hurdles a president's administration has to overcome to pursue its strategies toward the ally is the intervening variable. The dependent variable is the variation in the types of inducements or coercive strategies that the administration actually pursued in an effort to restrain the ally's nuclear weapons program.

The Nature of Strategic Environments and the Degree of Systemic Clarity

Neoclassical realism presents a more nuanced conception of the international system than do variants of structural realism, such as hegemonic theories and balance-of-power theories. Ripsman, Taliaferro, and Lobell contend that a state's strategic environment refers to the magnitude and the imminence of the external threats and opportunities that state faces at any given time. More imminent and larger threats and opportunities indicate a more restrictive strategic environment. More remote and smaller external threats and opportunities indicate a more permissive strategic environment. One might think of the nature of a state's strategic environment as an idealized continuum from restrictive to permissive. The degree of permissiveness or restrictiveness of a state's strategic environment is not necessarily synonymous with its share of relative power. For example, the types and the magnitude of external threats and opportunities that might indicate a restrictive strategic environment for a middle-ranked power or a small state would not necessarily be indicative of a restrictive strategic environment for a great power.[28]

Hegemons often have strategic interests in various geographic regions. Consequently, they simultaneously face different strategic environments in different geographic regions. For example, in the early 1850s, Britain faced a relatively permissive strategic environment in Atlantic and North America, thanks to the Royal Navy's dominance of the high seas. It also faced a relatively permissive strategic environment with respect to its interests in Western Europe, since France was in no position to make a renewed bid to dominate the continent. Britain, however, faced an increasingly restrictive environment with respect to its interests in the eastern Mediterranean and the Balkans due to Russia's encroachments on the Ottoman Empire, which precipitated the outbreak of the Crimean War in 1853.

Similarly, during the Cold War, the US concurrently faced a permissive strategic environment in the Western Hemisphere and more restrictive strategic environments with respect to its interests in East Asia, the Middle East, and Western Europe. The US faced relatively few threats to its military security and economic prosperity from within the Western Hemisphere. In Western Europe, East Asia, and the Middle East, by contrast, the US policymakers generally encountered more restrictive strategic environments due to those regions' proximity to the Soviet Union or China, the loss-of-strength gradient, and the patterns of rivalry among local states. It is also important to note that the nature of the strategic environment that an outside power faces in a region can vary over time and can shift depending upon alignment patterns within that region.

The degree of systemic clarity is the second explanatory variable. Clarity comprises three elements: (1) the extent to which policymakers can readily discern threats and/or opportunities to their interests; (2) the time horizons over which policymakers anticipate those threats and/or opportunities will materialize; and (3) whether policymakers agree upon an optimal strategy to redress the threat or exploit the opportunity. 'Whereas clarity and uncertainty pertain to the scope of information that the [international] system provides, the strategic environment pertains to the content of that information."[29] States, especially great powers and hegemons, do not face imminent threats to their physical survival very often. Yet, the degree of systemic clarity can also pertain to the content of information about dilemmas that clearly do not rise to the level of existential threats. Hegemonic states encounter varying degrees of systemic clarity with respect to the threats and opportunities, time horizons, and identification of optimal strategies with respect to their interests in distant regions. Denying the Soviet Union access to the Middle East and to South Asia was an overriding interest of successive US administrations.

Israeli Prime Minister David Ben-Gurion authorized a secret nuclear program in 1955, ostensibly to meet civilian energy needs and agricultural purposes, but with the option of eventually developing nuclear weapons.[30] It had been US foreign policy since the Truman administration to avoid selling arms to either side in the Arab–Israeli conflict. While the US and Israel had friendly relations, the Eisenhower and the Kennedy administrations did not necessarily want to forge a military alliance with Israel for fear of driving the Arab states—especially Egypt, Syria, and after 1958, Iraq—to seek a military alliance with the Soviet Union. A de facto and highly asymmetric alliance between Israel and the US gradually came into existence during the Johnson administration.[31]

Other alliances were formed and were important in the nuclear age. Pakistan was a founding member of the Central Treaty Organization (CENTO) or Baghdad Pact, a US-led multilateral alliance with states as diverse as Iran and the United Kingdom (UK), to contain Soviet influence in the Near East through providing mutual aid and support. Nonetheless, the US denied Pakistan military assistance through CENTO in its 1965 and 1971 wars with India. During the 1965 India–Pakistan war, President Lyndon B. Johnson imposed an arms embargo on both sides that remained in place until President Gerald Ford lifted it in 1975.[32] In the aftermath of defeat in the 1971 war, Pakistan initiated a secret nuclear weapons program. Prime Minister Zulfikar Ali Bhutto had long advocated developing nuclear weapons and famously said that the Pakistani people would obtain the bomb even if they had to 'eat grass'.[33] Although CENTO continued to exist on paper until its dissolution in 1979, the alliance was irrelevant in addressing Pakistani fears of India and effectively moribund by the mid-1960s.

US diplomats in Oslo, Paris, and Tel Aviv first learned about Israeli contracts to purchase Norwegian heavy water and French reactor technology in 1959, but the Central Intelligence Agency (CIA) and other agencies did not deliver this intelligence to senior policymakers until late summer 1960.[34] Had Eisenhower and his national security team received this intelligence in 1958 or 1959, it is conceivable that they could have pressured France or Norway to cancel those contracts, thus strangling the proverbial Israeli nuclear baby in its cradle.[35] With respect to South Asia, the CIA identified India and Pakistan as potential nuclear proliferators in the 1960s, but the timing of India's detonation of a nuclear device in May 1974 took intelligence analysts by surprise. An interagency working group convened by Secretary of State Henry Kissinger immediately after the Indian detonation concluded, 'Pakistan is seeking security assistance from the US and other major powers, a relaxation of US arms restrictions, and possibly in time, its own nuclear test program.'[36] Since 'limiting the number of nuclear weapons states' and 'attaining a peaceful and stable South Asia' remained major US interests, it was crucial to dissuade Pakistan from following India's example.[37] In December 1975, US intelligence confirmed the secret Pakistani contract to purchase a French uranium reprocessing plant, in addition to the contract to purchase a heavy water production facility from West Germany.[38] As in the Israeli non-proliferation case a decade earlier, senior policymakers did not receive actionable intelligence until Pakistan's efforts to acquire sensitive nuclear technology from abroad were already underway.

After the initial revelations about the Israeli and Pakistani nuclear programs, averting containment failure in the Middle East and South Asia became the overriding concerns of policymakers in Washington. A Special National Intelligence Estimate (SNIE-100-8-60), released on 8 December 1960, concluded, 'On the basis of all available evidence, including the configuration of the complex, we believe that plutonium production for weapons is at least one major purpose of this effort.' The SNIE also stated, 'In lieu of providing nuclear weapons or assistance, the USSR would almost certainly give general assurances and support to the UAR (Egypt).'[39] During a meeting in New York on 30 May 1961, President John F. Kennedy told Ben-Gurion, 'It is to our common interest that no one thinks that Israel is involved in the proliferation of atomic weapons. Obviously the UAR [Egypt] would not permit Israel to go ahead in this field without getting into it itself.'[40] In June 1964, President Johnson warned Israeli Prime Minister Levi Eshkol that the US was 'violently against nuclear proliferation', but he added, 'we are not being naive about [President Gamal Abdel] Nasser [of Egypt]. What we want to do is to try and prevent him from leaning over too far towards the Russians.'[41]

President Ford delivered a similar message in a March 1976 letter to Bhutto, writing, 'the establishment of sensitive nuclear facilities under national control inevitably gives rise to perceptions in many quarters that . . . non-peaceful uses may be contemplated'. Pakistan's contracts to acquire a uranium reprocessing plant from France and a heavy water facility from West Germany 'could erode' American support for Pakistan.[42]

Domestic Mobilization Hurdles

The two explanatory variables—the degree of systemic clarity and the nature of the strategic environment the hegemon faces in a particular region—pertain to the international system. Neoclassical realism posits four clusters of domestic-level variables—leader images (e.g., individual belief and cognitive biases), strategic culture (e.g., ideologies, shared ideas, belief systems), state–society relations (e.g., regime legitimacy, political fragmentation, sectoral conflict), and domestic institutions (e.g., the extractive capacity of state institutions and degree of executive autonomy)—intervene between the international system on the one hand and the foreign policies that states actually pursue on the other hand. The salience of each cluster of intervening variables depends largely upon time span. Since intra-alliance coercion in the area of nuclear non-proliferation is likely to unfold over the course of months and years, the state–society relations and the domestic institutions clusters of variables are more salient.[43]

While the members of any state's FPE has privileged information about the international system, they generally do not have instantaneous access to the material and/or human resources required to pursue their preferred foreign and defence policies. The FPE, therefore, has to mobilize domestic support for their preferred foreign policies and the resources required to carry them out. At a minimum, policymakers need to diffuse the opposition to their initiatives. This process often entails bargaining with relevant societal actors or with other parts of the state apparatus.[44]

In order to pursue its preferred nuclear non-proliferation strategies toward an ally, administration officials have to bargain with Congress and/or with lobbying groups who may act on behalf of an ally. The degree of congressional opposition to or support for the administration's proposed foreign policy initiatives, as well as the degree of lobbying group involvement on behalf of an ally, is contextual; it cannot be specified *a priori.* Congress has always had some leverage over an administration's foreign policies through its oversight committees and its control of appropriations. For example, following India's detonation of a nuclear device in 1974, Congress began to enact non-proliferation legislation that raised the hurdles the Ford, Carter, and Reagan administrations needed to overcome to pursue their preferred strategies in South Asia. The 1976 Symington Amendment to the Foreign Assistance Act of 1961 required the administration to terminate US economic and military aid to states that failed to comply with International Atomic Energy Agency (IAEA) regulations and inspections of their nuclear facilities.[45] The 1977 Glenn Amendment prohibited any military or economic aid to states that acquired and/or transferred nuclear technology or exploded a nuclear device after 1 January 1977. The 1985 Pressler Amendment required any president to annually certify that Pakistan did not possess a nuclear explosive device before any US military and economic assistance could be sent. Lastly, the 1985 Solarz Amendment stated that absent a presidential waiver, the US had to terminate military and economic aid to any state that illegally exported or imported nuclear technology. Congress passed the Pressler and Solarz amendments following two high-profile court cases involving efforts by Pakistani agents to smuggle sensitive technologies out of the US.[46]

The administration of Jimmy Carter succeeded in pressuring France to terminate a contract to sell Pakistan a uranium reprocessing plant in August 1978.[47] In April 1979, however, Carter and his national security team felt compelled to invoke the Symington Amendment after intelligence and media reports of Pakistani attempts to build a uranium enrichment facility. In a letter to NATO leaders informing them of his decision, Carter warned Pakistani efforts to acquire a nuclear weapons capability would 'disturb the stability of the sub-continent and the region' by provoking a nuclear arms race in South Asia and reactive nuclear proliferation in the Middle East.[48] The Reagan administration, however, did persuade Congress to alter the Symington Amendment to include a five-year presidential waiver and to approve a five-year $3.2 billion package of military and economic aid for Pakistan in 1982.[49]

Additionally, some allies are better able to mobilize their domestic supporters in the US than others. From the mid-1960s onward, for example, Israeli officials began to leak selective information to the US media and mobilize Israel's supporters to lobby Congress in an effort to moderate the Johnson administration's efforts to link US conventional weapon sales to Israeli concessions on the nuclear program and other issues. For example, Johnson's proposed sale of tanks and armoured personnel carriers (APCs) to Jordan in spring 1966—in a bid to forestall Amman's purchase of Soviet-made tanks and APCs from Egypt—faced intense opposition from Israel's supporters on Capitol Hill. During a meeting in the Oval Office on 9 February 1967, Johnson asked the Israeli foreign minister, Abba Eban, to restrain 'well-meaning friends of Israel' and to get them 'to stop coming in the back door, or writing, or sending telegrams, or talking to the newspapers.'[50] Similarly, in November 1968, the Johnson administration abandoned efforts to make the sale of fifty F-4 Phantom fighter jets to Israel contingent on the Levi Eshkol government's commitment to sign the NPT, in part due to the intervention of Israel's supporters in Congress.[51]

Intra-alliance Coercion and Inducements

The dependent variable is the variation in the coercive strategies or inducements the US employs to thwart the nuclear weapons programs of its allies.

I define alliance coercion as the use of conditional threats and promises by the stronger party in an alliance for the express purpose of inducing a change in the cost–benefit calculations of the weaker party. I agree with Gene Gerzhoy, formerly of Harvard's Belfer Center, on the two necessary conditions for intra-alliance coercion: first, the client or weaker party must have some level of military dependence on the hegemon or patron; and second, the hegemon's threats and inducements must be conditional on the client's behaviour.[52] I part company with Gerzhoy, however, in not defining intra-alliance coercion as being synonymous with conditional threats of abandonment. Forward base arrangements, integrated military command structures, intelligence sharing, and foreign military sales are all vehicles that not only enable the US armed forces to command the global commons, but also enable Washington policymakers to restrain allies. The US has in-curred significant sunk costs in many of these alliances, a fact not lost on allied governments. Therefore, explicit threats of abandonment may only be credible in limited circumstances.

Intra-alliance inducements and coercive strategies can vary along a contin-uum from 'strong' to 'weak'. Strong strategies are those that entail relatively high military, economic, political, or opportunity costs for the US. Weaker strategies are those that entail low or marginal military, economic, political, or opportunity costs for Washington. The anticipated costs are contextual, depending upon the ally's degree of security dependence, the extent of US strategic interest in that region where the ally is located, the perceived strategic implications of an overt rupture in bilateral relations, and the per-ceived domestic political costs to the presidential administration stemming from such an overt rupture.

Kennedy, for example, repeatedly pressed Ben-Gurion to invite scientists from the US Atomic Energy Commission (AEC) to 'visit' the Dimona reac-tor, developed at an Israeli nuclear installation located in the Negev desert. The president warned the Israeli prime minister in a May 1963 letter that the US's support for Israel 'would be seriously jeopardized . . . if it should be thought this Government was unable to obtain reliable information on . . . Israel's efforts in the nuclear field'.[53] The bilateral agreement for twice-yearly inspections of the Dimona reactor began to fall apart in 1964 and

1965.[54] Yet, even as the inspection regime languished due to Israeli delays in scheduling visits to Dimona and a denial and deception campaign, the Johnson administration continued to deliver demarches to Israeli officials. For example, in February 1966, Secretary of State Dean Rusk told Eban that 'the only major question that could have a disastrous effect on US–Israeli relations was Israel's attitude on proliferation', adding, 'Israel should expect the US to be extremely clear and utterly harsh on the matter of non-proliferation.'[55]

A similar pattern of demarches and the establishment of red lines characterized the Carter and the Reagan administrations' handling of the Pakistani nuclear program in the latter seventies and eighties. For example, in March 1979, Deputy Secretary of State Warren Christopher travelled to Islamabad to tell Zia that unsafeguarded uranium enrichment would trigger the invocation of the Symington Amendment. Pakistani Foreign Minister Agha Shahi, who was present at the meeting, characterized Christopher's words as an 'ultimatum'.[56] Despite Christopher's demarche, Pakistani uranium reprocessing continued and President Carter invoked the Symington Amendment in April 1979.[57] Similarly, in the 1980s, various Reagan administration officials repeatedly warned Zia, Shahi, and other Pakistani officials that continued uranium enrichment, clandestine efforts to import sensitive nuclear technologies, and other activities risked a congressionally mandated termination of US military and economic assistance.[58]

In the Israeli and Pakistani proliferation cases, US administrations began to offer conventional arms sales as an inducement for nuclear restraint. The Kennedy administration, somewhat reluctantly, approved the sale of MIM-23 Hawk surface-to-air missiles to Israel in September 1962 as an inducement for the Dimona 'visits' to continue and in an effort to head off Ben-Gurion's request for a mutual security treaty.[59] Opening the door to weapons sales to Israel, however, had the paradoxical effect of raising the domestic mobilization hurdles the Johnson administration and later the Nixon administration would need to overcome to pursue coercive strategies to forestall the Israeli nuclear program.

On 10 March 1965, Eshkol signed a memorandum of understanding (MOU) stating Israel 'would not be the first to introduce nuclear weapons into the Arab–Israeli area' and acquiesced to US arms sales to Jordan. In return, the Johnson administration said it recognized an 'effective Israeli deterrence . . . as a major factor in preventing aggression' and agreed to supply Israel ninety tanks by 1966 and an additional one hundred M48 tanks superior to those sold to Jordan.[60] A little over a year later, Johnson approved the sale of forty-eight A-4 Skyhawk attack aircraft to Israel to achieve three goals: (1) to mollify Israel's congressional supporters over the proposed tank sale to Jordan; (2) to redress the perceived imbalance in Arab–Israeli air capabilities; and (3) to exert leverage over the Israeli nuclear program.[61] In exchange, the Eshkol government reaffirmed the 'no introduction of nuclear weapons' pledge, recognized the sale did not create a precedent, and agreed to not consider the US its principal arms supplier and that it would continue to seek Western European suppliers for the majority of Israel's military requirements.[62]

By mid-July 1969, senior officials in the Nixon administration concluded it was no longer possible to forestall Israel crossing the nuclear threshold; instead, the most that could be done was to contain the damage from the public becoming aware of Israel's nuclear capabilities. According to a July 1969 State Department assessment, the main negative consequences of overt Israeli nuclear weapons possession were a heightened risk of US–Soviet military confrontation in the Middle East, a sharp reduction in the near-term chance for an Arab–Israeli peace settlement, accusations of American complicity in the Israeli nuclear effort, and the collapse of the NPT.[63] Nixon and Kissinger's first concern was averting containment failure in the Middle East; maintaining the credibility of the NPT was secondary. As Kissinger wrote in a memo to Nixon on 16 July, 'Israel's secret possession of nuclear weapons would increase the potential danger in the Middle East, and we do not desire complicity in it.' Kissinger then went on to make an important distinction: 'In this case, public knowledge is almost as the possession itself', since the former 'might spark a Soviet nuclear guarantee for the Arabs, tighten the Soviet hold on the Arabs, and increase the danger of our involvement'.[64]

Although there is no record of the Oval Office meeting between Nixon and

Israeli Prime Minister Golda Meir on 29 September 1969, it is understood they reached the following understanding: Israel would neither confirm nor deny its possession of nuclear weapons and delivery systems, but Israel would refrain from detonating a nuclear device or using any US-made aircraft to carry nuclear weapons.[65] In exchange, the US agreed to become Israel's principal supplier of sophisticated conventional weapons and promised not to press Israel to sign the NPT.[66]

The Ford administration adopted a two-pronged strategy to forestall Pakistan's nuclear development: first, the use of diplomatic pressure on allies to enforce export controls on sensitive nuclear technologies, and second, the resumption of US arms sales to Pakistan in exchange for its compliance with IAEA safeguards. Ford offered to sell Pakistan one hundred A-7 attack aircraft in exchange for cancelling the reprocessing plant contract with France.[67] In October 1976, Kissinger told Pakistani Ambassador Sahabzada Yaqub Khan that the nuclear program had become an issue in the US presidential campaign. He warned, 'If the Democrats win, you will face an assault and they will attack you. Credit and arms sales will be much more difficult, even impossible.'[68] Following Carter's election victory, Kissinger met with Yaqub Khan to offer the A-7s, and even US financing for a French-built nuclear reactor, in exchange for Bhutto quietly terminating the reprocessing contract. Kissinger warned, 'Early in January and it will be a new administration which was elected on a plank of non-proliferation. And I think I can assure you that it won't avail itself of escape clauses, or Symington amendments.'[69]

In the 1980s, the Reagan administration resumed the strategy of using US conventional arms sales as an inducement for Pakistani nuclear restraint. Reagan met with Zia in the Oval Office in December 1982 and personally established four red lines for the Pakistani nuclear program: (1) no reprocessing of spent uranium fuel into plutonium, (2) no assembly of a nuclear explosive device, (3) no testing of a nuclear explosive device, and (4) no transfer of sensitive nuclear technologies to other countries.[70] The administration also provided tangible inducements in the form of a $100 million aid package in the financial year (FY) 1982, split equally between economic assistance and military equipment sales (on a cash basis) and a

$3.4 billion six-year package of economic assistance and foreign military assistance from FY 1983 to FY 1987 that included forty F-16 fighters, 2,000 M48A5 tanks, 1,000 Improved TOW anti-tank missiles, twenty AH-1S Cobra attack helicopters, 500 AIM-9L Sidewinder air-to-air missiles, and 120 Stinger basic tactical anti-aircraft missiles.[71]

The Pakistani nuclear program did not cross Reagan's second and third red lines (no assembly of a nuclear explosive device and no testing of a nuclear explosive device) in the 1980s. The Pakistanis did, however, routinely violate the fourth red line (no transfers of sensitive nuclear technologies), as well as a fifth red line (no uranium enrichment above the 5 percent level) established in Reagan's letter to Zia on 21 September 1984.[72] When the Pakistanis crossed these lines, however, administration officials thwarted congressional efforts to cut off military and economic assistance to Islamabad. For example, in January 1988, in the aftermath of the Arshad Pervez nuclear smuggling case, Reagan invoked the Solarz Amendment and then promptly waived it.[73] In doing so, he allowed for the continuation of military and economic assistance to Pakistan. From January 1981 until August 1988, when Zia and Arnold Raphel, the US ambassador to Pakistan, were killed in a plane crash, the Reagan administration had three strategic objectives in South Asia: to continue the flow of covert military aid (via Pakistan) to the Afghan Mujahidin, to bolster Pakistan's conventional military capabilities as a hedge against further Soviet expansion in South Asia, and to restrain the Pakistani nuclear program. When the first two strategic objectives came into conflict with the third, the administration consistently favoured the first two.

Conclusion

As a hegemon, the US has an incentive to promote nuclear proliferation in order to minimize the twin risk of containment failure and access denial in various regions. This is consistent with hegemonic and nuclear domino theories, but arguably anomalous from the standpoint of balancing or power equilibrium theories. The non-proliferation strategies undertaken by the Eisenhower, Kennedy, Johnson, and Nixon administrations toward Israel between 1960 and 1969 and by the Ford, Carter, and Reagan administrations toward Pakistan between 1975 and 1988 were driven by the same strategic objective: a desire to avert containment failure in two volatile regions.

The specific mix of coercive strategies and inducements these administrations pursued toward Israel and Pakistan differed, as did the longer-term outcomes for bilateral relations. I argued that a neoclassical realist theory might account for that variation in US non-proliferation strategies. In both cases, policymakers in Washington confronted increasingly restrictive strategic environments in South Asia and the Middle East and increasing levels of clarity regarding the magnitude of threats to US interests in those regions, as well as optimal strategic responses to those threats. The types of domestic mobilization hurdles the Kennedy, Johnson, and Nixon administrations had to overcome were different from the ones the Ford, Carter, and Reagan administrations had to overcome. Whereas the three earlier administrations had to overcome increased congressional support for conventional arms sales to Israel and opposition to arms sales to Jordan, the three latter administrations had to circumvent non-proliferation legislation forcing them to cut off conventional arms sales to Pakistan.

The 1969 Nixon-Meir understanding has endured for forty-seven years, at least in part because the US became Israel's principal arms supplier, thus enabling the Israelis to maintain a decisive conventional force advantage over their Arab adversaries. Conventional arms sales to Pakistan by the Ford, Carter, and Reagan administrations were always more conditional. During the 1980s, the continuation of US military assistance to Zia's regime was always contingent on the Reagan administration's ability to circumvent non-proliferation legislation and never redressed Pakistan's conventional force imbalance with neighbouring India. Moreover, the generous US military and economic aid packages the Reagan administration provided to Islamabad as a hedge against Soviet expansion ended when the Soviet army withdrew from Afghanistan in 1989. Pakistan detonated its first nuclear explosive device in May 1998 in response to India's resumption of nuclear testing after a twenty-four-year moratorium. At least with respect to non-proliferation, it was never the objective of the US to bring 'peace' to the

Middle East in the 1960s or to South Asia in the 1970s and 1980s, but rather to minimize its own risk of containment failure in those regions.

In the twenty-first century, adversaries like Iran and North Korea, instead of allies, pose the immediate nuclear proliferation challenge for the US. Minimizing the risk of access denial in the Persian Gulf and East Asia has been the strategic objective of the administrations of presidents Bill Clinton, George W. Bush, Barack Obama, and Donald J. Trump. All four administrations have pursued a range of strategies including multilateral and unilateral economic sanctions, export controls on dual use technologies, sabotage, and diplomacy to thwart Iran's and North Korea's nuclear ambitions. The neoclassical realist theory outlined above may offer some policy insights in addressing these challenges.

In June 2015, Iran signed the Joint Comprehensive Plan of Action (JCPOA) with the five permanent members of the UN Security Council and Germany (P5 + 1), whereby Tehran agreed to eliminate its stockpile of highly enriched uranium and to accept strict limitations on its remaining nuclear facilities for a period of sixteen years in exchange for relief from economic sanctions imposed by the US, the EU, and the UN Security Council. The Trump administration, however, withdrew from the JCPOA in June 2018. President Trump criticized the agreement for not imposing restrictions on Iran's long-range missile programs and support for Hezbollah and other proxies in the region, as well for the 'sunset' provisions on the Iranian nuclear program. In November 2018, the Trump administration re-imposed US sanctions on Iran.

In 2017, North Korea conducted a series of long-range missile tests and at least one nuclear weapons test. After months of escalating tension in East Asia, Trump met with North Korean leader Kim Jong-un in Singapore in June 2018. The two leaders signed a declaration calling for the complete 'denuclearization' of the Korean peninsula. While North Korea has not resumed missile tests or nuclear detonations since the Trump-Kim summit, there is no agreement between the two sides over what the term 'denuclearization' actually means. Moreover, the North Korean regime has not yet provided a full accounting of its nuclear arsenal and delivery systems and the scope of its nuclear program's infrastructure.

The argument advanced above suggests that domestic politics may make it far easier for future US administrations to offer inducements for Middle Eastern and East Asian allies threatened by a potential resumption of Iranian and North Korean nuclear and missile activities than to provide inducements for Iran or North Korea to comply with any future agreements regarding their nuclear weapons programs.

Notes

1. Francis J. Gavin, 'Strategies of Inhibition: U.S. Grand Strategy, the Nuclear Revolution, and Nonproliferation,' International Security 40, no.1 (2015): 9–46. For an analysis of how the maintenance of power preponderance became a core objective of US grand strategy after World War II, see Melvyn P. Leffler, A Preponderance of Power: National Security, the Truman Administration, and the Cold War (Stanford, CA: Stanford University Press, 1992).

2. Thucydides, *The Landmark Thucydides: A Comprehensive Guide to the Peloponnesian War*, Robert B. Strassler, and Richard Crawley, eds. (New York: Free Press, 1996).

3. Richard Ned Lebow and Simon Reich, 'The Quest for Hegemony: A Threat to the Global Order' (Nobel Institute Symposium no. 167: The Causes of Peace, Os Commune, Norway, 2016), 41.

4. Stephen G. Brooks and William C. Wohlforth, 'Assessing the Balance,' *Cambridge Review of International Affairs* 24, no. 2 (2011): 201–19; Stephen G. Brooks and William C. Wohlforth, 'The Rise and Fall of the Great Powers in the Twenty-First Century: China's Rise and the Fate of America's Global Position,' *International Security* 40, no. 3 (2016): 7–53.

5. See Robert O. Keohane, *After Hegemony: Cooperation and Discord in the World Political Economy* (Princeton, NJ: Princeton University Press, 1984); G. John Ikenberry, *After Victory: Institutions, Strategic Restraint, and the Rebuilding of Order after Major Wars* (Princeton, NJ: Princeton University Press, 2001); Ikenberry, *Liberal Leviathan: The Origins, Crisis, and Transformation of the American World Order* (Princeton, NJ: Princeton University Press, 2011); Robert Gilpin, *War and Change in World Politics* (Cambridge: Cambridge University Press, 1981); Stephen D. Krasner, *Defending the National Interest: Raw Materials Investments and U.S. Foreign Policy* (Princeton, NJ: Princeton University Press, 1978); Robert Gilpin and Jean M. Gilpin, *The Political Economy of International Relations* (Princeton, NJ: Princeton University Press, 1987); Stephen G. Brooks and William C. Wohlforth, *World out of Balance: International Relations and the Challenge of American Primacy* (Princeton, NJ: Princeton

University Press, 2008); and Wohlforth, *America Abroad: The United States' Global Role in the 21st Century* (New York: Oxford University Press, 2016).

6. See, for example, Thomas P. Cavanna, 'Geopolitics over Proliferation: The Origins of US Grand Strategy and Their Implications for the Spread of Nuclear Weapons in South Asia,' *Journal of Strategic Studies* 41, no. 4 (2016): 576–603; Or Rabinowitz and Nicholas L. Miller, 'Keeping the Bombs in the Basement: U.S. Nonproliferation Policy toward Israel, South Africa, and Pakistan,' *International Security* 40, no.1 (2015): 47–86; Gene Gerzhoy, 'Alliance Coercion and Nuclear Restraint: How the United States Thwarted West Germany's Nuclear Ambitions,' *International Security* 39, no. 4 (2015): 91–129; and Se Young Jang, 'The Evolution of US Extended Deterrence and South Korea's Nuclear Ambitions,' *Journal of Strategic Studies* 39, no. 4 (2016): 502–20.

7. See for example, Jeremy Pressman, *Warring Friends: Alliance Restraint in International Politics* (Ithaca, NY: Cornell University Press, 2008); Evan N. Resnick, 'I Will Follow: Smart Power and the Management of Wartime Alliances,' *Journal of Strategic Studies* 38, no. 3 (2015): 383–409; and Thomas J. Christensen, *Worse Than a Monolith: Alliance Politics and Problems of Coercive Diplomacy in Asia* (Princeton, NJ: Princeton University Press, 2011).

8. Gavin, 'Strategies of Inhibition,' 11. On the extension of security assurances, see Jeffrey W. Knopf, 'Security Assurances: Initial Hypotheses,' in *Security Assurances and Nuclear Nonproliferation*, ed. Jeffrey W. Knopf (Stanford, CA: Stanford University Press, 2012), 13–38. For analyses of cases where US policymakers contemplated preventive military action, see Marc Trachtenberg, 'Preventive War and U.S. Foreign Policy,' *Security Studies* 16, no. 1 (2007): 1–31; Sarah E. Kreps and Matthew Fuhrmann, 'Attacking the Atom: Does Bombing Nuclear Facilities Affect Proliferation?' *Journal of Strategic Studies* 34, no. 2 (2011): 161–87; and William Burr and Jeffrey T. Richelson, 'Whether to Strangle the Baby in the Cradle: The United States and the Chinese Nuclear Program, 1960–64,' *International Security* 25, no. 3 (2000): 54–99. For an examination of interdiction efforts and export controls see William Burr, 'A Scheme of "Control": The United States and the Origins of the Nuclear Suppliers' Group, 1974–1976*,' *The International History Review* 36, no. 2 (2014): 252–76.

9. See, for example, Alexander Lanoszka, 'Protection States Trust? Explaining South Korea's Nuclear Behavior' (PhD dissertation, Princeton University, 2012), 418; Yang Bonny Lin, 'Arms, Alliances, and the Bomb: Using Conventional Arms Transfers to Prevent Nuclear Proliferation' (PhD dissertation, Yale University, 2012), 319.

10. This is the main conclusion of Or Rabinowitz, *Bargaining on Nuclear Tests: Washington and Its Cold War Deals* (Oxford: Oxford University Press, 2014).

11. Kenneth N. Waltz, *Theory of International Politics* (Reading, MA: Addison-Wesley, 1979), 169–79.

12. See, for example, Kenneth N. Waltz, 'The Spread of Nuclear Weapons: More May Be Better,' *Adelphi Papers No. 171* (London: International Institute for Strategic Studies,

1981); Scott D. Sagan and Kenneth N. Waltz, *The Spread of Nuclear Weapons: A Debate Renewed* (New York: Norton, 2003).

13.   John J. Mearsheimer, *The Tragedy of Great Power Politics* (New York: Norton, 2014), 157–67, 252–61.

14.   For a detailed analysis, see Barry R. Posen, *Restraint: A New Foundation for U.S. Grand Strategy* (Ithaca, NY: Cornell University Press, 2014).

15.   Gavin, 'Strategies of Inhibition,' 15–16.

16.   For a discussion of US command of the commons, see Barry R. Posen, 'Command of the Commons: The Military Foundation of U.S. Hegemony,' *International Security* 28, no. 1 (2003): 5–46. For a discussion the conclusion of bilateral alliances with Japan, South Korea, and Taiwan as mechanisms for US control, see Victor D. Cha, 'Powerplay: Origins of the U.S. Alliance System in Asia,' *International Security* 34, no. 3 (2010): 158–96.

17.   See Michael Beckley, 'The Myth of Entangling Alliances: Reassessing the Security Risks of U.S. Defense Pacts,' *International Security* 39, no. 4 (2015): 7–48.

18.   On the strategy of deep engagement, see Stephen G. Brooks, G. John Ikenberry, and William C. Wohlforth, 'Don't Come Home, America: The Case against Retrenchment,' *International Security* 37, no. 3 (2012): 7–51; and Brooks, Ikenberry, and Wohlforth, *America Abroad*, 88–102.

19.   Evan Braden Montgomery, *In the Hegemon's Shadow: Leading States and the Rise of Regional Powers* (Ithaca, NY: Cornell University Press, 2016), 12.

20.   Ibid., 12–13.

21.   Miller, 'Nuclear Dominoes,' 33–35.

22.   See Matthew Kroenig, 'Force or Friendship? Explaining Great Power Nonproliferation Policy,' *Security Studies* 23, no. 1 (2014): 1–32.

23.   See James Cameron and Or Rabinowitz, 'Eight Lost Years? Nixon, Ford, Kissinger and the Non-Proliferation Regime, 1969–1977,' *Journal of Strategic Studies* 40, no. 6 (2016): 839–66; Roland Popp, 'Introduction: Global Order, Cooperation between the Superpowers, and Alliance Politics in the Making of the Nuclear Non-Proliferation Regime,' *The International History Review* 36, no. 2 (2014): 195–209; Dane Swango, 'The United States and the Role of Nuclear Co-Operation and Assistance in the Design of the Non-Proliferation Treaty,' *The International History Review* 36, no. 2 (2014): 210–29; and William Burr, 'A Scheme of "Control",' 252–76.

24.   Mark S. Bell, 'Beyond Emboldenment: How Acquiring Nuclear Weapons Can Change Foreign Policy,' *International Security* 40, no. 1 (2015): 87–119, especially 91–92. Also see S. Paul Kapur, *Dangerous Deterrent: Nuclear Weapons Proliferation and Conflict in South Asia* (Stanford, CA: Stanford University Press, 2007).

25.   Jan Melissen, 'The Restoration of the Nuclear Alliance: Great Britain and Atomic Negotiations with the United States, 1957–58,' *Contemporary Record* 6, no. 1 (1992): 72–106; and John Baylis, 'The 1958 Anglo-American Mutual Defence Agreement: The Search for Nuclear Interdependence,' *Journal of Strategic Studies* 31, no. 3 (2008): 425–66.

26. See Marc Trachtenberg, *A Constructed Peace: The Making of the European Settlement, 1945–1963* (Princeton, NJ: Princeton University Press, 1999), 146–200.

27. Gerzhoy, 'Alliance Coercion and Nuclear Restraint,' 111–24.

28. Norrin M. Ripsman, Jeffrey W. Taliaferro, and Steven E. Lobell, *Neoclassical Realist Theory of International Politics* (New York: Oxford University Press, 2016), 52–53.

29. Ibid., 56.

30. Cohen, *Israel and Bomb*, 57–78.

31. Yaacov Bar-Siman-Tov, 'The United States and Israel since 1948: A "Special Relationship"?' *Diplomatic History* 22, no. 2 (1998): 231–62.

32. '193. National Security Decision Memorandum 289, Washington, 24 March 1975,' *FRUS, 1969–1976, vol. E-8: Documents on South Asia, 1973–1976* (Washington, DC: GPO, 2007), https://history.state.gov/historicaldocuments/frus1969-76ve08/d193.

33. Quoted in Feroz Hassan Khan, *Eating Grass: The Making of the Pakistani Bomb* (Stanford, CA: Stanford University Press, 2012), 7.

34. 'Department of State Instruction a-128 to U.S. Embassy Israel, "Atomic Energy Developments," 7 March 1958, Confidential,' in *NSA Electronic Briefing Book no. 510*, eds. Avner Cohen and William Burr (Washington, DC: National Security Archive, 2015), http://nsarchive.gwu.edu/nukevault/ebb510/docs/doc%201A.pdf; 'U.S. Embassy Tel Aviv Dispatch No. 652 to State Department, "Israeli Exchanges with Other Countries Relating to Atomic Energy," 16 April 1958,' in *NSA Electronic Briefing Book no. 510*, eds. Avner Cohen and William Burr (Washington, DC: National Security Archive, 2015), http://nsarchive.gwu.edu/nukevault/ebb510/docs/doc%201B.pdf; 'U.S. Joint Atomic Energy Intelligence Committee, Post-Mortem on SNIE 100-8-60: Implications of the Acquisition by Israel of a Nuclear Weapons Capability, 31 January 1961, Draft, Secret,' in *NSA Electronic Briefing Book no. 510*, eds. Avner Cohen and William Burr (Washington, DC: National Security Archive, 2015), http://nsarchive.gwu.edu/nukevault/ebb510/docs/doc%2027A.pdf; and 'Memorandum, Phillip Farley to Hugh Cumming, Director of Intelligence and Research, "Post-Mortem on SNIE 100-8-60," 28 January 1961,' in *NSA Electronic Briefing Book no. 510*, eds. Avner Cohen and William Burr (Washington, DC: National Security Archive, 2015), http://nsarchive.gwu.edu/nukevault/ebb510/docs/doc%2027B.pdf.

35. Avner Cohen and William Burr, 'The Eisenhower Administration and the Discovery of Dimona: March 1958–January 1961,' in *NSA Electronic Briefing Book no. 510*, eds. Avner Cohen and William Burr (Washington, DC: National Security Archive, 2015), http://nsarchive.gwu.edu/nukevault/ebb510/.

36. 'Memo from Sidney Sober to Henry A. Kissinger, Re: Indian Nuclear Development—NSSM 156 [Includes Revised Report; Annex Not Included], 31 May 1974,' *DNSA Collection: Presidential Directives, Part II* (Washington, DC: Digital National Security Archive, 1974), 67, http://search.proquest.com/docview/1679070697.

37. Ibid.

38. 'Memorandum to Holders, Special National Intelligence Estimate, "Prospects for Further Proliferation of Nuclear Weapons," SNIE 4-1-74, 18 December 1975,' in *NSA*

Electronic Briefing Book no. 333, ed. William Burr (Washington, DC: National Security Archive, 2010), http://www.gwu.edu/~nsarchiv/nukevault/ebb333/doc01.pdf.

39. 'Special National Intelligence Estimate Number 100-8-60, "Implications of the Acquisition by Israel of a Nuclear Weapons Capability," 8 December 1960, with Memoranda to Holders Attached, 22 and 29 December 1960, Attached, Secret, Excised Copy,' in *NSA Electronic Briefing Book no. 510*, eds. Avner Cohen and William Burr (Washington, DC: National Security Archive, 2015), http://nsarchive.gwu.edu/nukevault/ebb510/docs/doc%208.pdf.

40. 'Memorandum of Conversation, "President Kennedy, Prime Minister Ben-Gurion, Ambassador Avraham Harman of Israel, Myer Feldman of the White House Staff, and Philips Talbot, Assistant Secretary, Near East and South Asian Affairs, at the Waldorf Astoria, New York, 4:45 P.M. To 6:15 P.M.," 30 May 1961, Secret, Draft,' in *NSA Electronic Briefing Book no. 547*, eds. Avner Cohen and William Burr (Washington, DC: National Security Archive, 2016), https://assets.documentcloud.org/documents/2806694/Document-9B-Memorandum-of-Conversation-President.pdf.

41. '65. Memorandum of Conversation, Re: Johnson/Eshkol Exchange of Views, 1 June 1964,' *FRUS, 1964–1968*, vol. XVIII: Arab-Israeli Dispute (Washington, DC: GPO, 2000), https://history.state.gov/historicaldocuments/frus1964-68v18/d65.

42. '225. Letter from President Ford to Pakistani Prime Minister Bhutto, Washington, 19 March 1976,' *FRUS, 1969–1976*, vol. E-8, *Documents on South Asia, 1973–1976* (Washington, DC: GPO, 2007), https://history.state.gov/historicaldocuments/frus1969-76ve08/d225.

43. Ripsman, Taliaferro, and Lobell, *Neoclassical Realist Theory of International Politics*, 58–79.

44. Thomas J. Christensen, *Useful Adversaries: Grand Strategy, Domestic Mobilization, and Sino-American Conflict, 1947–1958* (Princeton, NJ: Princeton University Press, 1996), 20–31; Fareed Zakaria, *From Wealth to Power: The Unusual Origins of America's World Role* (Princeton NJ: Princeton University Press, 1998), 38–41; and Aaron L. Friedberg, *In the Shadow of the Garrison State: America's Anti-Statism and Its Cold War Grand Strategy* (Princeton NJ: Princeton University Press, 2000), 22–33, 45–50.

45. 'Assistant Secretaries Alfred L. Atherton and Douglas J. Bennet, Jr. through Mr. Habib to the Acting Secretary, "Pakistan's Purchase of a Nuclear Fuel Reprocessing Plant: The Symington Amendment and Consultations with Congress," 23 June 1977, Confidential, with Cover Note from Christopher to "Roy" Atherton,' in *NSA Electronic Briefing Book no. 333*, ed. William Burr (Washington, DC: National Security Archive, 2010), http://nsarchive.gwu.edu/nukevault/ebb333/doc03.pdf.

46. 'Arms Control and Disarmament Agency, Memorandum from Norman Wulf for Under Secretary of State for Political Affairs, Next Steps on Pakistan-Solarz and Symington, 21 December 1987, Secret,' in *NSA Electronic Briefing Book no. 446*, ed. William Burr (Washington, DC: National Security Archive, 2013), http://nsarchive.gwu.edu/nukevault/ebb446/docs/25.pdf; 'Department of State, Memorandum from INR Director Morton Abramowitz to Mr. Armacost, "Pakistan-Pervez Case and Solarz

Amendment," 29 December 1987, Secret,' in *NSA Electronic Briefing Book no. 446*, ed. William Burr (Washington, DC: National Security Archive, 2013), http://nsarchive .gwu.edu/nukevault/ebb446/docs/26.pdf.

47. 'U.S. Embassy Paris Cable 24312 to State Department, "French Go Public (Partly) on Reprocessing Issue with Pakistan," 3 August 1978, Secret,' in *NSA Electronic Briefing Book no. 333*, ed. William Burr (Washington, DC: National Security Archive, 2010), http://nsarchive.gwu.edu/nukevault/ebb333/doc09.pdf; 'U.S. Embassy Islamabad to Cable 8167 to State Department, "Reprocessing Plant," 21 August 1978, Secret,' in *NSA Electronic Briefing Book no. 333*, ed. William Burr (Washington, DC: National Security Archive, 2010), http://nsarchive.gwu.edu/nukevault/ebb333/doc14.pdf.

48. 'Paul H. Kreisberg to Mr. Newsom, "Presidential Letter on Pakistan Nuclear Program to Western Leaders," 30 March 1979, Secret,' in *NSA Electronic Briefing Book no. 333*, ed. William Burr (Washington, DC: National Security Archive, 2010), http:// nsarchive.gwu.edu/nukevault/ebb333/doc33.pdf.

49. 'Size and Timing of '82 Security Assistance Amendment for Pakistan, Internal Paper, Secret, Bureau of Near East and South Asia Affairs, Department of State, 24 February 1981,' *DNSA collection: Nuclear Nonproliferation* (Washington, DC: Digital National Security Archive, 2016), 6, http://search.proquest.com/docview/1679125035; 'Security Assistance for Pakistan, Secret, Action Memorandum, 16 February 1981,' *DNSA collection: Nuclear Nonproliferation* (Washington, DC: Digital National Security Archive, 2016), http://search.proquest.com/docview/1679139930.

50. '268. Memorandum for the Record, President's Talk with Israeli Foreign Minister Eban, 9 February 1966, *FRUS, 1964–1968*, vol. XVIII, *Arab-Israeli Conflict, 1964–1967* (Washington, DC: GPO, 2000), https://history.state.gov/historicaldocuments /frus1964-68v18/d268.

51. '297. Telegram from the Department of State to the Embassy in Israel, Re: F-4 Negotiations, 31 October 1968,' *FRUS, 1964–1968*, vol. XX, *Arab-Israeli Dispute, 1967–1968* (Washington, DC: GPO, 2001), https://history.state.gov/historicaldocuments /frus1964-68v20/d297; '290. Action Memorandum Rostow to President Johnson, Re: Strong Israeli Reaction to Eban Talks Here, 25 October 1968, 2:20 P.M.,' *FRUS, 1964– 1968*. Vol. XX, *Arab-Israeli Dispute, 1967–1968* (Washington, DC: GPO, 2001), https:// history.state.gov/historicaldocuments/frus1964-68v20/d290; '295. Memorandum from the Assistant Secretary of Defense for International Security Affairs (Warnke) to Secretary of Defense Clifford, Re: F-4 Negotiations with Israel, 28 October 1968,' *FRUS, 1964–1968*. Vol. XX, *Arab-Israeli Dispute, 1967–1968* (Washington, DC: GPO, 2001), https://history.state.gov/historicaldocuments/frus1964-68v20/d295; and '299. Memorandum of Telephone Conversation between Secretary of State Rusk and Secretary of Defense Clifford, 1 November 1968,' *FRUS, 1964–1968*. Vol. XX, *Arab-Israeli Dispute, 1967–1968* (Washington, DC: GPO, 2001), https://history.state.gov /historicaldocuments/frus1964-68v20/d299.

52. Gerzhoy, 'Alliance Coercion and Nuclear Restraint,' 92–93.

53. Avner Cohen, *Israel and the Bomb* (New York: Columbia University Press, 1998), 128–129.

54. Ibid., 175–193.

55. '269. Memorandum of Conversation, Secretary of State Rusk and Israel Foreign Minister Abba Eban, 9 February 1966,' *FRUS, 1964-1968*, vol. XVIII, *Arab-Israeli Conflict, 1964–1967* (Washington, DC: GPO, 2000), https://history.state.gov /historicaldocuments/frus1964-68v18/d269.

56. 'Handwritten Notes, Warren Christopher Meetings with General Zia and Foreign Minister Shahi, 1 and 2 March 1979,' in *NSA Electronic Briefing Book no. 333*, ed. William Burr (Washington, DC: National Security Archive, 2010), http://nsarchive.gwu .edu/nukevault/ebb333/doc26b.pdf.

57. 'Paul H. Kreisberg to Mr. Newsom, "Presidential Letter on Pakistan Nuclear Program to Western Leaders," 30 March 1979, Secret,' in *NSA Electronic Briefing Book no. 333*, ed. William Burr (Washington: National Security Archive, 2010), http://nsarchive .gwu.edu/nukevault/ebb333/doc33.pdf.

58. 'U.S. Embassy Pakistan Cable 10239 to State Department, "My First Meeting with President Zia," 5 July 1982, Secret,' in *NSA Electronic Briefing Book no. 377*, ed. William Burr (Washington, DC: National Security Archive, 2012), https:// assets.documentcloud.org/documents/347027/doc-13-a-7-5-82.pdf; 'U.S. Embassy Pakistan Cable 15696 to State Department, "Pakistan Nuclear Issue: Meeting with General Zia," 17 October 1982, Secret' in *NSA Electronic Briefing Book no. 377*, ed. William Burr (Washington, DC: National Security Archive, 2012), https://www .documentcloud.org/documents/347029-doc-14-a-10-17-82.html; 'State Department Cable 299499 to U.S. Embassy Islamabad, "Pakistan Nuclear Issue: Meeting with General Zia," 25 October 1982, Secret,' in *NSA Electronic Briefing Book no. 377*, ed. William Burr (Washington, DC: National Security Archive, 2012), https:// www.documentcloud.org/documents/347030-doc-14-b-10-25-82.html; 'Embassy Islamabad Telegram 16556 to Department of State, "Under Secretary Armacost Meeting with Zia," 5 August 1987, Secret,' in *National Security Archive Electronic Briefing Book no. 446*, ed. William Burr (Washington, DC: National Security Archive, 2013), http://nsarchive.gwu.edu/nukevault/ebb446/docs/14B.pdf.

59. '327. Memorandum from the Department of State Executive Secretary (Read) to the President's Special Assistant for National Security Affairs (Bundy), 20 September 1963, Re: Israel Security Guarantee: Reply to Ben-Gurion's May 12 Letter,' *FRUS, 1961–1963*, vol. XVIII (Washington, DC: GPO, 1995), https://history.state.gov /historicaldocuments/frus1961-63v18/d327; '332. Telegram from the Department of State to the Embassy in Israel, 2 October 1963, Re: Text of President Kennedy's Letter to Israeli Prime Minister Eshkol,' *FRUS, 1961–1963*. Vol. XVIII (Washington, DC: GPO, 1995), https://history.state.gov/historicaldocuments/frus1961-63v18/d332.

60. '185. Telegram from the Embassy in Israel to the Department of State, Re: Text of Signed Memorandum of Understanding, 11 March 1965, 2 AM,' *FRUS, 1964–1968*,

vol. XVIII, *Arab-Israeli Dispute, 1964–1967* (Washington, DC: GPO, 2000), https://history.state.gov/historicaldocuments/frus1964-68v18/d185.

61. Zach Levey, 'The United States' Skyhawk Sale to Israel, 1966: Strategic Exigencies of an Arms Deal,' *Diplomatic History* 28, no. 2 (2004): 255–76.

62. '283. Memorandum from the Assistant Secretary of Defense for International Security Affairs (McNaughton) to Secretary of Defense McNamara, 31 March 1966,' *FRUS, 1964–1968*, vol. XVIII, *Arab-Israeli Conflict, 1964–1967* (Washington, DC: GPO, 2000), https://history.state.gov/historicaldocuments/frus1964-68v18/d283.

63. 'Summary of Intelligence Information Gained Concerning Israel's Nuclear Capability, and Its Impact Upon US-Israeli Relations, Top Secret, Department of State, 19 July 1969,' *US Declassified Documents Online* (Farmington Hills, MI: Gale, 2007), http://tinyurl.galegroup.com/tinyurl/3bptP6.

64. 'Memorandum from Henry Kissinger to President Nixon, "Israeli Nuclear Program," N.D., with Enclosures Dated 19 July 1969, Top Secret, Excised Copy,' in *NSA Electronic Briefing Book no. 485*, eds. William Burr and Avner Cohen (Washington, DC: National Security Archive, 2014), http://www2.gwu.edu/~nsarchiv/nukevault/ebb485/docs/Doc%2010%207-19-69%20circa.pdf.

65. Cohen, *Israel and the Bomb*, 336–37; and Rabinowitz, *Bargaining on Nuclear Tests*, 88–89.

66. 'National Security Decision Memorandum No. 81, Re: US Arms Transfer Policy toward Israel, 6 November 1969, Secret/Sensitive,' *US Declassified Documents Online* (Farmington Hills, MI: Gale, 2009), http://tinyurl.galegroup.com/tinyurl/3k7Jv9; 'National Security Decision Memorandum (NSDM) No. 82, Re: US Economic Assistance Policy toward Israel, 6 November 1969, Secret/Sensitive,' *US Declassified Documents Online* (Farmington Hills, MI: Gale, 2009), http://tinyurl.galegroup.com/tinyurl/3k7Jw7; and 'National Security Decision Memorandum (NSDM) No. 87, Re: Military and Financial Assistance to Israel, 15 October 1970, Secret/Nodis,' *US Declassified Documents Online* (Farmington Hills, MI: Gale, 2009), http://tinyurl.galegroup.com/tinyurl/3k7Jx5.

67. 'Memo of Conversation in Brent Scowcroft's Office, Re: Progress on Proposal to Sell 110 A-7s to Pakistan and Problem Concerning Nuclear Sale by France to Pakistan, 20 September 1976,' *US Declassified Documents Online* (Farmington Hills, MI: Gale, 1996), http://tinyurl.galegroup.com/tinyurl/3cbYd1.

68. '236. Memorandum of Conversation, New York, 6 October 1976, 10:30–11:28 A.M.,' *FRUS, 1969–1976*, vol. E-8, *Documents on South Asia, 1973–1976* (Washington, DC: GPO, 2007), https://history.state.gov/historicaldocuments/frus1969-76ve08/d236.

69. '239. Memorandum of Conversation, Washington, 17 December 1976, 3:20–4 P.M.,' *FRUS, 1969–1976*. Vol. E-8, *Documents on South Asia, 1973-1976* (Washington, DC: GPO, 2007), https://history.state.gov/historicaldocuments/frus1969-76ve08/d239.

70. 'National Security Council, Memorandum from Shirin Tahir-Kheli to Robert Oakley, "Dealing with Pakistan's Nuclear Program: A US Strategy," 23 July 1987, Secret,' in

NSA Electronic Briefing Book no. 446, ed. William Burr (Washington, DC: National Security Archive, 2013), http://nsarchive.gwu.edu/nukevault/ebb446/docs/9.pdf.

71. 'Size and Timing,' 6.

72. 'US Arms Control and Disarmament Agency, Memorandum from Kenneth Adelman for the Undersecretary of State for Political Affairs, "the Pakistani Procurement Cases," 23 July 1987, Secret,' in *NSA Electronic Briefing Book no. 446*, ed. William Burr (Washington, DC: National Security Archive, 2013), http://nsarchive.gwu.edu /nukevault/ebb446/docs/8.pdf.

73. 'Presidential Determination No. 88-5 of January 15, 1988,†*Federal Register*, Vol. 83, No. 24, 5 February 1988,' in *NSA Electronic Briefing Book no. 446*, ed. William Burr (Washington, DC: National Security Archive, 2013), http://nsarchive.gwu.edu /nukevault/ebb446/docs/27A%20Statement%20on%20Reagan%20determinaton %201-15-88.pdf.

Ideology and Peace

5.

Ideology and Peace: Historical Perspectives

Niall Ferguson

Introduction

In 1971, Woody Allen parodied Henry Kissinger in a half-hour 'mockumentary', *Men of Crisis: The Harvey Wallinger Story*, made for PBS. It was due to air in February 1972 but was almost certainly pulled for political reasons.[1] In one scene, Wallinger is asked to comment on President Nixon's (authentic) statement that 'we shall end the war [in Vietnam] and win the peace'. Allen mumbles, 'What Mr. Nixon means is that, uh, it's important to win the war and also win the peace; or, at the very least, lose the war and lose the peace; or, uh, win at least part of the peace, or win two peaces, perhaps, or lose a few peaces but win a piece of the war. The other alternative would be to win a piece of the war, or lose a piece of Mr. Nixon.'[2]

The early 1970s was one of those periods in modern history when pacifism was all the rage. Despite Tom Lehrer's remark that 'political satire became obsolete when [in 1973] Henry Kissinger was awarded the Nobel peace prize',[3] satirists continued to hammer the Nixon administration for failing to end the Vietnam War sooner. On the whole, however, the tone of the anti-war movement of that era was more solemn than satirical. As an undergraduate, a graduate student, and then a professor at Harvard, Kissinger had grown accustomed to peace protesters issuing po-faced condemnations of war. On the day of his graduation in 1950, there had been a demonstration against the commencement speaker, Dean Acheson, by a so-called peace group, the Massachusetts Action Committee for Peace, led by the

Reverend Robert H. Muir, an Episcopalian clergyman from Roxbury.[4] One of the demonstrators' placards read, 'Acheson, Peace Not Bombs'. Another urged him to 'End War Talks'.

This was on the eve of the Korean War. By the time of Vietnam, pacifism on American campuses was more vociferous and, ironically, more violent. In November 1966, Defense Secretary Robert McNamara narrowly escaped assault by members of Students for a Democratic Society (SDS).[5] In September 1969, members of SDS and the so-called Weather Underground stormed the Harvard Center for International Affairs, where Kissinger had worked since its creation in 1958, accusing its staff of being 'hired killers'. There were recurrent attacks on the CFIA offices—notably in April 1970, when the offices were 'trashed', and six months later, on 14 October 1970, when a bomb exploded on the third floor. [6] The building was ransacked once again in April 1972 in a protest against 'America's genocidal war against the people of Indochina'.[7]

Militarism and Pacifism

Clashes between absolutist proponents of peace and governments engaged in statecraft have been a recurrent feature of the modern age. For most of history, the legitimacy of war itself was not much contested, even if its harsh consequences were often lamented. Pacifism as an ideology or component of an ideology is in fact of relatively recent origin. So too is militarism, which saw war as beneficial precisely because of its consequences. Both of these extreme theoretical positions attracted adherents at a time when military technology was exponentially increasing the destructive power of states. Indeed, the two terms 'pacifism' and 'militarism' were in most frequent use in the era of the two most destructive wars in human history (see figure 5.1).

Pacifism as a political movement in the nineteenth and twentieth centuries had its roots in certain strains of Christianity, notably Quakerism, but drew sustenance from Cobdenite liberalism, which foresaw global free trade as the precursor of world peace, and from Marxism, with its emphasis on the international character of the proletariat and the malign, imperialist character of war, as well as from feminism. The world wars were trying times for

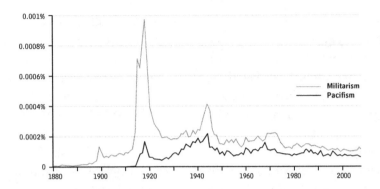

FIGURE 5.1. *Google Ngram of the relative frequency of the words 'militarism'
and 'pacifism' in English-language books, 1880–2008.*

pacifists, who were subjected to prosecution and even execution for their
'conscientious objection' to bearing arms. The era of the Cold War provided
a more benign environment, partly because the advent and proliferation
of nuclear weapons reduced the need for mass conscription, but also because both sides in the Cold War insisted in their propaganda that they
themselves were pro-peace. As a young man, I remember being sent by a
newspaper to cover a conference of 'Generals for Peace' in Vienna. It took
me some time to realize that the conference was a KGB operation, though
I do not doubt the sincerity of the former North Atlantic Treaty Organization (NATO) generals who had been persuaded to participate.

One of the simplest lessons that history teaches is that an absolute insistence on peace at any price is not a good basis for the foreign policy of a
country that wishes to retain its independence or, indeed, to preserve peace.
The more difficult challenge is how best to ensure that those states not willing to renounce violence can minimize their use of it. As outlined in other
sections, American theorists of international relations often distinguish
between realist and idealist solutions to this problem, the former focusing
on national interests and capabilities, the latter on international institutions
and laws. I have come to doubt the usefulness of this distinction. In sections 2 and 3, I use the work of Henry Kissinger—whose biography I am
halfway through writing[8]—to illustrate how idealist and realist elements
are necessarily combined in any serious theory of peace without weakness.

I then show how Kissinger's doctrine was fundamentally rejected by the anti-war generation that came to the fore on university campuses during and after 1968. The final section asks which made the greater contribution to reducing conflict between the 1970s and the present: the statesmen or the pacifists. The chapter concludes by briefly considering other non-ideological explanations for the decline of war in the past fifty years.

In December 1975, two years after his appointment as the fifty-sixth US secretary of state, Henry Kissinger travelled to his birthplace, the Franconian industrial town of Fürth, to receive a citizen's gold medal.[9] Before an audience of Bavarian worthies, he and German Foreign Minister Hans-Dietrich Genscher exchanged what today might seem like diplomatic platitudes:

> In the shadow of a nuclear catastrophe [declared Kissinger] . . . we must not bow to the supposed inevitability of historical tragedy . . . Our shared task is to collaborate in building a system of international relations which ensures the stability of continents and the security of peoples, which binds the peoples of the world together through their common interests, and which demands restraint and moderation in international affairs. Our goal is a peace for which all of us work—small as well as big states—a peace that is enduring because all wish to uphold it—strong as well as weak states.[10]

A more memorable speech was the unscheduled one given by Kissinger's father, Louis, making his first visit to Germany since 1938, when he and his family had emigrated to the United States to escape persecution by the National Socialist regime. A teacher and a scholarly man, Louis Kissinger took the opportunity to compare his son to Trygaeus, the hero in Aristophanes's comedy *Peace*. Like Trygaeus, the elder Kissinger said, his son

> has seen it as his life's work to dedicate his time and energy to furthering and maintaining peace in the world. Working together with the President of the United States, he has the great idea of ushering in an era of understanding and peaceful collaboration between nations . . .

It is a gratifying feeling for us parents that today the name Kissinger is seen around the world as interchangeable with the term 'peace'; that the name Kissinger has become a synonym for peace.[11]

Peace was certainly not the synonym for 'Kissinger' that Woody Allen or Tom Lehrer would have chosen. Yet the claim was not altogether an outlandish one. In an address to the United Nations General Assembly two years before, on 24 September 1973, Kissinger had quoted Immanuel Kant's prediction:

> that perpetual peace would come eventually—either as the creation of man's moral aspirations or as the consequence of physical necessity. What seemed utopian then looms as tomorrow's reality; soon there will be no alternative. Our only choice is whether the world envisaged in the [United Nations] charter will come about as the result of our vision or of a catastrophe invited by our shortsightedness.[12]

Such a catastrophe did not seem at all remote in the mid-1970s. The world today is a good deal more peaceful than it was then, surprising as that may seem to those who watch television, where journalists routinely assert that we live at a time of 'unprecedented upheaval'. In reality, the Nixon-Ford-Carter years were far more violent than the Bush-Obama years. For example, there were more than 2 million battle deaths due to state-based armed conflict in the 1970s, compared with approximately 270,000 in the 2000s. Vietnam was a vastly more lethal war than Iraq (47,424 US combat deaths compared with 3,527).

In December 1975, when Kissinger and his father returned to Fürth, Angola was sliding into civil war, less than a month after the end of Portuguese colonial rule. The Pathet Lao, supported by Vietnam and the Soviet Union, had just overthrown the king of Laos, and the Indonesian military had invaded the briefly independent state of East Timor. Just five days after the Fürth medal ceremony, the Central Intelligence Agency's head of station in Athens was shot dead. The newspapers that month were full of terrorist outrages: by the Irish Republican Army in London, by the Palestine Liberation Organization in Vienna, by South Moluccan separatists in the Netherlands. There was even a fatal bomb explosion at New York's LaGuardia airport. To some young German Social Democrats, it seemed incongruous to honour the American secretary of state at such a time.[13]

Perhaps only the older Germans present understood the significance of Kissinger's call for 'a world, in which it is reconciliation and not power that fills peoples with pride; an era, in which convictions are a source of moral strength and not of intolerance and of hate.'[14] Those born before WWII had lived through far worse times. First as a refugee, then as an infantry rifle-man, and finally as a counter-intelligence agent hunting down Gestapo and SS personnel, Henry Kissinger had experienced first-hand the disastrous consequences of the policies of appeasement, which had not only failed to avoid WWII but had given Hitler the time to start the war in more advantageous circumstances than would have been the case in 1936 or 1938. 'We like to smile now at Baldwin and Chamberlain in 1938', Kissinger remarked in an interview in 1957, 'but they thought of themselves as tough realists.'[15] The assumption that realism had failed in the 1930s underpinned much of his early work, including even his famously dense senior thesis, 'The Meaning of History', a work that affirms the centrality of the idea of individual freedom to the quest for peace. Aside from its significance in the realm of ethics, Kissinger argued, the categorical imperative provided 'the framework for Kant's philosophy of history', for

> If the transcendental experience of freedom represents the condition for the apprehension of the greater truth at the core of all phenomenal appearances, then its maxims must [also] constitute norms in the po-litical field. Peace is therefore the noblest goal of human endeavor, the affirmation of the ultimacy of man's moral personality.[16]

In Kissinger's eyes, the pursuit of peace was the noblest of all acts of free will, rather than part of an inexorable historical process.

Similar themes can be found in Kissinger's 1954 doctoral thesis, 'Peace, Legitimacy, and the Equilibrium (A Study of the Statesmanship of Castlereagh and Metternich)', which—it is worth noting—won the Senator Charles Sumner Prize, awarded each year by the Harvard Department of Government for the best dissertation 'dealing with any means or measures tending toward the prevention of war and the establishment of universal peace'.[17] Published three years later—almost unaltered—as *A World Restored*, the dissertation offers an alternative to the Kantian notion of a predestined era of perpetual peace. Why, Kissinger asked, had the period from 1815 to 1914 in Europe been 'a period of stability . . . without a major war or a permanent revolution'?[18] His answer lay in a paradox: 'Those ages which in retrospect seem most peaceful were least in search of peace. Those whose quest for it seems unending appear least able to achieve tranquility.' For Kissinger, the practical significance of the era of Lord Castlereagh and Klemens von Metternich was that they had pursued achievable stability rather than perpetual peace. Perhaps the most memorable lines in the book are these: 'Whenever peace—conceived as the avoidance of war—has been the primary objective of a power or a group of powers, the international system has been at the mercy of the most ruthless member of the international community. Whenever the international order has acknowledged that certain principles could not be compromised even for the sake of peace, stability based on an equilibrium of forces was at least conceivable.' The allusion was to the failure of appeasement in the 1930s; the implication was that the statesmen of the 1950s must do better. But how exactly?

A World Restored

The argument of *A World Restored* most directly relevant to the early Cold War was about how a revolutionary period can be ended and stability reestablished. The key to stability was that it came from 'a generally accepted legitimacy . . . [which] implies the acceptance of the framework of the international order by all major powers, at least to the extent that no state is so dissatisfied that . . . it expresses its dissatisfaction in a revolutionary foreign policy'.[19] The century of stability after 1815 was proof in itself that a legitimate order had been established.[20]

This could not be said of the time of Kissinger's writing. In 1954 the Soviet Union still seemed to be a revolutionary state, though not for the same reasons that Germany had been after 1919. As Kissinger noted, 'the motivation of the revolutionary power may well be defensive [and] it may well be sincere in its protestations of feeling threatened'. But

> the distinguishing feature of a revolutionary power is not that it feels threatened—such feeling is inherent in the nature of international relations based on sovereign states—but that nothing can reassure it. Only absolute security—the neutralization of the opponent—is considered a sufficient guarantee, and thus the desire of one power for absolute security means absolute insecurity for all the others . . . Diplomacy, the art of restraining the exercise of power, cannot function in such an environment . . . [And] because in revolutionary situations the contending systems are less concerned with the adjustment of differences than with the subversion of loyalties, diplomacy is replaced either by war or by an armaments race.[21]

Here, albeit in cryptic form, was a critique not just of the policies of the 1930s, but also of the 1950s. In particular, Kissinger was pouring cold water on those who insisted that dialogue with the Soviet Union would yield anything other than (as he put it) 'sterile repetitions of basic positions and accusations of bad faith, or allegations of "unreasonableness" and "subversion"'.[22] So long as there was a revolutionary power at large, conferences could be nothing more than 'elaborate stage plays which attempt to attach as yet uncommitted powers to one of the opposing systems'. In particular, he heaped scorn on those who favoured 'treating the revolutionary power as if its protestations were merely tactical; as if it really accepted the existing legitimacy but overstated its case for bargaining purposes; as if it were motivated by specific grievances to be assuaged by limited concessions'.[23] As he put it in a 1956 article that made the parallel with contemporary superpower talks quite explicit, 'the negotiators at Vienna did not confuse the atmosphere of the conference table with the elements of stability of the international system'.[24]

Elsewhere in this first book, Kissinger drew an explicit contrast between Vienna in 1814 and Versailles in 1919, which had important implications for his view of Europe after Potsdam in 1945. The logic of total war implied a punitive peace.[25] The choice was between a retrospective and vindictive peace or a prospective and magnanimous peace. The former—as at Versailles—'seeks to crush the enemy so that he is unable to fight again; its opposite will deal with the enemy so that he does not wish to attack again'.

A retrospective peace inadvertently created a new revolutionary situation 'because the defeated nation, unless completely dismembered, will not accept its humiliation'. A prospective peace, by contrast, recognized 'that the task of statesmanship is not to punish, but to integrate': only a settlement accepted by the vanquished power can hope to be the basis for a legitimate international order.[26] In such an order, no one—neither the winners nor the losers of the war—can have 'absolute security', which is a chimera:

> The foundation of a stable order is the relative security—and therefore the relative insecurity—of its members. Its stability reflects, not the absence of unsatisfied claims, but the absence of a grievance of such magnitude that redress will be sought in overturning the settlement rather than through an adjustment within its framework. An order whose structure is accepted by all major powers is 'legitimate'.[27]

A legitimate international order, Kissinger argued, was not based on a mechanical or a mathematical balance, much less on some shared aspiration to harmony. Rather, it required an almost constant process of adjustment between multiple actors—each actuated by its own historical vision of itself—who agreed only on the broad rules of the game.

This explains why Castlereagh, more than Metternich, was the true hero of *A World Restored*. It was Castlereagh, Kissinger argued, who achieved the compromises over Poland and Saxony that made the settlement possible. It was Castlereagh who violated his own instructions from London and dissolved the victorious wartime coalition. It was Castlereagh who, after Napoleon's return from Elba, pressed for moderation when others were demanding the dismemberment of France. Metternich, by contrast, grew ever more dogmatic, aspiring to an illusory restoration of the old order.[28] Ultimately, Britain could not commit itself to uphold a counter-revolutionary European order of the sort Metternich aspired to create, and which he encouraged the Tsar to believe was his own idea. Political crises in Spain, Naples, and later Piedmont were, in Metternich's eyes, life-threatening menaces to the new order; to the British they seemed like little local difficulties, intervention in which might unbalance that same order.[29] At Troppau—the high point of Metternich's diplomatic skill—he was able to represent his doomed 'battle against nationalism and liberalism' as a European rather than an Austrian enterprise.[30] Castlereagh saw only too clearly that Russia would be equally willing to intervene on the side of nationalism if, as in the Balkans, it was directed against the Ottoman Empire. But on 12 August 1822, Castlereagh, exhausted and despairing, cut his own throat with a penknife, his tragedy complete. All that remained after the Congress of Verona was 'the legitimizing principle'—at once counter-revolutionary and anti-French—as the basis for the Holy Alliance between Austria, Prussia, and Russia.[31]

To a significant extent, *A World Restored* was a critique of the peace treaties that followed World War I. 'Collective security' as embodied by the League of Nations (and, by implication, its successor, the United Nations) was one of many aspects of the interwar order that Kissinger excoriated. But the book was also an oblique indictment of post-1945 American policy. The lesson Kissinger wished to draw from the Congress of Vienna was that US policy should aim to create an 'international order [in which] no power [was] so dissatisfied that it did not prefer to seek its remedy within the framework of the . . . settlement rather than in overturning it'—in other words, a 'political order [that] did not contain a "revolutionary" power'.[32] However, that could be achieved only with Metternich's skill and Castlereagh's wisdom. The mistake had already been made of imposing unconditional surrender on the Third Reich and partitioning Germany. The danger therefore existed of a revanchist Germany emerging once again as the revolutionary power, intent on overturning the international order. Simply because we now know that did not happen does not mean it was a danger Kissinger and his contemporaries could disregard—and it was clearly Kissinger's intention to devote much of his next historical volume to 'the German Question' and Otto von Bismarck's answer to it (see below).

More importantly, it was inconceivable that the same kind of victory could ever be won over the Soviet Union as had been won over Napoleonic France. The only way of establishing international order must therefore be by converting the Soviet Union from a revolutionary power—which it certainly still was under Stalin—into a status quo power. Here was the seed of the policy that would come to be known as détente. What made that seed flourish in Kissinger's mind was the mounting evidence, even before Stalin's death, that the leaders of the Soviet Union were no longer true revolutionaries and were certainly not the 'prophets' whom Kissinger considered the statesman's mortal enemies.[33] Unlike those strategists—notably George Kennan—who saw the Soviet regime as having an ideologically driven insecurity, to which American 'containment' was the correct response, Kissinger from an early stage saw the possibility that Moscow could become a 'normal' geopolitical actor with a stake in a legitimate post-war order.

In the course of the 1950s, Kissinger began to write more explicitly about contemporary problems of US foreign policy. A recurrent theme of this early writing was the folly of wishful thinking on the subject of peace. In a letter to Arthur Schlesinger in 1954, Kissinger wrote,

> While I agree with [Adlai] Stevenson that we must not bomb Moscow if Italy goes Communist, I think it equally senseless to announce beforehand that we would not bomb Moscow under any circumstances. Nor do I think it wise to fight any more Koreas.

> I also wish the candidates would finally quit talking about a 'peace to be won' as if on a certain date 'peace will break out' and tensions will magically disappear. I know of no period in which this was true in all history except under the Roman Empire. I can conceive no settlement with Russia which will permit us to say that there will be no longer any tensions, and this would be true even if the Kremlin were ruled by arch-angels. For in a world of two superpowers under conditions of sovereignty, tensions are inevitable.[34]

The year before, in a memorandum on 'the Soviet Peace Offensive', Kissinger had argued that the death of Stalin had presented a 'great opportunity' for US diplomacy 'boldly [to] capture the peace offensive' by calling a four-power meeting to discuss European problems, in particular Germany. At this meeting, the United States should propose 'the conclusion of a treaty of peace and all-German elections'—in other words, German reunification. Such a scenario was, Kissinger argued, 'less to be feared by us than by the

USSR.[35] In September 1954, in an essay entitled 'The Impasse of American Policy and Preventive War',[36] Kissinger warned that

> the USSR has managed to capture the peace offensive so that all over the world the US increasingly appears as the obstacle to peace; it has made great strides in the development of its nuclear weapons and thus confronted Western Europe at least with imminent neutralization; it holds the diplomatic initiative in every corner of the globe with the US vacillating between bombast and pliability but in any case reduced to relative ineffectiveness.

Hegemony and Peace

The Eisenhower administration had underestimated the appetite of the rest of the world for peace and their 'reluctance . . . to believe in unbridgeable schism'. In terms of psychological warfare, the US had been wrong-footed by the Soviet 'peace offensive' that had followed the death of Stalin.

Kissinger had a second, and in many ways more powerful, criticism of the Eisenhower administration. By relying exclusively on the threat of massive retaliation, Kissinger argued in a *Foreign Affairs* article published in 1955, Eisenhower was inevitably undermining the system of American alliances, as 'either our Allies will feel that any military effort on their part is unnecessary, or they may be led to the conviction that peace is preferable to war almost at any price'.[37] Kissinger made a similar point a year later:

> The real significance of thermonuclear weapons may well be that they place a premium on a strategy which shifts the risk of their use to the other side . . . If we stake everything on an all-or-nothing military policy one of two consequences becomes inevitable: either our allies will feel that peace is preferable to war almost at any price; or they reduce their military expenditures on the assumption that events cannot be affected by their action.[38]

This was the prelude to the argument, most famously made in his 1957 book *Nuclear Weapons and Foreign Policy*,[39] that the United States must be prepared to wage a 'limited nuclear war' in order to give itself an option between all-out Armageddon and capitulation. As Kissinger wrote to Schlesinger,

> It is one thing to say that Quemoy and Matsu [islands controlled by Taiwan, which had been shelled by the People's Republic of China in 1954] are not worth a nuclear war; it is quite another to assert that we can never threaten war at all. The slogan 'there is no alternative to peace' [used by Eisenhower at the time of Geneva] amounts to giving the Soviets a blank check, at least for this election year.[40]

In short, both of the Eisenhower administration's trademark phrases—'there is no alternative to peace' and 'massive retaliation'—were dangerous, the former because it removed 'a powerful brake on Soviet probing actions and any incentive for the Soviet Union to make concessions', the latter because it posed 'risks for us out of proportion to the objectives to be achieved'.[41]

To be a proponent of limited war—and especially of limited nuclear war—was to invite criticism, even if the logic of Kissinger's position was the classical *si vis pacem, para bellum*. 'We have been more concerned with peace,' Kissinger argued on *Face the Nation* in 1957, 'while our opponent has been more concerned with victory, which has created a psychological inequality.'[42] A year later, Kissinger was accused by ABC's Mike Wallace of offering only 'war policies' and no 'positive peace policies'. Kissinger rounded on him, rejecting the dichotomy as a false one:

> Defense policies are essential to maintain the peace. They are not, however, going to solve the political problems of the world. They are only going to give us a shield behind which we can engage in constructive measures. What is essential right now is that we identify ourselves with the tremendous revolution that is sweeping across the world, that we have some image for the construction of the free world which is based on other motives than simply defending the world against communism. We must make clear what we are for rather than what we are against. If we were clearer about the kind of world we want to bring about, if we could project this concern to other people, then we wouldn't always

seem so intransigently militant, then we would be identified with positive measures rather than simply with military alliances.[43]

As Kissinger put it in a letter to Nelson Rockefeller a month later, 'the great
problem of the West is a peace which preserves our values. We can also
have peace by surrendering, of course. In order to preserve our values,
however, we may have to face a seeming paradox. We must do everything
we honourably can to avoid war. At the same time, we must not stigmatize
nuclear weapons to the point where we create the conditions for Communist nuclear blackmail.'[44]

By the mid-1960s, Kissinger found himself making somewhat similar arguments with regard to Vietnam. Already in 1965, increasing US involvement
in propping up the government of South Vietnam and directly fighting
North Vietnamese and Vietcong forces was leading to demands for peace
talks. On the basis of his first visit to the country that year, Kissinger could
see that the prospects for military success and a political stabilization of the
Saigon government were bleak. Yet he once again warned against loose talk:

'Unconditional negotiations', 'cease fire', 'tacit mutual concessions' are
useful phrases if some concrete meaning attaches to them. Otherwise
they can be turned against us, and confuse and demoralize our friends.
It is true that we cannot know all the elements of a negotiating position in advance. But we do know that we will have to adopt an attitude
towards the NLF [National Liberation Front, i.e., the pro-Communist
elements in the South]; we must know whether we will strive for an
all-Vietnamese or simply a South Vietnamese solution; we must have
ideas on how to police an agreement. If we cannot be precise on these
issues, there is a grave danger that negotiations will primarily concern
the extent of our concessions . . . [We] must recognize that they begin
a new phase of the struggle rather than mark its end.[45]

Kissinger's key insight in the 1960s was that the United States would not be
able to extricate itself from Vietnam without altering the structure of great-
power politics in its favour. Either the Soviet Union or, less plausibly, China
would need to be induced to reduce support for North Vietnam, in order

to strengthen the US bargaining position vis-à-vis Hanoi. The opportunity for translating this theoretical insight into practice would be presented by the transformation of Sino-Soviet tensions into full-blown war in 1969. The insight, like so much of Kissinger's thinking, had its origins in the study of history. Although never published (aside from a fragment in article form), Kissinger's book-length study of Bismarck provides a missing link in the evolution of his thinking. As noted above, this book was intended to be the first of two sequels to *A World Restored*, the second of which was to cover the period from Bismarck's dismissal in 1890 to the outbreak of the First World War. Put differently, the Bismarck volume would have been the centrepiece of a triptych 'on the maintenance of a hundred-year peace in Europe through a system of alliances based on a balance of power'. (That, in any event, was what Kissinger's London publisher, George Weidenfeld, was led to expect.)[46] Although the book was never completed, much less published, one of its core arguments later surfaced in works written after Kissinger had left office, notably *Diplomacy* and *World Order*. In both works, Kissinger argued that the European order established by Castlereagh and Metternich at the Congress of Vienna broke down in the wake of Bismarck's foundation of the German Reich, because 'with Germany unified and France a fixed adversary, the system lost its flexibility'.[47] After 1871, a more rigid pentarchy of great powers (to use Leopold von Ranke's term, referring to Austria, Britain, France, Germany, and Russia) depended on the virtuoso diplomat Bismarck to keep it in equilibrium. The key stratagem was the Secret Reinsurance Treaty that Bismarck signed with Russian Foreign Minister Nikolay Girs in June 1887.

Why did Kissinger attach so much importance to this somewhat obscure diplomatic document? Under its terms, Germany and Russia each agreed to observe neutrality should the other be involved in a war with a third country, unless Germany attacked France or Russia attacked Austria-Hungary. This committed Germany to neutrality if Russia sought to assert control over the Black Sea Straits. But the real point was to discourage the Russians from seeking a mutual defence treaty with France, which was exactly what happened after Bismarck's fall from power led to the non-renewal of the Secret Reinsurance Treaty. 'Paradoxically', as Kissinger later put it, 'it was precisely that ambiguity which preserved the flexibility of the European equilibrium. And its abandonment—in the name of transparency—started a sequence of increasing confrontations, culminating in World War I.'[48] After Bismarck had gone, Kissinger argued, the great-power system 'aggravated' rather than 'buffered' disputes. Over time, 'political leaders lost control over their own tactics' and 'in the end, the military planning ran away with diplomacy'.[49]

Kissinger's preoccupation with the ambiguity of Bismarck's policy provides an important insight into the strategy he pursued under both Richard Nixon and Gerald Ford. In effect, it might be argued, the opening to China of 1972 created a kind of Secret Reinsurance Treaty, whereby the United States and China each effectively agreed to remain neutral if the other became involved in a conflict, but at the same time détente committed the United States to improving relations with the Soviet Union on a range of issues, notably strategic arms limitation. Just as the most flammable conflict in the 1880s had been between Russia and Austria-Hungary, so in the 1970s it was the one between Russia and China. Like Bismarck, Kissinger did not want to choose a side in the conflict; he wanted to have relations with both sides—to be, as he frequently put it, closer to each of the rival Communist powers than they were to one another. This was surely the guiding principle of US foreign policy in the period of his ascendancy. But this realism complemented rather than contradicted the idealism of Kissinger's early work.

Cold War, Hot Peace

As the Cold War recedes from memory into history, the most important thing to remember about it is that it *was* a war. It was not a Hot Peace. The second most important thing to remember about it is that it was never the war that its many prophets foresaw from the moment the phrase 'Cold War' was first borrowed from George Orwell by the journalist Herbert Bayard Swope and popularized by Walter Lippmann. Through the distorting rearview mirror of hindsight, we see either a classical tale of two rival empires or a Manichaean struggle between two incompatible ideologies. On closer inspection, what happened was rather peculiar. Most of those who predicted a US–Soviet conflict in the later 1940s assumed that it would at some point manifest itself as a full-scale 'Third World War'—nuclear and/or conventional—with Europe as the principal battleground. To Kissinger and the other members of the class of 1950, the probability of a 'Long Peace' lasting until the late 1980s and ending with the kind of Soviet collapse Kennan had predicted in the Long Telegram seemed very low indeed.

To the generation that had fought the Germans and the Japanese, the Korean War looked very much like the prelude to the next global conflagration. From the 1950s until the 1980s, the generals on both sides prepared for World War III—but that was precisely the war that did not happen. Instead, the Cold War was fought as a series of localized conflicts almost everywhere except Europe, with Asia as the main war zone. American and Soviet forces never directly fought one another, but at least one of the sides in every war fought between 1950 and 1990 was—or was believed to be—a superpower proxy. The result was a global Cold War—the conflict between the superpowers for predominance in the Third World—that might equally well be called the Third World's War.[50] If the threat of mutually assured destruction ultimately sufficed to produce a Long Peace for the United States, the Soviet Union, and a divided Europe, the same was not true for much of Africa, Asia, Latin America, and the Middle East. There the struggle between the superpowers had a shockingly high cost in human life.

Still, the worst did not happen in the Cold War. No collision between the superpowers escalated to the point of even a limited nuclear war, much less a full-scale conflict. Nor did any of the mishaps and false alarms of the period have catastrophic consequences. Yet that is not to say that the probability of thermonuclear war was zero throughout the period. On the contrary, humanity came perilously close to the verge of Armageddon on more than one occasion during the Cold War. The 'doomsday clock', adjusted twice a year by the Science and Security Board of the *Bulletin of the Atomic Scientists*, implied that the risk of 'technology-induced catastrophe' reached its peak in the years 1953 to 1959, when the clock showed two minutes before midnight.

Perhaps reflecting their political biases, the scientists turned the clock back to 23.48 during the presidency of John F. Kennedy. In reality, it was in the autumn of 1962 that the knell of a nuclear 'midnight for . . . civiliza-tion' came closest to sounding.[51] Kennedy himself put the odds of disas-ter—meaning a thermonuclear war that could have claimed the lives of 100 million Americans, more than 100 million Russians, and comparable millions of Europeans—at 'between one out of three and even'.[52] Arthur Schlesinger later called it simply 'the most dangerous moment in human history'.[53]

Armageddon kept not happening. Writing in 1968, Kissinger noted that

> Deterrence is tested negatively by things which do *not* happen. But it is never possible to demonstrate *why* something has not occurred. Is it because we are pursuing the best possible policy or only a marginally effective one? . . . The longer peace is maintained—or the more suc-cessful deterrence is—the more it furnishes arguments for those who are opposed to the very premises of defense policy. Perhaps there was no need for preparedness in the first place.[54]

Because people are always reluctant to think counterfactually—to consider the importance of the things that do not happen—it was getting easier every day to talk about 'banning the bomb', especially as the bombs kept getting more destructive. Here was a central problem for the administration Kissinger was about to join as national security advisor. To the generation that had fought World War II, the logic of deterrence was compelling. They had seen what conventional and atomic bombing of cities could achieve. They had faith that Hanoi could be bombed to the negotiating table. To the next generation, conceived as that war was ending or in the early years of peace, the logic was much more elusive: bombing—and indeed war itself—simply seemed abhorrent. Both Kissinger and Nixon valiantly tried to explain their position to the unruly baby-boomers. In the small hours of 9 May 1970, Nixon even ventured out of the White House to confront a group of student protesters who were camped out in the Lincoln Memorial. As he told them,

> I was sorry they had missed it [his press conference the previous day] because I had tried to explain . . . that my goals in Vietnam were the

same as theirs—to stop the killing, to end the war, to bring peace. Our goal was not to get into Cambodia by what we were doing, but to get out of Vietnam.

There seemed to be no—they did not respond. I hoped that their hatred of the war, which I could well understand, would not turn into a bitter hatred of our whole system, our country and everything that it stood for.

I said, I know you, that probably most of you think I'm an SOB. But I want you to know that I understand just how you feel.[55]

Perhaps Nixon did understand how the protesters felt. But, as they subsequently made clear to the reporters who descended on them, they did not remotely understand how he felt.

In the end, the pacifists of 1970 got a good deal of what they wanted. The world became a good deal more peaceful in their lifetimes. Interstate war today is at far lower levels than in the 1970s. All the major data series available make this clear—for example, the one produced by the Peace Research Institute of Oslo (PRIO), which estimates total battle deaths arising from state-based armed conflict. Between 1956 and 2007, the peak years were 1971 (around 380,000 fatalities) and the years from 1982 to 1988, when the annual average was close to 250,000. Between 2002 and 2007, by contrast, the average was just under 17,000. The 'war magnitude' index calculated by the Center for Systemic Peace (CPA) in Vienna, Virginia, rose steadily from the 1950s to the mid-1980s, then fell steeply—by more than half—after the end of the Cold War in 1991, as did the CPA's estimates for the percentage of states experiencing warfare and the number of armed conflict events. A broader measure of 'annual deaths from political violence', which includes the victims of genocide, ethnic cleansing, and the like, tells a similar story, with the global death rate peaking in the early 1970s and then declining more or less steadily, aside from the spike due to the 1995 genocide in Rwanda. The frequency of revolutions, military coups, and political assassinations is also lower than it was in the twentieth century. Even homicide has declined.[56]

In short, the world has become a much more peaceful place than it was in the 1970s. But is that because the anti-war movement triumphed over Nixon? Does today's relatively peaceful world represent a victory for pacifism? I cannot think of any serious study that makes such a claim. There are at least five answers available to the question of why violence has declined in recent history:

1. The psychologist Steven Pinker has recently revived Norbert Elias's idea of a long-run civilizing process, beginning with state formation and continuing through the Enlightenment to our own 'rights revolution', as he terms it. There has been a sustained accumulation of restraints on our violent impulses, reducing not only warfare but once widespread forms of violence like capital punishment and torture.

2. Another, more institutional, explanation is that the spread of democracy and the proliferation of international or supranational institutions have inhibited political leaders from making war.

3. Technology, beginning with the atomic bomb and continuing through television to the internet, has reduced the incentives for large-scale warfare by creating large asymmetries between superpowers and other states, while at the same time increasing the accountability of governments.

4. The ideologies that did so much to encourage violence in the twentieth century—fascism and communism—were emphatically defeated, a point made as long ago as 1989 by Francis Fukuyama.[57]

5. Finally, there is the more old-fashioned (and politically contentious) answer that the leaders of the superpowers in the 1970s and the 1980s did a remarkably good job of ending the nuclear arms race, the multiple conflicts of the Third World, and ultimately the Cold War itself.

In none of these explanations do the peace movements of the Cold War era play a meaningful role.

Is our present era of relative tranquillity the harbinger of 'perpetual peace', as envisioned by Kant? Or is it just a quiet interlude? The answer depends on how enduring one considers these various pacifying trends. The trend away from violence, identified by Pinker, may not stand up to close statistical scrutiny.[58] Twentieth-century history suggests that advances in democracy and in international institutions can be reversed, particularly in the wake of major economic shocks. Technology, too, may be making new kinds of conflict (terrorism, cyber-warfare) easier, while proliferation may in fact be increasing the risk of a nuclear war. Fascism and communism may have declined as ideologies, but the rise of radical Islam since the Iranian revolution in 1979 has provided a new and potent source of inspiration for acts of organized violence. As for the good judgment of political leaders, it is getting steadily harder to be optimistic.

Conclusion

Henry Kissinger's father was wise to remind his listeners in 1975 of Aristophanes's *Peace*. In the play, the ironical and genial Trygaeus succeeds in ending the Peloponnesian War after ten years of conflict between Athens and Sparta. It is no easy task. He achieves it by flying to Mount Olympus on the back of a giant dung beetle. He finds the home of the gods all but deserted, apart from Hermes, who explains that the goddess Peace has been thrown into a deep pit by the monster War and that the prolongation of her captivity is the fault of certain Athenian politicians—the human 'pestles' with which War grinds up the Greek people in his bloody mortar. Assisted by a chorus of his fellow citizens, as well as by Hermes, Trygaeus succeeds in liberating Peace. But his success—though crowned by his marriage to Harvest (symbolizing post-war prosperity) and celebrated by the farmers who can return to their fields—is not unalloyed. For Aristophanes's real theme is not so much peace as the sheer difficulty of stopping war. The play concludes with an ambivalent exchange between the peacemaker and the people:

Chorus: Yes, a man like this one is good for all the citizenry.

Trygaeus: When you gather your vintage, you'll realize much better what a man I am.

Chorus: Even now we plainly see, for you've become a saviour for all mankind.

Trygaeus: That's what you'll say when you drink off a cup of new wine![59]

It was the fate of those who sought to reduce conflict and establish stability during the Cold War that they were not thanked for their efforts, least of all when the 'peace dividend' brought ordinary Americans and Europeans the equivalent of Aristophanes's post-war vintage in the form of reduced defence budgets and diminished geopolitical risk. Far from seeking to learn from the achievements of Western diplomacy in the 1970s and 1980s, a generation of scholars who had come of age in the anti-war protests published polemics accusing Kissinger and others of war crimes.[60] More generally, the study of diplomatic history all but ceased at major institutions of higher education. In that sense alone, the ideology of pacifism achieved a victory. However, if the result of that victory is to efface the memory of statecraft itself, it may all too swiftly prove to have been Pyrrhic.

Notes

1.   Barbara Stewart, 'Showering Shtick on the White House: The Untold Story; Woody Allen Spoofed Nixon in 1971, But the Film Was Never Shown,' *New York Times*, December 4, 1997.

2.   Woody Allen, 'Men of Crisis The Harvey Wallinger Story' 1971. Online, https://www .youtube.com/watch?v=qyuCjDiqX58

3.   'Did Tom Lehrer Really Stop Writing Protest Songs Because Henry Kissinger Won the Nobel Peace Prize?' Online, http://legendsrevealed.com/entertainment/2013/12 /05/did-tom-lehrer-really-stop-writing-protest-songs-because-henry-kissinger-won -the-nobel-peace-prize/

4.   'Peace Group Pickets Acheson at Harvard,' *Boston Traveler*, June 23, 1950.

5.   Robert J. Samuelson, 'Mill Street: Chronicle of a Confrontation,' *Harvard Crimson*, November 15, 1966.

6. David C. Atkinson, *In Theory and Practice: Harvard's Center for International Affairs, 1958–1983* (Cambridge, MA: Harvard University Press, 2007), 150.

7. Ibid., 153.

8. Niall Ferguson, *Kissinger, 1923–1968: The Idealist* (New York: Penguin Press, 2015) is the first of two projected volumes.

9. 'Grosser Bahnhof für Henry Kissinger,' *Fürther Nachrichten*, December 15, 1975.

10. 'Henry A. Kissinger in Fürth,' *Amtsblatt der Stadt Fürth*, December 19, 1975, 338.

11. Kissinger family correspondence, Louis Kissinger, Rede anlässlich die Verleihung der 'Goldenen Bürgermedaille' an Dr Henry Kissinger, December 15, 1975.

12. US Department of State, Office of the Historian, *Foreign Relations of the United States* [FRUS], *1969–1976*. Vol. XXXVIII, part 1, *Foundations of Foreign Policy, 1973–1976*, Document 17, Address by Henry A. Kissinger [HAK], 'A Just Consensus, a Stable Order, a Durable Peace,' September 24, 1973.

13. 'Beide Parteien distanzieren sich,' *Fürther Nachrichten*, December 15, 1975.

14. 'Henry A. Kissinger in Fürth,' *Amtsblatt der Stadt Fuerth*, December 19, 1975, 339.

15. 'Kissinger Speaks,' *New York Herald Tribune*, October 14, 1957. See also 'Dr Kissinger Amplifies,' *New York Herald Tribune*, October 17, 1957.

16. Henry A. Kissinger, 'The Meaning of History (Reflections on Spengler, Toynbee and Kant)' (Senior thesis, Harvard University, 1950), 260f.

17. *Kissinger Papers*, Yale University [formerly Library of Congress], MDC-101, Sargent Kennedy to HAK, June 2, 1954.

18. Henry A. Kissinger, *A World Restored: Metternich, Castlereagh and the Problems of Peace, 1812–22*, Kindle ed. (London: Weidenfeld & Nicolson, 1957), Kindle Line (KL) 172–81.

19. Ibid., KL 102–19.

20. Ibid., KL 172–81.

21. Ibid., KL 140–48.

22. Ibid., KL 119–40.

23. Ibid.

24. Henry A. Kissinger, 'The Congress of Vienna: A Reappraisal,' *World Politics* 8, no. 2 (January 1956), 280.

25. Kissinger, *A World Restored*, KL 2837–61.

26. Ibid., KL 2923–33.

27. Ibid., KL 2974–3022.

28. Ibid., KL 4178–85.

29. Ibid., KL 5377–78, 5389.

30. Ibid., KL 5396–99.

31. Ibid., KL 6398–400.

32. Ibid., KL 3478–505.

33. Ibid., KL 3812–19.

34. Kissinger Papers, Kent 63, HAK to Schlesinger, March 10, 1954.

35. Kissinger Papers, Kent 63, HAK, 'The Soviet Peace Offensive and German Unity,' June 3, 1953.

36. Kissinger Papers, Kent 63, HAK, 'The Impasse of American Policy and Preventive War,' September 15, 1954.

37. Henry A. Kissinger, 'Military Policy and the Defense of the "Grey Areas",' *Foreign Affairs* 33, no. 3 (April 1955), 419.

38. Henry A. Kissinger, 'Psychological and Pressure Aspects of Negotiations with the USSR,' NSC Series 10, *Psychological Aspects of US Strategy* (November 1955).

39. Henry A. Kissinger, *Nuclear Weapons and Foreign Policy* (New York: Harper and Brothers, 1957).

40. Arthur Schlesinger papers, Box P-17, HAK to Schlesinger, January 24, 1956, John F. Kennedy Presidential Library, Boston.

41. Henry A. Kissinger, 'Force and Diplomacy in the Nuclear Age,' *Foreign Affairs* 34, no. 3 (April 1956), 350ff.

42. Kissinger Papers, *Face the Nation*, November 10, 1957, transcript.

43. American Broadcasting Company and The Fund for the Republic, *Survival and Freedom: A Mike Wallace Interview with Henry A. Kissinger* (1958), 9f.

44. Kissinger Papers, Kent 64, HAK to NAR, June 1, 1961.

45. Lodge Papers, Vietnam, Reel 20, HAK to Lodge, September 7, 1965, Massachusetts Historical Society, Boston,.

46. George Weidenfeld, *Remembering My Good Friends: An Autobiography* (New York: HarperCollins, 1995), 384f.

47. Henry A. Kissinger, *World Order* (New York: Penguin Press, 2014), 78.

48. Ibid., 233.

49. Ibid., 80, 82.

50. Odd Arne Westad, *The Global Cold War: Third World Interventions and the Making of Our Times* (New York: Cambridge University Press, 2005); Niall Ferguson, *The War of the World: Twentieth-Century Conflict and the Descent of the West* (New York: Penguin, 2006), 596–625.

51. '1953: It is 2 Minutes to Midnight,' *Bulletin of the Atomic Scientists*, http://thebulletin .org/clock/1953.

52. Graham Allison, 'The Cuban Missile Crisis,' in *Foreign Policy: Theories, Actors, Cases*, 2nd ed., eds. Steve Smith, Amelia Hadfield, and Tim Dunne (Oxford: Oxford University Press, 2012), 256.

53. Arthur M. Schlesinger Jr, Foreword to *Thirteen Days: A Memoir of the Cuban Missile Crisis* by Robert Kennedy (New York: Norton, 1999), 7.

54. Henry A. Kissinger, 'Central Issues of American Foreign Policy' in *American Foreign Policy: Three Essays* (New York: Norton, 1969), 61.

55. 'New Nixon Tapes Reveal Details of Meeting With Anti-War Activists,' *PBS News Hour*, November 25, 2011, transcript, http://www.pbs.org/newshour/bb/white_house -july-dec11-nixontapes_11-25/.

56. Steven Pinker, *The Better Angels of Our Nature: Why Violence Has Declined*

(New York: Viking, 2011). See also http://www.slate.com/articles/news_and_politics
/foreigners/2014/12/the_world_is_not_falling_apart_the_trend_lines_reveal_an
_increasingly_peaceful.html.

57. Francis Fukuyama, *The End of History* (New York: Free Press, 1992).

58. Pasquale Cirillo and Nassim Nicholas Taleb, 'On the Tail Risk of Violent Conflict and its Underestimation' (research paper, NYU School of Engineering, 2015).

59. Aristophanes, *Peace*, trans. Jeffrey Henderson (Cambridge, MA: Loeb Classical Library, 1998).

60. Christopher Hitchens, *The Trial of Henry Kissinger* (New York: Verso Books, 2001).

6.

The Paradox of American Diplomacy in the Cold War

Fredrik Logevall

I

Like other great powers throughout history, the US frequently relies on deterrence in dealing with adversaries on the international stage. Very often, however, US leaders neglect to pair it with diplomacy, with the result that conflicts fester and often intensify. This neglect of diplomacy is not altogether surprising, for a cardinal rule of American politics is to talk tough at all times on foreign policy and to amplify threats. Flexibility is equated with weakness, conciliation is derided, and every sort of iniquity is ascribed to overseas adversaries. However, the easy bravado and 'never give an inch' bluster of the campaign trail can come back to haunt later, when victory has come, and one has to go about the business of governing. The pressure can be intense to maintain one's position, even to harden it, lest hawks on Capitol Hill and elsewhere get to noisily wonder where the steadfastness has gone.

The story is more complicated, however, for there's a paradox in the historical record. Although that record suggests that, historically, Americans have been deeply suspicious of negotiations with foreign foes, those leaders who have broken free from the shackles of this thinking have achieved real and sustainable national security gains. Notables on this list include John F. Kennedy, Richard M. Nixon, and Ronald Reagan, all of whom came to believe that it makes little sense to assume that bargaining with foes necessarily jeopardizes US security; that maintaining manoeuvrability by broadening the range of options is usually a much better way to get what one wants; and that diplomacy, though subject—like any other instrument of statecraft—to failure and to unrealizable expectations, can bring lasting success. Barack Obama, too, believed this, it seems—he came into office in 2009 committed to a policy of diplomatic engagement with adversaries and was awarded the Nobel Peace Prize in significant part because of that promise. The awarding of the prize was controversial, but Obama in office followed through to a significant extent on his diplomacy pledge. My guess is that history will judge this part of his legacy favourably as a result.[1]

My aim in this chapter is to explore this paradox in American diplomacy, with particular emphasis on the Cold War. I define 'diplomacy' narrowly, as the dialogue between independent states, rather than employ the word as a synonym for the 'foreign policy' or, broader still, the 'foreign relations' of a state. Although it is accepted form to blur these distinctions, it can be beneficial—if only for clarity of thinking—to pull them apart, and to speak of 'diplomacy' as the process of dialogue and negotiation by which states in a system conduct their relations.[2]

Under this definition, it can be asserted that the US had no meaningful diplomacy with Communist foes through long stretches of the Cold War. Though successive administrations after 1945 engaged in near-perpetual negotiations with allied and non-aligned governments in Western Europe and elsewhere, for a long time, Washington officials generally forswore negotiations with Communist leaders, including, most notably, those in Moscow. The Containment doctrine that emerged by 1947 was vague and imprecise in several respects, but it was unambiguous on one point: cooperation with the Kremlin was impossible at present and for the foreseeable future, for its leaders possessed an omnivorous appetite for power. The only language they understood was deterrence and preponderant military force. Soviet–American tension, therefore, did not result from clashing national interests, but from the moral shortcomings of Soviet leaders, which in turn meant that negotiations were pointless until such a time as the regime underwent a transformation and scrapped its ideology. In Henry Kissinger's apt formulation, 'containment allowed no role for diplomacy until the climactic final scene in which the men in the white hats accepted the conversion of the men in the black hats.'[3]

On very rare occasions, American statesmen would depart from this received wisdom and engage in face-to-face meetings with their counterparts in Moscow—but the key word is 'very', particularly with respect to the early Cold War. There was but a single East–West foreign ministers' meeting between the one in London in December 1947 and that in Berlin in January 1954, and no heads-of-government summits at all in the decade between the Potsdam Conference in 1945 and the Geneva Summit in 1955. Nor were these rare encounters serious affairs, aimed at gaining substantive negotiated agreements involving mutual concessions; summit meetings like those in Geneva in 1955, Paris in 1960, and Vienna in 1961 were mostly about placating domestic and international public opinion and about scoring propaganda points against the other side. Only in 1963 did there emerge a spirit of compromise, as reflected in the tenor of the Soviet–American exchanges and the Limited Test Ban Treaty. Not until 1969 did a US president, in the form of Richard Nixon, speak of an 'era of negotiations'—to distinguish it from what went before. Even after that point, indeed right up to the end of the Cold War, the American reluctance to engage in substantive diplomacy with Moscow remained pronounced.

Although my focus in this chapter is on the US, it should be noted up front that the story of diplomacy (or, as it were, non-diplomacy) in the Cold War is a two-sided and at times a multi-sided affair. The Soviets had their own fears of diplomatic compromise, and at various moments other players in the international system made their presence felt in critical ways. The same was true of leaders in Beijing, in Hanoi, and elsewhere in the Communist world.

A second caveat: though I explore the reasons for, and implications of, the American diplomatic disinterest during the post-WWII era, I fully acknowledge that Containment, in a fundamental way, succeeded: the policy obstructed the expansion of Soviet Communism for four-plus decades without blowing up the world and without demolishing civil society at home. The Soviet empire collapsed, and the USSR itself vanished from the map. Still, it remains an open question whether there were other roads to a peaceful resolution of superpower differences, whether indeed Containment as it developed after 1947 served to lock in existing circumstances far longer than otherwise might have been the case. Moreover, there is the fundamental question of why American policymakers defined their choices so narrowly, why diplomacy with foes held almost no place in US foreign policy, not merely in the fluid context of the late 1940s but later, not merely before Stalin's death in 1953 but for many years thereafter—indeed, within some circles in Washington, down to the present day.

II

It makes sense to start in September 1938, at the Munich Conference, where British Prime Minister Neville Chamberlain, along with his French counterpart, Édouard Daladier, agreed to let Adolf Hitler's Germany annex a large chunk of Czechoslovakian territory in return for a pledge of peace. Chamberlain returned triumphantly to England proclaiming that his so-called appeasement policy had produced 'peace for our time'. Less than a year later, Europe was at war.

It should be remembered that in the US President Franklin Roosevelt (FDR) initially greeted the signing of the Munich accord with equanimity, and that Hitler was infuriated by it. Like many informed Americans—and Europeans—Roosevelt suspected that Britain and France were unready for war, and he knew that the US public had no desire to be drawn into another European conflict. Negotiations seemed the best course to take. 'Good man' FDR famously cabled Chamberlain before the conference, even as he privately acknowledged that the Englishman was 'taking very long chances'.[4] Hitler, for his part, was angry that he had allowed himself to be manoeuvred into a diplomatic agreement. He wanted war. The deal bought the democracies time, the Führer understood, and as such, it stood in the way of his territorial ambitions.

For Chamberlain, meanwhile, Munich represented a tactical victory of sorts. It provided Britain with a breathing spell to build its strength in preparation for the inevitable showdown with the Nazi juggernaut. There was a certain logic in this position, both then and in retrospect. When war came the following year, however, instantly Munich became the ultimate symbol of naïveté, implying a craven willingness to barter away a nation's vital interests for empty promises. By the time Chamberlain died in November 1940, his reputation was in tatters. 'Few men can have known such a tremendous reverse of fortune in so short a time', he said of himself not long before his death.[5]

In short order, President Roosevelt articulated the new meaning of Munich. 'Normal practices of diplomacy . . . are of no possible use in dealing with international outlaws', he declared repeatedly as he tried to convince an isolationist Congress and an anxious public of the need for deeper US involvement in the anti-Axis struggle.[6] With dictatorship and tyranny, there could be no negotiated settlements, no deals, only capitulation. This led logically to the policy of 'Unconditional Surrender', announced at the meeting of the Allied leaders at the Casablanca Conference in 1943 and achieved in 1945.

At war's end, the division of Europe and the slide into Cold War solidified the no-more-Munichs maxim in American political discourse. The basic US strategy was laid out in George F. Kennan's famous 'X' article in July 1947, in *Foreign Affairs*. Variously referred to as the 'bible', the 'blueprint', or, in Barton Bernstein's phrase, 'the near-canonical expression' of Containment, Kennan's article, 'The Sources of Soviet Conduct', brought together the various strands of US post-war thought under a single heading. To meet the Soviet threat, Kennan wrote, it would be necessary to pursue 'a policy of firm containment, designed to confront the Russians with unalterable counter-force at every point where they show signs of encroaching upon the interests of a peaceful and stable world'. The challenge would not be easy, and the Western powers could expect perpetual crises and ceaseless efforts by the Soviet Union 'to make sure it has filled every nook and cranny available to it in the basin of world power'.[7]

Why was Stalin uncooperative? Not primarily because of historic Russian fears of invasion, Kennan maintained, but because of the nature of Communist philosophy and the Kremlin's domestic imperatives. 'There is ample evidence that the stress laid in Moscow on the menace confronting the USSR from the world outside its borders is founded not on the realities of foreign antagonism but in the necessity of explaining away the maintenance of dictatorial authority at home.' Stalin was not reckless, however; indeed he was cautious, which for Kennan meant that the US could afford to be patient, secure in the knowledge that strains on Soviet society would inevitably grow until they caused either the mellowing or the breakup of the entire Soviet system.

For now, however, and for the foreseeable future, vigilance was the watchword and diplomacy a waste of time. Soviet hostility to the West was irrational, Kennan maintained, justified neither by America's wartime policies nor by its earlier actions, and thus Moscow leaders could not be reasoned with; negotiations, in other words, would not ease or eliminate the hostility and end the Soviet–American confrontation. Kremlin leaders, Kennan declared, were 'committed fanatically to the belief that with the United States there can be no permanent *modus vivendi*, that it is desirable and necessary that the internal harmony of our society be disrupted, our traditional ways of life be destroyed, the international authority of our state be broken, if Soviet power is to be secure'.

One can picture *Foreign Affairs* readers nodding in agreement as they read these words. For by the time Kennan's article appeared, anti-Soviet sentiment was a staple of both policy documents and much journalistic reporting. Few readers, it's safe to assume, would have troubled themselves over the article's lack of a specific policy prescription or its failure to explain how Stalin and his lieutenants could be at once fanatical and cautious. One who did was the journalist Walter Lippmann, who hit the 'X' article hard in a series of columns in the *New York Herald Tribune* in September and October, to be scrutinized in chancelleries the world over—for such was Lippmann's global reach. The columns were then gathered together in a slim book whose title popularized the name of the Soviet–American competition. Whereas Kennan had emphasized Marxist ideology as the foundation of Soviet foreign policy, Lippmann saw Stalin's government as a successor to the Czarist regimes that, seeking to protect their western flank against European foes, had also pushed into Eastern Europe, and had also sought power in the Mediterranean. 'Mr X has neglected even to mention the fact,' he wrote, 'that the Soviet Union is the successor of the Russian Empire and that Stalin is not only the heir of Marx and Lenin but of Peter the Great, and the Czars of all the Russians.'[8]

Lippmann's critique of the emerging Containment strategy was wide-ranging—he charged that it mistook Soviet hostility for intentions, not to mention capability, and that its implementation would bankrupt the treasury. Of particular interest here, the columnist castigated both the Truman Doctrine and the 'X' article for envisaging no role for good-faith negotiations with the Kremlin. This made little sense. 'The history of diplomacy', he wrote, 'is the history of relations among rival powers, which did not enjoy political intimacy, and did not respond to appeals to common purposes. Nevertheless, there have been settlements. Some of them did not last very long. Some of them did. For a diplomat to think that rival and unfriendly powers cannot be brought to a settlement is to forget what diplomacy is all about. There would be little for diplomats to do if the world consisted of partners, enjoying political intimacy, and responding to common appeals.'[9]

Lippmann was saying that you don't have to like the Soviets, and you don't have to trust them; you just need to talk to them. He had zeroed in on a key feature of Kennan's notion of Containment: that built into it was, as historian Anders Stephanson has put it, 'a deliberate moment of diplomatic refusal, a period of recharging the western batteries and rearranging the power configuration'.[10] Kennan did not initially deny this interpretation of his position, but in later years he would insist that he always wanted the period of diplomatic refusal to be brief and that he in fact sought early Soviet–American negotiations. And indeed, though Kennan in the second half of 1947 passed up the opportunity to clarify his meaning in the 'X' article, we know that he agreed with many elements of Lippmann's analysis and was stung by the columnist's harsh critique. Earlier in the year, for example, Kennan had told a meeting of the Russian Study Group of the Council on Foreign Relations in New York that Russian diplomacy had always been characterized by both cautiousness and flexibility and that, therefore, the Truman administration should be forthright in its dealings with Moscow and always be willing to negotiate while never appearing false or weak or arrogant. 'Nothing is to be gained', the diplomat told his audience, by 'fatuous concessions without receiving a *quid pro quo*. They balance their books every night and start over every morning . . . They expect you to proceed in a hard-boiled way and not to give them things without getting something from them.'[11] The passage could have come straight from a Lippmann column.

Already in 1947, Kennan was uncomfortable with the extravagant rhetoric of the Truman doctrine (in which the president declared, 'I believe that it must be the policy of the United States to support free peoples who are resisting attempted subjugation by armed minorities or by outside pressures'), and over the next year he grew confident that the Soviet campaign against the West was essentially political. 'The Soviets don't want to invade anyone', he wrote in an unsent letter to Lippmann in April 1948, adding that his intention in the *Foreign Affairs* article had been to make Americans aware that they faced a long period of difficult diplomacy when political arts and skills would dominate. Once Western Europe had been shored up, he assured the columnist, negotiations under qualitatively new conditions could follow.[12]

Worthy sentiments all, but as Kennan surely knew, the political sentiment in official Washington was rapidly moving in another direction, as developments abroad mixed with domestic politics at home to make the danger of negotiations with the Communists seem ever greater. The victory of Mao Zedong in China's civil war in 1949 and the outbreak of the Korean War in 1950 gave Republicans the opening they sought. Having already begun using the 'soft on communism' charge against Democrats in the years prior, they now bludgeoned Truman's administration for 'losing' China. Senator Joseph McCarthy ratcheted up the pressure by hunting for Communist spies in the US government, sensationally charging Democrats—the very architects of the Containment policy—with 'twenty years of treason'. Although McCarthy's Senate career ended in disgrace, his four years of insinuating attacks, together with the debilitating 'Who lost China?' debate, cast a long shadow over American foreign policy.[13] A generation of politicians learned a simple lesson: a Communist gain anywhere by political means, under anyone's watch, would be met with charges of appeasement—now equated not just with spineless gullibility, but treacherous disloyalty. This heated atmosphere narrowed the range of acceptable policy choices available to a sitting president. Diplomacy lost out.

A strange thing occurred: the US was least willing to negotiate with the USSR when the US was strongest. In the 1940s and throughout the 1950s, the American strategic arsenal surpassed that of the Soviet Union in all but one category—the number of men under arms. In terms of nuclear warheads, missiles, bombers, submarines, warships, military bases, points for logistical support—to say nothing of its vastly superior economic strength and ideological appeal—the United States far surpassed the Soviet Union. What's more, American officials knew it. Declassified documents testify to the US preponderance of power, and to planners' knowledge of the fact. Behind closed doors, they conceded that there was little threat of war with the USSR. Publicly, however, politicians and government officials articulated a different line: that the threat was as great as ever, that Moscow's ambitions were global, its capabilities immense.

To be sure, they could find support for their position among some specialists. According to Ferguson's chapter in this book, Kissinger in the mid-1950s took a dim view of those who believed dialogue with Moscow would yield anything other than, as Kissinger put it, 'sterile' repetitions of basic positions and accusations of bad faith, or allegations of 'unreasonableness' and 'subversion'. Conferences with such an adversary would be nothing but 'elaborate stage plays which attempt to attach as yet uncommitted powers to one of the opposing systems'. Kissinger had no use for those like Lippmann, who favoured 'treating the revolutionary power as if its protestations were merely tactical; as if it really accepted the existing legitimacy but overstated its case for bargaining purposes; as if it were motivated by specific grievances to be assuaged by limited concessions'.[14]

To which Lippmann would have replied that Kissinger was missing the point: dialogue with Moscow was necessary precisely in order to determine how revolutionary were its leaders, how accepting or unaccepting of the 'existing legitimacy', how willing or unwilling to bargain over specific grievances.

III

How to explain this tendency toward threat inflation in US foreign policy in the decades after WWII is a complex question. One could look, perhaps, to geography and history, and to the effects of the nation's long experience with what Yale historian C. Vann Woodward called 'free security'.[15] America's immediate neighbours were weak, and through the early years of the twentieth century, the country was to a large extent shielded from predatory powers by two vast oceans that served as giant moats. Then, during the period of the two world wars, America's wealth and power grew enormously just as the strength of many other large states was declining; in a short period of time, it went from a position of limited engagement to one of informal but recognized hegemony over a good portion of the globe. The result: both before and after attaining great-power status, Americans lacked the necessity to negotiate and compromise continually in order to survive and prosper. Though they professed to be pragmatists, seeking the most efficient solution to problems, their pragmatism was parochial, corresponding as it did to an experience that in international terms was not normative. It left little room for cooperation with states that did not share in the American consensus and that saw global affairs from a different point of view.

This long experience of security had another effect as well: it made Americans more sensitive to new dangers, more fearful of even the possibility of defeat, than were peoples more conditioned to the cycles of ups and downs in their national traditions and more gloomily modest in their expectations. It reinforced Americans' moralistic tendency to see any hostility directed toward the United States as illegitimate, and to want to frame those conflicts that did arise in Manichaean terms, as pitting good against evil, angels against devils, in which the very survival of civilization was at stake. For after all, an illegitimate enemy is an absolute enemy, with whom you can have no dialogue or interaction until he disappears or is wholly transformed, abandoning his hostility. In Richard Hofstadter's words, for many Americans international politics is a struggle against an enemy who 'is a perfect model of malice'.[16]

To allied government leaders in Europe and elsewhere. it was a source of continual puzzlement, this American penchant for interpreting world affairs in black-white terms and for ruling out negotiations with foes, for disavowing compromise. Thus, in London in the early 1950s, for example, Winston Churchill and Anthony Eden struggled to comprehend the seeming support in Middle America for extreme Red-baiters such as McCarthy, and the unwillingness of the Truman and Eisenhower administrations to recognize the People's Republic of China or admit her into the United Nations. The two Tory leaders shook their heads at the periodic anti-British broadsides in Congress and in the American press—especially the Scripps-Howard and Hearst chapters—over Britain's willingness to engage with Moscow and Beijing.

One could also look to the American political structure. As scholars have long shown, power is more widely dispersed in the US political system than in relatively more centralized parliamentary systems, where control over foreign policy is strongly concentrated in the executive. American political parties are weak, and political leaders depend for their positions on popular support. From the development of the two-party system in the 1790s to the present day, the parties have jockeyed for advantage; many times, leaders have found that the most effective way to get the attention of a generally parochial public and Congress, and to score points against the other party, is to exaggerate a given threat and portray it in the most vivid terms possible.

This strikes me as important. Any satisfactory answer to the question at hand must give due attention to the 'uses of alarmism', to the manipulation of fear by officials and interest groups to gain political and institutional advantage. For, as it turns out, what had been true for most of the nation's history before WWII was also true after: the United States during much of the Cold War and beyond was objectively safe from external attack, as safe as any nation could realistically hope to be.[17] Its security was seldom directly imperilled, a reality that distorted US foreign policy in the ways that worried thoughtful critics near and far, many of whom have been lost to history. From an early point, American planners had the luxury of blurring the distinction between policy and politics, so that governing became less about the common good and more about achieving partisan and personal goals. Or, as the international relations theorist Kenneth Waltz has put it, 'absence of threat permits policy to become capricious'.[18]

Indeed, the politicians and operators in Washington who exploited America's Cold War perceived an even deeper reality—namely, that their fundamental interest lay in denying that the nation was secure, no matter what was happening overseas. Talking up the threat, perpetuating 'the politics of insecurity'—as Campbell Craig and I have called it—became the mission.[19]

The result was a militarization of American politics. Contrary to myth, foreign policy after 1945 was never uncontaminated by domestic politics.[20] Throughout the era, each new generation of politicians in Washington rediscovered the winning political formula of talking tough on Communists, both foreign and domestic, often irrespective of what was happening overseas. Politicians who were accused of being insufficiently vigilant against the Reds were put on the defensive and often found it irresistible to call for a more militaristic waging of the Cold War, whatever they actually thought about the merits of such a policy.

In this way, one can speak of an anti-Communist crusade inside the US that paralleled the Cold War abroad, a crusade that contained a large element of practical politics—and that had no real likeness anywhere else in the Western world, in either scope or intensity.[21] David Halberstam said of the phenomenon, 'Rather than combating the irrationality of the charges of softness on communism and subversion, the Truman Administration, sure that it was the lesser of two evils, moved to expropriate the issue, as in a more subtle way it was already doing in foreign affairs. So the issue was legitimized; rather than being the property of the far right, which the centrist Republicans tolerated for obvious political benefits, it had even been picked up by the incumbent Democratic party.'[22]

Halberstam made this assertion in the introduction to *The Best and the Brightest*, his sprawling, mesmerizing account of America's descent into Vietnam, and there's no question that US intervention in Indochina cannot be understood apart from a close consideration of the domestic political context in which that intervention occurred. Indeed, one could go so far as to say that for all six presidents who dealt with the struggle in a direct way—from Truman through Ford—Vietnam mattered in large part because of the damage the outcome there could do to their political standing at home in the United States.

John F. Kennedy and Lyndon B. Johnson, for example, both harboured private doubts about the importance of the Vietnam struggle to US national security and about whether the war could be won in any meaningful sense, even with the introduction of American air power and ground forces. Neither needed convincing that the South Vietnamese government was a weak reed on which to build an effective counter to Ho Chi Minh's Hanoi government. Both men ruled out seeking a negotiated settlement in Vietnam, despite the urgings of European allied leaders. In 1962, JFK expanded the US military commitment to Saigon substantially, and in 1964–1965 Johnson took the fateful step into large-scale war. In the midst of the Gulf of Tonkin incident in August 1964, Johnson phoned Secretary of Defense Robert McNamara to say that Americans 'want to be damned sure I don't pull 'em out and run, and they want to be damned sure that we're firm. That's what all the country wants because Goldwater's raising so much hell.'[23] The meaning was clear: there could be no negotiated solution to the conflict in Vietnam, no talk of withdrawal; LBJ would demonstrate that he 'wasn't any Chamberlain umbrella man'.[24] In July 1965, when he announced a major escalation of the US troop commitment, he referred confidently to the lessons of history: 'We learned from Hitler at Munich that success only feeds the appetite for aggression. The battle would be renewed in one country and then another country, bringing with it perhaps even larger and crueler conflict, as we have learned from the lessons of history.'[25]

This didn't mean Johnson shunned all talk of negotiations. On the contrary, after mid-1965 he constantly pressed Undersecretary of State George Ball and others for new negotiating ideas—though, as Ball later said, 'he really meant merely new channels and procedures'. The administration, Ball told his colleagues, was 'following the traditional pattern for negotiating with a mule; just keep hitting him on the head with a two-by-four until he does what you want him to do. But that was useless with Hanoi; the mule's head was harder than the two-by-four.'[26]

Even after negotiations with Hanoi finally commenced in mid-1968, Johnson stuck to an unyielding diplomatic posture. The North Vietnamese representatives refused to discuss anything but the unconditional and permanent cessation of the bombing attacks on the North, and their US counterparts—under orders from the White House—said the bombing would not stop without 'reciprocation' by North Vietnam. This the Hanoi representatives refused, on the grounds that the bombings had no legitimate basis and Washington was in no position to demand anything in exchange for stopping them. And so, the fighting dragged on, year after bloody year. Not until January 1973, in the second term of a new administration, would a peace agreement be reached. By then, some 3 million Vietnamese had perished (2 million of them civilians), along with 58,000 Americans. In April 1975, Saigon fell to North Vietnamese forces.

IV

To a degree—but only to a degree—the Vietnam misadventure transformed the politics of appeasement. Up until 1969–1970, liberals and moderates had played the appeasement game, or some variation of it, almost as well as their conservative counterparts. With Vietnam exposed as a wholesale misapplication of the Munich analogy, those on the left became less likely to evoke the comparison and more vulnerable to political attack. For the right, however, the power of Munich had not diminished. Savvy Democrats understood this and remained wary of risking the charge of appeasement by appearing too eager to negotiate with Communist foes. They reasoned, why take the chance? This political reality produced a striking outcome: henceforth it would be easier for Republicans to pursue negotiations with an adversary than it would be for Democrats to do so.

This was the reason why, as the saying goes, only Nixon could go to China. Only a Republican with strong anti-Communist credentials—and Nixon's were second to none—could withstand the charges of weakness that would come from conservative hard-liners. Democrats had already paid their pound of flesh for 'losing China'; they wouldn't do it again.

So it was that Nixon, who had blasted first Truman and Adlai Stevenson and then Kennedy and Johnson for being muddle-headed appeasers, made the first big breakthrough in Cold War diplomacy. In his 1969 inaugural address he announced a new 'era of negotiation' to replace the old one of 'confrontation', then made good on that claim by working to repair two decades of frozen relations between Washington and Beijing. In addition, along with National Security Adviser Kissinger, he presided over détente, a relaxation of Cold War tensions that sparked, among other things, a productive round of arms control agreements with Moscow and the Anti-Ballistic Missile Treaty.[27] (Kennedy and Soviet leader Nikita Khrushchev had helped paved the way, with their tentative steps toward improved bilateral relations following the Cuban Missile Crisis and their agreement on a Limited Test Ban Treaty.) These Nixonian moves showed that diplomacy with adversaries could work, for the actions served American interests on several levels. The opening of China led to the beginning of a vital commercial relationship that, despite occasional tensions, has served the American economy well over the years. It has also acted as a force for liberalization within China itself, gradually easing the repressive structures built by Mao Zedong. Much the same could be said about the impact of détente on the Soviet Union. The 1975 Helsinki Agreement, finalized by Kissinger and Nixon's post-Watergate successor, Gerald Ford, provided a mechanism for advancing human rights within the Soviet bloc. Historians now recognize that Helsinki sowed many of the seeds for change that would bear fruit a decade later under Mikhail Gorbachev.[28]

Still, détente did not sit easily with the right wing of the Republican Party. Nixon's seeming acknowledgment of the Soviet Union as an equal and his tacit recognition of Kremlin domination of Eastern Europe smacked too much of a pact with the devil. Amoral realism seemed the order of the day, with nary a reference to the godless Soviets and their wholesale violations of human rights. Grassroots conservatives who paved the way for the New Right revival of the 1980s attacked détente and the China opening with unrelenting rage. The firebrand Phyllis Schlafly, a leading voice of the New Right who later became famous for her opposition to the Equal Rights Amendment, led a revolt against Nixon's leadership of the GOP. 'Civilized people don't dine with murderers and criminals', she said, as she compared Nixon to, yes, Neville Chamberlain, and condemned the ABM Treaty as yet another Munich. 'The delusion that America can be defended by treaties instead of by weapons is the most persistent and pernicious of all liberal fallacies', Schlafly declared.[29]

Such arguments gained traction as the years went on. One who suffered the consequences was Jimmy Carter. He entered the White House in early 1977 determined to build on the détente policy engineered by Nixon and continued under Gerald Ford. But embracing the policies of his Republican predecessors opened him up to attack from, oddly enough, his Republican opponents. Neoconservative intellectuals such as Norman Podhoretz— later to be credited with coining the term 'Islamofascism'—complained about a 'culture of appeasement' that was encouraging Soviet adventurism in the Third World and turning a blind eye to Russia's growing strength.[30] Candidate Reagan sensed an opportunity. He focused his quest for the White House in large part on wooing grassroots conservatives by attacking détente and playing up the present danger. Asked what he thought of détente, Reagan quipped, 'Isn't that what a farmer has with his turkey—until Thanksgiving?'[31]

Carter sensed the political reality and toughened his foreign policy accordingly—setting in motion the arms build-up, the secret war in Afghanistan, and other tough policies often generally ascribed to his successor. Prodding Carter along was National Security Adviser Zbigniew Brzezinski, who repeatedly lectured his boss on the politics of foreign policy. 'It is important that in 1980 you be recognized as the President both of *peace* and of *resolve*', Brzezinski advised in April 1979.[32] 'For international reasons as well as for domestic political reasons', he later elaborated, 'you ought to deliberately toughen both the tone and the substance of our foreign policy.'[33] To win re-election, Carter needed to talk and act tough.

In the end, Reagan played to Brzezinski's script better than Carter did, and rode his message of hard-hitting anti-communism and hyper-patriotism into the Oval Office. He did so in part by expanding upon the meaning of Munich. If it had once represented the folly of negotiations, it now also became a symbol of the importance of strength. On the campaign trail, Reagan fused the meaning of World War II with that of Vietnam. 'There is a lesson for all of us in Vietnam', he announced in the summer of 1980.

'If we are forced to fight, we must have the means and the determination to prevail or we will not have what it takes to secure the peace.' In virtually the same breath, Reagan spoke of World War II. It came about 'because nations were weak, not strong, in the face of aggression'. One war began because of weakness; another was lost because of it. Both taught the very same lesson: the importance of standing firm in the face of aggression.[34]

In time, however, Reagan changed, and his actions came to belie his campaign words. He entered office sounding very much like the antithesis of Carter; by the time he left, he looked more like Carter than either liberals or conservatives today care to admit. His anti-communism did not diminish, but his sense of how to best contend with Soviet power evolved. Negotiations, formerly anathema to him, came to hold promise, particularly after Mikhail Gorbachev rose to power in Moscow. Reagan reached out to Gorbachev, and the two men initiated a series of stunning diplomatic breakthroughs that laid the groundwork for the end of the Cold War. Thus, in 1987, they signed the Intermediate-Range Nuclear Forces (INF) Treaty banning all land-based intermediate-range nuclear missiles in Europe. As bilateral relations warmed, Gorbachev also unilaterally reduced his nation's armed forces, helped settle regional conflicts, and began the withdrawal of Soviet troops from Afghanistan.

Reagan had come to see, in other words, what other US leaders have found when they break free of the never-negotiate straitjacket: that diplomacy can be a vital tool for enhancing American interests. Although Reagan had once attacked détente for perpetuating the Kremlin's immoral rule, as president he came to realize that by relaxing tensions, he could actually destabilize the Soviet regime's grip on power. As he wrote in his diary, 'if we opened them up a bit, their leading citizens would be braver about proposing changes in their system'.[35] By negotiating with Gorbachev, Reagan strengthened the Soviet leader's position in the Kremlin. He allowed Gorbachev to reassure sceptical colleagues in the Communist Party that further reforms could be pursued without any danger. This, in turn, emboldened Gorbachev to move ahead with his reforms, measures that ultimately paved the way—against his expectations and desires, for he hoped to revitalize socialism in the USSR—for the Soviet Union's demise.

Nor was it just Cold War manoeuvring that led Reagan to retreat from the hard-line obstinacy that had characterized much of his political career. The more he talked with Kremlin leaders, the more he came to grasp 'something surprising'. He later recalled, 'Many people at the top of Soviet hierarchy were genuinely afraid of America and Americans. Perhaps this shouldn't have surprised me, but it did.' He realized he could stabilize the international system and reduce the threat of war by giving the Soviets fewer reasons to fear American power and more reasons to cooperate. In other words, he showed empathy, the capacity to see things from another's perspective, which is arguably the essence of statecraft. As Reagan once said about negotiations, 'You're unlikely to get all you want; you'll probably get more of what you want if you don't issue ultimatums and leave your adversary room to maneuver; you shouldn't back your adversary into a corner, embarrass him, or humiliate him; and sometimes, the easiest way to get things done is for the top people to do them alone and in private.'[36]

Conservatives in his own party didn't see it that way. Like Nixon, Kennedy, and others before him, Reagan came under fire for being an alleged appeaser. The Conservative Caucus pulled out the stops, running a full-page newspaper ad juxtaposing photos of Reagan and Gorbachev with photos of Neville Chamberlain and Adolf Hitler.[37] The conservative icon William F. Buckley, Jr. chimed in, alleging that Reagan fundamentally misunderstood the Gorbachev regime: 'To greet it as if it were no longer evil is on the order of changing our entire position toward Adolf Hitler.'[38] As early as 1983, when Reagan was embarking on the largest peacetime military buildup in US history, Podhoretz was comparing Reagan to Chamberlain and complaining that 'appeasement by any other name smells as rank, and the stench of it now pervades the American political atmosphere.'[39] Reagan had become a 'Carter clone', he later griped, warning—less than two years before the fall of the Berlin Wall—that 'the danger is greater than ever.'[40]

Viewed from the perspective of history, what seems most striking about these critics is how utterly mistaken they were. Declassified documents from Soviet and American archives reveal that it was the deep structural problems in the Soviet system, more so than Reagan's bellicose rhetoric and military build-up, that paved the way for the USSR's collapse. These same documents demonstrate that the president's willingness to engage Gorbachev diplomatically only hastened the process. Soviet documents also reveal something counterintuitive: Gorbachev became more open to negotiating with the West not because of Russia's military weakness, but in fact because of its strength. He came to realize that he could accept deep cuts in his nuclear arsenal and loosen his grip on Eastern Europe because Soviet military power remained sufficient to guarantee his country's security.[41] This is not as startling as it may seem. If Americans were comfortable with 'peace through strength', why would it be any different for American adversaries?

V

On 16 September 2015, about half an hour into a debate among Republican presidential candidates at the Ronald Reagan Library in California, there occurred a quite remarkable exchange. In response to Carly Fiorina's assertion that she would not talk to Russia's Vladimir Putin, 'because the only way he will stop is to sense strength and resolve on the other side', Senator Rand Paul offered a rejoinder: 'Well, think if Reagan had said that during the Cold War?' He went on, 'We do need to be engaged with Russia. It doesn't mean we give them a free pass, or China a free pass, but [we need] to be engaged, to continue to talk. We did throughout the Cold War, and it would be a big mistake not to do it here.'[42]

Paul found little support on the stage that evening, and his candidacy soon fizzled. But the man he was seeking to succeed would have agreed with his every word. Since concluding the nuclear agreement with Iran some months earlier, Obama had endured the now-familiar attacks— 'The deal is an American Munich', thundered former UN Ambassador John Bolton. 'Barack Obama is trying to appease the mullahs in Tehran by making one concession after another.' Senator Ted Cruz, who hadn't even read the agreement, called it a 'catastrophe on the order and magnitude of Munich'.[43] Obama now enlisted two Republican predecessors in defending it. 'I have a lot of differences with Ronald Reagan', Obama told *New York Times* columnist Thomas Friedman, 'but where I completely admire him was his recognition that if you were able to verify an agreement that you would negotiate with the evil empire that was hellbent on our destruction and was a far greater existential threat to us than Iran will ever be [then it would be worth doing]. I had a lot of disagreements with Richard Nixon, but he understood there was the prospect, the possibility, that China could take a different path.'[44]

From his own party, Obama might have referenced President Kennedy, who in the aftermath of the Cuban Missile Crisis endured withering Republican attacks for his decision to negotiate with Nikita Khrushchev. The denunciations have long since passed from memory, but the diplomatic achievements live on. It brings to mind JFK's powerful formulation from his first year in office, when superpower tensions flared over Berlin: 'Let us never negotiate out of fear, but let us never fear to negotiate.'

Diplomacy will not always succeed, and even when it does, we make a mistake when we promise too much for it, as Niall Ferguson wisely reminds us in this volume. Barack Obama, too, understood this, as he acknowledged to Friedman: 'Part of our goal here has been to show that diplomacy can work. It doesn't work perfectly. It doesn't give us everything that we want.' But, he added, 'what we can do is shape events in ways where it's more likely that problems get solved, rather than less likely, and that's the opportunity we have now'.[45]

That seems right. The post-war American presidents who have managed to escape the 'no more Munichs' constraints and withstood the inevitable charges of appeasement have often achieved real and lasting national security gains—and, in the process, bolstered their historical reputations. Conversely, those leaders who have chosen the alternative of relying on ultimatums, on threats and 'comply or else' bluster, too often have painted themselves into a corner—if their bluff is called, they will feel intense pressure to take the next step, to escalate the confrontation, culminating quite possibly in the resort to major military force. (Exhibit A: Lyndon Johnson and Vietnam.) Ultimatums can work in international politics, but the risks for disaster are immense. (Exhibit B: George W. Bush and Iraq.) Moreover, an inflexible hard-line approach typically generates a hard-line response. Relations become frozen and stagnant. Inflexibility begets inflexibility.

As presidents from Kennedy to Nixon to Reagan to Obama have come to understand, maintaining manoeuvrability by broadening the range of options is usually a better way to get what you want.

Or as Winston Churchill put it some seven decades ago, in the first volume of his monumental history of the Second World War, 'Those who are prone by temperament and character to seek sharp and clear-cut solutions of difficult and obscure problems, who are ready to fight whenever some challenge comes from a foreign power, have not always been right. On the other hand, those whose inclination is to bow their heads, to seek patiently and faithfully for peaceful compromise, are not always wrong. On the contrary, in the majority of instances, they may be right, not only morally but from a practical standpoint.'[46]

Wise words then as now.

Notes

1. The historiography on American diplomacy (in the strict sense used here) during the Cold War is surprisingly thin. The reasons are varied, but certainly it has something to do with what Niall Ferguson laments in his chapter in this book: the diminished place of diplomatic history in American universities in recent decades. The field that, in the past, would have been called 'US diplomatic history' or 'US foreign relations history' is now generally referred to as 'The US and the World,' and many practitioners centre their research not on high politics and statecraft (sometimes derided as 'what one diplomat said to another') but on cultural relations, transnational movements, and non-government organizations. Still, some general histories of the Cold War give attention to the subject of the present essay; see e.g., John Lewis Gaddis, *The Cold War: A New History* (New York: Penguin, 2005); Melvyn P. Leffler, *For the Soul of Mankind: The United States, the Soviet Union, and the Cold War* (New York: Hill and Wang, 2007); and Campbell Craig and Fredrik Logevall, *America's Cold War: The Politics of Insecurity* (Cambridge, MA: Harvard University Press, 2009).
2. On the diplomatic method in modern times, see Harold Nicolson, *Diplomacy*, 3rd ed. (Oxford: Oxford University Press, 1963); Hedley Bull, *The Anarchical Society* (London: Macmillan Press, 1977); F.H. Hinsley, *Power and the Pursuit of Peace* (Cambridge: Cambridge University Press, 1963); Adam Watson, *Diplomacy: The Dialogue Between States* (New York: McGraw-Hill Book Company, 1983). My definition here follows Watson, 11.

3. Henry Kissinger, *Diplomacy* (New York: Simon & Schuster, 1994), 471. This section of the present essay draws in significant part from my Stuart L. Bernath Lecture to SHAFR, 'A Critique of Containment,' in *Diplomatic History* 28, no. 4 (September 2004): 473–99.

4. Warren Kimball, *Forged in War: Roosevelt, Churchill, and the Second World War* (New York: William Morrow, 1997), 26.

5. David Reynolds, *Summits: Six Meetings that Shaped the Twentieth Century* (New York: Basic Books, 2007), 101.

6. FDR Fireside Chat, 11 September 1941, in *The American Presidency Project* by John T. Woolley and Gerhard Peters, http://www.presidency.ucsb.edu/ws/?pid=16012.

7. 'X' (George F. Kennan), 'The Sources of Soviet Conduct,' *Foreign Affairs*, 25, no. 4 (July 1947); Barton Bernstein, 'Containment,' in *Encyclopedia of American Foreign Policy*, 2nd ed. Vol. 1, eds. Alexander DeConde, Richard Dean Burns, and Fredrik Logevall (New York: Scribner, 2002), 346.

8. Walter Lippmann, 'The Cold War: A Study in U.S. Foreign Policy,' *New York Herald Tribune*, 1947. There were fourteen columns in all, the first appearing on 2 September the last on 2 October.

9. Ibid., 60.

10. Anders Stephanson, 'Fourteen Notes on the Very Concept of the Cold War,' H-Net Diplomatic History List (H-Diplo), 24 June 1996 (Note #13).

11. David Mayers, 'Containment and the Primacy of Diplomacy: George Kennan's Views, 1947–1948,' *International Security* 11 (Summer 1986): 134–35. See also George F. Kennan, *Memoirs 1925–1950* (Boston: Little, Brown, 1967), 359–61.

12. The letter to Lippmann is analysed in Mayers, 'Containment and the Primacy of Diplomacy.' For a differing depiction of Kennan's thinking, see Niall Ferguson's chapter in the present volume.

13. See Campbell Craig and Fredrik Logevall, *America's Cold War* (Cambridge, MA: Harvard University Press, 2012).

14. See page 132.

15. C. Vann Woodward, 'The Age of Reinterpretation,' *American Historical Review* 66 (October 1960): 2–8.

16. Richard Hofstadter, *The Paranoid Style in American Politics and Other Essays* (New York: Knopf, 1965), 31.

17. This is a theme in Craig and Logevall, *America's Cold War*.

18. Kenneth Waltz, 'Structural Realism after the Cold War,' in *America Unrivaled: The Future of the Balance of Power*, ed. G. John Ikenberry (Ithaca, NY: Cornell University Press, 2003), 53.

19. Craig and Logevall, *America's Cold War*.

20. Julian E. Zelizer, *Arsenal of Democracy: The Politics of National Security from World War II to the War on Terrorism* (New York: Basic Books, 2009).

21. Only in the United States among the Western democracies, Eric Hobsbawm has written, was the 'communist world conspiracy' a serious part of domestic politics.

Eric Hobsbawm, *The Age of Extremes: A History of the World, 1914–1991* (New York: Vintage, 1994), 236–37. See also 234.

22. David Halberstam, *The Best and the Brightest*, 20th anniversary ed. (New York: Random House, 1992), 108–109.

23. John Prados, 'LBJ Tapes on the Gulf of Tonkin Incident' (3 August 1964), *The White House Tapes* (New York: The New Press, 2003), National Security Archive, http://www.gwu.edu/~nsarchiv/NSAEBB/NSAEBB132/tapes.htm.

24. Geoffrey Wheatcroft, '"Munich" Shouldn't Be Such a Dirty Word,' *Washington Post*, 28 September 2008.

25. LBJ press conference, 28 July 1965, quoted in Yuen Foong Khong, *Analogies at War: Korea, Munich, Dien Bien Phu, and the Vietnam Decisions of 1965* (Princeton, NJ: Princeton University Press, 1992), 179. On LBJ's aversion to negotiations in 1964–65 and the consequences, see Fredrik Logevall, *Choosing War: The Lost Chance for Peace and the Escalation of War in Vietnam* (Berkeley, CA: University of California Press, 1999).

26. George W. Ball, *The Past Has Another Pattern: Memoirs* (New York: Norton, 1982), 405.

27. Richard Nixon Inaugural Address, 20 January 1969, The American Presidency Project, http://www.presidency.ucsb.edu/ws/?pid=1941.

28. Michael Cotey Morgan, 'The United States and the Making of the Helsinki Final Act,' in eds. Fredrik Logevall and Andrew Preston, *Nixon in the World: American Foreign Relations 1969–1977* (New York: Oxford University Press, 2008), 164–82.

29. Donald Critchlow, *Phyllis Schlafly and Grassroots Conservativism: A Woman's Crusade* (Princeton, NJ: Princeton University Press, 2005), 204–6.

30. Norman Podhoretz, 'The Culture of Appeasement,' *Harper's*, October 1977; Podhoretz, *World War IV: The Long Struggle Against Islamofascism* (New York: Vintage, 2007).

31. Quoted in Gaddis, *The Cold War*, 217.

32. Memo, Brzezinski to Carter, 12 April 1979, Subject: 'NSC Weekly Report #93–1. Opinion: Foreign Policy and Domestic Politics,' Jimmy Carter Library, Atlanta.

33. Memo, Brzezinski to Carter, 13 September 1979, Brzezinski Donated Files, box 2, Carter Library, Atlanta.

34. Ronald Reagan Address to the Veterans of Foreign Wars Convention in Chicago, 18 August 1980, The American Presidency Project, http://www.presidency.ucsb.edu/ws/?pid=85202.

35. Melvyn Leffler, *For the Soul of Mankind* (Hill and Wang, 2008), 358–9.

36. Ibid, 358–59, 381.

37. Glenn Greenwald, 'Ronald Reagan: Chamberlain Appeaser of the 1980s,' *Salon*, May 17, 2008, http://www.salon.com/opinion/greenwald/2008/05/17/reagan/.

38. Dinesh D'Souza, 'How Reagan Won the Cold War,' *National Review*, November 24, 1997, reprinted at http://www.nationalreview.com/flashback/dsouza200406061619.asp.

39. Norman Podhoretz, 'Appeasement by Any Other Name,' *Commentary* 76 (July 1983),

cited in Andrew Bacevich, *The New American Militarism: How Americans are Seduced by War* (New York: Oxford University Press, 2005), 236 n11.

40. Norman Podhoretz, 'How Reagan Succeeds as a Carter Clone,' *New York Post*, October 7, 1986, cited in Bacevich, *New American Militarism*, 78–79, 237 n28. See also Craig and Logevall, *America's Cold War*, 337, 347.

41. The sense that nuclear weapons ensured Soviet security also conditioned Moscow's willingness to watch passively as the Berlin Wall was torn down in 1989. See Leffler, *For the Soul of Mankind*, 436.

42. 'CNN Library Debate: Later Debate Full Transcript,' CNN, September 16, 2015, http://cnnpressroom.blogs.cnn.com/2015/09/16/cnn-reagan-library-debate-later-debate-full-transcript/.

43. Bolton and Cruz quoted in Samuel Kleiner and Tom Zoellner, 'Republicans' "Munich" fallacy,' *Los Angeles Times*, July 20 2015, http://www.latimes.com/opinion/op-ed/la-oe-zoellnerandkleiner-munich-and-iran-20150720-story.html.

44. Thomas L. Friedman, 'Obama Makes His Case on Iran Nuclear Deal,' *New York Times*, July 14, 2015, http://www.nytimes.com/2015/07/15/opinion/thomas-friedman-obama-makes-his-case-on-iran-nuclear-deal.html.

45. Friedman, 'Obama Makes His Case on Iran Nuclear Deal.'

46. Winston Churchill, *The Second World War*. Vol. 1, *Gathering Storm* (New York: Holt, Rinehart & *Winston*, 1948), 287.

SECTION IV

Democratic Peace

7.

A Somewhat Personal History of the Democratic Peace and Its Expansion to the Kantian Peace

Bruce Russett

Introduction[1]

The scientific study of what has come to be known as the democratic peace (DP), and subsequently the Kantian peace (KP), had early theoretical roots in the twentieth century.[2] It can be traced to Clarence Streit's book *Union Now*, published in 1939 as World War II began.[3] Streit called for a union of democracies that would feature (1) union citizenship, (2) a mutual defence force, (3) a customs-free union of free market economies, (4) a common currency, and (5) a postal and communication system. It is easy to see there the intellectual roots of the European Union. After the war's end, leading Christian Democrats in France (Jean Monnet and Robert Schuman), Germany (Konrad Adenauer), and Italy (Alcide De Gasperi) strove to make those ideas a reality. Their initial step was the formation of the European Coal and Steel Community in the early 1950s, which then became the basis for the European Union. Its appearance in social scientific theory and research about the causes of peace and war, however, did not occur until the 1960s.

The first statistical analysis of the democratic peace was by Dean Babst in *The Wisconsin Sociologist*.[4] That journal was unknown to most political scientists. A few, however, paid attention to his results, including Melvin Small and J. David Singer, whose analysis appeared to confirm Babst's research.[5] Nevertheless, Small and Singer dismissed their own results. Singer, who would be instrumental in the development of the Correlates of War project, held firmly to this position for the rest of his life, insisting that only the power structure of the international system mattered and a state's internal political structure was irrelevant. We see this in the ongoing debate between those who define themselves as realists on one side and idealists, mostly liberals, on the other. While the rhetorical concept of idealism may contrast well with a realist outlook, the scientific work of idealists over the last quarter of a century shows them to be every bit as realistic as the realists.[6]

A key element enabling the growth (in both the depth and breadth) of the study of the DP, notably its expansion into the KP, was the application of what can reasonably be called Big Science to the study of international conflict. It began more than half a century ago, and in the twenty-first century has become even more notable for two characteristics.

(1) A greatly expanded infusion of financial support from multiple, and sometimes competing, sources. This has meant money for data collection and the creation of databases, developing new research tools, supporting research assistants and collaborators, conference travel, and funding to support teaching leave and summer salary add-ons. It has been made available to all sides of the various debates I will be discussing below. This, in turn, has made possible the internationalization of the discussion. American scholars welcomed the enriching contribution of major established institutions in Europe, notably the PRIO, the Department of Peace and Conflict Research in Uppsala, the Richardson Institute for Conflict and Peace Research in England, and the Peace Research Institute Frankfurt,[7] as well as less formal groups in Israel, Japan, and elsewhere.

(2) Changes in norms and practices of transparency, both regarding the sources of funding (foundations, government agencies, own university) and *especially* the emergence of norms regarding the public availability of all data and computational routines on a permanent website for easy consultation, replication, and improvement (correction and expansion). Nils Petter Gleditsch was one of the first journal editors to champion these

norms and insist on their implementation when he edited the *Journal of Peace Research*. Full replication files have enabled those responding to a new claim or critique to closely examine data and specifications to find potential errors—where the bodies are buried, so to speak. Quantitative social science can be a rough contact sport, like football (in both its North American and European varieties such as rugby), but it is a 'game' with very high stakes, both in its personal/professional and policy implications. The replication norm is a vital contribution in keeping the players both honest and informed. Good critics, and critiques, are essential to the development of any scientific endeavour and should be regarded as adversarial partners with the shared goal of advancing knowledge, not as enemies.

Point 1 above applies across fields of inquiry, but point 2, regarding the norms of transparency, is an innovation that began specifically in the study of international politics, and as a norm, it has since spread to other subfields of political science and to economics. It is not practised in many areas of the physical and biological sciences, or even in all areas of international relations. This norm, combined with the confrontational nature of the debates surrounding the DP and KP, may have important implications for progress in the field. In his sweeping survey of standards of evidence applied by many schools of international relations theory, Fred Chernoff argues, 'The DP debate has exhibited more progress than those over alliance formation and nuclear proliferation. And authors in the DP debate share more fully reliance on particular criteria of a good explanation. One of the reasons that there has been progress . . . may well be the closer agreement on what makes for a good explanation.'[8]

The Evolution of Democratic Peace Research

Michael Doyle drew the attention of contemporary scholars to Kant with two articles in *Philosophy and Public Affairs* in 1983 and another in the *American Political Science Review* in 1986.[9] The 1983 material was largely unknown outside the field of political philosophy; the APSR article drew wider attention, but not much—perhaps because it lacked the useful data he had compiled for his previous articles. Yet, in retrospect, this article is noteworthy as an important theoretical basis for the DP and the KP.

Scholars and policymakers have long invoked a vision of a peace among democracies as part of a larger structure of institutions and practices to promote peace among nation-states. Kant in 1795 urged that peace could be based partially upon states sharing 'republican constitutions'.[10] As the components of such a constitution, he identified freedom, legal equality of subjects, representative government, and separation of powers. The other key elements of his perpetual peace were cosmopolitan law, embodying ties of international commerce and free trade, and a pacific union or confederation established by treaty among sovereign republics. Kant understood that not all countries might be in a pacific union, but that those who were could avoid war among themselves even while remaining vigilant against outsiders. In the twentieth century, the principal founders of what became the European Union expressed a similar vision as a means to end the perpetual cycle of war on their continent. The term 'democratic peace' was coined only in the early 1990s, to characterize the observed phenomenon that stable democracies rarely, if ever, fight wars against each other. Without the DP label, Zeev Maoz and Nasrin Abdolali pioneered the quantitative study of the phenomenon in an article for the *Journal of Conflict Resolution* in 1989.[11] Then, one evening over a fish dinner in Haifa, Israel, Zeev and I agreed to pursue the issue, and did so first in 'International Conflict: Alliances, Contiguity, Wealth, and Political Stability' (1992), and then in 'Normative and Structural Causes of Democratic Peace' (1993), which was published at the same time as my *Grasping the Democratic Peace* (1993).[12] We noted the pacific effects both of democratic institutions and norms of behaviour without making a stronger case for one or the other, probably because each might play the stronger role depending on circumstances. David Rousseau, in *Democracy and War: Institutions, Norms, and the Evolution of International Conflict*, also makes a persuasive argument for the importance of both norms and institutions.[13]

Right after publication of *Grasping the Democratic Peace*, John Oneal, while then unaware of Doyle's work, picked up the idea of adding trade variables to the initial specifications of what we still called the DP to find out whether trade, or economic interdependence, would have a greater effect than democracy. I agreed, but I remained sceptical because we needed a good theoretical basis to test the primacy of trade over democracy, not to mention that it would require another huge data-gathering effort. We did it anyway, and when we did, we found that trade and democracy had about equal effects.

I think it was then that Oneal discovered Kant's essay on perpetual peace and urged me to read it. He was less enthusiastic about adding international, or intergovernmental, organizations (IOs) as the third leg, but we did so nonetheless as a modern version of Kant's emphasis on a pacific union. We continued to find evidence for democracy and trade, but support for IOs was somewhat ambiguous. Different specifications yielded results with different statistical significance, and we lacked a way to distinguish between different types of IOs. Research continues on the role of IOs, for example, in Charles Boehmer and colleagues' 'Do Intergovernmental Organizations Promote Peace?' Jon Pevehouse and Russett's 'Democratic International Organizations Promote Peace', and Pevehouse's *Democracy from Above: Regional Organizations and Democratization*. Daniela Donno, in 'Who Is Punished? Regional Intergovernmental Organizations and the Enforcement of Democratic Norms' and *Defending Democratic Norms: International Actors and the Politics of Electoral Misconduct* also made important contributions.[14] Joshua Goldstein, in *Winning the War on War*, credits the United Nations for its peacekeeping efforts and other activities.[15]

In the contemporary era, 'democracy' denotes a country where nearly everyone can vote, elections are freely contested, its chief executive is chosen by popular vote or by an elected parliament, and civil rights and liberties are substantially guaranteed. The Polity Project, working out of PRIO and the University of Maryland, gives states a yearly score on an ordinal scale from +10 for the most democratic to –10 for the most authoritarian. It is not the only such effort to score states on their democratic characteristics, but its conceptual framework and data, primarily the measurement of institutions, are the international standard. The project started under Ted Gurr and was aimed at scholars of comparative politics, which means the data are not biased by IR scholarship. Using them protects against possible subjective bias, for example, by using a dataset designed according to existing conceptions of the democratic peace.

If wars are defined as conflicts with 1,000 or more battle deaths between internationally recognized states, then established democracies, measured according to Polity's criteria, fought no wars against one another during the entire twentieth century. Wars are relatively rare phenomena, but the generalization about democracy and conflict largely applies to many types of lower-level militarized disputes with far fewer casualties. It is clear from the data that democracies are unlikely to engage in any kind of militarized disputes with other democracies. Since the end of the nineteenth century, dictatorships have been seven times more likely than democracies to use military violence against each other. The democratic peace has subsequently become a major focus for much political science research about the causes of war. The research program has largely confirmed the relatively pacific character of relations between democracies, has added new insights not initially anticipated, and has strengthened the interest in the domestic influences on foreign policy among IR scholars.

Continuing Development of the Discussion

I will not discuss further the earlier critiques and rejoinders to the DP because I and others (my co-authors writing with me, or alone, as well as other scholars writing entirely independently) have rebutted these critiques. Rather, I will discuss some of the many contributions of the past decade or so. First, DP is not a law in the sense that we might talk about a law of physics. Nearly all its advocates regard it as a probability statement, with inevitable false negatives and false positives due to the influences of variables excluded from statistical models because of problems with theory, or due to difficulties in measurement, either through human error or the absence of a sound empirical proxy for theorized variables. These problems are to be expected in social and observational research. This is something that Joanne Gowa and I agree on. Any social scientist who claims to have discovered a law does so at great peril: the social/political world is not that simple.

Numerous critiques and new puzzles about the causes and consequences of the DP and KP continue to arise. One such puzzle is that of identifying the causal processes that produce the DP. Consensus about these causal processes is less complete than it is regarding the empirical generalization.

Three common schools of thought exist regarding the sources of the democratic peace: institutions, norms, and economics.

Political institutions impose constraints on democracies' decisions to go to war. They ensure that any two democracies with a conflict of interest can expect sufficient time for nonviolent conflict resolution processes to be effective. Moreover, the general population frequently stands to gain fewer of the spoils of war, and to pay more of its costs, than does the political leadership. In democracies, the ability of the populace to hold the leadership accountable through elections provides a strong incentive for leaders to avoid engaging in wars—particularly costly wars and wars they are likely to lose. At the same time, democratic leaders in one country know that their counterparts in other democracies have similar constraints. Since democracies choose their wars carefully (they win about 90 percent of the wars they initiate, against only about 60 percent when they are targets), they avoid fighting each other.[16]

Some scholars argue that dictators are better able to resist being deposed and so are less restrained in their actions by fear of popular reprisal.[17] If they win, then they can appropriate the spoils of victory; if they lose, they need little more than to retain the support of their cronies and their police and military forces to stay in power. However, others have argued that while dictators may not worry about losing elections, they do risk much more violent ends if their 'audience' or support coalition decides to turn on them.[18] This may lead to caution about going to war in certain types of authoritarian regimes. While Jessica Weeks challenges 'audience cost' theory as it applies specifically to democracies, it is important to note that the logic behind this argument, supported by the statistical evidence, is the same as arguments regarding democratic accountability and restraint, reinforcing institutional explanations for the DP.[19]

Finally, and similarly, during international negotiations or escalating crises, democratic institutions may give their leaders a far better ability to signal threats and commitments credibly when the political opposition can be seen as supporting the government. If the opposition disagrees, it will be harder for the government to commit itself credibly to fight, and hence it will be less likely to escalate the conflict by bluffing.[20] The free press that often flourishes in democracies may also be a vehicle by which transparency of intention is improved when two democracies enter into negotiations.

A second view is that peace between democracies derives from normative restraints on conflict and preferences for nonviolent conflict resolution. That explanation posits that democracies extend the cultural norms of peaceful conflict resolution that operate within them to the international arena. In their relations with one another, democracies expect that domestic political norms of negotiation and mutual respect will carry over into their international behaviour. By contrast, democracies do not expect authoritarian leaders to follow such norms. Rather, they expect dictatorships to often act aggressively and use force.

These influences reinforce one another. Where normative constraints are weak, democratic institutions may provide the necessary additional constraints on the use of violence against other democratic states. There is not yet agreement among scholars as to which influences are strongest. Pinker's magisterial survey, *The Better Angels of our Nature*, makes a good case for both, but emphasizes the development of strong societal norms of nonviolence.[21] Most research has been devoted to institutions, partly because that is where the best data exist, but Michael Tomz and Jessica Weeks used survey data to demonstrate a role for norms of nonviolent conflict resolution at the individual level of analysis.[22] An important article by Rachel Stein also presents a normative argument for the democratic peace by cleverly adding a variable measuring norms against vengeance characterized by popular approval of capital punishment.[23]

Addressing the effect of inequality of income and/or wealth in reducing the effect of democratic institutions has now become possible, over time and across countries, thanks to the magnificent work by Thomas Piketty and his colleagues in Luxembourg.[24] Our initial results show that the pacific effect of democratic institutions is reduced in democracies (coded as such by the institutionally oriented Polity dataset) with high levels of inequality. Is it because economically powerful elites undermine democratic norms, or perhaps because they restrict access to democratic institutions, such as citizenship and voting, by low-income individuals such as immigrants, former felons, and ethnic minorities? Or is it both? It is hard to identify the relevant agents and causal mechanisms, and for now, we have only our conjectures.

Are Democracies Simply Peaceful?

Another puzzle concerns whether democracies are more peaceful in general—with all states, not just with one another. This question shifts the focus from dyads, or pairs of states, to monads, or individual states.

Much of the research on the DP, and its fundamental logic, focuses on relationships between pairs of states or dyads as the unit of analysis.[25] The question of whether democracies are more peaceful in general at the monadic level, that is, with all states and not just with one another, is still disputed. Democracies, especially powerful ones, do initiate many military disputes and wars with autocratic states, which might suggest that democracies are not more peaceful in general than autocracies. Because countries behave differently toward some countries than toward others, the interaction of two governments is typically required to make a quarrel or establish a peaceful relationship. The more democratic each state in the pair is, the more peaceful their relations are likely to be. Democracies more often employ democratic means of peaceful conflict resolution. They are readier to reciprocate each other's behaviour and to accept third party mediation, arbitration, and adjudication in settling disputes.[26] Because democratic leaders must obtain political support among their electorates in order to ratify international agreements, they can more credibly commit to keeping the commitments they make.[27] Careful statistical analyses show that the relatively peaceful relations of democracies toward each other are not spuriously caused by other influences such as rapid growth, high levels of wealth, or alliances. The phenomenon of peace between democracies is not limited just to the rich industrialized states, nor was it enforced solely by the pressure of having a common adversary during the Cold War.

Some writers have concluded that modern democracies are somewhat more peaceful in general than are autocracies.[28] The scholarly consensus on such a monadic assertion, however, is not as great as on the dyadic proposition that democracies are more peaceful with each other. The monadic statistical generalization is fairly weak, with numerous exceptions. Great powers, for example, have both wide interests across the world and the capability to fight distant adversaries. Thus, great powers may engage in many military conflicts, even if they are democracies. Here the realist emphasis on relative power and the structure of that power remains important, and measures of such realist variables as alliances, relative power, and geographical distance are incorporated in our models along with liberal variables.[29] Alliances consistently have little effect, but other realist variables are significant but do not notably reduce the significance of the liberal influences. Finally, democracies are less likely to initiate crises in the first place, but once a military or severe diplomatic crisis arises, democracies are in general—though not with one another—as likely as autocracies to escalate the conflict to full-scale war.[30]

Democracies, especially powerful ones, do initiate many military disputes and wars with autocratic states, which might suggest that democracies are not more peaceful than autocracies in general. The history of imperialism by Western democracies might argue that they were not especially peaceful. Nevertheless, there is reason to be cautious in reaching such a conclusion. Many of the recorded examples of acts of imperialism by democracies in the nineteenth century involved states that, while considered to be democratic by the standards of their time, would not be considered very democratic by contemporary standards. They had heavily restricted voting franchises: women, certain ethnic and racial groups, and people who did not own property were often denied the vote. For example, it was not until 1920 that women achieved the right to vote and hold office in the United States, and in the United Kingdom this did not come about until 1928. After the US Civil War, the 15th Amendment to the US Constitution forbade denying voting rights based on 'race, color, or previous condition of servitude'. However, this right was widely flouted, especially in the South, and to this day is diminished by various means.

Since the evidence indicates that the more democratic both states in a pair are, the more peaceable they will be with each other, it should not be surprising that in general the moderately democratic states of the nineteenth century were less peaceful than their more democratic successors in the twentieth century. This difference could also explain why more alleged exceptions, or near exceptions, to the 'democracies don't fight each other' generalization arose in the nineteenth century.

Democracies might also feel dragged into conflicts with autocracies despite wanting to avoid such confrontations. If the norms and institutions of democracies make them reluctant to fight, then autocratic states might use this reluctance as a lever to force democracies into making heavy concessions to avoid war, believing democracies are more likely to appease aggression than confront it. The population of a democracy might then be persuaded to resist such pressure not merely because this would go against their pacific tendencies but also as a reaction to an attempt to exploit them, whereas if confronted by a similarly minded democracy they might not feel these pressures. If war ultimately does result when a democracy refuses to make any more concessions, the democracy may well have been provoked into fighting.

If democracies are more peaceful, especially with each other, one might expect less war in the world if democracies increase as a proportion of all states. The road to greater peace may not be smooth, however. Autocracies are more likely to fight each other than are democracies. However, democratic–autocratic dyads are also prone to fight because their norms and institutions clash. In a world composed solely of democracies, peaceful conflict resolution should prevail. Near the other extreme, a world composed mostly of autocracies would exhibit much violent conflict. This is a reasonable characterization of international relations in previous centuries, where wars between autocracies were fairly frequent, and while the few democracies would not fight each other, they would often fight autocracies. The most conflict-prone international system could be one with roughly equal numbers of democracies and autocracies: a system marked by a large number of conflicts among the autocracies and very many conflicts between democracies and autocracies.

This picture also seems consistent with what we find in particular regions of the world. This is instructive because most wars arise between countries that are geographically proximate: neighbours can fight each other easily and often have issues (borders, ethnic conflicts, control of natural resources) that provoke conflict. In regions composed almost entirely of democracies (such as Western Europe since WWII or Latin America more recently) there is little fighting between neighbours or within the region in general, but in regions such as the Middle East, where democracy is rare, war is much more common. A similar phenomenon arises for the few countries that count as major powers, with global interests and military capabilities. In every international system, the most powerful nations, democracies included, have been more involved in war than have most of the less dominant states. Overall, peace would become more common only if a solid majority of countries in each region, as well as in the global system, became democratic and their dyadic ties could operate widely.

One further objection arose from the contention that, whereas stable democracies do not go to war with each other, states in transition from autocratic regimes toward democracy may be more war-prone, as Edward Mansfield and Jack Snyder proposed.[31] If true, this would raise serious doubts about whether, at least in the short run, creating more democratic states in the world would make the world more peaceful. In any event, the accuracy of this observation has been hotly contested. It depends heavily upon how the transition is measured and how long it lasts. Out of more than 500 liberalizing transitions, only about 2 percent resulted in war. Moreover, war may be equally common, or more common, under transitions from democratic to autocratic regimes; if so, political instability and transition in general, not democratization in particular, would be the culprit.[32] The coup de grâce to Mansfield and Snyder's proposition was delivered by Vipin Narang and Rebecca Nelson, who question the empirical finding itself and argue that the cases in question are dependent on historical context, notably the disintegration and dismemberment of the Ottoman Empire.[33]

Finally, one must look not just at the general behaviour of democratizing states, but also at their relations with particular types of neighbours.[34] Newly democratizing states surrounded by established democracies or other democratizing states (for example, much of Central Europe since 1989) may fight much less often than do those with authoritarian neighbours.[35] As often as possible, one must ask whether it was the democracy or its autocratic neighbour that initiated the conflict; dictators may feel their own security in office is threatened by the example of a potentially successful democracy nearby and take action to quash the transition.

Modelling the Democratic Peace

Beyond the simple statement that pairs of democracies are likely to live in peace, a wide variety of related propositions can be derived and tested. Some of these suggest that democracy and the expectation of international peace feed on each other. These analyses use a system of separate structural equations dealing with one issue at a time. This issue was addressed in an extended discussion between Oneal and colleagues and Patrick James and colleagues in *Defence and Peace Economics*.[36] I have serious doubts about the specification of James and his co-authors and have not seen it again in the literature. Russett and Oneal agree regarding the value of multiple separate reciprocal relationships in the expansion of the DP to the KP.[37] Håvard Hegre and colleagues concluded that it could be done satisfactorily with care.[38]

But analysing the whole Kantian system in one set of equations is too complex to be done reliably. A distinguished economist, Christopher Sims, once warned me that to do so would leave me defending it for the rest of my life. It is much safer to analyse reciprocity in one leg of the Kantian triangle at a time (see below). Democracies win their wars much more often than do authoritarian states, in part because democratic leaders, requiring consent from the populace, try not to start wars they cannot win. Free speech and debate may make them more accurate and efficient information processors. They may also be more effective in marshalling their resources. Authoritarian governments that lose wars may often be replaced by democratic regimes. As the politically relevant international environment inhabited by democracies becomes composed of more democratic and internally stable states, democracies tend to reduce their military expenditures and conflict involvement. A less menacing international system can permit the emergence and consolidation of democratic governments. Arms races and protracted international threats—real or perceived—strengthen the forces of secrecy and authoritarianism. Relaxation of international threats to peace and security reduces the need, and the excuse, for repressing democratic dissent.

The theory around why democracies behave peacefully needs to be carefully developed, taking into equal consideration their patterns of strategic interaction with different types of states. Research needs to be done both at the macro level, to identify broad patterns of behaviour in large-scale statistical studies, and at the micro level, to identify, in carefully constructed case studies, the processes and mechanisms by which leaders and their people perceive and behave toward other countries.

The Kantian Peace Revisited

As explained above, democracy alone is not sufficient for peace in Kant's vision. The relationship of all three elements of that vision—democracy, trade, and international organizations (IOs)—among themselves, and each with conflict—needs to be examined thoroughly. As Kant suggested, trade and IOs (especially IOs composed largely of democracies) also reduce conflict between states. Democracy, trade, and IOs are more likely to flourish in an environment of peaceful relations. Democracies typically trade more with each other than with autocracies; democracies and trading partners are more likely to join IOs.[39] In recent decades, more countries have become democratic, international trade has reached higher levels as a proportion of countries' income, and IOs have become stronger and more inclusive. A graphic image of the Kantian vision of an international society, very unlike Hobbes's realist depiction of a war of all against all, is sustained by a complex set of mutually supporting relationships. This complexity is shown in figure 7.1.

Many of these relationships are well established. Not all countries are part of the Kantian system, but it has the capacity to expand over time, as governments and citizens come to see its benefits.[40] Yet another way of dealing with some of these questions is network analysis, which, especially after Maoz's *Networks of Nations*, has been used widely and productively.[41]

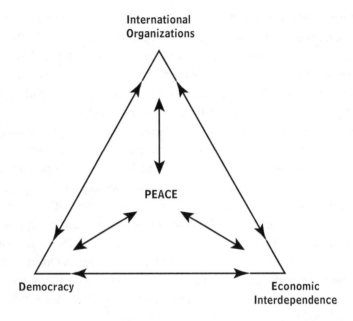

International
Organizations

PEACE

Democracy

Economic
Interdependence

FIGURE 7.1. *The Kantian triangle.*

The weakest links are mostly related to those to or from IOs, partly because of technical difficulties with model specification and partly because the measures often do not distinguish well the functions of different IOs. Oneal and I recognized those limitations in *Triangulating Peace* but could not solve them. Much progress breaking down the categories of IOs and using them in new research has since been made by other authors who have worked to code IOs more appropriately, and many more to explore the effects of IOs.

Here I will concentrate on two relatively recent challenges, because earlier ones have been largely refuted or at least have led to clarification of the DP/ KP paradigm. One of these is Douglas Gibler's claim that sharing stable borders is more important than democracy in *The Territorial Peace: Borders, State Development, and International Conflict*.[42] However, much of his research has, in turn, been critiqued, with some of his data and analysis found not to be replicable.[43]

One of the most persistent challenges to the democratic peace has come in the form of an economic argument regarding the pacific effects of capitalism, international trade, and economic interdependence. This argument derives from the classical liberal tradition, which sees market forces as potentially beneficial and which stipulates that people involved in mutually beneficial economic processes are less likely to become involved in violent conflict because of a reluctance to disrupt those mutually beneficial processes. That is consistent with the Kantian peace position. However, Michael Mousseau insists that what might be seen as a partially defining aspect of 'democracy', namely the rule of law—especially regarding financial and other economic transactions—is the factor with the most important pacifying impact.[44] For some of Mousseau's earlier arguments and rebuttals, see Allan Dafoe and Russett, 'Does Capitalism Account for the Democratic Peace? The Evidence Still Says No', Dafoe, Oneal, and Russett, 'The Democratic Peace: Weighing the Evidence and Cautious Inference', and Dafoe and Kelsey, 'Observing the Capitalist Peace: Examining Market-Mediated Signaling and Other Mechanisms'.[45]

Mousseau has proposed various measures for this idea, but now focuses on 'contract intensity' within a society, as indicated by the value of life insurance contracts as a percentage of GNP. He argues that contract intensity causes both democracy and peace, thus rendering the correlation between democracy and peace spurious. This argument is dubious because his new measure of contract intensity is so complex as to make his theoretical argument implausible, since it depends on leaders, interest groups, and the general public in different states being able to consistently identify each other as 'contract intensive'. Moreover, his argument withstands empirical scrutiny only if a number of controversial theoretical and methodological issues are resolved in ways that allow him to completely disentangle 'democracy' and 'contract intensity' despite the distinct possibility that they are inextricably intertwined. *Conflict Management and Peace Science* has published the latest version of Mousseau's endeavour, with the theoretical and methodological issues addressed in the same issue by James Ray and Dafoe; thus, the debate continues.[46]

I have not yet discussed Joanne Gowa's past and current work because her chapter in this book provides an opportunity to address both. I start with two positive remarks. First, we agree on one fundamental principle: the democratic peace is not an empirical law, nor is it intended to be. It is a probability statement to which there will be exceptions. International relations research cannot, and should not, make claims to non-trivial 'laws'. Second, and more important, is that research must take into account changes in the structure of the international system, and this is the dominant and consistent theme of her critiques of the DP—but it is not enough.

Gowa has consistently held that the DP cannot be found in certain historical periods, and that is the essential argument in Henry Farber and Gowa (1997), and Gowa (1999), especially chapter 4, co-authored with Farber.[47] The best support for this is that there is no evidence for a lower rate of armed conflict for democracies than for other pairs of states before World War I. However, it is hardly surprising if one remembers that the franchise in many countries was sharply restricted. We will recall from earlier in the chapter that, in the US at that time, women could vote only in a few states and, contrary to the intent of the 15th Amendment to the US Constitution, measures to prevent blacks from voting were common. The UK likewise limited women's rights to vote and hold public office, and also had restrictions based on property and place of residence. Many other European democracies limited women's voting rights. The standard Polity IV scoring of regime type (used by both Gowa and myself) does not reflect these historical changes. This matters because there is no reason to expect women and other restricted voters to hold the same attitudes toward war as those who could vote. In fact, they are usually more dovish.[48]

In this book, Gowa and colleagues continue the effort to find changes in the effect of democracy by focusing on the differences during and then after the Cold War. Unfortunately for their argument, the post-Cold War years they analyse run only from 1992 to 2005, a relatively short period from which to generalize (see their note to figure 8.7 and figure 8.7 itself), contra their claim to be analysing the post-Cold War period between 1992 and 2010. In fact, the necessary data to run their analysis to 2010 were available when their chapter was completed.

Their multivariate analysis raises several questions about the choice of variables. A serious problem arises with their use of Polity scores, which is a bit opaque. Instead of using Polity's full scale from 0 to +10 for the democratic scale and to −10 for authoritarian states, they combine all states from +7 to +10 as democratic and make a similar combination for the most autocratic states. This reduction of a continuous variable to two binary scores loses important information, notably for all the states in the large middle sector. A second problem arises from their measurement of national power by the Correlates of War's National Capabilities scores, which over-weights population and so exaggerates the power of China and the USSR. A more relevant index would have been GDP or military spending.[49] Perhaps the oddest thing about this chapter is that, although figure 8.7 appears to be derived from a multiple regression equation, we never see a table of co-efficients and their error ranges per standard operating procedure in the field. Finally, there is no reference to a replication site where a reader can check the data and computations (see point 2 in the introduction above). With all these problems, the verdict on Gowa and Pratt's chapter must be the Scottish 'not proven'.

Conclusion

In sum, the democratic peace/Kantian peace has been heavily critiqued and refined, but not overturned. Still, much more work needs to be done by academic advocates and critics to uncover robust mechanisms, develop better data, and come up with stronger research designs that allow for more confident inference. The Kantian vision of an international society, very unlike Hobbes's image of a war of all against all, is sustained by a complex set of mutually supporting relationships. Not all countries are yet part of it. The Kantian peace might be unravelled by wars between great powers and/ or a global depression deeper than the recent recession and near stagnation. Scholars and practitioners must persist. One of my mentors in college, William Parker, had a plaque on his desk saying, 'Every good thing must be renewed each day.'

Notes

1. I thank Joshua R. Goodman (Yale graduate student) for his excellent stylistic and substantive editing on this chapter.
2. The literature on this topic is enormous, so with a few exceptions I have limited this review to work employing or seriously engaging with quantitative research. That segment alone is also enormous, so the review is also selective, but I hope it includes representatives of most of those that have been prominent.
3. Clarence K. Streit, *Union Now* (London: J. Cape, 1939).
4. Dean Babst, 'Elective Governments—A Force for Peace,' *The Wisconsin Sociologist* 3, no. 1 (1964): 9–14.
5. Melvin Small and J. David Singer, 'The War-Proneness of Democratic Regimes, 1816–1965,' *Jerusalem Journal of International Relations* 1, no. 4 (1976): 50–69.
6. A good review of the early development of this debate, including Rudolph J. Rummel's considerable contribution to the claim that domestic structures matter greatly, is in chapters 2 to 4 of his *Power Kills: Democracy as a Method of Nonviolence* (Piscataway, NJ: Transaction, 1997). His first journal article with a relevant statistical analysis was 'Dimensions of Conflict Behaviour,' *Journal of Conflict Resolution* 10, no. 1 (1966): 65–73.
7. The principal European critics have come from the Peace Research Institute Frankfurt. A relatively early example is Anna Geis, Lothar Brock, and Harald Müller, eds., *Democratic Wars: Looking at the Dark Side of Democratic Peace* (London: Palgrave Macmillan, 2006). It too often critically cites actions by the United States at the expense of rigorous comparative analysis. A better book, but still with the same flaws, is A. Geis, H. Müller, and N. Schörnig, eds., *The Militant Face of Democracy: Liberal Forces for Good* (Cambridge: Cambridge University Press, 2013).
8. Fred Chernoff, *Explanation and Progress in Security Studies: Bridging Theoretical Divides in International Relations* (Stanford: Stanford University Press, 2014), 240. Chernoff covers many of the debates discussed here along with others. This book deserves close attention.
9. Michael W. Doyle, 'Kant, Liberal Legacies, and Foreign Affairs,' parts I and II, *Philosophy & Public Affairs* 12, nos. 3 and 4 (1983): 205–235, 323–353; M.W. Doyle, 'Liberalism and World Politics,' *American Political Science Review* 80, no. 4 (1986): 1151–69.
10. Immanuel Kant, *Perpetual Peace: A Philosophical Sketch*, trans T. Humphrey (Indianapolis, IN: Hackett, 1970 [1795]).
11. Zeev Maoz and Nasrin Abdolali, 'Regime Types and International Conflict, 1816–1976,' *Journal of Conflict Resolution* 33, no. 1 (1989): 3–35.
12. Zeev Maoz and Bruce Russett, 'Alliance, Contiguity, Wealth, and Political Stability: Is the Lack of Conflict among Democracies a Statistical Artifact?' *International Interactions* 17, no. 3 (1992): 245–67; Zeev Maoz and Bruce Russett, 'Normative and Structural Causes of Democratic Peace, 1946–1986,' *American Political Science Review* 87, no. 3 (1993): 624–38; Bruce Russett, *Grasping the Democratic Peace: Principles for a Post-Cold War World* (Princeton. NJ: Princeton University Press, 1993).

13. David Rousseau, *Democracy and War: Institutions, Norms, and the Evolution of International Conflict* (Stanford: Stanford University Press, 2005).

14. Charles Boehmer, Erik Gartzke, and Timothy Nordstrom, 'Do Intergovernmental Organizations Promote Peace?' *World Politics* 57, no. 1 (2004): 1–38; Jon C. Pevehouse and Bruce Russett, 'Democratic International Governmental Organizations Promote Peace,' *International Organization* 60, no. 4 (2006): 969–1000; Jon C. Pevehouse, *Democracy from Above: Regional Organizations and Democratization* (Cambridge: Cambridge University Press, 2005); Daniela Donno, 'Who Is Punished? Regional Intergovernmental Organizations and the Enforcement of Democratic Norms,' *International Organization* 64, no. 4 (2010): 593–625; and Daniela Donno, *Defending Democratic Norms: International Actors and the Politics of Electoral Misconduct* (Oxford: Oxford University Press, 2013).

15. Joshua S. Goldstein, *Winning the War on War: The Decline of Armed Conflict Worldwide* (London: Penguin, 2011).

16. Dan Reiter and Allan C. Stam, *Democracies at War* (Princeton, NJ: Princeton University Press, 2002).

17. Bruce Bueno de Mesquita, Alastair Smith, Randolph Siverson, and James Morrow, *The Logic of Political Survival* (Cambridge, MA: MIT Press, 2003).

18. Jessica L.P. Weeks, 'Strongmen and Straw Men: Authoritarian Regimes and the Initiation of International Conflict,' *American Political Science Review* 106, no. 2 (2012): 326–47.

19. James D. Fearon, 'Domestic Political Audiences and the Escalation of International Disputes,' *American Political Science Review* 88, no. 3 (1994): 577–92.

20. Kenneth A. Schultz, *Democracy and Coercive Diplomacy* (Cambridge: Cambridge University Press, 2001).

21. Steven Pinker, *The Better Angels of Our Nature: The Decline of Violence in History and its Causes* (London: Penguin, 2011).

22. Michael R. Tomz and Jessica L.P. Weeks, 'Public Opinion and the Democratic Peace,' *American Political Science Review* 10, no. 4 (2013): 849–65.

23. Rachel M. Stein, 'War and Revenge: Explaining Conflict Initiation by Democracies,' *American Political Science Review* 109, no. 3 (2015): 556–73.

24. Thomas Piketty, *Capital in the Twenty-first Century* (Cambridge, MA: Belknap, 2014).

25. David Kinsella, 'No Rest for the Democratic Peace,' *American Political Science Review* 99, no. 3 (2005): 453–57.

26. William J. Dixon, 'Democracy and the Peaceful Settlement of International Conflict,' *American Political Science Review* 88, no. 1 (1994): 14–32.

27. Charles Lipson, *Reliable Partners: How Democracies Have Made a Separate Peace* (Princeton, NJ: Princeton University Press, 2013).

28. Rummel, *Power Kills*.

29. Consequently, John Oneal and I refer to our specification as liberal/realist.

30. Paul K. Huth and Todd L. Allee, *The Democratic Peace and Territorial Conflict in the Twentieth Century* (Cambridge: Cambridge University Press, 2002).

31. Edward D. Mansfield and Jack Snyder, *Electing to Fight: Why Emerging Democracies Go to War.* (Cambridge, MA: MIT Press, 2005).

32. John R. Oneal, Bruce Russett, and Michael L. Berbaum, 'Causes of Peace: Democracy, Interdependence, and International Organizations, 1885–1992,' *International Studies Quarterly* 47, no. 3 (2003): 371–93.

33. Vipin Narang and Rebecca M. Nelson, 'Who Are These Belligerent Democratizers? Reassessing the Impact of Democratization on War,' *International Organization* 63, no. 2 (2009): 357–79.

34. Nils Petter Gleditsch and Håvard Hegre, 'Peace and Democracy: Three Levels of Analysis,' *Journal of Conflict Resolution* 41, no. 2 (1997): 283–310.

35. Kristian Skrede Gleditsch, *All International Politics Is Local: The Diffusion of Conflict, Integration, and Democratization* (Ann Arbor, MI: University of Michigan Press, 2009). Also see Lars-Erik Cederman's work on diffusion as in *Emergent Actors in World Politics: How States and Nations Develop and Dissolve* (Princeton: Princeton University Press, 1997) and, most recently, Ewan Harrison and Sara McLaughlin Mitchell, *The Triumph of Democracy and the Eclipse of the West* (London: Palgrave Macmillan, 2014).

36. Patrick James, Eric Solberg, and Murray Wolfson, 'An Identified Systemic Model of the Democracy and Peace Nexus,' *Defence and Peace Economics* 10, no. 1 (1999): 1–37; John R. Oneal and Bruce Russett, 'Why "An Identified Systemic Analysis of the Democracy-Peace Nexus" Does Not Persuade,' *Defence and Peace Economics* 11, no. 1 (2000): 197–214; and Patrick James, Eric Solberg, and Murray Wolfson, 'Democracy and Peace: Reply to Oneal and Russett,' *Defence and Peace Economics* 11, no. 1 (2000): 215–229.

37. Bruce Russett and John R. Oneal, *Triangulating Peace: Democracy, Interdependence, and International Organizations* (New York: Norton, 2001).

38. Håvard Hegre, John R. Oneal, and Bruce Russett, 'Trade Does Promote Peace: New Simultaneous Estimates of the Reciprocal Effects of Trade on Conflict,' *Journal of Peace Research* 47, no. 6 (2010): 763–74.

39. Russett and Oneal, *Triangulating Peace.*

40. Lars-Erik Cederman, 'Back to Kant: Reinterpreting the Democratic Peace as a Macrohistorical Learning Process,' *American Political Science Review* 95, no. 1 (2001): 15–31; Lars-Erik Cederman and Kristian Skrede Gleditsch, 'Conquest and Regime Change: An Evolutionary Model of the Spread of Democracy and Peace,' *International Studies Quarterly* 48, no. 3 (2004): 603–29.

41. Zeev Maoz, *Networks of Nations: The Evolution, Structure, and Impact of International Networks, 1816–2001* (Cambridge: Cambridge University Press, 2010).

42. Douglas M. Gibler, *The Territorial Peace: Borders, State Development, and International Conflict* (Cambridge: Cambridge University Press, 2012).

43. Jae Park and Michael Colaresi, 'Safe Across the Border: The Continued Significance of the Democratic Peace When Controlling for Stable Borders,' *International Studies Quarterly* 58, no. 1 (2014): 118–25; and Douglas M. Gibler, 'Contiguous States, Stable

Borders, and the Peace Between Democracies,' *International Studies Quarterly* 58, no. 1 (2014): 126–29.

44. Michael Mousseau, 'The Democratic Peace Unraveled: It's the Economy!' *International Studies Quarterly* 57, no. 1 (2013): 186–97; Michael Mousseau, 'Grasping the Scientific Evidence: The Contractualist Peace Supersedes the Democratic Peace,' *Conflict Management and Peace Science* 75, no. 2 (2018): 175–92.

45. Allan Dafoe and Bruce Russett, 'Does Capitalism Account for the Democratic Peace? The Evidence Still Says No,' in *Assessing the Capitalist Peace*, eds. Nils Petter Gleditsch and Gerald Schneider (London: Routledge, 2013), 110–26.; Allan Dafoe, John R. Oneal, and Bruce Russett, 'The Democratic Peace: Weighing the Evidence and Cautious Inference,' *International Studies Quarterly* 57, no. 1 (2013): 201–14; and Allan Dafoe and Nina Kelsey, 'Observing the Capitalist Peace: Examining Market-Mediated Signaling and Other Mechanisms,' *Journal of Peace Research* 51, no. 5 (2014): 619–33.

46. Mousseau, 'Grasping the Scientific Evidence'; James Lee Ray and Allan Dafoe, 'Democratic Peace versus Contractualism,' *Conflict Management and Peace Science* 35, no. 2 (2018): 193–203.

47. Henry S. Farber and Joanne Gowa, 'Common Interests or Common Polities? Reinterpreting the Democratic Peace,' *The Journal of Politics* 59, no. 2 (1997): 393–417; and Joanne Gowa, *Ballots and Bullets: The Elusive Democratic Peace* (Princeton, NJ: Princeton University Press, 1999).

48. Carole K. Chaney, R. Michael Alvarez, and Jonathan Nagler, 'Explaining the Gender Gap in US Presidential Elections, 1980–1992,' *Political Research Quarterly* 51, no. 2 (1998): 311–39.

49. William Nordhaus, John R. Oneal, and Bruce Russett, 'The Effects of the International Security Environment on National Military Expenditures: A Multicountry Study,' *International Organization* 66, no. 1 (2012): 491–513.

8.

The Democratic-Peace Debate

Joanne Gowa and Tyler Pratt

Introduction

Students of international relations have engaged in a long and heated debate about democratic-peace theory. Many among them now take for granted the idea that democracies are less likely to engage each other in conflict than are members of other country pairs. Mansfield and Snyder, for example, observe that the theory has become 'an axiom for many scholars'.[1] Savun and Tirone describe the theory as 'one of the most well-established findings in international relations'.[2] Dafoe agrees, labelling the existence of a democratic peace as among 'the most thoroughly established empirical relationships in international relations'.[3]

Even a casual inspection, however, makes clear that a sizeable number of sceptics remain. Some among them express qualms about the integrity of the theory itself. Although they regard the empirical evidence as consistent with it, they nonetheless consider its theoretical foundations fragile. Baum and Potter, for example, view democratic-peace theory as largely a 'post hoc explanation for empirical findings'.[4] Chan believes that 'observations of empirical regularities' have 'tended to precede explicit theories to explain them'.[5] Joining the choir, Gates, Knutsen, and Moses conclude that 'no agreed-upon explanation has been devised which can account for the statistical relationship between regime type and bellicosity'.[6]

Other sceptics argue that the theory rests on fragile empirical foundations.

Erik Gartzke contends that high levels of trade and capital flows have produced what is a capitalist rather than a democratic peace.[7] Patrick McDonald regards the supporting evidence as 'so weak that it is largely nonexistent.'[8] Steven Pinker notes that wars have become exceedingly rare among all major developed countries (not just democracies) since 1945.[9] Michael Mousseau concludes that 'economic norms, specifically contractualist' economies, explain both democracy and conflict rates.[10] Farber and Gowa find that cross-dyadic dispute rates shift with the structure of the international system.[11,12]

Whether a democratic peace exists matters both within the ivory tower and outside of it. Students of international relations have long debated the relative explanatory power of different theories about state behaviour. Democratic-peace theory delivers a severe blow to the 'third image' interpretation that Kenneth Waltz, among others, argues trumps theories based on leader characteristics or domestic regime types.[13] Realist theory maintains that international systems determine state behaviour. The premise of democratic-peace theory, in contrast, is that politics within rather than between countries plays the dominant role. It exemplifies what Waltz long ago referred to as 'second image' theory, in which state behaviour is a function of politics at home rather than the pressures the international system exerts.[14]

Democratic-peace theory is also one of the rare instances in which an idea has crossed the equivalent of the blood-brain barrier between academics and policymakers. A 2014 survey of current and former US national security officials, for example, finds that more than 60 percent of them believe in democratic-peace theory.[15] Some among them occupy positions at the pinnacle of power. UK Prime Minister Margaret Thatcher, for example, urged former Soviet bloc members to democratize because 'democracies don't go to war with each other.'[16] US President Bill Clinton argued that foreign policy should support the adoption of democracy abroad because 'democracies don't attack each other.'[17] George W. Bush agreed with his predecessor, pointing out that democracies 'don't go to war with each other.'[18]

Because of the importance of democratic-peace theory, we first examine the extent to which a consensus about it actually exists. Based on the evidence we describe below, we find that a large majority of academics do indeed believe that a democratic peace exists. This review also revealed a striking finding about the empirical foundations of the theory: the data it relies upon are highly skewed toward the bipolar era. This asymmetry implies that Cold War era observations dominate the findings of democratic-peace studies irrespective of whether an analysis also includes the years before or after it. Below, therefore, we reanalyse the data, taking explicitly into account shifts between international systems. We find no evidence of a separate peace among democratic states after the Cold War, and we conclude by discussing the implications of this chapter for democratic-peace theory.

The Status of the Democratic Peace

We evaluate the views of students of international relations about democratic-peace theory using three approaches. First, we review all the articles about the democratic peace that the ten most highly regarded journals in political science published in the last fifteen years. Then, we present the results of a 2016 survey that asked faculty specializing in international relations whether they believe that a democratic peace exists. Finally, we interrogate the views of the authors of the almost 200 papers that cite Jack Levy's now classic statement that the democratic peace is the 'closest thing we have to an empirical law in international relations'.[19] All three sources converge on the same conclusion: approximately two-thirds of academics agree that a democratic peace exists.

Drawing on the work of Garand and Giles, we first selected the ten most influential peer-reviewed journals that publish articles in international relations.[20] They are the *American Political Science Review* (APSR), *American Journal of Political Science* (AJPS), *Journal of Politics* (JOP), *World Politics* (WP), *International Organization* (IO), *British Journal of Political Science* (BJPS), *International Studies Quarterly* (ISQ), *Journal of Conflict Resolution* (JCR), *International Security* (IS), and *Journal of Peace Research* (JPR).

We reviewed all research articles that appeared in these journals between 2000 and 2015 that referred at least once to democratic-peace theory. To identify them, we searched for the term 'democratic peace' using the home website of each journal. With two exceptions, we include all articles that our search produced. First, we exclude articles that mention the democratic peace only in passing—for example, they cite a reference to democratic-peace theory but do not otherwise discuss it. Second, we exclude references to related concepts (e.g., the 'domestic democratic peace') that do not directly address the impact of regime type on the probability of interstate disputes.

We identified 265 unique scholarly articles that reference the democratic peace. The sample includes both empirical analyses and papers that do not present original empirical evidence but do refer to the democratic peace as a theory or empirical regularity. The 265 articles represent an average of approximately 1.6 articles per journal per year since 2000. Thirty-nine of them (14.7 percent) subject the democratic-peace hypothesis to large-N empirical tests. Figure 8.1 displays the distribution of the articles across the ten most influential journals.

We divide the papers into two groups: (1) theoretical or conceptual papers and (2) empirical studies. For each group, we determine whether the authors express confidence in democratic-peace theory. We first create a dichotomous variable, DISSENT, which is equal to one if an article cites at least one paper sceptical about the existence of a democratic peace and is zero otherwise. By design, this is a very low threshold that is biased against finding support for the theory. We create another dummy variable, GRANTED, that takes a value of one if the article depicts the democratic peace as an established and unchallenged fact.

Our review of the 226 theoretical or conceptual articles reveals strong and widespread confidence in the democratic-peace hypothesis. These articles are unlikely to cite sceptics of the democratic peace: more than 60 percent fail to provide any reference to papers critical of the democratic peace (DISSENT = 0). In addition, almost a third (32 percent) of the conceptual articles portray the democratic peace as a finding that enjoys universal acceptance (GRANTED = 1).

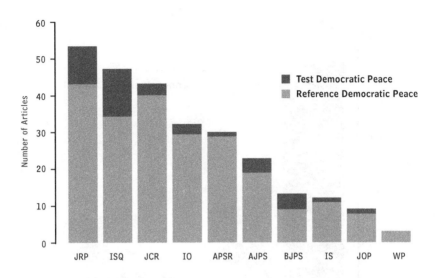

FIGURE 8.1. The total number of democratic-peace articles in top ten journals, 2000–2015. The dark grey bars represent the number of articles that test the relationship between joint democracy and conflicts; other articles are in light grey.

In contrast, considerable heterogeneity exists among empirical studies. About 56 percent of the thirty-nine large-N studies we review report empirical results consistent with the democratic peace. The others find no evidence of an inverse relationship between democratic dyads and dispute rates. The vast majority of empirical studies (86 percent) cite at least one critic of the democratic peace, and very few (10 percent) regard the evidence as incontrovertible. Figure 8.2 shows the rates at which empirical and non-empirical articles cite democratic-peace sceptics (left column) and take the hypothesized empirical relationship for granted (right column). Thus, the academic literature about the democratic peace—and especially the set of academic articles that do not directly test democratic-peace theory—reveals a strong belief in the validity of the theory.

We also asked the administrators of the Teaching, Research, and International Policy (TRIP) polls to include a question in their February 2016 survey about beliefs in democratic-peace theory. The survey, sent to all international relations faculty at US colleges or universities, asked this question:

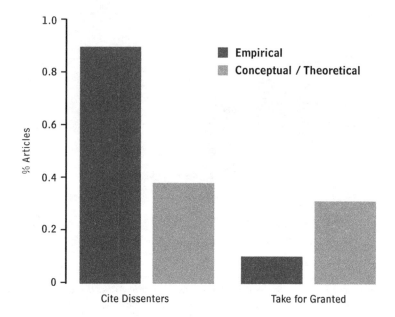

FIGURE 8.2. Percentage of empirical and theoretical papers that cite dissenters and take the existence of the democratic peace for granted.

A large body of research exists that supports the idea of a democratic peace—i.e., the idea that democracies are less likely to engage each other in military conflict than are members of other pairs of states. Do you agree with this view?

Respondents had a choice among three answers: (1) yes, consistently across time periods, (2) yes, in some time periods but not others, and (3) no, in no time periods. As figure 8.3 shows, about two-thirds (66 percent) of the 701 respondents indicated that they agreed with the democratic-peace hypothesis in all or some years. Among them, 80 percent chose the first option; the remainder opted for the second. Only about one-third of respondents agreed that no democratic peace existed in any time period.[21]

These results are consistent with a 2004 TRIP survey that asked respondents to indicate the five research programs they viewed as among the 'most

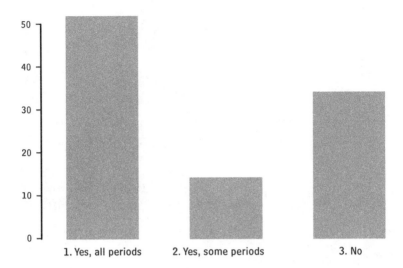

FIGURE 8.3. *Distribution of TRIP poll responses regarding agreement with the democratic peace. See text for full survey question. 1 = yes, consistently across time periods; 2 = yes, in some time periods but not others; 3 = no, in no time periods.*

productive controversies/research programs in international relations in recent years'. The democratic-peace debate was the most popular choice by a significant margin.[22] Almost half of the 827 respondents (48 percent) included the democratic peace among their top choices.

To gain further insight into the beliefs of scholars, we examine the sources that Google Scholar reports as citing Levy's now iconic statement that the democratic peace is 'as close as anything we have to an empirical law in international relations'.[23] This criterion selects papers that differ from those in our initial sample of academic articles. For example, some appeared before 1995 and some appeared in journals other than the top ten. We exclude books, which generally do not provide text for download, and articles written in languages other than English. We use a quantitative discourse model[24] to examine a three-sentence text string in the 175 articles returned in our search. The string includes the Levy quote and the sentences immediately before and after it. The model then uses the words

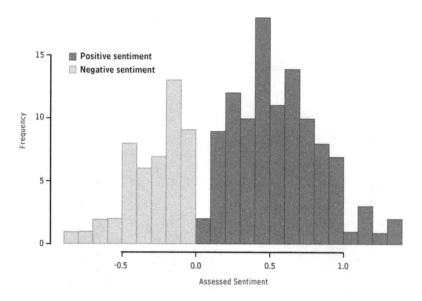

FIGURE 8.4. *Sentiment associated with the diffusion of Levy's statement on the democratic peace. Higher scores represent more positive sentiment (neutral sentiment = 0).*

in these text strings, along with a user-specified sentiment lexicon,[25] to assign a sentiment score to each quote. Negative sentiments, representing texts that disagree with the Levy quote, receive negative scores (< 0); neutral attitudes receive a 0; favourable sentiments receive a positive score.

The results of the sentiment analysis of the papers that cite the Levy quote are consistent with the other sources we used. Figure 8.4 shows the distribution of assessed sentiments for the 175 articles. Negative sentiments are displayed in light grey; positive sentiments are in dark grey. The x-axis records the sentiment score assigned to each article. The more strongly an article endorses the quote, the higher the positive score it receives. The y-axis indicates the number of articles that received the same score. Note that the number of papers that receive a positive score is more than twice as high as the number that are coded as expressing negative views. Fully 70 percent of the papers express positive sentiments. As a whole, then, the available evidence is consistent with a strong consensus among political scientists that a democratic peace exists.

The Data

In addition to allowing us to assess scholarly opinion about democratic-peace theory, our literature review gave us the data necessary to assess the empirical foundations of the theory. Our investigation of the evidence revealed an important feature of the data that, to our knowledge, has never before been reported. Not surprisingly, we found that each of the thirty-nine empirical articles in our review includes either all or most observations from the Cold War era. A substantial number of them also include years before and after the Cold War. Figure 8.5 depicts the years each study includes, indicating that the evidence extends from 1816 to 2003.

Examining the distribution of country dyads from 1816 to 2003 makes it clear, however, that the distribution of observations across time is extremely uneven. Figure 8.6 recreates the previous plot but transforms the time period each study includes to a distribution of dyadic observations per year. It shows that more than fourteen times as many observations exist in

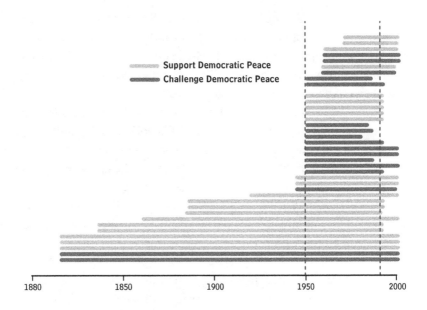

FIGURE 8.5. *Time coverage of democratic-peace studies reviewed. Time period examined in thirty-nine prominent empirical studies. The vertical dotted lines demarcate the Cold War era.*

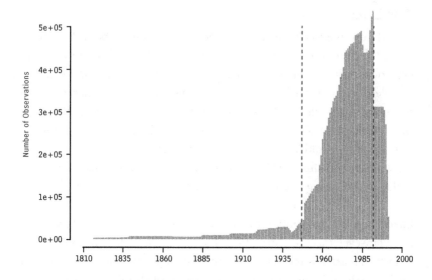

FIGURE 8.6. *The distribution of country pairs in democratic-peace studies.*

an average year during the East–West conflict than before 1914. The skew exists because almost all analyses of democratic-peace theory employ a dyad-year as the unit of analysis—that is, an observation records whether the members of a country pair in a given year engaged each other in a dispute. Between 1816 and 1914, the total number of dyad-years is about 55,000. During the Cold War (1950–1991), the corresponding statistic is about 337,000. The difference between them is attributable primarily to the large increase in independent states that post-war decolonization produced and to a relative dearth of post-Cold War evidence. As the figure shows, findings about the relationship between polities and peace depend heavily on the patterns that prevailed during the Cold War period, irrespective of the time period they nominally include, making the bipolar era the empirical core of democratic-peace theory.

This implies that there may be more variation in the extent to which the democratic peace prevails across time than studies that include the Cold War era suggest. That this is so is evident from the relatively rare cases in which analysts disaggregate the data in order to study the impact of changes in the international system on patterns of cross-dyadic disputes. Studies that examine only the years preceding 1914, for example, find no evidence of a democratic peace.[26] Pooling the pre-1914 years with the Cold War years, however, reproduces the conventional wisdom.[27] The difference is due to the overwhelming number of observations that originate in the bipolar world relative to its multipolar predecessor.

Here, we complement existing studies with an analysis of whether the effect of joint democracy also varies between the bipolar era and its unipolar successor. To do so, we use an empirical specification that is common in the literature to gauge whether the effect of joint democracy on conflict changes during this period. We estimate a separate model for each year of the post-war era using eleven-year rolling time windows.[28] We make use of data that has recently become available that allow us to study the period between 1992 and 2010. Previous studies of the post-Cold War era end in 2001.[29]

As is the industry standard, an observation in our dataset is a record of whether a dispute begins between two states in a given year. Some analyses of the democratic peace include only 'politically relevant' dyads—that is, country pairs that include either a major power or contiguous states.[30] Including only these country pairs reduces the size of the 1950–2010 sample by about 90 percent and the number of disputes by about one quarter. It also results in a 16 percent drop in democratic dyads and an increase of about 3 percent in the rate at which members of autocratic dyads engage each other in disputes. Given the potential of an arbitrarily defined 'politically relevant' sample to bias the findings about dyads and disputes, we include all country pairs in our analyses.[31]

The dependent variable is the onset of a militarized interstate dispute (MID). As is common in the literature,[32] we use volume 4.1 of the Correlates of War project to record the occurrence of a MID, defined as an overt, government-sanctioned 'threat, display or use of military force' by one state against 'the government, official representatives, official forces, property, or territory of another state'.[33] As Russett notes in his contribution to this volume, it is common to include all MIDS rather than just wars. Wars, he observes, are 'relatively rare phenomena, but the generalization also applies as a strong probability for the many lower-level militarized disputes with far fewer casualties'.[34] Democracies, he notes, 'are quite unlikely to engage in any kind of militarized disputes with other democracies'.[35]

We record the onset of MIDs because the democratic-peace debate is about the incidence rather than the duration of conflict. We code subsequent observations of the same dispute between members of a given country pair as zeroes.[36] A dichotomous variable takes on a value of one when two countries first become involved in a MID and is zero otherwise. There are 1612 MIDs in the Cold War sample, a dispute incidence of 0.48 percent. During the post-Cold War period, the corresponding statistics are 827 and 0.32 percent.

We use the Polity IV database 'commonly used to generate measures of democracy'[37] to record the regime type of a state.[38] Polity scores reflect the 'competitiveness of political participation, the openness and competitiveness of executive recruitment, and the level of constraints on the chief executives' in each year.[39] Information about polity type exists for about 96 percent of the observations in the sample. When data are missing, it is commonly because states have populations of less than 500,000, the level required to gain entry into Polity IV. In 1980, for example, polity type is missing for such states as the Bahamas, Barbados, Iceland, and St. Lucia.

The dataset assigns governments an annual score ranging between zero and ten on each of the democracy and autocracy scales. This produces 'a single regime score that ranges from +10 (full democracy) to –10 (full autocracy)'.[40] We define a polity as democratic if it scores at least a seven on the democracy scale. This means that a state is designated a democracy here only if it has a 'highly coherent set of institutional structures', including a competitive polity, an elected leader, and constraints on executive power'.[41] This measure excludes any government that Jaggers and Gurr regard as 'particularly vulnerable' to regime reversal[42] or that Mansfield and Snyder code as 'democratizing'.[43] It codes cases of foreign 'interruption'— e.g., occupied states—as missing.[44]

We code a country pair as jointly democratic in year *t* if each of its members scores at least a seven on the Polity IV scale in that year.[45] We distinguish democratic dyads from two other types of country pairs. Mixed dyads are country pairs in which one state is a democracy and the other is not. We separate these dyads here because the waging of the Cold War involved a large number of proxy wars. Previous studies also report that the rate at which members of these dyads engage each other in MIDs differs from that of both democratic and nondemocratic country pairs.[46] Nondemocratic dyads—that is, pairs of states that both score below seven—compose the base group. A negative and significant coefficient on only those dyads that include two democracies is consistent with the existence of a democratic peace.

We include a range of control variables to account for potential confounders. They include whether states in a dyad are contiguous. Using the COW Direct Contiguity dataset (version 3.0),[47] we code states in a dyad as contiguous if they share a land border or if 150 miles or less of water separates them. The limited ability of almost all states to project power suggests that disputes are more likely to occur between states that are relatively close to each other. Indeed, between 1950 and 1991, about 2.7 percent of dyads include contiguous states, yet these dyads account for more than half of all disputes.

Three variables control for the relative power of states. Two dichotomous variables indicate whether one or both members of a dyad are major powers. As is well known, major powers have a relatively high propensity to engage each other, as well as relatively small states, in conflict. We define the set of major powers here in accord with the COW project.[48] It labels Britain, China, France, Germany, Russia, and the US as being major powers during the entire post-war period, while Japan joins as of 1991. During the Cold War, members of country pairs that include either one or two major powers engage each other in disputes more than seven times as often as do dyads in which neither state is a major power. Although dyads that include at least one major power represent only about 8 percent of the sample, they account for about 36 percent of MIDs.

Another power variable uses the National Material Capabilities dataset (version 3.02) to construct a measure of relative power using the composite index of national capability scores (CINC).[49] To construct a dyadic measure of relative power, we take the ratio of the larger state's capability index to the sum of both states' indices in year t. This variable ranges in value from 0.5 to 0.99. As the power ratio increases, disputes should decline, as the outcome of any conflict becomes easier for the states involved to forecast.

We also control for alliance memberships. Using the COW dataset on formal alliances,[50] we construct two variables to represent alliances: the first takes on a value of one if a defence pact joins dyad members and is zero otherwise; the second takes on a value of one if states participate only in lower-level alliances—e.g., ententes, neutrality agreements, or nonaggression pacts. Defence pacts account for almost 90 percent of all alliance dyad-years during the Cold War, occurring in almost 8 percent of dyad-years between 1950 and 2010. The corresponding statistic for lower-level alliances is about 3 percent. Although it seems likely ex ante that defence pacts exert stronger effects on conflict rates than do other alliance ties, we let the data address this question.

Figure 8.7 displays the results of a logistic regression model that estimates the effect of joint democracy on the likelihood of a MID from 1950–2010.[51] For each year in the 1955–2005 time period, we subset the data to include the five previous and five subsequent years, for a time span of $(t - 5)$ to $(t + 5)$. The figure shows the estimated effect of joint democracy on the probability of a MID. Confidence intervals are obtained via quasi-Bayesian Monte Carlo simulations. It makes clear that the conventional wisdom is correct during the bipolar era: joint democracy tends to exert a negative and significant impact on the probability of a MID. Thereafter, however, it exerts either no effect on the likelihood of a dispute or its effect is actually positive.

The contrast that is evident during and after the Cold War shows that regime type does not have the consistent effect that democratic-peace theory posits. Figure 8.7 shows clearly that its impact varies across the bipolar and unipolar worlds. As we noted above, earlier studies show that a difference also exists between the Cold War era and the multipolar world that

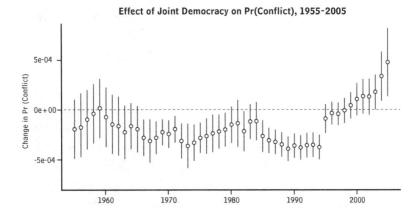

FIGURE 8.7. *Effect of joint democracy on conflict, 1955–2005. The plot shows the estimated effect of joint democracy on MIDs for each year in the 1955–2005 time period. Data are from 1950–2010; point estimates for the years 1955–2005 are obtained using observations within an eleven-year rolling window. Ninety-five percent confidence intervals are obtained via quasi-Bayesian Monte Carlo simulations.*

preceded it. These studies imply that the pattern of cross-dyadic dispute rates corresponds to shifts in the international system, a finding that challenges the core of democratic-peace theory. Existing explanations for the pacifying effect of democracy cannot account for these significant changes over time, suggesting the theory does not rest on strong theoretical foundations. We turn next to examine these foundations in detail.

Dispute Settlement: War and Peace

In the literature about war, the prevailing wisdom is that all states, not just democracies, prefer to settle disputes between themselves peacefully rather than engage in an armed contest.[52] The logic is simple. Fighting a war burns resources, reducing the size of the pie that is at stake in the conflict. Thus, states are better off if they can agree upon a peaceful division of the pie between them. Their ability to reach an agreement depends on the width of the bargaining range—i.e., the set of negotiated outcomes both sides prefer to a costly war—that exists between them. The larger the bargaining range, the easier it should be for states to resolve the issue in dispute without recourse to armed conflict. Problems of information and credibility can preclude successful agreements despite the existence of a feasible pre-war bargain.

Formally, the width of the bargaining range is the distance between the expected utilities that accrue to each state if it engages another state in war. The expected utility of war to State A is the sum of three quantities: (1) the probability, p, that it wins the war times the value of the pie it gains control over; (2) the probability it loses the war $(1 - p)$ times the utility of doing so; and (3) the cost, ca, it incurs in waging the war. Suppose, for example, the winning state receives a value of one and the losing state receives zero. Then, the expected utility of State A to fighting the war is $p \times 1 + (1 - p) \times 0 - c_a$ or $(p - c_a)$. By analogy, the expected utility to State B of fighting the war is $p \times 0 + (1 - p) \times 1 - c_b$ or $(1 - p - c_b)$. Thus, any peaceful division of the pie that lies between $(p - c_a)$ and $(1 - p - c_b)$ makes both states better off than the expected utility the states would gain if they engaged each other in war. This makes clear that as the costs of war rise, the bargaining range expands, increasing the set of peaceful settlements that both states would prefer to war.[53]

In this framework, the argument that democracies face higher costs of war than do other states is equivalent to the claim that a larger bargaining range exists between them, all else equal, than it does between the members of other country pairs. As a result, democracies have more opportunities to reach a peaceful settlement between themselves than do other states. Democratic-peace theorists frequently point to two reasons to explain why this is so. The first is that checks-and-balances systems prevail in democracies, requiring their leaders to gain the assent of the governed before they wage war, since their tenure in office depends on public support. The resources that they must expend to do so raise the costs of going to war relative to a system in which the ruling group is small and tightly knit.

In the democratic-peace literature, the relationship between a checks-and-balances system and the ability of leaders to wage war is almost invariably expressed in much the same language Kant used long ago. In states that are not republics, Kant observed, a decision to wage war is the 'easiest thing in the world to decide upon, because war does not require of the ruler, who is the proprietor and not a member of the state, the least sacrifice of the pleasure of his table, the chase, his country houses, his court functions, and the like'.[54] In democratic states, however, the leader is accountable to the voters that bear the costs of war, tying his hands in a way that has no counterpart in autocracies.

Based on what is essentially the Kantian logic, Kriner and Shen observe that 'one of the most important constraints on a democratic executive's freedom of action in the realm of military affairs is domestic political opinion'.[55] Because 'the public bears the human costs of war, they note, 'it is particularly sensitive to combat casualties—this assumption is implicit in virtually all international relations studies that assert differences in conflict behaviour between democracies and nondemocracies'.[56] Democratic leaders, therefore, will 'be loath to rush into conflict because the costs and even the outcome of war are—as Winston Churchill presciently warned—inscrutable'. This makes public opinion 'a critically important democratic brake on aggressive military policy'.[57] As a result, democratic leaders engaged in a dispute with each other recognize that neither is anxious to wage war. This expands the bargaining range and decreases the prospect that disputes between democracies will end in armed conflict.

Yet, as Kriner and Shen point out, the argument about checks and balances rests on what is more often than not a very tenuous assumption about the distribution of the costs of war across the population. The assumption is that the costs of fighting wars conform to 'long standing democratic norms of equality in military sacrifice'.[58] Because fighting a war produces a public 'bad', a robust basis exists for mass political protests against an unpopular war that can topple an elected leader and, in expectation, deter the leader from engaging in war.

This argument is more persuasive in theory than in practice, however. It assumes that democratic leaders do not act strategically—that is, they do not manipulate the extent to which the costs of war are distributed across the public. However, ample evidence exists that leaders can allocate the costs of war in a way that minimizes the risk of creating broad-based political opposition. In fact, the US citizens who have gone to war since

1945 are disproportionately from low-income communities.[59] This is so, in part, because the economic incentives to join the military are much more appealing to residents of low-income communities than to their counterparts in higher-income areas. Replacing conscription with a volunteer force is another way to dampen political opposition to an elected leader's decision to wage war.[60]

The allocation of personnel within the military reinforces these inequalities. The military distribution of labour relies on the logic of comparative advantage: it assigns more highly educated recruits to desk jobs distant from the front lines and assigns recruits with less education and fewer skills to the infantry. During the Korean War, for example, ground combat forces were 'mainly' composed of recruits from relatively low socioeconomic groups. The same process occurred during the Vietnam War: the 'relatively poor and less educated were more likely to end up in the infantry than in other branches of the military'.[61]

Together, these factors produce a 'casualty gap'—that is, 'a disparity in the concentration of wartime casualties among communities at different points on the socioeconomic ladder'.[62] This, in turn, loosens the political constraints that a checks-and-balances system imposes on leaders of democracies in theory. It does so because the skewed distribution of the costs of war undercuts the potential for the widespread and effective political backlash that is a basic premise of the checks-and-balances argument. As is well known, individuals from lower socioeconomic brackets are less likely to engage in political activity of all kinds than are their higher-income counterparts.

It is worth quoting Kriner and Shen at length on this point. While acknowledging that US citizens do react to wartime casualties by decreasing their support for military operations and political leaders, Kriner and Shen point out that the decline in support is not uniform across the population. Rather, the backlash is most intense among citizens who have experienced the costs of war most intimately through the lens of their local communities. Beginning with the Korean War, the casualty gap has concentrated these costs disproportionately in socioeconomically disadvantaged communities and insulated many other Americans from direct exposure to the human costs of war. Because residents of socioeconomically disadvantaged communities possess fewer of the resources needed to engage in politics, the casualty gap decreases the political pressure that is brought to bear on military policymakers to change course. If the casualty gap did not exist, swing voters in affluent parts of the country, which exhibit higher levels of political participation, would be more exposed to local casualties. So primed, our analyses suggest that these Americans would be more likely to raise concerns about the costs of America's war efforts and ratchet up the pressure on the nation's political leader.[63]

This process of cost-shifting is clearly neither new nor limited to the US. Because of the correlation between political participation and income,[64] the distribution of military exemptions politicians extend tends to favour higher income, better-educated members of the draft-age population. France, for example, pioneered the replacement system in 1793, allowing a potential conscript to supply a substitute to serve in his stead. Adopted by Sweden, Holland, Spain, Belgium, and other European countries, the French system supplied both the necessary troops and an 'alternative to propertied citizens who might otherwise resist conscription politically, avoid the draft altogether, or desert.'[65] During the Vietnam War, President Johnson decreased the measured intelligence level required to enter the armed services, partly to avoid drafting much more politically active college students.[66]

The ability of leaders to engage in strategic behaviour with respect to the socioeconomic composition of the military suggests that the bargaining range that exists between democracies may not be much larger than it is between other states. When strategic leaders can shift the costs of war onto citizens who are unlikely to possess the resources to organize political opposition to the war, the public is a much less powerful domestic brake on recourse to war than democratic-peace theory assumes. Moreover, as the process of fighting wars becomes more capital intensive, the number of infantries deployed shrinks accordingly. This, too, depresses public opposition to waging a war.

Democratic-peace theorists also underestimate the costs autocrats incur. Autocracies are typically assumed to lack the checks-and-balances mechanisms that characterize democracies. This presumably lowers their costs of going to war, narrowing the bargaining range and raising the probability of armed conflict between them. Their leaders are assumed to be much less vulnerable to the political pressure of their public at large, because their tenure in office does not depend upon the widespread support of those who bear the costs of waging a war. In short, they are not hostages to public opinion. As Jessica Weeks observes, 'the stereotypical autocrat in the international relations literature resembles Saddam Hussein or Kim Jong-il crushing domestic rivals and co-opting political institutions'.[67]

As Weeks points out, however, 'such despots are a minority among non-democratic leaders'.[68] Most autocratic leaders depend for their political survival on some coalition of elite supporters 'who act as audiences in much the same way as voting publics in democracies'.[69] 'Rivals-to-rule', in short, exist not only in democratic polities but in autocracies as well. Members of the leader's 'selectorate', or group of elite supporters, can effectively substitute for domestic political pressure if they can solve the coordination problem that overthrowing an incumbent leader requires. Their return on doing so, of course, can be higher for each member of the successful elite than for mass publics in democratic states. This, in turn, implies that the costs of engaging in war can also be quite high for leaders of autocracies.

For these reasons, the costs that confront democracies when they wage war against each other need not exceed the costs that autocrats absorb when they opt for recourse to armed force to settle a dispute between them. A priori, it is impossible to know that the bargaining range is uniformly wider when two democracies confront each other than when two autocracies do so.

Democratic Norms

The second major theoretical argument advanced in support of a democratic peace involves norms that operate in democratic political systems.[70] Norms are defined as 'rules for conduct that provide standards by which behaviour is approved or disapproved.[71] In the literature under review here, the norm that wields the principal explanatory power governs appropriate methods of resolving conflicts at home. According to Maoz and Russett, domestic norms influence international outcomes because states 'externalize . . . the norms of behaviour that are developed within and characterize their domestic political processes and institutions.[72] Thus, if a norm mandates the peaceful resolution of disputes within two states, it will also mandate the peaceful resolution of disputes between them.

Two aspects of this argument are murky. First, the mechanism that generates 'externalization' is opaque. The international environment differs from domestic political systems in fundamental ways that make behaviour in one context difficult to export to the other. In domestic systems, peace prevails because the state has the means to sanction unauthorized recourse to force among their populations. In contrast, the 'ordering principle' of the international system is anarchy.[73] This difference calls for caution about arguments that assume that domestic norms—and especially norms of peaceful conflict resolution—seamlessly transition to the international system.

A second issue that afflicts the use of norms to explain the existence of a democratic peace is whether they differ in any fundamental way from interests. The conclusion that norms and interests differ follows from the interpretation of norms that dominates the democratic-distinctiveness literature. However, norms can also be seen as reflections of interests because it is the expectation of external sanctions rather than internalized values that explains adherence to norms. As John Finley Scott maintains, for example, 'the learning of norms is never complete, and always involves expectations that sanctions will be applied. Thus even when norms are thoroughly learned, when moral commitment is strong and a sense of obligation is keenly felt, the maintenance of both conscience and conformity depends on the exercise of sanctions.[74]

Because interests drive norms, little, if any, distinction exists between them. Were this the interpretation adopted in the literature, the norm-based explanation could be rewritten in terms of the interests of states and the logic of their situations. The interests of states in a peaceful resolution of disputes, as opposed to armed conflict, would follow from the relative price of those options: bargaining is less costly than war. From this perspective, what seems problematic is not the interest of states in settling disputes short of war but their failure to do so.

This discussion, then, suggests that the norm-based explanation common in the literature is not necessarily distinct from the interest-based explanations advanced in realist theory. In the latter, interests are understood to be independent of the idiosyncrasies of the particular states involved. This implies in turn that the outcomes of armed disputes should not vary as a function of domestic regime type, consistent with empirical studies that find that the relationship between polities and peace varies across time.

Conclusion

Using a variety of sources and methods to establish the contemporary status of the democratic-peace literature, we find that a large majority of contributors to the literature, including, of course, Bruce Russett, continue to believe that democracies are significantly less likely to engage each other in conflict than are members of other country pairs. The existence of this widespread consensus has consequences, both within and outside of the ivory tower. As we observed at the outset, it affects both the research agenda that students of international relations pursue and the beliefs of national-security policymakers.

The evidence we present here, however, is inconsistent with the prevailing consensus. This is at least in part the result of the extent to which observations from the bipolar world dominate the evidence used to study the democratic peace. We show here that different cross-dyadic dispute-rate patterns exist across time, making clear that these patterns depend on shifts in the international system rather than on the regime type of the states involved. This implies that the two most common explanations of democratic-peace theory are not invulnerable to criticism. We hope that this chapter helps to inspire the existing consensus to crumble.

Notes

1. Edward D. Mansfield and Jack Snyder, 'Democratization and the Danger of War,' *International Security* 20, no. 1 (1995): 790.

2. Burcu Savun and Daniel C Tirone, 'Foreign Aid, Democratization, and Civil Conflict: How Does Democracy Aid Affect Civil Conflict?' *American Journal of Political Science* 55, no. 2 (2011): 234.

3. Allan Dafoe, 'Statistical Critiques of the Democratic Peace: Caveat Emptor,' *American Journal of Political Science* 55, no. 2 (2011): 259.

4. Matthew Baum and Philip Potter, *War and Democratic Constraint: How the Public Influences Foreign Policy* (Princeton: Princeton University Press, 2015), 43.

5. Steve Chan, 'In Search of Democratic Peace: Problems and Promise,' *Mershon International Studies Review* 41, no. 1 (1997): 62.

6. Scott Gates, Torbjørn L. Knutsen, and Jonathon W. Moses, 'Democracy and Peace: A More Skeptical View,' *Journal of Peace Research* 33, no. 1 (1996): 3.

7. Erik Gartzke, 'The Capitalist Peace,' *American Journal of Political Science* 51, no. 1 (2007): 167. See Dafoe, 'Statistical Critiques of the Democratic Peace' for a critical assessment of the Gartzke paper.

8. Patrick J. McDonald, 'Great Powers, Hierarchy, and Endogenous Regimes: Rethinking the Domestic Causes of Peace,' *International Organization* 69, no. 3 (2015): 558.

9. Steven Pinker, *The Better Angels of Our Nature: Why Violence Has Declined* (New York: Viking, 2011), 251. For a critique, see Bear Braumoeller, 'Systemic Trends in War and Peace,' this volume.

10. Michael Mousseau, 'Grasping the Scientific Evidence: The Contractualist Peace Supersedes the Democratic Peace,' *Conflict Management and Peace Science* 35, no. 2 (2018): 1.

11. Henry S. Farber and Joanne Gowa, 'Polities and Peace,' *International Security* 20, no. 2 (1995): 123–46.

12. Henry S. Farber and Joanne Gowa, 'Common Interests or Common Polities? Reinterpreting the Democratic Peace,' *The Journal of Politics* 59, no. 2 (1997): 393–417.

13. Kenneth N. Waltz, *Theory of International Politics* (NY: Norton, 1979).

14. Ibid.

15. Paul C. Avey and Michael C. Desch, 'What Do Policymakers Want From Us? Results of a Survey of Current and Former Senior National Security Decision Makers,' *International Studies Quarterly* 58, no. 2 (2014): 227–46.

16. Margaret Thatcher, 'Managing Conflict—The Role of International Intervention' (speech, Aspen, CO, August 4 1995), Margaret Thatcher Foundation, https://www.margaretthatcher.org/document/108346.

17. William J. Clinton, 'State of the Union Address' (speech, Washington, DC, January 25, 1994), *The Washington Post*, https://www.washingtonpost.com/wp-srv/politics/special/states/docs/sou94.htm. It is, of course, very hard to distinguish between cases in which policymakers actually believe what they say and cases in which they say what they believe will rally popular support for actions they take for reasons

that are orthogonal to democratic-peace theory. In both cases, however, the theory serves political ends.

18. George W. Bush, 'Transcript: President and Prime Minister Blair Discussed Iraq, Middle East' (Washington, DC, November 12, 2004), The White House, https://georgewbush-whitehouse.archives.gov/news/releases/2004/11/20041112-5.html.

19. Jack S. Levy, 'Domestic Politics and War,' in *The Origin and Prevention of Major Wars*, ed. Robert I. Rotberg and Theodore K. Rabb (Cambridge: Cambridge University Press, 1988), 88.

20. James C. Garand and Micheal W, Giles, 'Journals in the Discipline: A Report on a New Survey of American Political Scientists,' *Political Science and Politics* 36, no. 2 (2003): 293–308. Garand and Giles survey 565 political scientists to calculate a unique 'impact rating' for 115 political science journals. The rating is based on the combination into a single 'impact' score of subjective evaluations of journal quality and respondents' familiarity with the journal. The text lists the ten highest impact journals in order.

21. We are grateful to Mike Tierney, Sue Peterson, and the TRIPs team for including this question. For additional information, see trip.wm.edu/home/index.php/data/snap-polls.

22. For full survey results, see 'Teaching and research practices, views on the discipline, and policy attitudes of international relations faculty at US colleges and universities,' http://www.wm.edu/about/search/index.php?q=survey+resultshttp://www.wm.edu/offices/itpir/_documents/trip/trip_summary2005.pdf.

23. Levy, 'Domestic Politics and War,' 88. We searched Google Scholar for the terms 'Levy' and 'to an empirical law in international relations,' resulting in 293 unique results (including articles and books but excluding patents).

24. Tyler W. Rinker, 'qdap: Quantitative Discourse Analysis Package 2.3.0,' 2017, Buffalo, New York, ttp://github.com/trinker/qdap.

25. We use the 'subjectivity' lexicon described in Theresa Wilson, Janyce Wiebe, and Paul Hoffmann, 'Recognizing Contextual Polarity in Phrase-level Sentiment Analysis' (proceedings of the Conference on Human Language Technology and Empirical Methods in Natural Language Processing, 2005) 347-354.

26. For examples, see Maoz, Zeev, and Nasrin Abdolali, 'Regime Types and International Conflict, 1816-1976.' *Journal of Conflict Resolution* 33, no. 1 (1989): 3-35; Farber and Gowa, 'Polities and Peace'; Farber and Gowa, 'Common Interests or Common Polities?'; Thompson, William R., and Richard Tucker, 'A Tale of Two Democratic Peace Critiques,' *Journal of Conflict Resolution* 41, no. 3 (1997), 428–54.

27. John R. Oneal and Bruce Russett, 'Is the Liberal Peace Just an Artifact of Cold War Interests? Assessing Recent Critiques,' *International Interactions* 25, no. 3 (1999): 213–41. Oneal and Russett pool the years between 1870 and 1989 and also examine separately the pre-1945 evidence. They find support for democratic-peace theory in both periods, but they include only sixteen countries in their analysis.

28. For each year *t*, we subset the data to include the five previous and five subsequent

years, for a time span of $(t - 5) - (t + 5)$. Using this subsample, we estimate the joint-democracy impact on MIDs.

29. For example, see Joanne Gowa, 'The Democratic Peace after the Cold War,' *Economics & Politics* 23, no. 2 (2011): 153–71.

30. Zeev Maoz and Bruce Russett, 'Normative and Structural Causes of Democratic Peace, 1946–1986,' *American Political Science Review* 87, no. 3 (1993): 624–38. The number of observations in the Maoz and Russett analysis of the years between 1946 and 1986 is 19,020.

31. For an illuminating article on the use of politically relevant dyads, see Bear F. Braumoeller and Austin Carson, 'Political Irrelevance, Democracy, and the Limits of Militarized Conflict,' *Journal of Conflict Resolution* 55, no. 2 (2011): 292–320.

32. Dan Reiter, 'Democratic Peace Theory,' *Oxford Bibliographies Online Research Guide*, Oxford University Press, 2012, http://www.oxfordbibliographies.com/view/document/obo-9780199756223/obo-9780199756223-0014.xml.

33. Daniel Jones, Stuart Bremer, and David Singer, 'Militarized Interstate Disputes, 1816–1992: Rationale, Coding Rules, and Empirical Patterns,' *Conflict Management and Peace Science* 15, no. 2 (1996): 163–213, www.correlatesofwar.org/data-sets/MIDs.

34. Ibid, 192.

35. Ibid., 192–93.

36. We do not code subsequent observations of a dispute as missing because in a nontrivial number of cases a new MID occurs the year after a different one began. A robustness test that codes subsequent observations as missing does not change our results.

37. Reiter, 'Democratic Peace Theory,' 32.

38. Monty G. Marshall, Ted Robert Gurr, and Keith Jaggers, 'Polity IV Project: Political Regime Characteristics and Transitions, 1800–2017,' *Center for Systemic Peace* (2017), http://www.systemicpeace.org/polity/polity4.htm.

   Zeev Maoz, Paul L. Johnson, Jasper Kaplan, Fiona Ogunkoya, and Aaron P. Shreve, 'The Dyadic Militarized Interstate Disputes (MIDs) Dataset Version 3.0: Logic, Characteristics, and Comparisons to Alternative Datasets,' *Journal of Conflict Resolution* (2018): 0022002718784158, www.correlatesofwar.org/data-sets/MIDs.

39. Keith Jaggers and Ted Robert Gurr, 'Tracking Democracy's Third Wave with the Polity III Data,' *Journal of Peace Research* 32, no. 4 (1995): 471.

40. Marshall, Gurr, and Jaggers, 'Polity IV Project,' 14.

41. Jaggers and Gurr, 'Tracking Democracy's Third Wave,' 479.

42. Ibid., 479.

43. Edward D. Mansfield and Jack Snyder, 'Democratization and the Danger of War.'

44. An interrupted polity 'cannot exercise relatively effective authority over at least 50 percent of its established territory' because, e.g., of foreign occupation (Marshall, Gurr, and Jaggers, "Polity IV Project", 14).

45. Because postwar Austria became independent only in 1955, we recode dyads that include it before then as missing.

46. For example, Zeev Maoz, 'The Controversy over the Democratic Peace: Rearguard Action of Cracks in the Wall?' *International Security* 22, no. 1 (1997): 171.

47. The Correlates of War Project, 'Direct Contiguity,' last accessed July 25, 2017, http://cow.dss.ucdavis.edu/data-sets/direct-contiguity.

48. The Correlates of War Project, 'State System Membership,' last accessed July 25, 2017, http://correlatesofwar.org/data-sets/state-system-membership.

49. J. David Singer, Stuart Bremer, and John Stuckey, 'Capability Distribution, Uncertainty, and Major Power War, 1820–1965,' in *Peace, War and Numbers*, ed. Bruce Russett (Beverly Hills: Sage, 1972).

50. Douglas M. Gibler, *International Military Alliances, 1648–2008*, version 4.1 (CQ Press, 2009).

51. While common in the literature, this specification does not take into account the issue of cross-sectional dependence. This is so because 'in the context of information-poor datasets such as the binary rare events international conflict data, common econometric solutions such as unit-specific intercepts ("fixed effects") may not be practical since they do not leave enough information to reliably estimate the coefficients of slowly changing international variables' (Dafoe, 'Statistical Critiques of the Democratic Peace,' 249; see also Green, Kim, and Yoon, 2001).

52. James Fearon, 'Rationalist Explanations for War,' *International Organization* 49, no. 3 (Summer 1995): 379–414.

53. For a clear exposition of the bargaining range, see Fearon, 'Rationalist Explanations for Wars'. Necessary conditions for peace include complete information about the other's side reservation value and the ability to make a credible commitment to adhere to the peace agreement. If democracies can more easily fulfil these conditions, a democratic peace would be more likely. But the variation in dispute rates across time suggests that democracies do not systematically do so.

54. As cited in Michael W. Doyle, 'Kant, Liberal Legacies, and Foreign Affairs,' *Philosophy & Public Affairs* 12, no. 3 (1983): 229.

55. Douglas L. Kriner and Francis X. Shen, *The Casualty Gap: The Causes and Consequences of American Wartime Inequalities* (Oxford: Oxford University Press, 2010), 153.

56. Ibid., 153.

57. Ibid., 152.

58. Ibid., 4.

59. Even in World War I, however, the US conscripted men explicitly on the basis of their so-called value to society, with those valued least drafted first. See Richard V.L. Cooper, 'Military Manpower Procurement: Equity, Efficiency, and National Security,' in *Registration and the Draft*, ed. Martin Anderson (Stanford: Hoover Institution, 1982), 346.

60. See, for example, Joseph Paul Vasquez III, 'Shouldering the Soldiering: Democracy, Conscription, and Military Casualties,' *Journal of Conflict Resolution* 49, no. 6 (2005): 119–40; and Michael C. Horowitz and Matthew S. Levendusky, 'Drafting Support for

War: Conscription and Mass Support for Warfare,' *Journal of Politics* 73, no. 2 (2011): 524–34.

61. Charles C. Moskos, *The American Enlisted Man: The Rank and File in Today's Military* (New York: Russell Sage Foundation, 1970), 16.

62. Kriner and Shen, *The Casualty Gap*, viii.

63. Ibid., 182.

64. Arend Lijphart, 'Unequal Participation: Democracy's Unresolved Dilemma: Presidential Address, American Political Science Association, 1996,' *American Political Science Review* 91, no. 1 (1997): 1–14.

65. Margaret Levi, *Consent, Dissent, and Patriotism* (Cambridge: Cambridge University Press, 1997), 88.

66. Charles C. Moskos, 'The Negro and the Draft,' *Selective Service and American Society* (New York: Sage, 1969), 157.

67. Jessica L. Weeks, 'Autocratic Audience Costs: Regime Type and Signaling Resolve,' *International Organization* 62, no. 1 (2008): 36.

68. Ibid., 36.

69. Ibid., 36.

70. This section is drawn from Joanne Gowa, 'Democratic States and International Disputes,' *International Organization* 49, no. 3 (1995): 514–16.

71. Michael Hechter, *Principles of Group Solidarity* (Berkeley: University of California Press, 1987), 62.

72. Maoz and Russett, 'Normative and Structural Causes,' 632.

73. Waltz, *Theory of International Politics*, 88.

74. John Finley Scott, *The Internationalization of Norms: A Sociological Theory of Moral Commitment* (Englewood Cliffs, NJ: Prentice Hall, 1971), viii.

Peace through Institutions

9.

Can Domestic Institutions Destroy the International Order?

Petr Kratochvíl

Introduction

At the heart of all types of institutionalism lies the simple and widely acknowledged insight that institutions matter. However, as with all simple statements, its meaning as well as its repercussions for the broader study of international relations are not simple at all. Two clusters of questions need to be answered to give us a more precise picture about the study of institutions. First, we need to clarify what institutions are and, related to this, what kind of institutions we have in mind when claiming that they matter. Second, we need to address the equally fundamental question about the aim of this study: for what or whom do institutions matter, and in what sense is this relevant for the study of IR?

The first of these two questions pertains to our definition of institutions.[1] The three most common types of new institutionalism give different answers to this query.[2] For some, the basic opposition is that between the state (as the principal) and the institutions (as its agents). In other words, the state gains a special status and it is not considered an institution, but rather the institutions' creator. For others, this distinction does not hold to historical scrutiny, as the state is without any doubt also a type of institution. Hence this broader definition erases not only the borders between principals and agents, but also historicizes the state and casts it as one form of political institutions among many others, albeit an important one.

The second question is related to the study of order in international relations. Saying that institutions matter is usually understood as that they matter for peace, stability, and the intensity of cooperation among states or as the *loci* where communication is easier, negotiations more intense, and interactions more complex. However, which of these particular phenomena is most intensely tied to the institutional milieu is a question on which institutionalists fundamentally disagree. So, for example, while institutions may make negotiations easier, this does not necessarily translate into a lower frequency of armed conflicts, as these negotiations might be limited to specific institutions (such as military alliances) or might be directly about declaring war against a third party.

It is not, however, my intention here to review the vast literature on these two key questions. Instead, I want to take these questions as a starting point for my argument that the study of institutions has gradually evolved into a rather narrow focus on the impact of international organizations and regimes on (both domestic and international) politics. While this is undoubtedly a highly relevant area of research, I believe that too little attention is dedicated to the limitations of this perspective. In particular, I am convinced that we should be prepared to engage the opposite question about when and under what conditions domestic politics and domestic institutions influence the functioning of the international order, international regimes, and international organizations. I am aware of the fact that this topic is not entirely absent from international studies, but I will try to show below that those engaged in answering this question focus on very specific aspects of this phenomenon, such as the role of the hegemon in sustaining international regimes or the foundation of international institutions as an expression of state preferences.

However, current global politics reminds us that there are other vital dimensions of the domestic-international institutional nexus that have so far remained underexplored. Most importantly, we know very little about how states can undermine established institutions and regimes. In other words, how do domestic preferences, or even the changes in the domestic institutional set-up, change the functioning of international institutions of which these states are members? How can, for instance, the growing

Euroscepticism and its presence in domestic institutions of EU member states hamper (or improve) the working of central EU institutions? How does the changing domestic political context in the UK impact European policymaking, particularly after the Brexit vote? How does the recent wave of renewed authoritarianism that is now sweeping through Chinese domestic institutions influence the (non)functioning of the regional institutions as well as the global ones? We should be aware that the answers to these questions never lie simply in the directly expressed changes of preferences; instead these changes are first expressed in normative and institutional changes domestically, and it is primarily on this basis that international institutions are influenced as well.

To put it simply, in this chapter, I will try to present the case for the study of domestic institutions' impact on the functioning of international institutions. As important as the transfer of international norms to domestic politics is, the vitally important ability of domestic institutions to hamper international institutions also needs to be given more attention. I will proceed in five steps. First, I will show how domestic institutions have been gradually side lined in institutionalism that turned them from agents who shape the international environment to those who are influenced and constrained by international structures. Second, I will explain that the arrival of constructivism to the study of institutions has not meant a fundamental reorientation of the field, nor has it changed the primary focus on international institutions. Third, I will offer several explanations why domestic institutions as agents remain of marginal interest for institutionalists. Fourth, I will show that the more recent scholarship does offer several starting points for a reorientation of the institutionalist research towards a greater appreciation of the agency of domestic institutions. Fifth, I will offer four pathways through which the impact of domestic institutions on international institutions and the international order is exerted.

Institutionalism and the Marginalization of Domestic Institutions—Why and How?

There is no doubt that in the initial phase of the study of international relations in the first half of the twentieth century, the connection between the way domestic institutions function and the stability and fairness of the international order was taken as an undisputed fact. Both the liberal internationalists and their realist critics acknowledged that international politics was to a large extent the mirror image of domestic preferences and that the nature of the domestic political regime is highly relevant for the way the country conducts its foreign policy.[3] Today, this connection is, somewhat unfairly, known under the label of the 'second image', a notion introduced by Kenneth Waltz. This label is, nevertheless, rather confusing and, indeed, detrimental to the whole debate. First, while Waltz was interested in the link between the domestic and the international environment, he had very little to say about international institutions, whose relevance he readily discarded.[4] Second, for Waltz, the main question was not the stability of the international order (possibly underpinned by functioning institutions), but rather the domestic causes of international conflict. Third, from the very beginning, the 'second image' has been perceived as inadequate in terms of its explanatory power in the realm of international relations: for Waltz, both the 'first image' and the 'second image' are expressions of reductionist thinking that should be replaced by a structural/systemic perspective on IR.

Waltz's argument has been so successful that from the 1970s onward, the 'second image' has been all but forgotten. Instead, IR scholars focused on the 'second image reversed'.[5] The classical question of the study of institutions remains, though—that is, even in the 1970s, scholars explored the link between institutions and international stability, security, and peace. However, the interconnections between the international arena and domestic institutions were almost entirely seen as a one-way street, with scholars being interested in the impact of international institutions and international norms on the domestic institutional set-up, and not vice versa. This one-sided approach has gone so far that the term 'institutions' ceased to mean both domestic and international institutions and instead started to mean only the latter. When, for example, John Mearsheimer speaks about the disagreement about 'whether institutions markedly affect the prospects for international stability',[6] he has exclusively international institutions in mind. As strange as this might sound, in terms of (positivistically understood) causality, domestic institutions cease to be the causes and instead become consequences of international institutions. As Gourevitch argues, 'Most of the literature concerned with the interaction of the international system and domestic structure is authored by writers with international concerns, and that literature therefore primarily looks at the arrows that flow from domestic structure toward international relations . . . Instead of being a cause of international politics, domestic structure may be a consequence of it. International systems, too, become causes instead of consequences.'[7]

Scholars who did acknowledge the dependence of institutions on the member states usually still put the stress on the primacy of the institutions and their ability to shape the political processes within the member states ('[Institutions] themselves shape those preferences and that power').[8] It is, however, even more surprising that even those who have been critical of the idea that international institutions influence states do not start their argument from the critical dependence of international institutions on the domestic institutions and their preferences.[9] To summarize the whole argument, starting from Waltz's unfortunate treatment of the 'second image' as lacking, and via the transfer of the scholarly attention exclusively to the international level, the trajectory led to the situation in which domestic institutions are effectively marginalized. The neoliberal–neorealist debate that followed built exactly on this understanding of institutions, and although neoliberal institutionalists formally acknowledged the relevance of domestic politics, in all practical matters they continued to ignore the connection between domestic and international politics. In this sense, Andrew Moravcsik's critique of neoliberals (or institutionalists/functional regimes theorists, as he calls them) for their insufficient attention to domestic preferences is well justified.[10]

From the 1990s onwards, this gap has been gradually acknowledged, and the efforts to redress the flaw have become more evident.[11] Two types of studies of the nexus between the international and domestic institutions have started to appear: the first of them in the positivist tradition, and the second those appropriating the emerging social constructivist research program. These studies differ in a number of ways: some focus more on the carrots that lead states to complying with international institutions' requirements, and some explore the sticks. The rationalists try to formulate as precise causal mechanisms as possible and test the related hypotheses, and the constructivists explore the compatibility of the international norms with the domestic identities and political normative contexts. However, the unifying theme is again the unidirectional understanding of the relationship between the international and the domestic—it is virtually always the international impact on the domestic affairs, the acceptance of international norms by states, and so on. The state of the debate about international institutions in the 1990s is summarized in the following table.

	Carrots	Sticks
Constructivists	Enhanced status, socialization, sense of belonging	Naming and shaming, symbolic isolation from the international community, etc.
Rationalists	Economic and security benefits from cooperation	Economic sanctions for non-compliance, decreased security

To illustrate the specific focus of the new approach to institutions, let us give a few examples of influential studies of both types. The analysis of domestic institutions is not entirely omitted here, but the domestic factors such as 'domestic salience of international norms' or 'the domestic structural context' are seen as conditions for the assessment of an international norm's influence on state behaviour.[12] A typical example is Dai's study that explores the domestic setting, in particular the domestic constituencies, but again, they are seen as relevant only as far as they can be empowered to promote the adoption of international norms and ensure greater compliance with an international regime.[13]

In other cases, domestic politics can function as an intermediary/intervening variable that can be influenced by international institutions and subsequently exert effects on the behaviour of political leaders who are bound by the emerging domestic constraints.[14] Also in the study of democracy, domestic institutions are seen as the to-be-democratized objects rather than active carriers of democracy, which explore the connection between international organizations and democracy.[15] In this particular context, this is even more surprising since democracy as a normative ideal is much more strongly present in domestic settings than in the international environment. Finally, positivist institutionalists are also interested in the ways through which one (international) institution can influence another (international) institution. Gehring and Oberthür come up with four such causal mechanisms: 'transfer of knowledge, commitments established under an institution, behavioural effects of an institution, and functional linkage of the ultimate governance targets of the institutions involved'.[16]

A New Constructivist Life for Domestic Institutions? Not Really

The arrival of social constructivism to the study of institutionalism was not such a radical break with the previous type of study as in the other subfields of international relations. This is so for several reasons. First, the students of institutions have always had a penchant for the relevance of norms, and the topics introduced by constructivists were thus not so novel in institutionalism after all. Second, social constructivist ideas had already had a firm place in the study of institutions before the arrival of constructivism, albeit under the label of sociological institutionalism.[17] While constructivists are in general more cautious about a clear-cut domestic–international divide, and while they subscribe to the most general understanding of institutions, thus including even the state among them, they nevertheless mainly focus on the same questions as their more rationalist institutionalist counterparts.[18] In the end, the transfer of international norms and their impact on domestic politics have become an even stronger hallmark for constructivism than for the other approaches. Thus, the domestic institutions are taken into account only as far as their socialization into the international normative order is concerned. International institutions are often seen in structural terms, as more or less unchanging 'social environments',[19] and although domestic institutions are regarded as actors, their agency is typically limited to different ways of accepting or rejecting the internationally transmitted norms.

The question, in what ways domestic institutions might also influence the international arena, had thus been conspicuously lacking for a long time.

The attention to what is called 'Europeanization uploading'[20] in European studies is much younger than the constructivist study of institutions, and until today, its applications remain more or less limited to the study of European integration. Similarly, Epstein and Sedelmeier, as well as Epstein, focus on the domestic impact and adoption of international norms in a constructivist manner.[21,22] Epstein does ascribe a higher level of agency to domestic actors, but here the actions of domestic agents are again seen through the prism of international norm adoption, and domestic politics can only create better or worse conditions for the adoption of these norms—for instance, the status of domestic institutions plays such a role.

'Socialization' has become the central term for constructivists. Thomas Risse and his colleagues, in their very influential collection of texts on the constructivist study of institutions, argue that the aim is to explore socialization and to show that global ideas can influence domestic institutions.[23] In other texts, Risse elaborates on the metatheoretical assumptions of constructivists and rationalists, but again these analyses serve only to prepare the ground for research into the impact of the international norms on domestic politics.[24] Indeed, the very term socialization already predetermines the path on which the study of institutions will go: the starting assumption is that of an unchanging normative and institutional structure into which political actors (states and domestic institutions) are to be socialized. Again, the unproblematic a priori existence of international norms is typically taken for granted as if their existence did not derive from the normative inputs by states and their institutions, or even other actors such as transnational networks, non-governmental organizations, or the nascent global public sphere.[25]

Hence, unlike in the so-called great debate between rationalism and reflectivism in international studies, in the study of institutions the new wave of constructivist theorizing did not mean a radical departure from the original rationalist analysis of institutions. Indeed, many leading constructivists in the subfield (such as Jeffrey Checkel) saw themselves as positivists and tried to formulate testable constructivist hypotheses about norm transfer and socialization.[26] Also, constructivists attempted to present comprehensive accounts of institutional impact, combining 'strategic calculation, role playing, and normative suasion'.[27] These types of studies have become more and more popular, and the distinction between rationalist and constructivist institutionalisms has become blurred.

In a similar vein, Judith Kelley, in her 2004 article 'International Actors on the Domestic Scene', puts forward an argument for the study of international norms and international institutions in domestic politics, discussing constructivism and rationalism.[28] Interestingly, both Checkel and Kelley depart from the strategy of earlier rationalists who attempted to formulate mutually exclusive hypotheses. Instead, Kelley argues in favour of combining both, claiming that in the case she studied, 'conditionality motivated most behaviour change', but 'socialization-based efforts . . . guided [the changes]'.[29] Kelley argues that incentives, which are seen as important by rationalist institutionalists, are absolutely fundamental since without them socialization works only under very favourable conditions (such as when there is little domestic resistance to the new norm). In other words, socialization is not a strong independent source of normative change, and institutional pressure based on socialization only would in most cases fail, or at least its effects would be only moderate.

Here lies the reason why constructivism is seen as uncontroversial in the study of institutions. Most influential constructivists in the subfield do not directly challenge the rationalist dogma. Instead, they see themselves as adherents of positivism, too, and they interpret the effects of socialization not as a contrary logic of institutional impact, but only as an additional bonus to the essentially important effects of material benefits and other incentives. In this sense, the constructivist contribution to the study of institutions is analogous to the view of ideas as expressed by Robert Keohane and Judith Goldstein[30]—they matter, but in no substantial way do they challenge the received wisdom of rationalists about how institutions and world politics work.

Why Are Domestic Institutions Ignored?

To sum up, the current state of the study of institutions in world politics is thus the following: the discipline does flourish, with all three major forms of new institutionalism contributing in equal measure to explaining various facets of institutional impact. The field is markedly less defined in terms of theoretical clashes than the general field of international relations. Even the arrival of constructivism has not substantially challenged the positivist mainstream—and we should add that the label of positivism is not very precise in institutionalism in any case. Yet, in spite of all their great achievements, current theories of institutions also have non-negligible limitations. The most important of these is the exclusive focus on international institutions and their impact on world politics, other international institutions, or domestic politics. Very little attention is dedicated to the current relevance of the 'second image', to the domestic roots of international norms and the many ways through which domestic institutions can establish, transform, or even destroy international institutions.[31]

Interestingly, those authors who do explore the link between domestic politics and the international arena in European studies sometimes end up relegating international institutions to a secondary place. Most prominently among these, Andrew Moravcsik does explore the domestic–international connection in much detail, but what he is interested in is the impact of domestic political arrangements and domestic institutions on the outcome of international bargaining.[32] International institutions come to the fore only when the credibility of the commitments is discussed, that is, only after the agreement about everything that matters has already been reached by the states. Hence, while Moravcsik's account is detailed and concise, the direct link between domestic and international institutions is not addressed.

The reasons for this omission are, I believe, sufficiently clear now. First, there is the disciplinary pressure since, for many, the field of IR is defined through 'the fundamental discontinuity in the nature of international relations'.[33] For the IR mainstream, to explore the impact of domestic institutions would simultaneously mean challenging the fundamental domestic–international binary, crossing the disciplinary borders and trespassing into the territory of foreign policy analysis.

Second, the search for a grand theory has been—at least for the time being— left by general IR scholars (see the special issue of *European Journal of*

International Relations of 2013, which discusses this topic),[34] but it still casts a long shadow, and one corollary of this is the continuing quest for finding a top–down, systemic explanation of how institutions work. In other words, Waltz's non-reductionism still haunts the discipline and precludes a more thorough analysis of the role of domestic institutions. Let us note that even those who are sympathetic to the cause of renewing the study of domestic institutions and their impact on international institutions have to start from the a priori assumption imported from the structuralist accounts of international relations. Barbara Koremenos and colleagues argue that international institutions are 'the self-conscious creation of the states (and, to a lesser extent, of interest groups and corporations)'.[35] But they have to start with saying that 'it is misleading to think of international institutions solely as outside forces or exogenous factors'.[36] Clearly, the focus on institutions as 'environments', 'backgrounds', or 'structural constraints' is so all-pervasive that even critics of such an interpretation cannot avoid this as their starting point.

The black boxing of domestic politics is, however, not the only problem caused by the scholarly argument with neorealists. While institutionalists typically couched their arguments in the critique of neorealist failings, many of them (typically those in the tradition of rationalist institutionalism, but also historical institutionalists)[37] adopted a number of key assumptions of neorealism, such as understanding states as goal-seeking utility maximisers, understanding anarchy as the ever-present feature of international politics and the secondary nature of domestic politics.[38] Interestingly, the principles of non-cooperative game theory such as individualism and utilitarianism, or the zero-sum principle, have also heavily influenced the study of domestic institutions. It is an ironic paradox that although the respective studies of domestic and international institutions have been in many ways disconnected, the underlying principles and basic theoretical assumptions have been near identical.[39] There is no doubt that the automatic acceptance of these assumptions has been declining in recent years. But even though the rise of constructivism has contributed to the strengthening of the sociological institutionalism, the overall utilitarianism as the basic explanatory tool has remained unchallenged until today.

None of this is to say that we should replace the one-sided orientation on top–down mechanisms with an individualist, actor-centred analysis. Instead, I believe that we should overcome the dichotomy, take the insights of structuration theory more seriously, and always complement the analysis of international institutional structures and their effects with the analysis of their origins and the actors who make these structures possible and who can also eventually transform them. Indeed, it is striking how little the agency-structure debate in IR has impacted the theoretical discussions in the study of institutions.

Re-introducing Domestic Institutions: The Starting Points

Although the mainstream study of institutions has thus side-lined the questions about the impact of domestic institutions on the international ones, references to the importance of domestic institutions are plentiful even in the most classic texts, and these can be used as starting points for our analysis of the domestic–international nexus. To start with, Robert Keohane, in spite of his priority attention to international regimes and organizations, did indicate several times that domestic institutions should not be summarily dismissed. International institutions are, according to him, embedded 'in pre-existing practices'[40]—this means, in the first place, that contemporary institutions did not arise *ex nihilo*, but also that we should take seriously the evolution of international institutions and the principals who established them. Similarly, Keohane cautions against the over-determination of actions by structural factors that became such a dominant explanatory factor in the 1980s, arguing that while environments are important, they cannot entirely explain the actions of states.[41]

Another promising line of thought that can be discovered in the classical discussions of the institutionalists of the 1980s is the debate about the role of the hegemon in establishing and sustaining the international order and its institutional underpinnings. While some (notably most realist and neo-realist thinkers of the time) argued in favour of the unique role of hegemony in providing the necessary international public goods and supervising the international order, neoliberals believed that international regimes can survive a diffusion of power in the international system and function as successfully maintained regimes with the help of a group of smaller powers.[42] In his classic work *International Institutions and State Power*, Keohane even dedicated several chapters to the influence of domestic politics on the international order, studying both the US hegemony and its consequences for international institutions and complex interdependence.[43] Irrespective of which side of the argument we choose, however, the common theme is the focus on the role of states and their vital importance for the survival of international institutions.

These scattered references are later transformed into a full confession in which Keohane, together with Lisa Martin, admits that the early institutionalists focused on 'institutions as dependent variables, examining the conditions under which they are created'. Suddenly, the realization that institutions emerge as a response to national preferences is acknowledged. Keohane and Martin then continue to argue that the focus on the conditions of the emergence of institutions and their transformation is not in any way incompatible with the institutionalist theory.[44]

From the second half of the 1990s onward, a minority of institutionalists have tried to take up the claim that domestic politics matter, even though they typically continue to compare the roles of international institutions and domestic politics in general rather than specifically domestic institutions. This is why some authors focus on the leaders and their usage of international norms or memberships in international organizations to convince domestic groups that resist a change of policy.[45] With a similar aim in mind, others, such as B.S. Chimni, explore the 'webs of sub-national authorities' from which the international order or, to use his neo-Marxist vocabulary, the nascent imperial global state can emerge.[46]

Only very few studies truly realize the relevance of the impact of domestic institutions on the international ones. One example of such a study, though, is the article by Lisa Martin and Beth Simmons in *International Organization* that summarizes the evolution of the study of institutions (albeit almost exclusively from the traditional, positivist perspective).[47] And yes, even though they decry the domestic blindness of the institutionalists caused by the encounters with their neorealist opponents, they do not further develop the idea and do not present even a hint of a more comprehensive account of the impact of domestic institutions on international politics. More promising is the line followed by Brett Leeds in 'Domestic Political Institutions'.[48] Here, she builds on game theory and develops several interesting hypotheses about the possible effects of domestic institutions on the ability of states and their leaders to cooperate internationally. Although Leeds distinguishes only two types of domestic institutional set-ups (democratic and autocratic), she convincingly shows that more cooperation among similar states (both democratic and autocratic) is invited when they have similar institutional arrangements than when they are institutionally different.

While Martin and Simmons's account represents the most comprehensive summary of the positivist tradition, Risse shows that the exploration of domestic institutions can be successfully conducted from the constructivist (but agency-centred) perspective too.[49] The great advantage of this type of theorizing here is that the constructivists are better capable of unpacking the black box of domestic politics. Unlike game-theoretical models that usually simplify the analysis into neat boxes, often in a dichotomous way, constructivism can explore a number of domestic actors, or indeed actors who transcend the easy division into the domestic and the international. This ability of constructivism to give more credence to the plurality of domestic and international as well as transnational actors is also one of the reasons constructivism has been so successful in the study of European integration. As already partially discussed above, constructivists can explore the supranational institutions of the EU, transnational advocacy networks, and also a variety of domestic institutions within one overarching framework of norm-guided behaviour and the mutual interactions and influences of all these actors.

Before moving on to the discussions of ways in which the impact of domestic institutions on the international ones can be studied, we need to turn for a moment to a basic limitation of such a discussion, which is the all too neat division of institutions into these two categories—that is, the institutions working in the international sphere and those functioning exclusively in the domestic arena.[50] While this division has been eroding for some time, and new types of trans-border actors have emerged, I still believe that the distinction makes sense, at least for some types of institutions. Clearly, a number of transnational movements, NGOs, or other entities such as churches and religious groupings have been as successful in promoting norms as states and formal international organizations. However, the question here is of a more direct impact of purely domestic institutions (such as those which are part of the state administration) on the institutions of which their mother country is a member state.

Again, the blurred border between national and international or transnational institutions is best seen in Europe. The EU has become a classic point of contention for those who discuss the limits to national sovereignty and explore the linkages between domestic and international politics. While the European Commission is certainly not a national institution, the policies and the legislation it adopts/initiates are often directly applicable in the member states. Even though the connections between the member states and EU institutions are well researched, they also show that the newly emerging overlapping jurisdictions make the neat boxes of the domestic and the international questionable in some cases. As Michael Zürn argues, 'West European national institutions and the EU institutions are so closely interwoven that they can no longer be conceived as separate political systems.'[51]

But even here, the question remains of how the interactions between institutions on the various levels of the EU's political system work. Indeed, there are several possible models within which this connection can be explored. One is the interpretation of the EU as a complex system of multi-level governance, which gave rise to a thriving subfield of European studies, and a vast amount of literature dedicated to this topic exists.[52] Even outside the EU, it is possible to explore institutions based on the type of activity they carry out and not primarily on whether they are domestic or international. For example, Daniel Drezner analyses how domestic groups can be persuaded or forced into compliance.[53] Although Drezner deals with domestic and international institutions, the key distinction is between 'policy initiators' and 'policy ratifiers'. Policy initiators may be domestic institutions, but also non-governmental organizations, various policy networks, transnational advocacy groups, and many other actors who wield sufficient influence to induce a policy change or the adoption of new legislation.

The Impact of Domestic Institutions: Four Pathways

Having shown that mainstream institutionalists have seriously neglected the influence of domestic institutions on international institutions, I want to turn to suggesting ways in which this influence may be exerted. However, I want to stress that my motivation and goal in this may be a bit different from the goals and motivations of what has been done so far. The scholarly attention has been mostly dedicated to the ways in which cooperation is fostered, international norms are successfully transferred, and socialization into new normative structures is completed.

We see, nevertheless, a trend across Europe and beyond in which domestic politics is in upheaval, and populists and right-wing extremists are on the rise. Frequently, Eurosceptic or anti-migration parties and movements are also implicitly anti-democratic, stressing the advantages of strong leaders and the clumsiness and ineffectiveness of democratic decision-making. The question we are facing every day in Europe is how far, in what ways, and how quickly these attitudes spill over from the national arenas to international and EU supranational institutions. If domestic institutions are 'captured' and re-modelled along the anti-liberal or anti-democratic lines (as we have recently seen such cases in Hungary and Poland), what are the channels through which these changes spread to international institutions and, most vitally, how can this influence be stopped?

This is the paradox we know so well from European studies: we have plentiful theories that discuss the deepening of integration, which is sometimes seen as a more-or-less automatic process (such as in functionalism) and sometimes as a consequence of a conscious decision taken by the key actors (such as in the liberal intergovernmental approach). However, all these theories explicitly or implicitly assume that we are talking about further integration, not disintegration. Attempts to theorize disintegration have been few, and their success has remained rather limited.[54] In spite of a high risk of disintegration in the EU, at least in some areas, we do not have at our disposal any comprehensive theory that could be used to explain this process.[55] The result of this absence was not only the inability to predict Brexit (but we have to bear in mind that for many theories, prediction is not considered their task), but also the absence of models that would explain the process of legal and institutional disentangling of the UK from the Union's structures. The same problem applies to international institutions. In practical terms, their ability to continue functioning as we have known them to may be threatened, and yet we do not possess robust models that would tell us why and how this is happening.

I want to propose four ways through which international institutions may change their behaviours, structures, or agendas as a consequence of domestic change. In other words, the source institutions are always the domestic ones, while the target institutions may vary more, as they may include international organizations, international regimes, supranational institutions of the EU, and so on.

1. Re-socialization

The broadest and most general phenomenon I want to point to is re-socialization. Socialization itself is a classic topic for constructivist institutionalists, and there exists a wealth of literature about the socialization of member states. Socialization explores the compliance of states with a broader normative and institutional environment.[56] The basic, if often unacknowledged, assumption here is that the normative structures are given, or change only very slowly, whereas the domestic institutions adapt relatively quickly. However, in some situations—for example, the eastern enlargement of the EU—the number and influence of non-socialized new members was so high that their combined pressure might lead to a normative re-orientation of the international institution itself. In other words, the institution as a social environment, as a normative structure, can change.

This does not pertain only to the official norms and values, but also to the political culture or the practical decision-making procedures within the international institutions. For instance, the shift to qualified majority voting in the Council of the EU is sometimes explained as a simple consequence of the growing number of member states and the impossibility of reaching consensual decisions with twenty-eight (or twenty-seven) EU member states. The ability to reach consensus is nevertheless not only a function of the number of voting agents, but also a function of their willingness and preparedness to accept a compromise solution. The new norm does not have to be necessarily the one introduced with the arrival of new members, but it may be a new norm nonetheless, taking into account the preferences of both previous and newer member states. As a consequence, the new members are socialized, but simultaneously, they transform the normative structure, and the older members, in their turn, have to re-socialize themselves into the new normative conditions. Needless to say, the re-socialization is typically more difficult for the old members as, in their case, the resistance to the normative change is higher and the expectations linked to the old structure more deeply embedded.

2. Reversed Nesting of Institutions

Nesting of institutions is based on a number of similar assumptions as those of socialization. Nested institutions are a specific case of one institution being 'nested' within a broader normative setting, such as an international organization in the broader international regime with the same focus area.[57] However, institutions can also be nested in the broader diplomatic relations of a particular group of countries. To give an example, in the post-Soviet space, there are a number of regional integration organizations, such as the Collective Security Treaty Organization and the Eurasian Economic Union, and while these organizations each have a different focus (economic, security-military, etc.), they all reflect the same skein of bilateral and multilateral relations in the particular regional context.

In our example, this may be the regional military dominance of Russia, the economic ties, and shared cultural frameworks. All these translate into similar patterns of interactions and similar institutional arrangements, and the 'nestedness' of these institutions also means that their seats are in Moscow or that Russian is used as their working language. Again, Brexit seems to be a particularly interesting case of reversed nesting: the UK's policies have become much more nested in EU structures than the Brexiters realized, and the process of 'un-nesting' is far more complex than anybody assumed. In other words, while nested institutions are usually understood as institutions embedded in a broader international context, I argue that institutions may be also nested in the implicitly shared understanding of how bilateral and multilateral diplomatic relations among the member states work. In the same vein, if domestic institutions are not entirely democratic in all the member states, the international institution is also nested in the shared understanding that democracy and democracy promotion will be off its agenda.

3. Agenda Replacement

Agenda replacement is another pathway that is closely related to the first one in that it also follows when a critical mass of new members joins an organization or when their internal priorities change. While re-socialization is concerned with formal and informal decision-making and the norms of political culture that characterize the particular institution, agenda replacement pertains to the substance of the institution's activities. The changing focus can simply mean that the stress is shifted from one policy area to another, but a more radical change can occur when the new agenda is— to some extent—contrary to the previous one.

For instance, the Visegrád Four, as an informal but slowly formalizing grouping of four Central European countries, was originally focused on the coordination of activities related to the preparation for their entry into the EU. However, with the rise to power of Fidesz in Hungary and the Law and Justice Party in Poland, the organization has become a platform for expressing Eurosceptic and, even more importantly in recent years, anti-immigration views. While the organization is almost as active as before and its members cooperate intensely, the coordination focuses on how to resist the diplomatic pressure from other EU member states, again most notably in the area of migration. To put it simply, coalitions are needed to enforce the change, and these often include not only the member states, but they can draw on transnational policy networks, advocacy groups, or lobbyists.

As far as agenda replacement is concerned, there is a strong link between domestic institutions and international institutions. Re-socialization can be driven by political elites, but agenda replacement is often a consequence of a direct intervention of domestic institutions, ministries of foreign affairs, or ministries of defence that, upon first agreeing a common position with their counterparts in other countries, then go on to propose a formal change at the institution's meeting, such as the Council of the EU or even the European Council.

4. Institutional Isomorphism

The changing functioning of an international institution can be more indirect than in the two previous cases. Institutions emulate the structures, procedures, and institutional forms of other institutions, for reasons of efficiency or due to cultural (or even emotional) attraction. Institutional isomorphism usually works along with conditionality. EU membership, for instance, is tied to a number of domestic reforms, including state, regional, and local administration reforms, as well as reforms of legal institutions. Although the reform requirements typically do not contain specific provisions about the necessary forms of these institutions, the accompanying processes, such as twinning, offer solutions that replicate the institutional designs from other EU member states. As a result, institutions start to resemble one another. Importantly, institutional isomorphism can also work the other way around. Newly established international institutions or specific parts of them draw inspiration from the domestic setting. As the burgeoning literature on the European External Action Service attests, the influence of domestic arrangements is the key determinant in explanations of its structure and its working.[58]

Interestingly, institutional isomorphism can be explained both in the rationalist and in the constructivist manner. For rationalists, institutions are motivated to reproduce successful patterns of optimum institutional design from abroad to make the reforms successful or to reap the benefits related to conditionality. For constructivists, the emulation is based on the desire to belong to the community and adopt similar roles as the role models among the older member states, and thus expand the we-feeling to include the candidate country and its refurbished institutions.

Again, while domestic institutions emulate the templates from abroad, domestic institutions do not typically copy the transnational or supranational institutions (such as the European Commission in the EU context), but other domestic institutions in other member states. Hence, the templates are domestic and only the pathways to institutional isomorphism are supra/trans/international. Institutional isomorphism, when combined with institutional nesting, may, additionally, lead to copying the successful examples of resistance to the dominant normative structure. The legal and institutional changes in Hungary to some extent replicate the experience of rising authoritarianism in Russia and are again replicated in Poland and elsewhere in the region. In this sense, institutional isomorphism is another channel for the influence of domestic institutions.

I would like to stress that all four of the pathways I described above are compatible both with the rationalist theories of institutional change and with their constructivist alternatives. This applies even to re-socialization, since the compliance with the changed norms may also be motivated by the prospect of greater benefits. Broadly speaking, most rationalist explanations revolve around the question of accountability and audience costs.[59] Political agents accept changes or promote them to satisfy the demands of domestic institutions or, more directly, the past and future voters. This is not to deny the influence of international/structural factors, as noted earlier. Constructivists can also easily explore the domestic–international nexus, building on the classical terms of social learning, persuasion, and identity politics. These notions can help to explain why cooperation is established and how international institutions influence domestic politics, but also how domestic institutions transform or re-orientate international institutions.

Conclusion

The aim of this chapter was to point out the one-sided nature of the debate among institutionalists. For a number of reasons, institutionalists either focus on international institutions only or look at their effects on domestic institutions. Overcoming this one-sidedness is the first challenge for all institutionalists. The second challenge for students of institutions lies in the fact that they normally explore the positive side: how institutions emerge, what conditions are conducive to cooperation, and how institutional arrangements can be further strengthened. As important as these questions are, the key problems today are, nevertheless, related to the destabilization of institutions: how far can a lower legitimacy of domestic institutions or a re-orientation of domestic politics transform international institutions as well?

The debate among rationalists and constructivists (or sociological institutionalists) regarding the nature of institutions and their effects on behaviour, which has defined the field, has not, however, changed this basic orientation of institutionalist research. In this chapter, I tried to show that in the vast amount of literature on institutions, there are promising starting points that could be tapped if we want to study meaningfully 'the second image' again. These promising points of departure are often derived from the study of mutual interactions of international institutions, or they are based on the reversal of the study of the institution's impact on domestic policy.

From the many pathways through which the changing domestic arrangement can have an impact on international institutions (both the formal and the informal ones), I focused on four. The broadest of these is re-socialization. The vast array of studies on socialization into international normative structures tells us a lot about how domestic institutions are socialized, but we know very little about how normative uploading takes place. Similarly, we tend to assume that institutions emerge from previous practices and that they are nested in broader normative structures. However, we also need to focus on whether and how institutions are nested in the shared interactions among the domestic institutions of the organization's member states. Next, I pointed to the very direct ability of domestic institutions to impose a new agenda in the international institutions if a similar domestic shift takes place in a critical number of member states. The final pathway is based on institutional isomorphism, which can clearly work from the international to the domestic context, but also in the reverse order.

Notes

1. For a concise overview of the basic theoretical positions here, see the chapter by Mai'a K. Davis Cross in this book.
2. Josef Bátora, 'The "Mitrailleuse Effect": The EEAS as an Interstitial Organization and the Dynamics of Innovation in Diplomacy', *Journal of Common Market Studies* 51 no. 4, (2013): 598–613. Also see Peter A. Hall, 'Political Science and the Three New

Institutionalisms' (paper presented at the Board's meeting of the MPIFG Scientific Advisory Board, Cambridge, Great Britain, May 9, 1996).

3. Alfred Zimmern, *The League of Nations and the Rule of Law 1918–1935* (London: Macmillan, 1936). See also: Andrew Moravcsik, 'Taking Preferences Seriously: A Liberal Theory of International Politics,' *International Organization* 51, no. 4 (1997): 513–53.

4. Kenneth N. Waltz, 'Structural Realism after the Cold War,' *International Security* 25, no. 1 (2000): 5–41.

5. Peter Gourevitch, 'The Second Image Reversed: The International Sources of Domestic Politics,' *International Organization* 32, no. 4 (1978): 881–912.

6. John J. Mearsheimer, 'The False Promise of International Institutions,' *International Security* 19, no. 3 (1994): 7.

7. Gourevitch, 'The Second Image Reversed,' 881.

8. Robert O. Keohane, 'International Institutions: Two Approaches,' *International Studies Quarterly* 32, no. 4 (1988): 382.

9. Mearsheimer, 'The False Promise,' 5–49.

10. Moravcsik, 'Taking Preferences Seriously,' 513–553.

11. See chapter 8 in Michael W. Doyle and John G. Ikenberry, *New Thinking in International Relations Theory* (Boulder, CO: Westview, 1997).

12. Andrew P. Cortell and James W. Davis, 'How Do International Institutions Matter? The Domestic Impact of International Rules and Norms,' *International Studies Quarterly* 40, no. 4 (1996): 451–78.

13. Xinyuan Dai, *International Institutions and National Policies* (Cambridge: Cambridge University Press, 2007).

14. See Songying Fang, 'The Informational Role of International Institutions and Domestic Politics,' *American Journal of Political Science* 52, no. 2 (2008): 304–21.

15. See Jon C. Pevehouse, 'Democracy from the Outside-In? International Organizations and Democratization,' *International Organization* 56, no. 3 (2002): 515–49.

16. Thomas Gehring and Sebastian Oberthür, 'The Causal Mechanisms of Interaction between International Institutions,' *European Journal of International Relations* 15, no. 1 (2009): 125.

17. See Hall, 'Political Science and the Three New Institutionalisms.'

18. Clearly, this is a different type of constructivists than those like Onuf or Kubálková, who have an entirely different view of institutions (cf. N.G. Onuf, 'Rules, Agents, Institutions: A Constructivist Account,' Working Papers on International Society and Institutions, Global Peace and Conflict Studies at University of California, Irvine, 1996; or V. Kubálková, N.G. Onuf, and P. Kowert, eds., *International Relations in a Constructed World*, (Armonk, New York: M.E. Sharpe, 1998).

19. Alastair I. Johnston, 'Treating International Institutions as Social Environments,' *International Studies Quarterly* 45 (2001): 487.

20. Tanja Börzel, 'Member State Responses to Europeanization,' *Journal of Common Market Studies* 40 (2002): 193–214; John Connolly, 'Europeanization, Uploading and

Downloading: The Case of Defra and Avian Influenza,' *Public Policy and Administration* 23, no. 1 (2008): 7–25.

21. Rachel A. Epstein and Ulrich Sedelmeier, 'Beyond Conditionality: International Institutions in Postcommunist Europe after Enlargement,' *Journal of European Public Policy* 15, no. 6 (2008): 795–805.

22. Rachel A. Epstein, *In Pursuit of Liberalism: International Institutions in Postcommunist Europe* (Baltimore: Johns Hopkins University Press, 2008).

23. Thomas Risse, Stephen C. Ropp, and Kathryn Sikkink, *The Power of Human Rights: International Norms and Domestic Change* (Cambridge: Cambridge University Press, 1999).

24. Thomas Risse, 'Constructivism and International Institutions: Toward Conversations across Paradigms,' in *Political Science: State of the Discipline*, ed. Ira Katznelson and Helen V. Milner (New York: Norton, 2002), 597–623.

25. For an exception, see Epstein, *In Pursuit of Liberalism*.

26. Jeffrey T. Checkel, 'Why Comply? Social Learning and European Identity Change,' *International Organization* 55, no. 3 (2001): 553–88.

27. Jeffrey T. Checkel, 'International Institutions and Socialization in Europe: Introduction and Framework,' *International Organization* 59, no. 4 (2005): 808.

28. Judith Kelley, 'International Actors on the Domestic Scene: Membership Conditionality and Socialization by International Institutions,' *International Organization* 58, no. 3 (2004): 425–57.

29. Ibid, 425.

30. Robert O. Keohane and Judith Goldstein, *Ideas and Foreign Policy: An Analytical Framework* (Ithaca, NY: Cornell University Press, 1993).

31. This is not to deny that other problems exist too. Some criticism has been levelled against the institutionalists for years and decades, without leading to a substantive response (this includes the longstanding feminist critique of institutionalism, cf. L.J. Shepherd, ed., *Gender Matters in Global Politics: A Feminist Introduction to International Relations* (London and New York: Routledge, 2014). Others are newcomers to the field, such as the actor network theory that, however, seriously challenge the very definition of what constitutes an institution. A typical example in this category is the actor network theory (cf. Bruno Latour, 'On Actor-Network Theory: A Few Clarifications,' *Soziale Welt* 47, no. 4 (1996): 369–81.

32. Andrew Moravcsik, *Choice for Europe: Social Purpose and State Power from Messina to Maastricht* (Ithaca, NY: Cornell University Press, 1998).

33. Gourevitch, 'The Second Image Reversed,' 908.

34. Special Issue: The End of International Relations Theory? *European Journal of International Relations*, September 2013, http://journals.sagepub.com/toc/ejta/19/3.

35. Barbara Koremenos, Charles Lipson, and Duncan Snidal, 'The Rational Design of International Institutions,' *International Organization* 55, no. 4 (2001): 762.

36. Ibid., 761–99.

37. For the latter, see Thomas Rixen, Lora Anne Viola, and Michael Zürn, eds., *Historical*

Institutionalism and International Relations: Explaining Institutional Development in World Politics (Oxford: Oxford University Press, 2016).

38. See Robert O. Keohane and Lisa L. Martin, 'The Promise of Institutionalist Theory,' *International Security* 20, no. 1 (1995): 39–51.

39. See Lisa L. Martin and Beth A. Simmons, 'Theories and Empirical Studies of International Institutions,' *International Organization* 52, no. 4 (1998): 729–57.

40. Keohane, 'International Institutions: Two Approaches.'

41. Robert O. Keohane, *International Institutions and State Power: Essays in International Relations Theory* (San Francisco: Westview Press, 1989).

42. See Robert O. Keohane, *After Hegemony: Cooperation and Discord in the World Political Economy* (Princeton, NJ: Princeton University Press, 1984).

43. See, in particular, chapters 9 and 10 in Keohane, *International Institutions and State Power.*

44. Keohane and Martin, 'The Promise of Institutionalist Theory,' 46.

45. Daniel W. Drezner, 'Introduction: The Interaction of Domestic and International Institutions,' in *Locating the Proper Authorities: The Interaction of Domestic and International Institutions*, ed. Daniel W. Drezner (Michigan: University of Michigan Press, 2002).

46. B.S. Chimni, 'International Institutions Today: An Imperial Global State in the Making,' *European Journal of International Law* 15, no. 1 (2004): 1–37.

47. Martin and Simmons, 'Theories and Empirical Studies of International Institutions,' 729–757.

48. Brett A. Leeds, 'Domestic Political Institutions, Credible Commitments, and International Cooperation,' *American Journal of Political Science* 43, no. 4 (1999): 979–1002.

49. Risse, 'Constructivism and International Institutions,' 597–623.

50. See Kjell Goldmann, 'The Line in Water: International and Domestic Politics,' *Cooperation and Conflict* 24, no. 3 (1989): 103–116.

51. Michael Zürn, 'Democratic Governance beyond the Nation-State: The EU and Other International Institutions,' *European Journal of International Relations* 6, no. 2 (2000): 185.

52. Beate Kohler-Koch and Berthold Rittberger, 'Review Article: The "Governance Turn" in EU Studies,' *Journal of Common Market Studies* 44 (2006): 27–49.

53. Drezner, 'Introduction.'

54. Also see the attempts to reformulate neo-functionalism for telling examples: Philippe C. Schmitter, 'Three Neofunctional Hypotheses about International Integration,' *International Organization.* 23 (1969): 297–317; Jeppe Tranholm-Mikkelsen, 'Neofunctionalism: Obstinate or Obsolete? A Reappraisal in the Light of the New Dynamism of the EC,' *Millennium* 20 (1991): 1–22; Philippe C. Schmitter, 'Neo-Neo-Functionalism,' in *European Integration Theory*, ed. Antje Wiener and Thomas Diez (Oxford: Oxford University Press, 2004).

55. For some recent attempts and contributions see Erik Jones, 'Towards a Theory of Disintegration,' *Journal of European Public Policy* 25 no. 3 (2018), 440–51; and Hans

276

Vollaard, *European Disintegration: A Search for Explanations* (London: Palgrave, 2018).

56. Checkel, 'Why Comply?' 553–88.

57. See Dexter C. Payne, 'Policy-Making in Nested Institutions: Explaining the Conservation Failure of the EU's Common Fisheries Policy,' *Journal of Common Market Studies* 38, no. 2 (2000): 303–24; David S. Meyer, 'Political Opportunity and Nested Institutions,' *Social Movement Studies* 2, no. 1 (2003): 17–34.

58. Bátora, 'Mitrailleuse Effect,' 598–613.

59. Leeds, 'Domestic Political Institutions,' 979–1002.

10.

EU Institutions and Peace

Mai'a K. Davis Cross

Introduction

The international system is in the midst of a long peace, the likes of which has not been seen since the Roman Empire. The most powerful actors in the international system—or, the forty-four richest countries in the world—have not gone to war with each other since WWII.[1] Much of this can be attributed to developments in Europe over the past seventy years. This chapter seeks to explain how and why EU institutions have brought about regional transformations that have significantly contributed to this long period of peace.[2]

Since at least the seventeenth century, temporary periods of peace and the gradual creation of diplomatic norms were often achieved through major multilateral diplomatic congresses such as those leading to the 1648 Treaties of Westphalia and the 1713 Treaty of Utrecht.[3] Beginning in the early nineteenth century, when the Congress of Vienna set up the Concert of Europe, a coalition of great powers sought to achieve a longer-term peace through more regular diplomatic interactions designed to maintain a balance of power.[4] However, it was really with the outbreak of war in 1939, and the devastating failure of the Treaty of Versailles, that it became clear to many that the existing system of diplomacy was profoundly insufficient. New leaders rose to prominence in the mid-twentieth century, inspired to create an entirely different form of political organization for the achievement of peace. Their ideas manifested in the establishment of a multitude of international and regional institutions to foster cooperation among states in an emerging era of global governance. During this time, it was not uncommon for leaders to talk about taking this even further, calling for the establishment of a world government. As Thomas Weiss, president of the International Studies Association, writes, 'Throughout the 1940s, it was impossible in the United States to read periodicals, listen to the radio, or watch newsreels and not encounter the idea of world government.'[5]

Indeed, in the 1940s one-worldism became quickly popular for a number of reasons, including widespread worries that WWIII was a distinct possibility and fears surrounding the advent of nuclear weapons.[6] The idealist proponents of a world federation were clear that what they wanted was not simply another League of Nations or United Nations, but a central body to which countries would give up their sovereignty and which countries would endow with real power to enforce world law, backed up by a world constitution. This notion was so popular in the US that a Gallup Poll in September 1947 showed 56 percent in favour of strengthening the power of the UN so that it could function as a world government. There was a hearing in Congress to consider the idea the next year.[7] There was even some discussion at the international level of abolishing the national veto in the UN.

While the establishment of a world government was perhaps too ambitious, especially given the fact that the Soviets would never have accepted such a transformation in the UN, a core group of European leaders was determined to make this a reality at the regional level through the pursuit of integration—the pooling of sovereignty—among states. They believed that only through ceding national sovereignty to the supranational level would peace truly be possible. Ultimately, this initiative, originating in Europe, became the most advanced and successful experiment in transforming a region with centuries of violent conflict into one of enduring, and even permanent, peace. In the twenty-first century, the EU is recognized as a model for how to achieve peace through institutions and was awarded the Nobel Peace Prize in 2012.

This chapter proceeds as follows. The first section reviews the more general debate in the international relations literature that seeks to explain how international institutions lead to peace, and then looks more specifically at the debate surrounding the nature of EU institutions. The second section provides an account of the development of the EU over time, from the 1940s to today, to shed light on the stability of the current institutional arrangement in Europe and, specifically, how the creation of EU institutions consolidated regional peace over time. The final section examines whether the character and quality of these institutions has consequences for democratic legitimacy in Europe.

Debating Institutions and European Peace

An international institution is a formal organization in which multiple states participate in the pursuit of commonly agreed-upon goals. With the flourishing of international institutions beginning in the mid-twentieth century, most states in the international system belong to several institutions, and membership in each comes with different rules and responsibilities. Altogether, this form of political organization at the international level has made the system more reliant on diplomacy, more stable, and less prone to war. International institutions encourage states to conceive of the world in terms of absolute gains (all states can benefit together), instead of just relative gains (when one state benefits, another loses). There are many explanations for how international institutions contribute to peaceful interactions among states. To simplify, these perspectives can be grouped into three main camps, based on how much of an independent role international institutions are seen to have, compared to states.

The first camp, *neoliberal institutionalism*, assumes that international institutions have little independent role. This approach departs from realism only insofar as its adherents recognize that international institutions allow cooperation through overcoming collective action problems, reducing transaction costs, and increasing transparency and information. Realists generally assume that temporary peace is only possible if there is a balance of power among two or more states, or if a dominant, hegemonic state is willing to maintain an international regime that prevents war. Like realists, neoliberal institutionalists stick closely to rationalist assumptions (i.e., that actors always pursue their individual self-interest), while seeking to understand the role international institutions might play. Much of this school of thought focuses on the economic dimension of interdependence. For example, taking one step beyond realist hegemonic stability theory, Duncan Snidal argues that cooperation takes up where hegemony leaves off.[8] He argues that with the decline of US hegemony, and persistence of a free-trade regime since the 1980s, hegemony is neither necessary nor sufficient to explain stability. Similarly, Keohane's book, *After Hegemony*, also bridges the gap between hegemonic stability theory and neoliberal institutionalism.[9] He argues that intensive interaction among a few players can substitute for the control of a hegemonic power creating an international regime. According to Keohane, the mechanisms for stability are thus the ability for states to adapt and engage in mutual adjustment, rather than simply pursuing their own rational self-interest.

The second camp, *liberalism*, sees more of an independent role for international institutions. It rejects the realist premise that states mainly seek to maximize material self-interest. This camp instead emphasizes that states may want to pursue a higher common interest that they share. Liberals believe that socialization and the spread of norms can actually change the preferences of states over time.[10] Rather than only focusing on short-term calculations, they argue that states are capable of long-term cooperation, and not just on economic issues, but on a range of common goals. They argue that international institutions do not simply alter the payoff structure for states but create predictability and legitimacy because states renounce the use of military force when they are able instead to work through these institutions. In other words, states are capable of changing their preferences over time such that they are not simply focused on national self-interest. For example, Stephen Krasner argues that beyond realist notions of self-interest and power, international regimes mitigate anarchy through their diffusion of norms, beliefs, customs, and knowledge.[11] Similarly, John Ikenberry argues that when the US encouraged the creation of international institutions it was also willing to bind its own power in an open, democratic, and non-discriminatory rules-based order, rather than using these institutions mainly to amplify its own power.[12] Jeffrey Taliaferro reviews the literature on democratic peace and 'pacific union' in his chapter in this volume. Going well beyond realist thinking, liberals tend to agree that three outcomes occur when states form international institutions. First, they agree to settle differences in a peaceful manner without the use of force. Second, they see national interest as aligned with the broader interests of the international community. Thus, if dealing with an aggressor, those states that are members of international institutions work together to defeat it. Third, they develop trust in each other over time. The longer states remain members of international institutions, the easier it is to trust one another.

The third camp, *institutionalism*, argues more strongly still that international institutions take on a life of their own, beyond states. Scholars in this camp focus on the internal workings of international institutions and the influence of the bureaucrats and experts that work within these institutions. Institutionalists have typically focused more on domestic institutions but have more recently turned their attention to the international level, as described in Petr Kratochvíl's chapter in this volume. Institutionalists are the furthest removed from realist explanations in that they find that institutions can become actors in their own right or are more than the sum of their parts. Oftentimes, those in the constructivist school of thought or the English School adhere to this approach. The emphasis is more on the importance of international society and the ability of international institutions to change the nature of states' identities. Ideas and norms spread and socialize new actors, processes of learning over time constitute the behaviour of states, and non-state actors can also be heavily influential in the international system. In particular, those bureaucrats and diplomats who work within international institutions actively shape the norms advanced by those institutions. For example, John Ruggie argues that the principled beliefs, communicative action, and ideas of individuals and epistemic communities matter in determining the outcomes of international institutions.[13] Even though states create institutions, institutions can re-create states and even bind them to certain standards of behaviour, because the people who compose institutions are effective at persuading and pushing for new norms. Michael Barnett and Martha Finnemore analyse international institutions as bureaucracies to argue that they have power in their own right. Bureaucrats often determine the rules of interaction among states.[14] Overall, this approach argues that institutions can create peace through human agency and that ideas matter.

Each of these three approaches might be appropriate to explain various institutions, but the EU is a special case as it is the most advanced example of the power of institutions. As the next section of the chapter will demonstrate, the EU fits best with institutionalist arguments as member states have formally given up some of their national sovereignty to these institutions, empowering certain key individuals and ideas. Given the importance of the EU, a literature has emerged specifically devoted to explaining it.

To name the most prominent approaches, the theory of *neo-functionalism*—spill over of integration from one policy area to another—was a reaction to the rapid integration that took place in the first decades of the European Economic Community.[15] In turn, *intergovernmentalism*, which re-emphasized the sovereignty of member states, was a reaction to the slowing of integration in the seventies and early eighties.[16] The rise in popularity of *supranationalism*, a form of institutionalism, clearly reflected an effort to explain the strengthening of EU institutions from the mid-eighties through the nineties, and emphasizes the impact of their particular internal characteristics.[17] Multi-level governance in the 2000s sought to put a range of previous theories together in a kind of 'catch-all' explanation.[18] Subsequently, *constructivists* have sought to explain the fine-tuning of EU integration, which has often involved informal processes and norm diffusion.[19]

This rich debate is valuable in understanding certain aspects of cooperation and integration in Europe. However, these perspectives tend to be fundamentally tied to the time period in which they arise and the policy area on which they are focused. For the purposes of explaining why international institutions contribute to peace more generally and why the European region has been so much more successful than other efforts, it is valuable to seek to understand the greater trajectory of the European project.

The next section examines the development of the EU, with a focus on how and why in the late 1940s and early 1950s European leaders were finally able to make long-held ideas about uniting Europe a reality. The case of the EU is ideal to consider given its pioneering progress in achieving peace. In an effort to shed light on the longevity of the European project, rather than a particular time period or policy area, the emphasis will be on the way in which the federalist idea drove the creation of these early institutions and continued to shape the EU into the actor that it is today.

European Institutions and the Power of Ideas

To comprehend the nature and strength of the current arrangement, it is necessary to consider the past. The goals set for the European project at its inception demonstrate the importance of how early versions of European institutions embodied the transformational ideas of key leaders at the time. In particular, the centrality of the idea of federalism for Europe was crucial and set the path for the future momentum of EU integration that continues today.[20]

The idea of a united Europe has had a long history, stretching back to at least the philosophers of the seventeenth century. Prior to 1947, it was more often than not considered a utopian ideal rather than an achievable goal. During the interwar period, however, ideas surrounding the establishment of a federal union flourished, and subsequently re-emerged with greater strength in the wartime resistance movement. The most influential examples of this were Richard Coudenhove-Kalergi's 1923 book, *Pan-Europa*, and Altiero Spinelli's 1941 Ventotene Manifesto, calling for the immediate creation of a federal constitution for Europe.[21] Some spoke of this in the context of world government, as mentioned in the introduction to this chapter, and others focused more on the possibility of transatlantic federalism or an Atlantic Union, and still others associated it more narrowly with regional federation: the UK and France at the core of what would become a United States of Europe.[22] In 1947, the federalist idea became far more of a potential reality. Open support for this at both the popular and elite level was astounding, especially by today's standards.

This section advances the argument that the idea of federalism is not a story of the rise and gradual decline of an idea, as is often assumed. Instead, the idea has fundamentally shaped the nature of EU institutions all along, contributing to peace among European states. In addition, the federalist idea has tended to galvanize more support when framed as transformational (i.e., bold and visionary) rather than just transactional (i.e., individualistic and incremental). Finally, opinion leaders who have been able to pursue transformational ideas outside of the EU's formal institutional structures have often been more effective in impacting institutions than those who have operated from the inside.

The European Movement and Council of Europe

Across Europe in the late 1940s and 1950s, a European federalist movement blossomed at the societal level.[23] Several leaders of various organizations that were in favour of a united Europe founded the European Movement in December 1947. The key leaders of this movement were highly politically prominent and had close ties to governments, which gave them access to decision makers. These individuals included Paul-Henri Spaak, Winston Churchill, Konrad Adenauer, Léon Blum, Alcide De Gasperi, Jean Drapier, Richard Coudenhove-Kalergi, and Robert Schuman. However, it is important to note that the various chapters of the movement extended well beyond the original six members of what would become the fledgling EU (France, West Germany, Italy, Belgium, Netherlands, Luxembourg) to include countries in Eastern Europe (Albania, Bulgaria, Estonia, Hungary, Latvia, Lithuania, Turkey, Yugoslavia, Czechoslovakia, Romania, Poland, and so on) as well as countries to the north (Great Britain, Ireland, Norway, Denmark, Sweden, and so on).[24] Indeed, the point of the European Movement was to bring all of the various federalist organizations across Europe under one umbrella. Young people were a major force behind the European Movement, with organizations such as Jeune Europe pushing for more vitality and action behind words. The European Movement's Action Committee for the European Supranational Community (founded in 1952) even aimed to take 'militant action' to push for more integration in the European Coal and Steel Community (ECSC). This group was a big proponent of the European Defence Community (EDC) before the latter failed to pass through the French parliament.[25]

It was very much expected among those in this European Movement that the Council of Europe, founded in 1949, would be the venue where European federalism would be achieved. The calibre and seriousness of the discussions in the Council of Europe about how to proceed with the creation of a United States of Europe is little recognized. However, during and immediately after WWII, the discourse surrounding the need to create a new political organization for Europe through the creation of new institutions was thought to be both necessary and urgent. Even as the EDC was proposed and failed, as the Western European Union was launched, and as the Organisation for European Economic Co-operation (OEEC) took on responsibilities, representatives at the Council of Europe continually emphasized their institution's core role in uniting Europe. The other institutions, including the ECSC and Euratom, were regarded as more specialist organizations that would work on certain issues in support of the Council of Europe's overall centrality.

In 1955, Harold Macmillan, then British Secretary of State for Foreign Affairs, reflected on these early years, capturing the climate of the times:

> The Council of Europe and, especially, the Consultative Assembly were born out of the European Movement. This arose after the war by an almost spontaneous surge of emotion. I well remember the first gathering at The Hague in 1948. This meeting was organized by purely unofficial and voluntary efforts and yet it comprised the leading men and women of many countries . . . Those were the glorious, exciting, sometimes disorderly, but memorable days when our Movement began and the Council of Europe was founded. We had made it, not the Governments. Indeed, we had almost forced it upon the Governments. It was not just a political or a parliamentary phenomenon. It touched the imagination and raised the hopes of men and women in all walks of life, far transcending the normal confines of the political world.[26]

After the devastation of the war, the view among the representatives at the first session of the Council of Europe was that there was no choice but to create a united Europe that would be federal in character. They met as 'representatives of Europe trying to consider and solve problems in the interests of Europe as a whole'.[27] On 16 August 1949, the first substantive topic discussed at the Council of Europe was the future political structure of the entire continent. André Philip, a French representative who was the first to address the council in this debate, said,

What has brought us together at Strasbourg on this occasion is not merely the hope of achieving an ideal which dates back a long time in the traditions of our Continent, but also our consciousness of a situation of extreme urgency. It is the fact that public opinion in all our countries now realizes that the economic and political unification of Europe has become a matter of life and death for us all, and that unless we make rapid progress towards that unification we shall very soon find ourselves in what may become a tragic situation.[28]

He goes on to argue that the shared goal had to be a supranational Europe, a point of emphasis that all subsequent delegates present echoed strongly.[29] In essence, the first debate in the Council of Europe, which was later recognized as a 'landmark' event,[30] featured unanimous support for a united Europe on a strong path to federalism.

Naturally, some views were more cautious, and others were more ambitious. Mr Cappi, an Italian representative, expressed the more cautious side of the spectrum, pointing out the risks at stake on the first day of deliberations. As if foreshadowing the failure of the European Defence Community and European Political Community just five years later, he said,

Wisdom teaches us that politics—and we are engaged in politics in the most sublime sense of the word—is the art of the possible. Indeed, if we wish great historical events to be abiding and fertile, they must ripen in spirit and in fact, that is to say, they should be justified by circumstances. If some attempts fail because they are too hasty, if they are followed by bitter disappointments, these disappointments might be used to our disadvantage by many sceptics and opponents to our idea of a united Europe.[31]

The risk was high because all present understood very clearly that they were *not* launching the Council of Europe merely to replicate a regional version of the League of Nations or UN. At the same time, there was recognition that this was not going to be the same as the United States of America.[32] To be sure, there were competing ideas—unionists, functionalists, federalists, and so on—but it was also understood that these camps were not truly in opposition. The unionists, like Churchill, wanted to unite Europe in a broad sense, while the federalists, like Spinelli and the Union of European Federalists, also wanted the same, but more specifically through the signing of a federal constitution.[33] The functionalists too wanted federalism, but thought that a gradualist approach to get there would be preferable. Thus, they all wanted to end up with a united Europe but differed somewhat on the best path to get there. The British, Irish, and some Scandinavian representatives were more cautious, while most continental Europeans were more ambitious.[34] In response to these variations in viewpoints, Mr Le Bail of France struck a strong chord at the end of the first day of debate in the Council of Europe:

> Those in favour of caution say we must beware of an Assembly which starts to look like a congress; beware of an enthusiasm which has no outcome, and we must not make a great deal of noise about nothing! However, those in favour of boldness also call on us to beware! Beware of these legal quibbles which harden and paralyse the highest ideals! . . . I must say at once that I am on the side of the bold and opposed to the cautious. What is to become of us, in a few months or a few years time, if we are already timid? A great impulse has gone forth—a great creative impulse. It must be maintained at any price. How can we do this? By clearly perceiving the aim, which is very easy. Europe will not be created unless it is constantly allowed to outstrip its previous achievements.[35]

However, as the first few days passed in these early sessions of the Council of Europe, the hope placed in achieving federalism through this venue began to wane. The assembly resolved to create a Committee on General Affairs, led by Georges Bidault, to come up with a resolution on the political structure of Europe. Only twenty days after the start of discussions, the final report was underwhelming and seemed to focus more on accounting for differences among viewpoints than consolidating a common goal. Italian representative Mr Parri described the resolution as a 'first-class funeral, especially when compared to the eloquent discussions which took place in this Assembly during the Debate'.[36] He went on to say that he was 'anxious that the Assembly of Europe should declare that it has not forgotten the reason for its existence.'[37] Similarly, French representative Mr Bardoux said, 'this text is not only summary and cursory, but it is also thin and meagre; it lacks body; it is lifeless and it makes no appeal to the imagination. Yet Napoleon said that 'it is through imagination that people can be led.'[38] This capitulation to differences and national sovereignty had already become a matter of concern for Paul-Henri Spaak, president of the Council of Europe, who told *Le Monde* the day before that 'Our task must surely be that of thinking and feeling as Europeans, in all the branches of the Assembly, whether in its Permanent Committee or on the floor of the house.'[39] Naturally, those who were not fully in the federalist camp were satisfied with the resolution, particularly as it had unanimous approval by the committee.

This brief look at the debate that launched the first effort at creating federalist institutions in Europe demonstrates how even with large-scale political will—both at the popular and elite levels—putting a transformational idea into practice can still be easier said than done. The next stage in this effort involved a more focused number of players whose ideas converged more closely.

European Coal and Steel Community

Just a few months after the opening session of the Council of Europe, French Foreign Minister Robert Schuman announced Jean Monnet's plan (known as the Schuman Plan) for the European Coal and Steel Community (ECSC), with France and West Germany at its core. Thus, in 1950, discussions in the Council of Europe shifted to how this other, much more limited, arrangement would come to embody true European political integration. The secretary-general of the Council of Europe later described the advent of the ECSC as the 'concrete expression to the political decisions taken by the Assembly in favour of creating a European Authority', in effect interpreting the ECSC as an offshoot of the Council of Europe.[40]

This was not necessarily an accurate portrayal. Although it seemed to be narrow in its aim, the ECSC was far more ambitious than the Council of Europe because it involved true supranationalism from the start. It would be more accurate to say that the early shortcomings of the Council of Europe inspired the launch of the ECSC. Indeed, Jean Monnet himself made a speech at the Council of Europe in 1950 calling upon the others to join the Schuman Plan. Several representatives, including the British, responded that their countries would not be able to join this new initiative, betraying the limits that had emerged in the first few months of the Council of Europe's activities. When the Council of Europe's president, Paul-Henri Spaak, resigned early in December 1951, it clearly signalled that the impetus had shifted to the ECSC.[41] To be sure, the process of launching the early stages of the European Community was not easy. It was preferable at the beginning to avoid settling for only a 'Little Europe', which included the original Six, but actually instead pushing for a community that would encompass Great Britain and Scandinavia as well. Given that these countries were most reluctant to embrace federalism, a Little Europe it was to be. As Carlo Schmid, a politician in the Social Democratic Party of West Germany, said during a radio interview on 25 January 1956, 'No politically responsible man dares to think of a freely elected All-European parliament today.'[42] Ultimately, even though ratification of the Schuman Plan among the Six had its stumbling blocks, these leaders determined that the ECSC would be the best place to build this idea in practice.

In particular, Jean Monnet, the architect of the ECSC, actually felt from the very beginning that the Council of Europe would go nowhere as long as it maintained the national veto.[43] By contrast, he designed the institutions of the ECSC without this possibility. Moreover, Monnet had a clear idea of how the federalist idea would reach fruition through this new organization. He said, 'By the pooling of basic production and the establishment of a new High Authority whose decisions will be binding on France, Germany, and the countries that join them, this proposal will lay the first concrete foundations of the European Federation which is indispensable to the maintenance of peace.'[44] He clearly saw this as 'the first step towards European federation' with an 'ultimate objective to contribute essentially to the creation of a United States of Europe.'[45] Thus, when Monnet spoke of the ECSC, he emphasized the importance of its institutions and the necessity of giving up some element of national sovereignty to them. He said, 'Any of these institutions may be changed and improved in the light of experience. What cannot be challenged is the principle that they are supranational—in other words, federal—institutions.'[46]

Again, just because the initial launch of the ECSC was limited to supranational control of coal and steel production did not mean that ambitions were modest. Many ardent federalists were pushing for more but came up against confederalists and functionalists who saw their proposals as too far-ranging. The failure of the European Defence Community, which would have created a full-scale European army, in the French Parliament was the ultimate expression of this. Nonetheless, the European Defence Community and European Political Community signalled the still highly political thinking of the EU's founding fathers. It was just that there were still difficult obstacles in these early years after the war. As Walter Hallstein said in 1961, 'Both failed—not so much because of a general lack of the will to achieve them, as because of particular political circumstances, among others a virulent and largely Communist inspired propaganda campaign against them.'[47] Even failed ideas matter, as they shape the terms of the debate and extend the parameters of what might be possible.

Action Committee for the United States of Europe

Once the ECSC was set up, Monnet was still not satisfied, and in November 1954 resigned his position as president of the High Authority in order to push for more European integration. The failure of the EDC had left public opinion uninterested in the prospects for real integration, and when the foreign ministers of the Six spoke to the press after the 1955 conference in Messina, Italy, they had an agreement to set up the European Economic Community, but without much enthusiasm.[48] In this context, and after the failure of the European Defence Community, Monnet saw the need to energize the European movement once more. When he stepped down from his post at the helm of the ECSC, he said, 'I think I can be of more use to you outside.'[49] His aim was to 're-launch' Europe,[50] and by resigning from the High Authority he was free to become more active. He did so as a private individual through the creation of the Action Committee for the United States of Europe on 13 October 1955, relying on funding from his family's cognac business.[51] Like with the Schuman Plan negotiations, Monnet adopted a particular kind of diplomatic approach that would favour some ideas over others. He kept the group small and focused on members of political parties and trade unions, but not neo-fascists, Communists, Gaullists, and other militant European groups.

Others in the European federalist movement were at first alarmed by Monnet's departure from the Authority, and the press also speculated that Monnet had abandoned the project. To the contrary, after months of bringing together nearly all of the leaders of the Socialist, Christian Democrat, and Liberal political parties,[52] as well as trade unions throughout Europe, the Action Committee's work began in January 1956, and it continued on for two decades.[53] The stated goal of the Action Committee was 'to arrive by concrete achievements at the United States of Europe.'[54] Significantly, membership in the committee rested with the organizations—political parties and trade unions—rather than the individuals who met on behalf of these organizations.[55]

The sheer amount of work Monnet put into this new push for a United States of Europe demonstrated that the momentum for the federalist idea had shifted to the Action Committee. The Action Committee met roughly once per year after its inception and held fourteen meetings between 1956 and 1970. The first ten were in Paris, followed by meetings in Bonn (1965), Berlin (1965), Brussels (1967), and London (1969). Each meeting was closed to the public, but upon its conclusion, a public announcement was made on the mutually agreed resolution. With all of the groundwork laid in advance of each meeting, most agreements were arrived at unanimously, but any abstentions or disagreements were noted in the public press conference. On occasion, national political parties also vetted some aspects of these agreements in advance, giving them stronger legitimacy.[56]

There were initially three main goals of the Action Committee. The first key task of the committee was to expand the supranational precedent set by the ECSC to the creation of Euratom—a federal approach to nuclear energy. Indeed, the first few meetings were virtually exclusively devoted to this. And, importantly, Monnet wanted to ensure that the institutional precedent set by the ECSC was the model for Euratom. The High Authority, in his view, needed to be endowed with significant federal power. The second main task was to ensure the establishment of the common market or European Economic Community (EEC). Third, the entry of Britain into this arrangement was a key goal.

In some respects, the proposal for a common market, and a shift towards economic goals, was a reaction to the failure of the European Defence Community. As Spaak, then Minister of Foreign Affairs of Belgium, put it in a speech on 21 October 1955, 'We then considered that having failed on the political plane, we should take up the question of the economic plane and use the so-called functional method, availing ourselves to some extent . . . of the admittedly successful experiment already made with the European Coal and Steel Community.'[57] However, Spaak, who later became known as one of the main founding fathers of the EU, went on to lament that it is much more difficult to arouse the interest and passion of the European public in following a functionalist instead of federalist path. In his words, 'The economic and functional method, therefore, is less likely to attract and retain the attention—let alone enthusiasm—of the masses than the constitutional method which is based on ideas of a more general nature and so easier to assimilate.'[58] He appealed to decision makers not to focus primarily on technical details, but instead on political resolve. He said, 'The day that this political resolve gathers its full force there will be no technical problem that cannot be solved.'[59]

European Economic Community

As Europeans proceeded on the basis of a gradualist approach to integration, the main idea driving these initiatives was still the creation of a federal United States of Europe, but it began to fade from prominence as the more direct benefits from integration began to be felt. Once the EEC was agreed upon, its striking success provided much momentum for the Six to surpass even their own goals. In 1960, trade among EEC member states was around 28 percent higher than the year before, and the community's international trade increased by around 23 percent. Industrial production was 11 percent higher and GNP was 6.5 percent higher in 1960 compared to 1959. This economic success far exceeded initial projections about the impact of the common market.[60]

The more functionalist logic focused on the need to create free movement of persons, services, and capital, and to prevent discrimination within the common market, such as financial penalties. As these more specific rationales began to take over, the idea of the far more ambitious United States of Europe began to recede, just as Spaak had predicted.[61] In 1961, Hallstein gave speeches in the US that focused on the EEC, with only indirect mention of a United States of Europe. Instead, he emphasized that political integration must exist alongside economic integration, a far less ambitious framing than before. However, he still noted that political integration would not be some kind of automatic process. A political choice had to be made. Moreover, he said, 'There are two words by which I should like to characterize the development of the European Community in the past years and months: these words are success and recognition.'[62] In the early sixties, documents from Monnet's Action Committee clearly betrayed a sense of disappointment with the lack of true federalism. Transactional ideas could not inspire the public in the same way as transformational ones, but integration was by this time infused into institutional life and continued forward, nonetheless.

Expanding Membership and Continued Integration

The achievement of federalism may not have happened all at once as some had hoped, but the idea had clearly put Europe's institutions on a strong trajectory towards more formal integration over time, even alongside the challenge of expanding membership from six to twenty-eight. From the 1970s onward, the EEC continued on a steady path of both enlargement and integration. At times, such as during the 1970s and early 1980s, progress towards integration slowed. At other times, such as during the late 1980s through to the early 2000s, with the signing of the 1986 Single European Act and the 1992 Maastricht Treaty, integration proceeded more rapidly. The relative speed of integration coincided with the rise and fall in popularity of the federalist idea, highlighting the ongoing centrality of the founding idea of federalism.[63] Importantly, federalism's popularity was not directly tied to increased economic gain as neoliberals might assume. For example, during the sixties and seventies, Europe fared better than the United States economically, and yet integration both accelerated (1960s) and slowed (1970s) during the same period.

Various informal pro-federalist organizations thrived in parallel to the formal evolution of EU institutions. These included the Crocodile Club, the Conference on European Federation, the Action Committee for the

United States of Europe, the European Movement, the European Union of Federalists, the Altiero Spinelli Action Committee for European Union, and the Spinelli Group, among many others. In particular, the Spinelli Group was where many ideas for advancing federalism were spawned and debated before being taken to the main floor of the European parliament. Many of the most prominent EU leaders were also members of these pro-federalist groups. With the precedent Monnet had set—pushing the federalist idea from outside of the formal institutions, rather than from within them—the importance of these informal groups in nurturing the federalist idea should not be underestimated. Support from across the Atlantic was also part of the backbone of integration. As Monnet said, 'This is the first time in history that a great power [the United States], instead of basing its policy on the keeping-up of divisions, has continuously and resolutely supported the establishment of a great community founded on union between peoples hitherto living apart.'[64] Indeed, the idea of European federalism so fascinated American elites that there was even serious talk of crafting a transatlantic union instead of leaving it just for Europeans to pursue. The European Movement itself had close ties to the American Committee for a United Europe, chaired by William J. Donovan, and it received funding from the Ford Foundation, which sponsored a series of publications on European federalism.[65]

In the lead-up to the 1990s, ongoing support for federalism finally broke through the barriers that had separated foreign and security policy from the integration process since the early failure of the European Defence Community and the European Political Committee in the 1950s. This was highly symbolic, as security is typically thought to be at the very core of national sovereignty.[66] It is noteworthy that in the 1960s, Monnet's new proposals to launch a common foreign policy and defence were a significant part of the Action Committee's work.

In 1970, the Six were able to put into place European Political Cooperation (EPC), but it was separated from European Community structures and not backed by treaty agreement. It was not really until after the Cold War and the 1992 Maastricht Treaty on European Union that the Common Foreign and Security Policy (CFSP) enshrined political and security cooperation into a treaty. There was even some debate over whether the word 'federal' would appear in this treaty, but it was ultimately taken out of the final text. Nonetheless, the fact that the idea was still part of formal discussion in the early nineties shows its endurance and influence in framing what was possible. With the advent of CFSP, the stage was set for more common external action. It called for the EU

> to assert its identity on the international scene . . . including the eventual framing of a common defence policy, which might in time lead to a common defence . . . The Member States shall support the Union's external and security policy actively and unreservedly in a spirit of loyalty and mutual solidarity. They shall refrain from any action, which is contrary to the interests of the Union or likely to impair its effectiveness as a cohesive force in international relations.[67]

Then, in December 1998, during a summit in Saint-Malo, France, French President Jacques Chirac and British Prime Minister Tony Blair agreed that the EU needed a true defence capability.[68] In other words, the two main security actors wanted the EU to 'have the capacity for autonomous action, backed up by credible military forces'.[69] Blair and Chirac were both witnessing Europe's utter inability to act in the midst of the crisis in Kosovo and the collapse of Yugoslavia. The Saint-Malo Declaration represented a big shift in British policy, as the UK had resisted the idea for decades.[70] In 1999, member states approved the European Security and Defense Policy (ESDP), reflecting the goals of Saint-Malo. Finally, in 2003, after decades of effort, the EU finally made ESDP (now CSDP) operational, sending troops out to conduct humanitarian operations under the EU flag. For the first time, the EU had not only articulated a desire for a common foreign policy, it had actually put concrete action behind these words, following this up with more than thirty military operations and civilian missions across three continents. Even now, there is debate over how strong the EU is on the international stage, with some arguing that its power is rather limited,[71] while others describing the EU as an emerging superpower.[72]

The federalist idea, in the second decade of the twenty-first century, is alive and well. However, getting here has been something of a rocky path, and as a result of a two-decade transformational period from the mid-eighties through to the first few years of the twenty-first century, the process has become more transactional. When the French and Dutch referenda rejected the 2005 Constitutional Treaty, the text of which invoked strong federalist symbolism, this signalled another turning point. Even though a nearly identical version of that treaty was approved as the 2009 Lisbon Treaty, the subsequent decade since the failure of the Constitutional Treaty has been one of scepticism about the future of federalism in the EU. For example, as Mark Mazower argues, 'Integration has been driven by a bureaucratic elite that continues to see national sovereignty as an obstacle to be overcome, but this elite has largely lost sight of the principles of social solidarity and human dignity that Spinelli wished to resurrect.'[73] This sense of disillusionment seems common, but is there any basis for it? As I discuss in the next section, there is little reason to assume that the EU lacks legitimacy. Some of the negativity surrounding the EU can be attributed to the media's tendency to exaggerate and sensationalize[74]—bad news sells—and some can be blamed on the recent dearth of inspirational leaders like Spinelli, Monnet, Spaak, Jacques Delors, and many others. Despite this, opinion polls consistently show that Europeans trust EU institutions more than their national institutions, and around 70 percent support a stronger EU foreign and security policy.[75]

While it is common to deride the EU as stumbling from crisis to crisis, especially in the twenty-first century, it is clear that the EU is remarkably resilient.[76] If one is to believe the press, doomsday scenarios abound: either certain key member states are ostensibly on the verge of leaving the EU, or the European economy is on the brink of collapse, or a cornerstone policy of EU integration—the euro, the Common Foreign and Security Policy, the common market, Schengen—is about to be thrown out. The instances are many and are typically described as such, with notable examples stretching from the 1965 Empty Chair crisis to the 1999 Commission resignation crisis, right up through the recent Greek debt and ongoing refugee crises.[77] Journalists, commentators, politicians, and other public figures quickly jump on the bandwagon, often invoking predictions about the imminent demise of the EU. Yet none of these predictions has actually come true.

At the same time, the creation and build-up of crises that seemingly threaten the very existence of the EU is only part of the story. What is perhaps equally interesting, and ultimately more important, is how Europeans then grapple with and overcome these crises. After these crises reach their height of intensity, seemingly bringing the EU to the brink of failure in the eyes of many, they then dissipate and leave in their wake a renewed will to find consensus. The EU has often been compared to a bicycle, in that if it stops moving forward, it might fall over. The release of the EU Global Strategy and French-German calls for the creation of a true defence union only days after the result of the Brexit referendum was known is a case in point. Indeed, European leaders repeatedly take some dramatic steps towards more integration in the wake of these sorts of existential crisis. It is often casually recognized, usually with the benefit of hindsight, that European actors seem to use crises as opportunities to further shape European order beyond what can be achieved incrementally. An article in *The Economist* quipped that 'Europe's model of change has long been based on lurch then muddle.'[78] The 1986 Single European Act, 2003 European Security Strategy, 2009 Lisbon Treaty, and 2011 Fiscal Compact, among many others, all followed seemingly serious existential crises.

The EU's founding fathers thought that by forming institutions, their ideas would live on. They were concerned that future leaders in Europe would not have the same far-reaching, transformational ideas. As this analysis shows, to a significant extent, the founders were right. EU institutions have served the role of holding on to what has already been agreed—especially the achievement of peace—creating a kind of path dependence. Ideas reside in leaders and in the people, as well as having an impact through institutions. Strong and enduring ideas help to frame the parameters of what is possible, even if sometimes behind the scenes. It may ultimately be that integration is beginning to slow down in the second decade of the twenty-first century and that the process is reaching a kind of equilibrium between the federalist idea and member-state sovereignty. If this is the case, the strength of the current quasi-federal system is likely strong enough to uphold peace over the long term. Some would argue that it might even get stronger and more cohesive with the departure of the UK, which has been a spoiler to many agreements from the beginning. Nevertheless, the EU is still a product of human agency as the various existential crises demonstrate, and the danger of self-fulfilling prophecies is ever-present.

Conclusion: Legitimacy through Institutions?

In sum, this chapter argues that ideas filtered through institutions can be highly influential, in line with the institutionalist school of thought. But is the EU also 'opaque and unrepresentative', in the words of one scholar?[79] I argue that even though this has been an elite-led integration process that is transactional at times, the EU is still remarkably legitimate and accepted at the popular level. Indeed, while the European public may not always be enthusiastic about the EU, they have nonetheless consistently supported its existence. As Fabio Serricchio, Myrto Tsakatika, and Lucia Quaglia write, there is 'a distinction between mass attitudes towards the current workings of the EU and mass attitudes towards the project of European integration.'[80] In other words, critics of the EU are not necessarily *against* the EU. For example, during the Eurozone crisis, Greek citizens had declining trust in the EU, but they still overwhelmingly wanted to stay in the EU and keep the Euro.[81] Kratochvíl's chapter in this book describes how the Visegrad countries formed their own institutional structure to seek change in the nature of EU institutions. Thus, critics often want to change the nature of the EU rather than dismantle it.

It is also important to recognize that as integration has increased over time, EU institutions have carefully cultivated democratic participation in tandem. The European parliament has grown in power and capacity, individuals can protect their rights directly through the European Court of Justice, various forums allow citizen participation, and the latest treaty enables Europeans to put forward proposals for new laws directly to the European Commission, among other things. In systematic comparisons of EU democracy with other federal systems like Switzerland and the US, the EU actually fairs well, if not better.[82] While some interpret routine breakdowns in consensus in Brussels as European dysfunction, in fact, such friction is a normal part of democracy. After all, it is to be expected that within democracies—particularly within twenty-eight different democracies—there will be debate, disagreement, and political gridlock. Comparison with the US is instructive—the polarization of just two political parties in the American system is often more of a problem than disagreement among twenty-eight EU member states over issues debated in Brussels. Unlike the US, the EU's government has never shut down.

Criticism of the EU is a healthy part of the democratic process. When put to the test, Europeans have repeatedly strengthened their resolve to continue with the project after each crisis. This has been most visible in the wake of major crises when Europeans face the possibility of dis-integrating. As Monnet remarked long ago, 'People only accept change when they are faced with necessity, and only recognize necessity when a crisis is upon them.' Even in transactional periods, crises seem to inspire transformation, but there is always the danger that the pull of national sovereignty will detract from the common goals of the EU. It is worth remembering that the original European Movement that spawned the Council of Europe and ECSC was fundamentally driven by a desire to prevent nationalism from sparking serious conflict among European countries again. In today's context, the more populist and nationalist sentiments rise to the surface in the member states, the more EU institutions are put to the test. Nonetheless, EU institutions were designed precisely to be the safeguard against nationalism, no matter how much far-right parties and leaders in Europe seek to frame them as the cause.

Notes

1. Steven Pinker, *The Better Angels of Our Nature: Why Violence Has Declined* (New York: Viking, 2011).
2. In referring to EU institutions, I also include their precursors: European Coal and Steel Community (ECSC), European Economic Community (EEC), and European Communities (EC).
3. Maïa K. Davis Cross, *The European Diplomatic Corps: Diplomats and International Cooperation from Westphalia to Maastricht* (Basingstoke: Palgrave, 2007).
4. Mark Mazower, *Governing the World: the History of an Idea, 1815 to the Present* (New York: Penguin, 2012).
5. Thomas G. Weiss, 'What Happened to the Idea of World Government,' *International Studies Quarterly* 53, no. 2 (2009): 253–71, 259.
6. Mazower, *Governing the World.*

7. Ibid.

8. Duncan Snidal, 'The Limits of Hegemonic Stability Theory,' *International Organization* 39, no. 4 (1985): 579–614.

9. Robert O. Keohane, *After Hegemony: Cooperation and Discord in the World Political Economy* (Princeton, NJ: Princeton University Press, 2005).

10. Joseph S. Nye Jr and David A. Welch, *Understanding Global Conflict and Cooperation: An Introduction to Theory and History* (London: Pearson Higher Ed, 2012).

11. Stephen D. Krasner, 'Structural Causes and Regime Consequences: Regimes as Intervening Variables,' *International Organization* 36, no. 2 (1982): 186

12. John G. Ikenberry, *After victory: Institutions, Strategic Restraint, and the Rebuilding of Order After Major Wars* (Princeton, NJ: Princeton University Press, 2009).

13. John Gerard Ruggie, 'What Makes the World Hang Together? Neo-utilitarianism and the Social Constructivist Challenge,' *International Organization* 52, no. 4 (1998): 855–85.

14. Michael Barnett and Martha Finnemore, *Rules for the World: International Organizations in Global Politics* (Ithaca, NY: Cornell University Press, 2004).

15. Ernst B. Haas, *Beyond the Nation State: Functionalism and International Organization* (Colchester, UK: ECPR Press, 2008).

16. Stanley Hoffmann, 'Obstinate or Obsolete? The Fate of the Nation-State and the Case of Western Europe,' *Daedalus* 95, no. 3 (1966): 862–915; Andrew Moravcsik, 'Preferences and Power in the European Community: A Liberal Intergovernmentalist Approach,' *Journal of Common Market Studies* 31, no. 4 (1993): 473–524.

17. George Tsebelis and Geoffrey Garrett, 'The Institutional Foundations of Intergovernmentalism and Supranationalism in the European Union.' *International Organization* 55, no. 2 (2001): 357–390; Peter L. Lindseth, 'Democratic Legitimacy and the Administrative Character of Supranationalism: The Example of the European Community,' *Columbia Law Review* 99 (1999): 628–738; Robert O. Keohane and Stanley Hoffmann. *Institutional Change in Europe in the 1980s* (London: Macmillan Education UK, 1994); Alec Stone Sweet and Wayne Sandholtz, 'Integration, Supranational Governance, and the Institutionalization of the European Polity,' *European Integration and Supranational Governance* 1 (1998).

18. Liesbet Hooghe and Gary Marks, *Multi-level Governance and European Integration* (Lanham, MD: Rowman & Littlefield, 2001); Liesbet Hooghe, *Cohesion Policy and European Integration: Building Multi-Level Governance* (Oxford: Oxford University Press, 1996).

19. Jeffrey T Checkel, 'Why Comply? Social Learning and European Identity Change,' *International Organization* 55, no. 3 (2001): 553–88; Jeffrey T. Checkel, 'International Institutions and Socialization in Europe: Introduction and Framework,' *International Organization* 59, no. 4 (2005): 801–26; Kathleen R. McNamara, *The Currency of Ideas: Monetary Politics in the European Union* (Ithaca, NY: Cornell University Press, 1998); Nicolas Jabko, *Playing the Market: A Political Strategy for Uniting Europe, 1985–2005* (Ithaca, NY: Cornell University Press, 2006); Mai'a, K. Davis Cross,

Security Integration in Europe: How Knowledge-Based Networks Are Transforming the European Union (Ann Arbor, MI: University of Michigan Press, 2011).

20. Michael Burgess, *Federalism and European Union: The Building of Europe, 1950–2000* (London: Routledge, 2000).

21. Desmond Dinan, *Ever Closer Union: An Introduction to European Integration* (New York: Palgrave, 1999), 12.

22. Richard Mayne and John Pinder, *Federal Union: The Pioneers* (New York: St. Martin's Press, 1990.

23. M. Serrarens (Netherlands), 'Official Report of the Fifth Sitting, 16th August 1949,' (Council of Europe documents: Nobel Peace archive), 103.

24. Foreign Service Despatch no. 918 from Sheldon B. Vance, Second Secretary of Embassy, American Embassy in Brussels to the Department of State Washington, February 21, 1956 (National Archives and Records Administration [NARA] of the United States).

25. Ibid.

26. Council of Europe Consultative Assembly, Seventh Ordinary Session (First Part), Official Report, Third Sitting, Wednesday, July 6th, 1955 at 9:30 am (NARA).

27. Council of Europe Secretariat-General, 'European Unity: Achievement and Prospects,' SG (58) I Part II, Strasbourg, April 25th, 1958 (Nobel Peace archive), 7.

28. Official Report of the Fifth Sitting, August 16, 1949, Council of Europe documents (Nobel Peace archive), 78.

29. Ibid, 80. Interestingly, countries that would not be part of the EU for several decades were just as fervent in their support of European unity and supranationalism as the others: Turkey, Greece, UK, Ireland.

30. Council of Europe Secretariat-General, 'European Unity: Achievement and Prospects,' SG (58) I Part II, Strasbourg, April 25, 1958. (Nobel Peace archive), 7.

31. M. Cappi (Italy), 'Official Report of the Fifth Sitting,' August 16, 1949, Council of Europe, 82.

32. M. Düsünsel (Turkey), ibid, 143.

33. Desmond Dinan, *Ever Closer Union: An Introduction to European Integration*, (New York: Palgrave, 1999), 13.

34. Mr. De Valera (Ireland), 'Official Report of the Sixth Sitting,' August 17, 1949, (Council of Europe documents), 141.

35. M. Le Bail (France), 'Official Report of the Sixth Sitting,' August 17, 1949 (Council of Europe documents), 119.

36. Parri (Italy), 'Official Report of the Fifteenth Sitting,' September 5, 1949, (Council of Europe documents), 481.

37. Ibid., 482.

38. Bardoux (France), ibid., 483.

39. As quoted by Bonnefous (France), ibid., 495.

40. Council of Europe Secretariat-General, 'European Unity: Achievement and Prospects,' SG (58) I Part II, Strasbourg, April 25, 1958 (Nobel Peace archive), 11

41. Desmond Dinan, *Europe Recast: A History of European Union* (Basingstoke: Palgrave, 2004), 25.

42. Foreign Service Despatch No. 1567 from Elim O'Shaughnessy, Counsellor of Embassy, American embassy Bonn to the Department of State, Washington. January 30, 1956 (NARA).

43. Jean Monnet, *Memoirs* (Arizona: Third Millennium Publishing), 273, 281.

44. Ibid., 298.

45. Statement before 'Randall Committee' investigating United States foreign trade policy, November 11, 1953, Paris (NARA).

46. Speech to the Council of Ministers, September 8, 1952 (NARA).

47. Walter Hallstein, 'Economic Integration and Political Unity in Europe,' speech before the joint meeting of Harvard University and the Massachusetts Institute of Technology, May 23, 1961, 9.

48. 'Note sure *l'histoire du comite*,' Jean Monnet Foundation, record code AMK 1/1/4.

49. Monnet, *Memoirs*, 405.

50. Clifford P. Hackett, *Monnet and the Americans: The Father of a United Europe and His U.S. Supporters* (Washington, DC: Jean Monnet Council, 1995), 22.

51. Colin Bingham, *Australian Financial Review*, February 2, 1961.

52. All non-Communist parties, representing around 60 million voters and 12 million trade unionists, equivalent to 67 percent of all citizens and 70 percent of organized labour.

53. Monnet, *Memoirs*, 405–17.

54. 'Action Committee for the United States of Europe,' note, 1970, Jean Monnet Foundation, record code AMK 1/2/11.

55. Walter Yondorf, 'Monnet and the Action Committee: The Formative Period of the European Communities,' *International Organization* 19, no. 4 (1965): 885–912.

56. 'Action Committee for the United States of Europe,' note, 1970.

57. Council of Europe Consultative Assembly, Seventh Ordinary Session, speech made by M. Paul-Henri Spaak, Minister for Foreign Affairs of Belgium at the Twenty-First Sitting of the Consultative Assembly, held on Friday, 21 October 1955 (NARA), 3.

58. Ibid., 4.

59. Ibid., 6.

60. 'The European Economic Community,' speech made by Walter Hallstein in Paris, January 23, 1961 (Monnet Foundation, Lausanne), 9.

61. Gilles Grin connects the decline of federalism with the development and growth of the EEC. See Gilles Grin, 'The Community Method: From Jean Monnet to Current Challenges,' *The EuroAtlantic Union Review* 2, no. 2 (2015): 15–29.

62. 'The EEC and the Community of the Free World,' speech made by Walter Hallstein in Zurich to the Schweizerische Europa-Union, November 24, 1961 (Jean Monnet Foundation), 2.

63. This can be traced through membership numbers in the Union of European Federalists over time.

64. Speech to the Common Assembly, Strasbourg, June 19, 1953 (NARA).

65. Foreign Service Despatch No. 918 from Sheldon B. Vance, Second Secretary of Embassy, American Embassy in Brussels to the Department of State Washington, February 21, 1956 (NARA).

66. Cross, *Security Integration in Europe.*

67. Treaty on European Union, Article J 1992.

68. The story behind how this agreement was reached is well told in Howorth 2004 and Mérand 2010.

69. Franco-British summit joint declaration on European defence, 1998.

70. Julian Lindley-French, *A Chronology of European Security & Defence* (Oxford: Oxford University Press, 2007), 247

71. Asle Toje, *The European Union as a Small Power: After the Post-Cold War* (Basingstoke: Palgrave, 2011).

72. John McCormick, *The European Superpower* (Basingstoke: Palgrave Macmillan, 2007); Andrew Moravcsik, 'Europe: The Quiet Superpower,' *French Politics* 7, no. 3 (2009): 403–22.

73. Mark Mazower, *Governing the World: The History of an Idea, 1815 to the Present* (New York: Penguin, 2012), 408.

74. Mai'a. K. Davis Cross and Xinru Ma, 'EU Crises and Integrational Panic: The Role of the Media,' *Journal of European Public Policy* 22, no. 8 (2015): 1053–70.

75. European Commission, Public Opinion, Standard Eurobarometer, accessed November 12, 2018, http://ec.europa.eu/COMMFrontOffice/publicopinion/index.cfm.

76. Mai'a K. Davis Cross, *The Politics of Crisis in Europe* (Cambridge: Cambridge University Press, 2017).

77. Wallace Thies, 'Is the EU Collapsing?' *International Studies Review* 14, no. 2 (2012): 225–39.

78. 'The European Union: Restoring Europe's Smile,' *Economist*, October 24, 2002.

79. Mazower, *Governing the World*, 412.

80. Fabio Serricchio, Myrto Tsakatika, and Lucia Quaglia, 'Euroscepticism and the Global Financial Crisis,' *Journal of Common Market Studies* 51, no.1 (2013): 51–64, 52.

81. Kyriaki Nanou and Susannah Vernet, 'The Eurozone Crisis Has Increased Soft Euroscepticism in Greece, Where Greeks Wish to Remain in the Euro, but No Longer Trust the EU,' *LSE European Politics and Policy (EUROPP) Blog*, March 2, 2013, http://blogs.lse.ac.uk/europpblog/2013/03/02/greece-euroscepticism/.

82. Thomas D. Zweifel, '. . . Who Is Without Sin Cast the First Stone: The EU's Democratic Deficit in Comparison,' *Journal of European Public Policy* 9, no. 5 (2002): 812–40; Frank Decker, 'Governance Beyond the Nation-State: Reflections on the Democratic Deficit of the European Union,' *Journal of European Public Policy* 9, no. 2 (2002): 256–72.

Peace and Development

11.

Fragile States and International Support

Paul Collier

Introduction: What Is a Fragile State?

Fragile states, like Tolstoy's unhappy families, have little in common. They are best defined by what they are not: they are neither cohesive common-interest states, nor effectively repressive autocratic states. These are the two types of state that are able to maintain order and achieve compliance from citizens, which enables a range of state functions. Given the economic opportunities now open globally, either of these types of state should normally be sufficient for the society gradually to grow out of mass poverty, though repressive states may struggle to rise above middle-income levels, and extremely repressive states, such as North Korea, may remain stuck in mass poverty. Fragile states are not necessarily in open conflict, but there is no clear bulwark against large-scale disorder. So defined, it is evidently useful to spell out how common-interest and repressive autocratic states each maintain order.

Common-Interest States

A common-interest state is the norm in the advanced Western societies, broadly coincident with the membership of the OECD. 'Common-interest' is the term used by Timothy Besley and Torsten Persson to define a state in which those in power adopt policies that are in the 'common' interest.[1] A more general form of a common-interest state is that people comply with the state without the high degree of open coercion needed for a repressive state, because they *perceive* those in power to be acting in the 'common interest'. The most reliable way in which this happens is if the perception is indeed correct. The condition under which it is *necessarily* correct is if the state is a well-informed democracy. However, more generally, democracy is neither necessary nor sufficient for a common-interest state. It is not necessary because those in power may act in the 'common' interest without being pinioned to such a course by democracy. China would be an example, as would Jordan and Morocco. Nor is it sufficient: if voters are sufficiently ill-informed, a minority may be able to run the state in their own interest, and if minority rights are not effective, majorities may be able to run the state to their own advantage. For example, throughout the Middle East, elections have failed as mechanisms to secure governments with sufficient acceptance to turn power into authority; only the monarchies have succeeded.

Cohesion is probably necessary for a common-interest state to function because many actions will not be in the individual interest of many people. For example, it is very hard to tell a story that it is in the individual interest of a rich person to pay for redistributive taxation. For non-coerced compliance, such people have to subsume their own interest in the collective interest: the 'common good'. For this, there has to be a 'common' to which these people belong: that is, there has to be a widely held sense of shared identity. This sense of shared identity and common interest is what turns power into authority: a radical reduction in the cost of enforcing compliance with the commands of the state.

The low cost of compliance resulting once power turns into authority makes it much easier to build the core organizations that are essential to an effective state: a tax administration and a security force. Building these institutions is an act of investment, (the key point of Besley and Persson), but the investment is much lower once the state functions by authority. Historically, the transition from power to authority has depended upon a very particular 'common interest', namely a narrative of collective defence against an external enemy. This is no longer a credible narrative in most fragile states where the predominant threats are internal rather than external.

Repressive Autocracies
Repressive autocracies depend upon two distinct forms of effective violence.

One is the capacity to defend the territory from organized violence per-petrated either externally or internally. The other is the capacity to inflict sufficiently severe penalties upon individual subjects that do not comply with a wide range of state commands that compliance becomes the rational action. The former type of capacity depends upon the localized extent of scale economies of violence, while the latter is about the capacity to build state information systems.

What is the condition that enables a territory to be defended from the threat of violence organized by some group within the society? It is that the scale economies of violence are sufficiently strong that its provision tends naturally to monopoly, so that a centrally financed army can defeat any regionally financed army. This situation can change as spatially distributed natural resources are discovered or become more valuable or as transport connections are built or decay.[2] In contrast, defence from external attack depends upon the opposite: that scale economies have been exhausted and union with another state would result in a territory that would be too large to be able to maintain an internal monopoly of violence.

This balance between internal and external violence occurs naturally in states that have gradually grown to their current boundaries and are in equilibrium, as in Europe. However, colonization followed by decolo-nization has created many states that are not militarily organic. Quite pos-sibly, they are both too large and too small at the same time, in the sense that, were they part of a much larger entity, scale economies would enable the entire territory to be secure, both internally and externally, but at their current size they are too large to maintain an internal monopoly of violence.

The capacity for coercion of individual subjects depends upon an adminis-tration that is able to marshal information about the assets and behaviour of individuals and then link it to the modest on-the-ground violence nec-essary to inflict coercive penalties.

Exploiting scale economies of violence and gathering information about assets both require large organizations: an army and a civil service. The ca-pacity to build such organizations depends both upon the underlying skill of the population and upon the ability to maintain motivation. Evidently, the skill needed for an army is less demanding that that for a civil service, but for both the key constraint is likely to be motivation.

An army faces an acute incentive problem: to win battles its soldiers must be prepared to risk their lives. It is radically difficult to incentivize people to take such risks: the rational behaviour for a soldier is to leave the dangerous stage of fighting to others, and if this is widespread the army will lose, regardless of its size. Indeed, large size may become an impediment to an effective force as the incentive for free-riding increases. Motivation in an army depends upon something other than material self-interest. It depends upon the soldier wanting the esteem of his peers, and the self-esteem that comes from actions that enact an identity that he has adopted. Most armies are effective and so building these sources of esteem cannot be very difficult. For self-esteem to motivate risk-taking requires the soldier to have adopted the identity of 'a good soldier'. Peer esteem requires that a sufficient number of soldiers have internalized the norm 'a good soldier is one who risks his life when necessary for the success of the army'. This identity and this norm have to be built by role models of 'heroes' and supporting narratives. In many cases the armies of fragile states are ineffective not primarily because they are too small, but because of a lack of motivation. The identity and norm have not been built.

A civil service faces a yet more acute problem of motivation. Many situations in which the state needs to coerce compliance depend upon a civil servant being assiduous in gathering information and honest in using it in the interest of the state rather than for personal gain. Being assiduous takes effort, which is costly, and being honest instead of exacting a bribe is likely to be even more costly. Hence, self-esteem and peer esteem need to be invoked, with their supporting mental constructs of an identity, 'I am a good civil servant', and norm, 'a good civil servant puts the state interest over his own'.[3]

Since a repressive state cannot rely upon the appeal to common interest, because most of its actions are not in the common interest, it will struggle to overcome either of these problems of motivation. The military motivation may be easier because the army can collectively be presented as an elite. The level of personal risk may rapidly become negligible if motivation can temporarily be overcome because the motivation of the army is difficult to observe by potential rebels (and costly to underestimate). While the civil service can also be presented as an elite, it is far larger (and so less elite), and its behaviour can be continually stress-tested by ordinary subjects at negligible personal cost: such cost depends not upon the civil servant refusing the bribe, but on successful prosecution.

Those repressive states that are effective have two means of building motivated cadres of soldiers and civil servants. Some, such as North Korea, rely on a sense of shared identity built on nationalism. In turn, nationalism is usually aroused by provoking an external threat that is presented as overarching and creates a common interest with those in power that trumps the many respects in which elite interest is opposed to the common interest.

Other repressive states, such as Saddam Hussein's Iraq, or apartheid-era South Africa, rely upon creating a clear identity for an ethnic or religious sub-group that is large enough to staff the army and the civil service. The sub-group is given some rewards.

Perhaps more potently, it is put in a position where, being complicit in the power of the autocracy, were the autocrat to be overthrown, the sub-group would become the victims of vengeance.

Why Fragile States Are Fragile
Having set out the two means of building states that securely maintain order, fragile states are the residual of those societies that are unable to pursue either route.

The common-interest state may be infeasible for four distinct reasons. First, the state may be controlled by an elite who serve their own interest (and who lack the means to deceive the population into thinking that they are doing otherwise). Second, even if the state is run in the common interest, the society may lack sufficient social cohesion to have a shared identity so that the key organizational building blocks of an army and a civil service do not function properly. If the polity has become a democracy prior to a shared identity being forged, it may be impossible to build shared identity. The political parties inherent to electoral democracy are most likely to be built on the existing fractures of identity, and the prevailing narratives of vilification of opposing parties, which democracy inevitably generates, will thereby work against the emergence of common identity. Third, the polity may be militarily unviable, either because it cannot control internal order or because it cannot protect against external threats. Finally, the society may lack the skills necessary to build an effective army or civil service.

The repressive autocracy may also be infeasible for four distinct, and somewhat similar, reasons. First, the revenues captured by the state might be insufficient to be able to reward a sub-group large enough to staff an army and a civil service of the required scale. Second, the society may lack social cohesion and the state cannot build a shared identity because there is no credible external enemy on which to build a sense of nationalism. Third, the polity may be militarily unviable, due to either internal or external threats. Finally, the society may lack the skills necessary to build an army or civil service.

The above yields eight varieties of fragile state. There may well be more. What all have in common is that they, or the collapse into state failure to which they are vulnerable, are equilibrium conditions: there is no clear autonomous process whereby such states become secure states, whether of the cohesive common-interest variety or the repressive autocratic variety. Fragile states are not simply at an earlier stage than secure states; they are stuck in circumstances that secure states were never in.

The emergence of the typical European state, an analysis pioneered by Tilly, set out a clear trajectory.[4] While that is not the only trajectory, it is an important one. Along it, states grew until the scale economies of violence were exhausted, national identities were built through interstate conflict, and effective armies and civil services emerged through a process of natural selection. Only after this did democratization take place, turning the states into common-interest ones. Today's fragile states are simply not on this trajectory.

So What Can Be Done for Fragile States?

On this analysis, fragile states will remain fragile unless some external intervention gives rise to substantial change. I will suggest three aspects of external intervention: political, security, and economic. In each case, the pertinent time frame is the short term. Visions of the long term are easy to conjure: in the long term, the society should look like a common-interest state. The challenge is to specify a viable path towards this end, and the most difficult steps are the first. The first steps are the most difficult because this is when the options are the most severely constrained. In a fragile state it is useless to navigate by what is wrong: almost everything is likely to be wrong. Yet because the state is a broken entity, its capacity to implement effective change is extremely limited. Further, because of past failure, people do not expect policy interventions to work, so that any intervention that is dependent upon a coordinated change in behaviour by many people is likely to fail. The route out of fragility is not an instant piecemeal leap into a common-interest state. Rather it is an ingenious search for the few actions that can actually be implemented and that will provide a rapid, perceptible improvement to many people's lives. The pertinent time frame is unlikely to be longer than two years. If the state manages its communications with citizens properly, it will lower expectations to only this very limited set of actions and pre-commit to doing them. As it delivers and claims the credit due, citizens and public officials will slightly revise their expectations of what government can achieve. This in turn modestly opens up the scope for slightly more demanding action, and step-by-step the state craws out of fragility. Along this arduous path, visions of the ultimate goal may be detrimental, because they tempt politicians into leaping ahead, at which point they return to failure.

Building the Polity

As Niall Ferguson discusses in Section III, the international promotion of peace has shifted from the robust pragmatism exemplified by Kissinger to an idealist ideology of values. This has been manifesting for the past twenty-five years in the strategy that international actors have promoted to build the polity in fragile states: they have idealized multi-party electoral democracy. Above, I have suggested why this is liable to be a cul-de-sac unless the society already has a shared identity. The disaster of democracy in Iraq is an example: the result was a Shia extremist government that lacked the military capacity to maintain order, resulting in large-scale violence. More generally, elections during the first post-conflict decade tend to raise, rather than lower, the risks of a reversion to violence.[5] Insistence upon early national elections is part of a larger strategy adopted by both donors and leaders to try to accelerate the construction of centralized authority by creating symbols of the nation-state: a directly elected president, an elected national assembly, and a conventional array of government ministries. This fails to achieve its objective of turning power into authority (because outside of exceptional circumstances such as international warfare, it is not possible to do this rapidly), but it does create delusions of legitimate power among national officeholders. Since it is not possible, at least in the short term, to govern a fragile state by means of central authority, it is safer to avoid the symbols that suggest that such authority exists. Heads of government and national assemblies are safer if they *manifestly* possess little legitimacy, so that it is evident to officeholders that the remit of political power is very limited, amounting to a few decisions that can be implemented because they are not significantly controversial.

While, to date, donors have made major mistakes in forcing polities into a form that is unlikely to be viable, nevertheless, they should play a central role in shaping the post-conflict polity. It is unlikely that any predominantly internal process will generate a viable outcome, because accumulated hatreds will typically prevent the give-and-take necessary for genuine negotiation, the continual failure to reach consensus in Libya being a current example. The donor error has not been to direct the outcome, but to impose an outcome that is usually unviable in a post-conflict context.

Government in a fragile state should, I think, be built on two pillars: power-sharing and decentralization. Only after a common identity has been built at the national level can national multi-party democracy work, and this is at best a slow process (and may turn out to be infeasible).

Decentralization

Fragile states typically start with a localized spatial structure of identities.

This structure is at best slow-changing, and so over the pertinent horizon—the early post-conflict years—it should be taken as a given. Mismatches between the spatial structure of power and that of identity lead to three types of state dysfunction: repression (the state exerts power through effective coercion), violent conflict (the state tries to exert power but is frustrated by violent opposition), and theatre (the state abandons the attempt to exert real power and settles for the appearance of power). Hence, in a fragile state decentralization is likely to be the least-bad option.

Nevertheless, decentralization of power carries risks that regional politicians may build self-serving autocracies. This can be moderated by requiring power-sharing at all levels of government, by making the regions somewhat dependent upon the centre for revenues, and by imposing effective donor scrutiny to maintain the integrity of budget processes.

Regions will vary greatly in their capacity to generate revenue, and there is no simple way of resolving the issue. While on some criteria the ideal is national pooling of all revenues and redistribution according to regional needs, attempting to impose this ahead of building shared identity would risk centripetal forces. Revenue and expenditure-sharing formulae have to recognize the spatial structure of identities and accommodate it. Restraint in prospecting is advisable because discoveries have the capacity to create strong secessionist pressures. Clearly, Iraq would have been less disastrous had generous revenue-sharing been agreed early on. The state may need to delay centralization until after it has become a cohesive common-interest polity.

Decentralized power-sharing may also enable good politicians to reveal their talents at the local level, gradually building the experience and reputation by means of which a subsequent phase of centralized power could become productive.

Power-Sharing

Almost inevitably, power-sharing at the national level will be both messy and unattractive. This is a further reason for favouring decentralization. It will be messy in that people who have opposing interests and hate each other will need to work together in government; they will do this only grudgingly, and so government will not work very well. The advantage, however, is that only by needing to work together (as a condition for aid and security assistance) can powerful people gradually learn the gains of cooperation, changing their mindsets from a zero-sum to positive-sum perspective on the world in which they operate.

It will be unattractive in that some truly unsavoury people will have to be included; representation will be closer to 'one gun, one vote' than 'one person, one vote'. Often, this will imply that 'transitional justice' will be little more than token: guilty people will not be punished. However, social psychological research has established that victims and culprits systematically assess the magnitude of appropriate punishments very differently. The human mind is ingenious at self-justification. Hence, the punishments regarded by victims as appropriate are seen by culprits as excessive. This then generates a further round of grievance and vengeance.[6] Consequently, pursued vigorously, transitional justice risks reigniting the conflict (as it did in Iraq). Inclusion of as many militarily significant groups as possible makes the security challenge more manageable. As Libya has demonstrated, leaving such interests excluded can lead to catastrophic outcomes.

While donor money is needed as the incentive for cooperation, I think it is important to impose financial integrity on the budget process. This is for instrumental rather than ethical reasons. Although, from a Western perspective, corruption is manifestly immoral, the ethical code prevalent in a fragile society is quite different: taking opportunities for public plunder that help the family is widely seen as reasonable. The instrumental reason to impose financial integrity is that if money is embezzled, it strengthens the position of crooked politicians who use the money to expand the patronage systems on which they depend. Only if starved of the money needed to maintain patronage networks may such politicians gradually be weakened so that honest competitors can emerge. Nevertheless, politicians in government may need to be paid generously. If there is no money to be made in government, then significant politicians are likely to withdraw and rely upon their localized military power to secure the revenues they need for patronage. The reward for being in government should enable personal enrichment, but not on a sufficient scale to maintain and expand a significant patronage network. In effect, participation replaces the need for such a patronage network. Gradually, such people become redundant.

Subject to the financial integrity of the budget process, so that neither revenues nor expenditures can be embezzled, politicians (both local and national) should be left to determine budgetary priorities and policies. Policy conditionality in any form—political, economic, environmental, or social—is a mistake: it inhibits social learning and confuses responsibility for outcomes. In many instances it actually impedes internalization of donor norms due to the well-understood psychological phenomenon of 'reactance', whereby people subjected to pressure to do an action re-establish autonomy by doing the opposite. In effect, donors should limit themselves to governance conditionality: the basic design of the polity (decentralization and power-sharing) and effective fiscal scrutiny (the integrity of revenues and expenditures, tempered by generous pay for senior politicians and officials).

Building Security

A pervasive sense of insecurity, generated by a recent history of violence and the credible prospect of further violence, is the essence of fragility. I will confine discussion to those fragile states that are at least momentarily at peace, or at least some approximation to it. Ending large-scale violent conflicts is a distinct challenge with a high degree of particularity.

Even at peace, fragile societies typically have considerable bottom-up violence. Traditional societies are usually characterized by cultures of violence, and the limited introduction of aid projects and other modern economic activity generates new opportunities for predatory criminal violence.[7,8] Political contestation sharply raises the returns to violence because of the benefits of capturing control of the state, and it is likely to infest ostensibly democratic national politics through the intimidation of voters.[9]

The fundamental technology of violence juxtaposes scale economies tempered by rising costs of spatial control. Large forces are likely to defeat small forces, but the cost of controlling territory rises with its area. In consequence, large low-income territories may only be able to sustain highly localized monopolies of violence, but these small forces are unable to protect their territories against sporadic attacks from much larger external forces.

The fragile state hence faces two distinct security problems: it does not have an effective monopoly of internal organized violence within its own territory whereby it can impose peace within the society, and it cannot protect its territory against external threat. These require very different solutions.

Maintaining a monopoly of internal organized violence depends upon nipping rival sources of violence in the bud before they can grow into substantial forces that could only be countered by major armed force. This requires an on-the-ground observational capacity throughout the territory, supported by the capacity to muster modest force fairly quickly once incipient organizations of violence are detected. Given the incapacity of the state to maintain effective repression (if it had this capacity it would be a repressive autocracy, not a fragile state), a ubiquitous observational capacity depends upon the cooperation of the local population. This in turn implies that coercive force can only be reactive, not pre-emptive. Pre-emptive force is the most effective means by which repressive autocracies maintain control, but since it punishes the innocent (alongside those who intend to engage in violence), it provokes outrage rather than cooperation. Even reactive force needs to be limited, for the same reason that transitional justice needs to be restrained: even when those who initiate violence recognize it as wrong, their estimate of the warranted punishment is self-serving, and exceeding this threshold risks generating a cycle of vengeance.

Any state-organized military force has the incentive to be predatory on the local populations it controls and to threaten the state itself. Thus, state provision of 'security' forces has the potential to worsen local and national insecurity.

The organizational form of the capacities needed for local security approximates to a gendarmerie. A well-functioning gendarmerie has a ubiquitous presence sufficiently embedded in localities to be able to observe information, a localized though modest coercive capacity, and an organizational culture that imposes voluntary restraints upon the exercise of coercion.

Building an organizational culture of restraint takes a long time. Fragile states do not have the luxury of being able to wait while long-term investments in security services come to fruition: they need interim solutions that provide security in the short term. A possible means of containing predation by public security forces against local communities is to decentralize the gendarmerie into local units that are subject to control by the decentralized political entities such as village councils. For example, the release of monthly payments to local gendarmes (perhaps effected by transfers of mobile money) could be made dependent upon approval by the village council. This makes clear that the security forces are there for the local population.

To counter the risk that such localized security forces become baronies that can threaten the nation, control can be shared with the national government that will, in any case, be the proximate source of finance for salaries of the security forces (the ultimate source may be donor funding). Fragmented localized security forces, subject to financial control shared between local communities and national government, limit the scope for a local commander to bid for national power.

However, making pay dependent upon satisfying the concerns of the local population will only work if the locality does not offer returns to predation that exceed the salary put in jeopardy. This depends in part upon salaries being reasonably high, but also on local opportunities for predation being modest. Since predation on a poor, heavily subsistence community is likely to be administratively difficult and to yield little, the main threat comes from high-value natural resources in remote locations. Such resources enable local non-government groups to grow their capacity for violence to a viable scale and tempt public security forces to go rogue and become predatory.[10] This suggests fragile states should postpone resource extraction until the security situation is firmly under control.

Evidently, while small, decentralized forces may be able to nip rebellion in the bud, they do not provide protection against external forces. This threat requires a completely different solution: where possible, regional cooperation between governments to establish a common force supported internationally. The rules for the use of such a force should be exclusively under the collective control of the participating governments in the region; otherwise, they would not trust it. Building such a force is a long-term project, but it can provide security immediately. Initially, the force securing the external safety of the territory is likely to be international, whether UN, France, or South Africa. However, rather than planning an 'exit' in favour of a supposedly revitalized national force, as is currently the norm, external forces should gradually evolve (over a decade or longer) into a standing regional force with an integrated command and clear regional political control, external involvement being confined to finance and logistics.

Building the Economy

Economic growth helps to gradually reduce fragility. Even some middle-income countries are fragile, so moderate economic prosperity is not a guarantee of stability, but poor societies are far more prone to fragility.

Typically, the economies of fragile states are so unproductive that there are many uncomplicated ways of raising productivity. The problem is not finding actions that would help. It is partly a matter of finding those few actions that pay off quickly, providing visible benefits to many people, and are implementable within a short horizon given very limited state capacities. It is partly a matter of creating an organizational form through which donor finance can be channelled with sufficient confidence that the money will be spent to good effect, and partly a matter of attracting the modern firms without which no economy can grow even to middle-income levels.

The foundations of productivity are energy and connectivity. Typically, in fragile states energy is unreliable and expensive, and connectivity in all its aspects is slow. Both can be improved quickly and simply. The key issues are not technical but political and organizational.

Technically Feasible Improvements in Energy and Connectivity

I first consider energy. It is usually technically feasible to transform the supply of electricity to the capital city within a two-year timescale. Electricity generation uses standard technologies and there are many reputable international companies that can build and operate energy provision. The usual impediments are a political quagmire of suspicion of foreign private enterprise, corruption in awarding contracts, mispricing of official supplies, and fear on the part of foreign firms that once they have made an irreversible investment, they will be subject to hold-up. For rural areas, grid-based power is uneconomic. The most appropriate technology for light is likely to be solar since unit costs are falling rapidly, but solar energy cannot meet the high-energy requirements of cooking. For this, the most viable option is likely to be a networked supply of bottled gas for cooking. The logistics network for bottled gas can be built quickly as a normal commercial venture.

Connectivity can be improved in a variety of ways. It is technically feasible to scale up mobile phone provision rapidly: this was one of the early successes in the recent opening of Myanmar. It is also technically easy to piggyback payment services onto a mobile phone system. Kenya is the model here and it scaled up very fast. The combination of rapid flows of information and payments can make a substantial difference to farms and small enterprises.

Three aspects of physical connectivity can all potentially be addressed. Rural-to-urban connectivity can be improved by simple road building; in post-conflict Uganda, early investment in such roads had an estimated rate of return of 40 percent, raising farm incomes through better access to urban markets and raising urban incomes by reduced food prices. Typically, the capital city of a fragile state has experienced rapid population growth with no concomitant investment in transport routes. An early private response to peace is for the middle classes to purchase cars. This completely congests the limited urban road network, causing gridlock for all users. From this disastrous situation, intra-urban connectivity can be improved rapidly by dedicating some roads to private minibuses to decongest them of private traffic. A further easy and rapid step is to legalize and encourage motorcycle taxis, which are far more efficient than cars. Connectivity to the world can be improved (if the country is coastal) by changing the management of the port, which is typically an epicentre of corruption.

The Organization of Public Service Delivery

Each of the above actions is technically feasible. The challenge is that the state lacks the organizational capacity to deliver any of the above improvements in energy and connectivity to an adequate standard, and building organizational capacity is a very long-term process. Meanwhile, the state typically blocks private provision in various ways. The domestic private sector is typically too underdeveloped to generate competent organizations that can provide the services, and so the only feasible option is foreign private provision, whether commercial or social enterprise. However, reputable foreign private firms are reluctant to operate in fragile states; they do not want to put either their staff or their reputations at risk. In some cases, NGOs may be more feasible providers, but they should be required to organize the supply of basic services at replicated scale rather than their normal model of photogenic and idiosyncratic boutique operations. Again, what is needed is not a long-term ideal but a practicable arrangement that can work rapidly and adequately even if it looks nothing like the long-term ideal.

The approach I favour is the independent service authority (ISA).[11] An ISA can take many forms (and names) but is basically an institution (or several of them) composed jointly of donors and the government (national or local). An ISA is a form of implementing agency. Policy decisions continue to be taken by political authorities, both national and local, but these decisions can then empower an ISA to implement them. For example, if the cabinet decides to permit the private generation of electricity, it can task an ISA with implementing it.

An ISA performs only three functions. First, it awards competitively bid contracts to private, social enterprise, community, and public-sector suppliers of specific services. Second, once contracts are signed, the ISA is the vehicle for providing ongoing financing; the money needed by the ISA comes initially entirely from donors and is routed by advance agreement through the national budget. Over time, some financing may also come from government domestic revenues if the government so chooses. Third, the ISA monitors the performance of the organizations contracted to deliver services. The ISA does not directly provide any services itself; its business is confined to contracting, financing, and monitoring the services of other organizations. All services are branded as government services, not as private or NGO services. The board of the ISA consists of both donor and government nominees. The number of nominees from each party is unimportant, but a decision rule might be that all board members have the power of veto. This gives donors the reassurance to provide adequate financing, firms the reassurance that contracts will be honoured, and government the ability to deliver fast on a limited range of government-branded critical services that make a rapid difference to citizens. ISA-provided services can operate alongside whatever the direct provision of government services might be and can be replaced by direct provision at the end of the specified contract period, but their operation is determined by the contract with the ISA, not by day-to-day government policies.

Because an ISA is freestanding, it is outside the civil service and so can be staffed to different rules and remuneration. Since it is newly created, it has an opportunity to build its own elite-organization, culture of effectiveness, and personal accountability. Since it is a hybrid between a government agency and a donor project, if it proves to be effective the government may decide to let it evolve into a permanent form of domestically financed public-service delivery.

One major advantage is that donors can have much greater confidence that their money is being spent effectively. Not only are they in the kitchen of the organization alongside government in day-to-day decisions, a core function of the organization is to monitor the performance of the organizations contracted to deliver services. As a result, donors can provide far more money than has typically been the case in fragile states.

ISAs are not an instant solution to the deep problems of organizing public-service delivery in fragile societies, but they are a flexible organizational form through which local initiatives can be empowered and all parties—government, donors, and service providers—can learn to improve. They are a fast-track alternative to the two standard approaches to the organizational deficiencies of fragile states: civil service capacity-building and project implementation units. The attempts to 'build capacity' in individual ministries have proved to be slow and usually unsuccessful.

Fundamental reform of dysfunction faces a binding coordination problem: in a large existing organization, staff seldom have any reason to expect that the behaviour of other workers will be different today from what it was yesterday, in which case it would be quixotic to change their own behaviour. Donor project implementation units face the severe limitations of being ad hoc, temporary, and lacking government ownership. As such, they are organizational cul-de-sacs.

Attracting Modern Firms

On the foundations of energy and connectivity, growth occurs predominantly by private activity harnessing the productivity gains from scale and specialization. These productivity gains are transformational: they are what lifts a society rapidly out of poverty. For example, in Ethiopian manufacturing, if we compare a relatively large informal artisanal enterprise of four workers with a modest modern enterprise of fifty workers, the modern firm achieves productivity per worker ten times that of the artisanal firm. This is the miracle of productivity offered by modern production for which Adam Smith was the first chronicler. Scale and specialization require modern modes of business organization; informality can only work if an organization stays small. Further, the transformation from informal to formal modes of operation is extremely difficult and rare: formal enterprises generally start out as formal, rather than growing out of informality.

Unfortunately, fragile states have very few formal firms, whether domestic or foreign. By far the fastest way to get more formal firms it to bring in established foreign ones but, understandably, such firms are reluctant to go to fragile states—markets are small, bureaucracies are dysfunctional and corrupt (exposing the firm to reputational risk), and staff may be endangered. Hence, the few formal firms that venture into fragile states are abnormal: often because they are run by predatory crooks who are comfortable in corrupt environments. These are obviously not the sorts of enterprises that fragile states need.

The problem of attracting reputable firms is compounded because most of the private investment possibilities in fragile states will be pioneering—the first such activity in the country. As such, there are many 'unknown unknowns' that can only be resolved by trying. In the act of trying, the pioneer investor generates information that is very useful to potential subsequent investors: if the investment is a success, it will get copied. This is good for the country, but bad for the pioneer—it is what economists term an 'externality', a benefit that does not accrue to the firm taking the decision. This is true of all pioneering investment, but fragile states are distinctive because a much higher proportion of investment is pioneering: in advanced economies most investment is routine, not pioneering. Yet, even in advanced economies, pioneering investment is recognized as socially valuable and is subsidized through various mechanisms. For example, Britain has a tax subsidy for investment in startups that amounts to around 40 percent. Clearly, the governments of fragile states cannot afford to provide such a subsidy, nor do they have the governance structures that would permit subsidies to be administered with integrity. However, there is scope for international aid to fragile states to administer subsidies properly through organizations such as the International Finance Corporation (IFC) of the World Bank.

Currently, however, aid can only be used for public spending, not as an incentive for attracting private investment. This is a severe limitation on aid effectiveness in fragile situations. One relatively easy way in which aid could be used would be to pay the premium on political risk insurance. Again, the World Bank has an organizational vehicle, the Multilateral Investment Guarantee Agency (MIGA), but as with IFC, currently no aid money can be used to subsidize it. A further limitation on MIGA's activities is that it is not permitted to ensure domestic firms, and so provides an advantage to foreign investors over domestic investors. Since surveys of investors reveal political instability to be the top perceived disincentive to investment in fragile states, this is an important matter. It is also distinctive:

political instability is not in the top three impediments for poor countries that are not fragile.

The prospect of subsidizing private investment triggers predicable antibodies: the political right castigates subsidies as wasteful and potentially corrupt, while the political left castigates them as helping foreign capitalists at the expense of the poor. Yet fragile states need modern firms but do not offer big opportunities to those that are reputable. An indication is the rate of return on the IFC portfolio. Since IFC screens firms carefully, the crooks are filtered out, so firms receiving IFC investment finance will overwhelmingly be reputable. Across the entire portfolio of developing countries, the rate of return on IFC investment has been around 4 percent, but in fragile states it has been −7.5 percent. That is why there are so few foreign firms. Yet without them, countries cannot grow out of fragility. The boards of private firms are legally required to manage their enterprises in the interests of shareholders: they can only scale up investment in fragile states if it is expected to be profitable. This will require that some of the risks be covered by public funds. Gradually, as the economy grows and becomes less fragile, such subsidies can be withdrawn.

Conclusion

Fragile states are the outstanding remaining development challenge. There is little reason to be confident that such societies will develop purely through autonomous internal mechanisms. Nor is there much reason to be confident that globalized market forces and conventional donor approaches will work. I have suggested that fragile states are a distinct category: neither cohesive common-interest states nor repressive autocracies. There is no natural path along which they evolve into either of these stable forms of government.

Pressured by OECD electorates, development agencies have adopted an approach that essentially tries to build the institutions of a cohesive common-interest state in a fragile state. I have argued that this approach inevitably fails: fragile states, though different one from another, lack key features that would enable such institutions to work as intended. Instead, the path out of fragility should be envisaged as a tortuous series of steps, each of which must pay off quickly, and the success of which is the precondition for further steps. The standard practice of swiftly installing a multi-party democracy with a government accountable to citizens through national elections may make it far more difficult to discover and follow such a path. Instead, the priorities should be to establish an interim political governance of power-sharing and decentralization, practical on-the-ground security for ordinary citizens, and basic improvements in energy and connectivity. Such a state will most likely tick few of the boxes that define governance in OECD societies. Onto this foundation, reputable private investment should be attracted by using aid to finance incentives that make it worthwhile.

Notes

1. Timothy Besley and Torsten Persson, *Pillars of Prosperity* (Princeton, NJ: Princeton University Press, 2011).

2. Nicholas Berman, Mathieu Couttenier, Dominic Rohner, and Mathias Thoenig, *This Mine Is Mine* (working paper, OxCarre, 2016).

3. Paul Collier, 'The Cultural Foundations of Economic Failure: A Conceptual Toolkit,' *Journal of Economic Behaviour and Organization* 126 (2016): 5–24.

4. Charles Tilly, *The Formation of Nation States in Western Europe* (Princeton, NJ: Princeton University Press, 1975).

5. Paul Collier, Anke Hoeffler, and Måns Söderbom, 'Post-conflict Risks,' *Journal of Peace Research* 45, no. 4 (2008): 461–78.

6. Jonathan Haidt, *The Righteous Mind* (London: Penguin, 2012).

7. Steven Pinker, *The Better Angels of Our Nature: Why Violence Has Declined* (New York: Viking, 2011).

8. Azar Gat, *The Causes of War* (Oxford: Oxford University Press, 2017).

9. Paul Collier and Pedro C. Vicente, 'Violence, Bribery and Fraud: The Political Economy of Elections in Sub-Saharan Africa,' *Public Choice* 153 (2012): 117–47.

10. Berman et al, *This Mine Is Mine.*

11. Collier, Paul. *The Bottom Billion.* (Oxford: Oxford University Press, 2007).

12.

Peace through Security-Development: Nebulous Connections, Desirable Confluences?

Maria Stern and Joakim Öjendal

Introduction

What are the causes of peace, the secret of achieving security, the recipe for development? Can peace be achieved without security and development? Is peace the same as security or development? Is there a sequence that we must follow—first, security, then development, then peace—or a hierarchy to achieve peace, for example, peace as an answer to the questions of security and development, or vice versa?

Questions such as these seem ever more pressing as the global landscape is increasingly painted with the colours of despair and hopelessness. Indeed, if you believe the newspapers, the world appears as an increasingly dangerous place and prospects for future generations as bleak. Those posed to respond to and redress the harms that befall people, society, and the planet appear to be ever more paralyzed or myopic. This decidedly pessimistic picture reflects a growing malaise that permeates news reporting, as well as global and local policy discussions—at least in the West. We are continually being informed that there is much to fear and lament: environmental degradation, natural disasters, global terrorism, mass displacement and migration, armed conflict, poverty, injustice, xenophobia and bigotry, corruption, gender-based violence, discrimination, social isolation, resource rivalry, ideational and religious clashes, identity politics, scarcity-based livelihood issues, the merging of crime and war, and global pandemics.

The Question of Peace: Revisiting Peace-Development-Security

How do we make sense of, and seek to redress, these problems? Does it matter what we call them, or through which frames we understand and seek to attend to them, both separately and as related issues? Can we *solve* them, and what would doing so imply? Surely, the hope for peace is expressed in various ways by many—from world leaders to vulnerable people fleeing drone attacks, the breakdown of all societal infrastructure, and oppressive extremism—and is surely embedded in the hearts of most. What causes peace, however, remains an open question, as does what we even mean by hoping for, speaking of, and acting towards achieving peace. Indeed, the question of peace is well-trodden terrain in history books, philosophical treatises, religious texts, and, more recently, the fields of international relations and peace and conflict studies—as well as in many more sites.[1] How this question is framed, as well as how it is answered, differs widely. Nonetheless, achieving peace remains a vital goal of policy at all levels or on all scales—sometimes to disastrous and violent effects.[2]

Equally clear, however, is the realization that peace, as an 'essentially contested concept',[3] can mean very different things to different people or bodies at different times, in different contexts, and at different scales of action.[4] Furthermore, even within and among the academic fields that study peace, its meaning diverges. Additionally, peace implicates other concepts (such as development, security) in the various lexicons in which it is employed.

Peace in the global policy world has become almost synonymous with a notion of (neo)liberal peace.[5] Peace in post-conflict societies, so understood and practised, is enabled and fostered through peacebuilding and reconstruction efforts that are regulated, and indeed governed, by intervening Western states. Furthermore, state-building in connection to peace-building has emerged as a way to tackle the security and development problems identified in 'developing' or 'fragile' states.[6] Yet, many have pointed out that peacebuilding efforts—efforts designed to address the pressing interconnections between peace, development, and security—often do not work.[7] Various reasons are proffered—and differences abound in how one identifies and offers remedies for the problems associated with 'failed' peacebuilding efforts and attending initiatives aimed at addressing the complex and interlinked problems of providing security and ensuring sustainable development.

This chapter seeks to reconsider the question of peace—especially in relation to that of development. However, we suggest that any answer to the question of the relationship between peace and development must also address the question of security. Hence, we embark on the somewhat cumbrous task of addressing three concepts or practices: peace, development, and security, and their interrelationships. We then probe 'peacebuilding' as a diagnostic site where these interrelationships are at the forefront and that we argue is ultimately failing in its ambitions. We do so in the hopes of better understanding the complexity involved in conceptualizing and 'implementing' peace-development-security in light of the pressing, yet all too daunting, task of solving the problems that peace-development-security efforts are meant to address.

The chapter proceeds as follows. First, we engage in a brief conceptual discussion about peace, development, and security by posing several interrelated questions that help us to examine how these terms are imbued with meaning, and to trace how these meanings slip and slide. Second, drawing upon the complexity of today's pressing globalized problems, as well as on trends in the global policy world that call for attention to be given to a 'security-development' nexus as the overarching policy directive, we argue that attention should be paid to the interlinkages of peace, development, and security in any attempt to understand or redress such problems. Third, we briefly explore some ways that scholars (and policy) have understood the interlinkages between peace-development-security, with a particular focus on the relations between peace and development. The groundwork in these three conceptual sections then allows us to turn, in the fourth section, to a critical discussion of peacebuilding (under the sign of the liberal peace) as the dominant vehicle for achieving peace-development-security.

We conclude by further calling into question the possibility of implementing the rationale of the security-development nexus through peacebuilding efforts and call for further empirically grounded and critical inquiry.

The Viability of a Security-Development Nexus

What is the nature of peace? Security? Development? Reader be warned: like many critical scholars before us, we do not attempt to define these concepts, but instead to gesture towards some of the ways that they have been/ could be defined both explicitly and implicitly. In so doing, we do not aim to imply that the terms are meaningless or that meanings differ so widely that we cannot engage in substantial conversations about them across, or within, disciplinary or sectorial boundaries.[8] Instead, we embrace the Foucauldian notion of the instability of concepts.[9] We can trace how they slip and slide in different discourses, and even within the same discourses,[10] in order to comprehend how meaning is being imparted (and deferred) and how other concepts inform those in question through their hauntings[11] and associations.[12] Importantly, as Dean explains, concepts metamorphose and are modified through 'careful processes of distinction between different rationalities and different regimes';[13] as they mesh, are borrowed, and are (re)adjusted, concepts become public in such a way that their proper use can never be dictated. 'They are always in this sense on loan . . . Empirical study and the production of concepts are one and the same process.'[14] Hence, querying how peace-security-development are being imbued with meaning also enables critical interrogation of different rationalities and governing regimes of power/knowledge.[15] As 'essentially contested concepts', peace, development, and security are the subject of much scholarly debate, and differences attributed to their meanings discern schools of thought as well as differences in policy orientation and goals.

One way to make sense of the meaning of the concepts/practices is by studying their genealogies throughout history,[16] as well as within certain academic traditions, such as international relations[17] or development studies.[18] We will not rehearse this rich scholarship here. Instead, we recall a set of questions that, although surely not comprehensive nor equally relevant in relation to the distinct concepts, nonetheless provide an overarching framework for delineating some of the basic ontological differences in the ways in which peace, development, and security are conceived in different academic traditions, as well as how they are understood and employed in the world of policy: *peace/security/development for whom or what? from whom/what? conceived how? by whom or what? through what measures?*

Out of possible answers to the above questions, one can compose different stories about 'peace', 'development', and 'security', which, in turn, can be combined in myriad ways to make sense of their interrelationships and, importantly, be used to guide policy.[19] For example, in one familiar liberal story, peace is conceived as the absence of war/direct violence.[20] The referent object is the state; the scale of action is the international system. Peace is delivered *from* war waged by other states; it is a desired state of being or condition that is measurable. According to this storyline, the international community and individual states make peace through treaties and implementing ceasefires. Post-conflict societies maintain peace by enacting (neoliberal) macro-reforms, implementing 'good governance' and democracy.[21] In another story—in which peace is envisioned as local, multi-scalar, and part of everyday life—peace needs to be felt among broad layers of the population. The local engaged citizen is an important referent and agent of peace. In such lines of reasoning, methods for achieving peace recognize that agency, participation, and (even diverging) opinions are seen as beneficial and need to be 'allowed' and encouraged.[22]

Given such a wide range of interpretations, how then can we understand the interrelationships between peace, development, and security—especially since the answers to the above questions differ within different discourses about security, development, and peace respectively? Surely, they are neither singular nor definitive. Furthermore, why do we insist on considering peace, development, and security together?

One answer is *empirical* and has to do with the kinds of violence, threats, and insecurities that people face today. Arguably, studying 'peace in our time' has become a daunting task, as it is not clear where or when peace is or potentially could be. Furthermore, notions of peace imply also an understanding of war or violence. Many argue that patterns of war and violence in the international system have undergone dramatic shifts during the last three decades,[23] changing first from international wars to civil wars and then from time-defined civil wars to what Mary Kaldor has (problematically) characterized as anarchic violence.[24] Additionally, not only are interstate wars transformed into internal wars, but in many contexts a war and crime blur, as do lines of distinction between the internal and external, as well as those between state-led and privately driven security efforts.[25]

Whether or not one espouses this version of the history of warring, it is abundantly clear that wars of today are not circumscribed by the tidy geopolitical boundaries that the field of IR, war studies,[26] international law,[27] and peace studies[28] expect them to.[29] Global terrorism, for example, has undoubtedly changed patterns of warfare, as have advancements in military and policing technology. Patterns of war and violence thus continually unsettle the political ordering that has been constructed (in part) to contain them.

Furthermore, war, largely understood as 'sustained coordinated violence between political organizations',[30] does not necessarily correspond with the variety of interrelated violence to which people are subjected and to which the global policy community seeks to respond.[31] Indeed, the danger, insecurity, threat, and misery associated with problems like those illustrated in the beginning of this chapter refuse familiar geographies of war and peace.[32] Today, instead of large-scale wars, complex emergencies as well as routine suffering make up the lion's share of contemporary violence and insecurities.[33] These problems are included under the remit of security as well as development. In other words, the study of peace—whether conceived as negative or positive peace,[34] liberal peace,[35] or local peace[36]—invariably involves questions about security and development. Furthermore, during the last decade, peace has been breached in atypical and unforeseen ways that may not resemble war in the traditional sense noted above, yet have had devastating consequences, with unexpected and violent effects, in South Sudan, Ukraine, Syria, and Libya—to mention but a few. Such breaches add to protracted conflicts, as has been the case in, for example, Iraq and Afghanistan.

The term 'security-development nexus' has emerged as a way of capturing this complexity.[37] The nexus has come to refer to a range of different meanings. For example, the complex of problems understood as produced by or productive of insecurity and underdevelopment and/or poverty; integrated holistic approaches and tools of policy; as well as the solutions that such policy is to bring forth. For well over a decade now, from the military strategists to grassroots NGO workers, from the Pentagon to the Development Assistance Committee (DAC) headquarters, the security-development nexus (as tool and solution) has been proffered as a key to peaceful recovery from violent conflict. Appeals to such a nexus are common in the policy world in order to justify one or another form of intervention. As is clear from the above, the nexus, as such, is loosely defined and, we argue, often used as a flag of legitimacy for particular purposes and for serving vested interests. We will return to this point below.

The idea of the security-development nexus is, however, not new. The argument that there is an interdependency between security and development emerged after the end of the Cold War and in light of a broadened understanding of security on the one hand and a reorientation of Western development policy towards conflict prevention on the other.[38] The World Bank report on its role in post-conflict reconstruction called for 'explicit recognition of conflict as an issue in development,'[39] thus paving the way for development interventions in the name of security.[40] This was followed with an even more conflict-focused WDR in 2001,[41] which called attention to different means to 'break cycles of violence' and to reduce the risk of violence. Appeals to the nexus quickly entered the mainstream with the call from the OECD's DAC on development actors to prepare for long-term engagement 'in and on conflicts rather than around them.'[42]

Since the terrorist attacks against the US in 2001, the statement 'no development without security' has served as a mantra in most security policies of Western states and international aid organizations, and has been firmly established as a premise of EU policy[43] as well as a pillar of UN rhetoric.[44] More recently, we have seen a new wave of integrated approaches to conflict (prevention), security measures, and long-term development—not least with the 2011 'Building Stability Overseas Strategy', jointly signed in the UK by the Ministry of Defence, the Foreign and Commonwealth Office, and the Department for International Development (DFID). In this regard and supporting the implementation of the British Strategic Defence and Security Review, DFID announced in 2012 that by 2014 the British government would earmark 30 percent of its Official Development Assistance (ODA) for fragile and conflict affected states.[45]

The discourse around the security-development nexus has largely been policy-oriented, and emphasis has been placed on globalized discussions among donor countries about how to best implement 'security' and 'development' in receiving countries. Indeed, there is a growing policy and academic commitment to understanding and addressing problems in comprehensive, holistic, or whole-of-government approaches, which involve a move away from sectored thinking and acting.[46] Sectored thinking means, in this sense, that traditional development problems (such as lack of clean water, education, and functioning infrastructure) are defined and addressed through development programs and budget allocation, while traditional security problems (such as armed group violence, terrorist activity, and buried landmines post-conflict) are defined and addressed through security programs and budget allocation. This contrasts with a security-development focus, which highlights their interconnection and suggests that a coordination and cooperation between development and security sector actors would best promote peace, security, development, and good governance. Peace, conflict, and development studies incorporate such lines of thinking, in, for example, the analysis of conflict cycles and peacebuilding, reconstruction, and democratization efforts and in a holistic focus on human security and development as integral to peace. (Recall, however, that the meanings imparted to these concepts slip and slide.)

Post-conflict peacebuilding has arguably become the site where the interrelations between peace, development, and security become most apparent and carry most purchase in the global policy market. Indeed, peacebuilding in a context of post-conflict reconstruction has gradually turned into a key ingredient in the global governance architecture. Internationally, the idea of peacebuilding and its various strategies has become institutionalized and now assumes a 'hegemonic status'[47] where every international organization 'from the United Nations to NATO' sees it as one of their primary activities. Interventions have become commonplace; operations to protect, prevent, and repair have been codified and turned into a UN-based norm through the Responsibility to Protect resolution.[48] From another angle, fragility[49] became a new focus for policy and research in the early 2010s.[50] Even more important, however, is the 2011 initiative labelled the New Deal for Engagement in Fragile States, a key global agreement between fragile and conflict-affected states, with stipulated peacebuilding and state-building goals, endorsed by the forty-three countries and the G7+ grouping.

Hence, that peace, development, and security are intimately interlinked has become a truism; numerous reports, resolutions, and speeches that have emerged in the global high policy arena rehearse variations of the statement that they are interrelated.[51] Yet, before we turn to a discussion of peacebuilding as a vital site of peace-development-security, we want to pause to further explore what can be meant by the interrelationships between peace, development, and security.

Unpacking Interrelationships: Understanding a Peace-Development-Security Nexus

What is meant when policy (or academics) refers to the connections between security and development or, for that matter, security and peace, or security, peace, and development?

If we recall the wide variety of answers to the questions about security, development, and peace noted above, the answer to this question becomes even more unwieldy. Interrogating the relations between peace and development has preoccupied many for decades[52] and even centuries.[53] Similarly, the interconnections between peace and security have, in different guises, been the subject of much debate.[54]

In correlation with the trends in the policy discourse noted above, there

338

is a growing body of scholarship that (critically) explores the relationship between security and development.[55] Few have explicitly addressed the question of the interrelations between all three concepts—peace, development, and security.[56] However, even if they are not addressed directly, the interlinking of the concepts is often embedded in attempts to address one or even the nexus of two. For example, in numerous accounts, (sustainable) human security and (sustainable) human development become interchangeable and provide the basis for a (sustainable) peace.[57] While there are, of course, myriad answers to the question of interrelationships in both academic work and policy texts[58]—and, importantly, these, in turn, are crafted differently depending upon how questions (noted briefly above) are posed and answered in the understandings of the concepts in themselves—we are nonetheless able to discern some common patterns in how these relationships are being depicted. Importantly, any picture that is painted of the interrelationships remains instable; they morph and are reconstituted within particular discourses and depending upon context, as well as through their operationalization into specific practices. As Hughes and Öjendal explain, 'peacebuilding contexts, like cultures, as James Clifford reminds us, "do not hold still for their portraits".[59]

In some accounts, the relations emerge as ones of *similitude*, albeit through different articulations. Galtung, for instance, outlined how peace and development—in their 'broad' interpretations—are 'the same thing'. For Galtung, the difference between the concepts lies in both the politics of naming and in the focus of concern regarding the 'narrow' definition of peace and development respectively. He explains that through the lens of 'structural violence' we are able to compare peace and development and to see them, in their preferred broad meaning, as essentially the same, although one is called 'misery' and the other 'war'.[60]

Such similitude becomes possible through casting peace and development as comparable (yet essentially 'the same') and as placed under another concept in a conceptual hierarchical order. In Galtung's account, the (absence of) structural violence serves as a broader concept that envelops peace and development, which are essentially synonymous yet expressed differently by people differently situated in terms of global capital. What of security in this constellation? Galtung's notion of (positive) peace can be seen as roughly synonymous with 'human security' (and 'human development'), although this is not explicit in the explanation of peace-development cited above. Hence, arguably, for Galtung, peace, development, and security, if interpreted thought the lens of (freedom from) 'structural' violence (and later in Galtung's work, also cultural violence), emerge as 'the same thing'.[61] As we shall see in the next section, a liberal peace has arguably become the overarching concept (within which 'good governance' acts as a vital component) that subsumes peace-development-security in the global policy landscape of today; peacebuilding has become its vehicle for deliverance.

In a slightly different move to Galtung's, Barnett takes his point of departure, in a critique of Galtung's theories of peace, as absence (either of direct, structural violence or cultural violence). He also seeks to equate peace and development by placing them under an umbrella concept: freedom (borrowing from Sen).[62] He thus defined these in close parallel with the notion of human security in which freedom from fear and want are central tenets.[63] Similarly, Hettne talks of peace and development being 'two sides of the same coin' and states that 'peace has been subsumed under a broader concept of security'.[64] While Hettne establishes the inherent interlinkages, even similitude of peace and development, he also maps how these interlinkages have been produced and equated or conflated into each other in different political economic contexts throughout European history. He thus critically assesses the 'assumed indivisibility' of development and peace by interrogating how their relations have been conceived in a succession of schools of thought. In a later piece, he similarly traces the macro-history of the evolution of the ways in which security and development have been conceived and practiced. Ultimately, Hettne advocates for a notion of global social development that also serves as an umbrella that encompasses security, development, and peace.[65]

In Hettne's earlier work, he outlined different ways in which peace and development are presented as *conditions of each other*—that is to say, in some accounts, development strategies (defined variably) are seen as a precondition for long-term peace—defined variably.[66] Importantly, according to Hettne, certain 'mainstream' modernist development strategies can lead to 'maldevelopment' and consequently structural violence and the use of direct force in 'internal and external' conflicts. 'Another development', on the other hand, could potentially lead to more balanced, grounded, and shared development and thus to 'peaceful economic, social and political structures'.[67]

Such notions of precondition and causality resonate with much of the reasoning in the policy world, as explained in the Brandt Report in 1980 and more recently in the UN's 2030 Agenda for Sustainable Development: 'There can be no sustainable development without peace and no peace without sustainable development'.[68] Hettne earlier explained that peace must also be sustainable and that a notion of security was integral to achieving sustainable peace: 'Without peace, there could be no development and without development, peace was not sustainable.' Similarly, he explained that 'development policy . . . in a context of "common security" was bound to become the peace policy of the future'.[69] This relationship of precondition can thus also be cast both ways. For example, number 16 of the UN Sustainable Millennium Goals reads, 'Promote peaceful and inclusive societies for sustainable development, provide access to justice for all and build effective, accountable and inclusive institutions at all levels'.[70]

As noted above, today, notions of the one (development, security, peace) being the *precondition* or the cause of the other(s), both in a positive sense or in the averse sense of a cascade of destructive processes—for example poverty, leading to conflict or war and then general insecurity; or conflict leading to insecurity, leading to poverty, leading to more insecurity, and so forth—are familiar in the conflict cycle analyses such as 'the conflict trap'.[71] Additionally, peace, development, and security have been conceived as *related or interlocking yet parallel processes, strategies, structures, practices, areas* for policy formulation or normative goals.[72] In such accounts, these surely influence each other but nonetheless emerge as *distinct* from one another, with their own histories, institutional frameworks, techniques of governance, and institutional homes.[73]

Peacebuilding: A Comprehensive Vehicle for Addressing Security-Development-Peace or an Impossible and Doomed Project?

Peacebuilding has traditionally been conceived as a phase following peace-making or a negotiated agreement between warring parties designed to put an end to the violence caused by the conflict.[74] As already noted, peace in the global policy world has become almost synonymous with a notion of (neo)liberal peace.[75] Peace in post-conflict societies, so understood and practised, is enabled and fostered through peacebuilding efforts that are regulated and, indeed, governed by intervening Western states.

Within the neoliberal hegemony, peacebuilding in the post–Cold War era has been experimental and has evolved over time. To some extent, both academics and the global policy community have learned from previous mistakes; however, when addressing one problem, peacebuilding initiatives soon ran into new dilemmas and difficulties. Crude and short interventions gave way to longer and more ambitious involvement. As a result of the evident failures of shallow interventions, *state-building* came to be seen as a necessity in order to consolidate peace (and democracy).[76] Since then, state-building has grown into an overarching framing of sorts, but it has also triggered critical calls for less state-centrism, more nuanced approaches,[77] and broader strategies.[78]

Hence, a 'first generation' of interventions for peacebuilding has been replaced with a second, and possibly with a third, and even the embryo of a fourth in an ongoing learning process of past failures.[79] In sum, the *first generation* was UN peacekeeping, which basically observed ceasefires (Cyprus, Lebanon, Korea). The *second*, commencing right after the end of the Cold War, was pursued with short interventions of a 'big bang' nature, with an over-belief in rapid democratization and the swift crafting of peace within a given and absolute time period (Cambodia, Mozambique, Somalia). A *third generation* shifted to more ambitious state-building processes where interveners stayed on, assumedly, until the task was/is completed (DRC, Afghanistan, Kosovo, Liberia). In this generation, interest turned more to comprehensive state-building, which included security sector reforms and state institution-building as key. Finally, as a *fourth generation*, peacebuilding is moving to more participatory and agency-oriented approaches, aiming at 'from below' and 'from within' in the spirit of John Paul Lederach.[80] Scholars, practitioners, and civil society alike have become vocal (some espousing postmodern/colonial perspectives) in calling for a thorough critique of the dominance (and violence) of the liberal peace[81] and for attention to turn to the local.[82] This approach is evolving gradually across the globe, but half-heartedly and with only limited impact in the policy world.

'Solutions' to state violence as well as the propensity to engage in acts of violence against other states (through the assumptions embedded in the familiar democratic-peace theory)[83] can be found in state-building.[84] Paradoxically, the state (in particular the African state) is routinely deemed to be incapable of building itself, and therefore requires external assistance.[85] In turn, the 'need' for external assistance and state-building as the 'solution' to violence combine to become a neat package of peacebuilding; in other words, peacebuilding has come to incorporate state-building, rendering it a far deeper, longer, and more complex endeavour than it was conceived to be in the mid-1990s.

Such state-building is intended to lead to improved governance on the part of the state in question. Democratization, good governance, the instalment of the rule of law and the respect of human rights, security sector reform (SSR), access to free and globalized markets, and neoliberal development are all understood as key elements of state-building and therewith, ultimately, of peace. Hence, in any empirical sense, the focus on peacebuilding and its connections to notions about state-building and the development of 'good governance' practices are key to understanding how the interrelations between security, development, and peace are being envisioned in today's global climate.[86]

In sum, peacebuilding is rooted in traditional security thinking, with its focus on peace agreements, interventions, and post-conflict reconstructions.[87] Additionally, as noted above, peacebuilding has with time assumed state-building ambitions and increasingly become a vital part of pursuing sustainable development. Hence, the peacebuilding package is presented as a clear-cut case of the security-development nexus[88] in practice. Peace-building emerges as perfectly positioned in an ideally seamless process of achieving security in the short term, and enabling sustainable development in the longer, which shall, in turn, guarantee security.[89] As such, peacebuilding epitomizes attempts to implement the logic behind such a nexus.

Peacebuilding as the Vehicle for Peace-Security-Development? Problems Abound

What then is the problem, or the problems, with peacebuilding as vehicle for peace-security-development? First, one vital problem has to do with ideas about causality and timing. In contemporary protracted conflicts, it is no longer realistic to delay the onset of development activities, transitional justice mechanisms, and social and political reconstruction and state-building until an undefined future point of peace. Recent research underlines that violence (in myriad forms and at myriad scales) does not stop, even when peace agreements are signed; it often endures and evolves despite ardent peacebuilding efforts and endangers the implementation and sustainability of peace agreements.[90] This becomes alarmingly evident if, for instance, we pay attention to the continuum of gendered violence that transgresses clear time frames (such as pre- or post-conflict) or familiar distinctions (such as the public/private) and that upsets any tidy notion of a peace that can be built and sustained through the peacebuilding mechanisms available.[91]

Second, as the situations in Syria, South Sudan, and Somalia[92] indicate, for example, in many contexts worldwide, the state system as we have come to perceive it is under violent transformation. This situation fundamentally alters the conditions for the peacebuilding process and challenges many of the dogmas about the relationships between peace-security-development that underpin peacebuilding since the end of the Cold War, including those related to liberal peace.

Third, the inherent paradox in the remit of state-building as peacebuilding persists. If we take the example of SSR, we see how the state is hailed as the solution to its own dysfunction or lack.[93] In addition to policy-oriented scholarship assessing the successes, failures, and challenges of SSR[94] there is a growing body of scholarship that critically appraises external interventions that are aimed at prompting and assisting so-called failed states in engaging in state-building reforms that will ensure 'good governance'.[95] Critical scholarship focusing on security governance explores the engagement of external actors (such as the EU, the UN, as well as individual state actors) in SSR and security-development efforts more generally as key techniques of governing these so-called failed states.[96] State-building through SSR shall, so the story goes, ensure good governance, entailing new techniques of governing by a plethora of different actors and the production of responsible subjects who are capable of self-governing in certain ways.[97] Yet external intervention, while envisioned as a step in the process towards the ownership of, and ultimate control by, the immanent sovereign national state, can become the condition of possibility for national state sovereignty. Furthermore, little attention is paid to how those who are to be reformed react to the efforts to reform them.

A fourth problem has to do with the ways in which the responses to the interconnected security and development problems of today have been confused at best, ranging from intensive bombing to international sanctions, from half-hearted interventions to disaster relief, and from full interventions to total neglect. These are often draped in a variety of other development responses and implemented through the regular UN system, bilateral and international NGOs.[98] Lack of coherence and coordination feeds into a widely acknowledged 'crisis' involving external intervention and peacebuilding, where negative experiences and broad confusion reign.[99]

In light of these problems, it is increasingly clear that the liberal peace is not working.[100] Liberal peace, critics argue, creates instability, alienation, and exclusion, followed by a higher level of social conflict. Ultimately, it serves to establish global hierarchies rather than achieving a sustainable peace—even in its liberal guise.[101] This has been discussed amply in the literature on peacebuilding from a variety of perspectives; even advocates admit that liberal peace is imprecise and needs 'saving'.[102]

Fifth, this confusion is further increased by the rising necessity to commence peacebuilding amidst continued high levels of violence,[103] as noted above—a context for which they were not designed, but which has to be accepted as unavoidable. Such a context renders a detached, tentative liberal peace extremely volatile. For instance, peacebuilding amidst violence requires a much closer collaboration between civilian and military actors than post-settlement peacebuilding called for in its original conception. Under a scenario of increased civil-military interaction, there is a higher degree of linkages between security forces on the one hand and traditional development efforts on the other, which creates a number of additional challenges for the peacebuilding process.[104]

In such circumstances, there is an intricate relation—and by necessity an intensive interaction—between civil and military actors, spheres, and interests related to the trade-off between security and development policies.[105] Actors in these fields are neither experienced nor comfortable in cooperating. Indeed, as we argued above, policies built on appeals to the 'nexus' of security and development often produce the opposite from their intended effects when understandings of the 'nexus' travel from well-intended policy documents to harsher realities in actual interventions.[106] Translations are impossible to avoid. The international community surely has debated the security-development nexus for almost a decade and has arrived at a consensus on the need to achieve a balance (interaction-communication-dialogue) between security and development, and a recognition that these concepts or practices are intimately intertwined. However, the relationship between actors from the development and security arenas and their goals, as well as the processes to achieve their goals, remains contentious and complicated. Their respective institutional 'homes' act on different mandates with different constituencies, binding them into particular approaches even if communication is open and mutual understanding is high.[107]

The balance and interaction, sometimes rewritten as linkages[108] between security and development, is implied in the ways that the security-development nexus as articulated in most policy texts is eschewed, often to the advantage of the 'harder' sectors such as military concerns, or activities related to national security. This occurs at the expense of sectors advocating development in different forms and guises. Most recent literature on the security-development nexus has furthermore pointed at an increasing shift towards the securitization of development, both in terms of international policy guidelines towards developing countries[109] as well as in terms of national policies.[110]

Peacebuilding in Practice: (Some) Lessons from Case Studies

Drawing on a case study of the allocation of economic development aid in Haiti, Shamsie illustrates the selectivity of how aid is allocated, thus challenging the notion that the security-development nexus 'fosters economic development that benefits the poorest and brings security to all' in. A focus on Haitian state fragility has influenced donor strategies of economic development. However, such strategies, he argues, have prioritized urban economic development at the expense of rural development, in turn resulting in greater food insecurity and an overall marginalization of the poorest segments of Haiti's population.[111] In a related vein, in a comparative study of East Timor and Solomon Islands, Derek McDougall illustrates long- and short-term problems relating to the issues of defining the means, directions, and focus of development, when considered a road to security. He argues that when proposed by external interveners, development strategies are likely to be defined in limited terms manifested as (neoliberal) state-(re)building attempts at a central level. Such development commitments, however, may result in a 'restoration of security in a minimal sense'[112] but they fail to achieve security on a long-term basis. A limited definition of development as state-(re)building creates fragile structures that 'lack deep roots in society'.[113]

Similarly, discussing the UK-led police reform in Sierra Leone, Krogstad illustrates how framing Sierra Leone as a 'fragile' and 'weak' state on the basis of its policing (in)capabilities informed a UK-led development strategy aimed to reform, retrain, and re-equip the Sierra Leone Police (SLP). Framing state fragility as the problem and police reform as the solution relates to the broader donor trend of conceiving SSR as a 'virtuous circle between security and development'.[114] However, it also begs the question of the goal and unintended consequences of promoting SSR in 'weak' states;

striking the balance between investing the state with coercive capabilities without making it oppressive is difficult, and Krogstad notes that there is a 'possibility that the coercive means supplied by donors may be harnessed to political logics very different from the one donors wish to promote'.[115]

Furthermore, the meshing of security and development, in practice, can readily lead to a situation in which development problems are only addressed through the lens of security policies where, for instance, poverty is treated as important only as a cause of conflict or terrorism.[116] Along this line of critique, development can thus become a counterinsurgency tactic, which is more about the intervening countries' security than the problems of the most vulnerable—again eschewing the idealized 'fit' of security and development, as well as fouling the idea of a tidy nexus.[117]

This disjunction coincides with powerful calls for a 'local turn' in peace-building (the so-called embryonic fourth generation of peacebuilding noted above) that renders peace tangibly present in the everyday life of people it is supposedly benefitting.[118] Such calls demand that peace is to be grounded and allows citizens to become involved in the making of their own peace—hard as that may be since security issues tend to exclude meaningful civic involvement.[119]

Furthermore, much criticism has been launched against donors' inward-looking concerns for self-image and the preservation of their power positions while they simultaneously disengage from serious policymaking in the developing world.[120] The donors, it is argued, pass responsibility on to other actors, thereby prioritizing rhetoric over policy responsibility. Thus, peacebuilding interventions and their attending development and security policies act increasingly in isolation from practice and the actual needs on the ground.

Conclusion

We began this chapter by posing the question of peace through also asking questions about the relationship between peace, security, and development. Clearly, *how* these relations are conceived, and indeed practised, varies depending upon one's ontological, epistemological, theoretical, and methodological assumptions as well as disciplinary (in academia) or sectional (in the policy world) vantage point. Importantly, the ways in which we approach the question of peace-security-development has much bearing upon how peace (and war/violence), security (and insecurity), and development (underdevelopment) are identified, political imaginaries crafted, and subjectivities produced, as well as how policy and specific measures are formulated and enacted, peoples and processes are governed, legitimacy is earned, resources are distributed, and who or what is held accountable when harm is done. In short, it has everything to do with politics and the political.

In light of this, we aimed to open space for critically reengaging with peace as it is imbued with meaning through the dominant global policy-framing of peacebuilding. To this end, we first embarked on a brief conceptual exploration of peace, development, and security, and their interrelations, and then further explored how particular articulations of security-development are manifested in peacebuilding practices. We then turned to the multifaceted problems inherent in peacebuilding (and attending implementation of security-development efforts) to date—both those that attest to peacebuilding efforts not delivering the 'peace' promised, as well as to those that gesture that such a promise is impossible under the sign of the liberal peace.

In sum, peacebuilding in the context of post-conflict reconstruction has received devastating critique, and its tight reliance on a liberal peace approach has been especially questioned. It is seen as too de-contextualized and over-reliant on the ability of a liberal order to reconcile differences between the demands of different sectors and between different actors. Peacebuilding is de facto pursued in violent contexts with unclear expectations on peace, which further weakens the capacity of the liberal peace framework to work in a universally applicable manner, detached from context. This framework rests on an unclear policy conception of a security-development nexus. The overall assumption is that governments in developing states tend to use the banner of the security-development nexus to first reconstruct and secure state power and territorial control before embarking on the quest to advance security and development, and therewith peace, for its citizens. In so doing, the state security apparatus is itself often implicated in producing insecurity for many rather than protecting citizens from threat.[121] State-building processes and bio-political forms of rule play an important role in this process.[122] Hence, critique has focused on the ways in which attention to the security-development nexus as a route to peace has been addressed in practice (e.g., mal-placed efforts, inadequate attention to demands of different time frames, poor identification of key actors and understandings of the complexity of the conflict patterns and political economic relations). There have also been questions about what is done in the name of the security-development nexus and in the 'building' of peace.

Furthermore, in questioning peacebuilding through development-security initiatives, we are struck by how little empirical research exists that interrogates how—in practice—security-development initiatives are being implemented, to what effect, and according to whom. There are few comprehensive studies on how the security-development nexus is actually perceived and implemented on the ground, and particularly missing are those cases where the nexus is implemented during ongoing violence, or that trace security-development (how it is understood and practised) from policy articulation to local implementation and local articulation.[123] This bodes poorly for the chances that peacebuilding effectively and ethically attends to the many complex and interrelated problems that people are facing globally.

Let us then return to the opening questions: what are the causes of peace, the secret of achieving security, the recipe for development? While hopes for an answer to these questions must persevere given the dire global landscape in which people are suffering and in which violence persists, critical inquiry into how they are being answered and to what effect remains just as crucial. While we are well aware that a direct flow from intention to articulation, implementation, and finally effect is never possible and that meanings shift and transmute along even the most seemingly certain trajectories, we nonetheless contend that attention to the details of such shifting and transmutations is needed. This is imperative, since, for instance, the continuation of rationales building on military solutions, backed by violence, may contribute to explain why campaigns at ending wars and conflicts often spin back into renewed violence.[124]

In the above, we have argued that a liberal peace emerges as the dominant framing through which answers to the above questions can be found and put into effect. Attention to the security-development nexus—or rather its endemic and collective reification—emerges as *the*, or at least *a*, golden solution for doing so and for the problems of hitherto inadequate or inefficient peacebuilding practices.[125] Yet we have also seen that this solution is not working well—not by any parameters. Hence the question is whether the security-development nexus, as it is currently constructed in certain policy texts, is at all possible to 'implement'?

It is paramount that we raise this question as creatively and clearly as possible. In a globalizing world with wide and deepening poverty, and with an international system in transition under a dysfunctional security architecture, neither the idea, nor the need, for a functional 'security-development nexus' is likely to go away. Hence the continuing need for critical inquiry that probes the core premises and practices of peace-security-development as they are being manifested in the daily lives of people in diverse contexts, and in a context of high-strung global political stakes, ideological practice mishmash, and very real life-and-death issues.

Notes

1. For an overview, see Oliver P. Richmond, Sandra Pogodda, and Jasmin Ramovic, eds., *The Palgrave Handbook of Disciplinary and Regional Approaches to Peace* (New York: Palgrave MacMillan, 2016).

2. See Séverine Autesserre, *Peaceland* (New York: Cambridge University Press, 2014); Roger Mac Ginty, 'Routine Peace: Technocracy and Peacebuilding,' *Cooperation and Conflict* 47, no. 3 (2012): 287–308; Roger Mac Ginty, 'Against Stabilization, Stability,' *International Journal of Security and Development* 1, no. 1 (2012): 20–30.

3. W.B. Gallie, 'Essentially Contested Concepts,' *Proceedings of the Aristotelean Society* 56 (1956): 167–98.

4. Maria Stern and Joakim Öjendal, 'Mapping Security-Development: A Question of Methodology?' *Security Dialogue* 42, no. 1 (2011): 105–10.

5. See Oliver .P. Richmond, *The Transformation of Peace* (Basingstoke: Palgrave Macmillan, 2005); Roger Mac Ginty and Gurchathen Sanghera, 'Hybridity in

Peacebuilding and Development: An Introduction,' *Journal of Peacebuilding & Development* 7, no. 2 (2012): 3–8; Vivienne Jabri, 'Peacebuilding, the Local and the International: A Colonial or a Postcolonial Rationality?' *Peacebuilding* 1, no. 1 (2013): 3–16. As claimed by Richmond, 'the liberal peace's main components—democratisation, the rule of law, human rights, free and globalised markets, and neo-liberal development—are increasingly being critiqued from several different perspectives. These critiques have focused upon the incompatibility of certain stages of democratisation and economic reform; the ownership of development projects and "thick and thin" versions of the neo-liberal agenda; the possible incompatibility of post-conflict justice with the stabilisation of society and human rights; the problem of crime and corruption in economic and political reform; and the establishment of the rule of law. These terrains are relatively well explored.' Oliver P. Richmond, 'The Problem of Peace: Understanding the "Liberal Peace,"' *Conflict, Security & Development* 6, no. 3 (2006): 291–314, 292

6. UNU-WIDER, *Aid, Governance and Fragility* (position paper, Helsinki: ReCom, UNU-WIDER, 2014); Sonja Grimm, 'The European Union's Ambiguous Concept of State Fragility,' *Third World Quarterly* 35, no. 2 (2014): 252–67; Yannick Hingorani, 'The New Deal for Engagement in Fragile States: Where Are We Now?' *Journal of Peacebuilding & Development* 10, no. 2 (2015): 87–93; Sarah Hearn, 'Preliminary Findings of the Independent Review of the New Deal for Engagement in Fragile States,' in *International Dialogue Steering Group Meeting*, ed. International Dialogue on Peacebuilding and Statebuilding (Paris, 2015); see also Tobias Nussbaum, Eugenia Zorbas, and Michael Koros, 'A New Deal for Engagement in Fragile States,' *Conflict, Security & Development* 12, no. 5 (2012): 559–87.

7. See Roger Mac Ginty, 'Routine Peace: Technocracy and Peacebuilding,' *Cooperation and Conflict* 47 no. 3 (2012): 287–308; Roger Mac Ginty, 'Against Stabilization,' *Stability: International Journal of Security and Development* 1, no. 1 (2012): 20–30

8. Faye Donnelly, 'Critical Security Studies and Alternative Dialogues for Peace: Reconstructing "Language Barriers" and "Talking Points,"' in *The Palgrave Handbook of Disciplinary and Regional Approaches to Peace*, eds. Oliver P. Richmond, Sandra Pogodda, and Jasmin Ramović (London: Palgrave Macmillan, 2016).

9. Michel Foucault, *The Archaeology of Knowledge and the Discourse on Language* (New York: Pantheon, 1972); Mitchell Dean, *Governmentality: Power and Rule in Modern Society* (Los Angeles: Sage, 2010), 13.

10. See Maria Eriksson Baaz, and Maria Stern, *Sexual Violence as a Weapon of War?* (London: Zed, 2013); Maria Stern and Joakim Öjendal, 'Mapping the Security-Development Nexus: Conflict, Complexity, Cacophony, Convergence?' *Security Dialogue* 41, no. 1 (2010): 5–29.

11. Avery F. Gordon, *Ghostly Matters: Haunting and the Sociological Imagination* (Minneapolis: University of Minnesota Press, 2008), 8.

12. Sara Ahmed, *The Cultural Politics of Emotion* (Edinburgh: Edinburgh University Press, 2004).

13. Dean, *Governmentality*, 13

14. Ibid.

15. See, for instance, Mark Duffield, *Development, Security and Unending War: Governing the World of Peoples* (Cambridge/Malden: Polity, 2007); Mark Duffield, 'The Liberal Way of Development and the Development—Security Impasse: Exploring the Global Life-Chance Divide,' *Security Dialogue* 41, no. 1 (2010): 53–76; Björn Hettne, 'Discourses on Peace and Development,' *Progress in Development Studies* 1, no. 1 (2001): 21–36; Björn Hettne, 'Development and Security: Origins and Future,' *Security Dialogue* 41, no. 1 (2010): 31–52.

16. See Hans G. Brauch, Ürsula Spring, Czeslaw Mesjasz, John Grin, Pál Dunay, Navnita Behera, Béchir Chourou, Patricia Kameri-Mbote, and P.H. Liotta, eds., *Globalization and Environmental Challenges: Reconceptualizing Security in the 21st Century* (Berlin: Springer, 2008), 151–65.

17. See Barry Buzan and Lene Hansen, *The Evolution of International Security Studies* (Cambridge and New York: Cambridge University Press, 2009); Oliver P Richmond, *Peace in International Relations* (Oxfordshire: Routledge, 2008); Oliver P. Richmond, 'A Post-Liberal Peace: Eirenism and the Everyday,' *The Review of International Studies* 35, no. 3 (2009): 557–80.

18. Jan Pieterse, *Development Theory* (London: Sage, 2009); Gilbert Rist, *The History of Development: From Western Origins to Global Faith* (London: Zed, 1997).

19. For instance, Maria Stern and Joakim Öjendal, 'Mapping the Security-Development Nexus: Conflict, Complexity, Cacophony, Convergence?' *Security Dialogue* 41 no. 1 (2010): 5–29, outline six (out of many possible) stories about security-development: security-development as modern (teleological) narrative; broadening, deepening and humanizing security-development; security-development as impasse; post- security-development; security-development as technique of governmentality; and, globalized security-development.

20. See Oliver P. Richmond, *Peace in International Relations* (Oxfordshire: Routledge, 2008).

21. Oliver P. Richmond, Sandra Pogodda, and Jasmin Ramovic, *The Palgrave Handbook of Disciplinary and Regional Approaches to Peace* (New York: Palgrave MacMillan, 2016).

22. See Autesserre, *Peaceland*.

23. Lotta Themnér and Peter Wallensteen, 'Armed Conflicts, 1946–2012,' *Journal of Peace Research* 50, no. 4 (2013): 509–21.

24. Mary Kaldor, 'In Defence of New Wars,' *Stability: International Journal of Security and Development* 2, no. 1 (2013): 1–16.

25. See Kaldor, 'In Defence of New Wars,' 1–16; Didier Bigo, 'Internal and External Security(ies): The Möbius Ribbon,' in *Identities, Borders, Orders*, eds. Mathias Albert, Yosef Lapid, and David Jacobson (Minneapolis: University of Minnesota Press, 2001); Joakim Berndtsson, 'Realizing the Market-State? Military Transformation and Security Outsourcing in Sweden,' *International Journal* 69, no. 4 (2014): 542–58. In

addition, Christine Sylvester, *War as Experience: Contributions from International Relations and Feminist Analysis* (London: Routledge, 2013), 618, for instance, speaks of the 'grey zones between war and peace, conflict and postconflict'.

26. Tarak Barkawi, 'Of Camps and Critiques: A Reply to "Security, War, Violence",' *Millennium: Journal of International Studies* 41, no. 1 (2012).

27. Wendy Lambourne, 'International Law: To End the Scourge of War . . . and to Build a Just Peace,' in *The Palgrave Handbook of Disciplinary and Regional Approaches to Peace*, eds. Oliver P. Richmond, Sandra Pogodda, and Jasmin Ramovic (New York: Palgrave MacMillan, 2016).

28. Richmond et al., *Palgrave Handbook*.

29. This storyline has been complicated by critical scholars who call attention to gendered violences that criss-cross geopolitical borders and the familiar lines of political orders such as that differentiating the public from the private and the domestic from the foreign (see e.g., Cynthia Cockburn, 'Gender Relations as Causal in Militarization and War,' *International Feminist Journal of Politics* 12, no. 2 [2010]: 139–57; Jean B. Elshtain, *Women and War* [Chicago: University of Chicago Press, 1995]; Cynthia Enloe, *Bananas, Beaches and Bases: Making Feminist Sense of International Politics* [Berkeley: University of California Press, 1990]). It has also been criticized by those who call attention to the ways in which geopolitical borders have been drawn, as well as the way we tell the history of state formation. See Tarak Barkawi, 'From War to Security: Security Studies, the Wider Agenda and the Fate of the Study of War,' *Millennium: Journal of International Studies* 39, no. 3 (2011): 701–16; Vivienne Jabri, *War and the Transformation of Global Politics: Rethinking Peace and Conflict Studies* (London: Palgrave Macmillan, 2007); Vivienne Jabri, 'Post-Colonialism: A Post-Colonial Perspective on Peacebuilding,' in *The Palgrave Handbook of Disciplinary and Regional Approaches to Peace*, eds. Oliver P. Richmond, Sandra Pogodda, and Jasmin Ramovic (New York: Palgrave MacMillan, 2016). See also Maria Stern, 'Gender and Race in the European Security Strategy: Europe as a "Force for Good"?' *Journal of International Relations and Development* 14, no. 1 (2011): 28–59, for an overview of post-colonial problematizations of peace in Europe.

30. Jack S. Levy and William Thomson, *Causes of War* (Oxford: Wiley-Blackwell, 2010); see also Laura Sjoberg, *Gendering Global Conflict* (New York: Columbia University Press, 2013).

31. Baaz and Stern, *Sexual Violence*; see also Claudia Aradau, *Good Practices in Response to Trafficking in Human Beings* (Copenhagen: Danish Red Cross, 2005); Maria Stern, *Naming Security—Constructing Identity: 'Mayan Women' in Guatemala on the Eve of 'Peace'* (Manchester: Manchester University Press, 2005).

32. Nick Megoran, Fiona McConnell, and Philippa Williams, 'Geography and Peace,' in *The Palgrave Handbook of Disciplinary and Regional Approaches to Peace*, eds. Oliver P. Richmond, Sandra Pogodda, and Jasmin Ramovic (New York: Palgrave MacMillan, 2016), 122–38. In addition, Sjoberg notes 'war [is] in women's living rooms, hair salons, and marriages in Iraq and the United States . . . in the way women prostitutes

use their bodies . . . [and] in International organizations but also in bars, in brothels . . . —in people's lives', Laura Sjoberg, *Gendering Global Conflict* (New York: Columbia University Press, 2013), 179–80. Harders notes that 'war (or violence), in this perspective [as a continuum], is not limited to enduring collective violence between states or organized groups' rather it should be framed as a violence 'shaped by social dynamics of escalation and de-escalation', Cilja Harders, *Gender Relations, Violence, and Conflict Transformation* (Berlin: Berghof Foundation, 2011), 135.

33. Therése Pettersson and Kristine Eck, 'Organized Violence, 1989–2017', *Journal of Peace Research* 55, no. 4 (2018), 535–547.

34. Johan Galtung, 'Violence, Peace, and Peace Research', *Journal of Peace Research* 6, no. 3 (1969): 167–91.

35. 'Liberal Peace . . . comprises a victor's peace aimed at security, and institutional peace to provide international governance and guarantees, a constitutional peace to ensure democracy and free trade, and a civil peace to ensure freedom and rights' Oliver P. Richmond, 'Peace in International Relations Theory', in *The Palgrave Handbook of Disciplinary and Regional Approaches to Peace*, eds. Oliver P. Richmond, Sandra Pogodda, and Jasmin Ramovic (London: Palgrave Macmillan, 2016).

36. See Roger Mac Ginty and Oliver P. Richmond, 'The Local Turn in Peace Building: A Critical Agenda for Peace', *Third World Quarterly* 34, no. 5 (2013): 763–83; Joakim Öjendal and Sivhouch Ou, 'The "Local Turn" Saving Liberal Peacebuilding? Unpacking Virtual Peace in Cambodia', *Third World Quarterly* 36, no. 5 (2015): 929–49.

37. See Stern and Öjendal, 'Mapping the Security-Development Nexus'; Stern and Öjendal, 'Mapping Security-Development'.

38. Björn Hettne, 'Development and Security: Origins and Future', *Security Dialogue* 41, no. 1 (2010): 31–52; UNDP, Human Development Report 1994 (New York: UN Development Programme, 1994).

39. The World Bank, *Post-Conflict Reconstruction: The Role of the World Bank* (Washington, DC: World Bank, 1998).

40. Caroline Hughes, 'Peace and Development Studies', in *The Palgrave Handbook of Disciplinary and Regional Approaches to Peace*, eds. Oliver P. Richmond, Sandra Pogodda, and Jasmin Ramovic (London: Palgrave Macmillan, 2016), 138–53.

41. The World Bank, *World Development Report 2000/2001: Attacking Poverty* (Washington, DC: World Bank, 2001).

42. OECD/DAC, *Helping Prevent Violent Conflict: The DAC Guidelines* (Paris: OECD, 2001), 17.

43. See European Parliament, *EU Policy Coherence for Development: The Challenge of Sustainability*, PE 535.022 (Directorate-General for External Policies, Policy Department, 2016).

44. See UN, *In Larger Freedom. Towards Development, Security and Human Rights for All* (New York: United Nations, 2005); The World Bank, *World Development Report: Conflict, Security, and Development* (Washington, DC: World Bank, 2011); USAID,

Foreign Aid in the National Interest Promoting Freedom, Security, and Opportunity (Washington, DC: US Agency for International Development, 2002).

45. DFID, *Preventing Conflict in Fragile States* (London: Department for International Development, 2012), doi:10.1017/S0260210510000057

46. See European Parliament, *EU Policy Coherence.*

47. Jabri, 'Peacebuilding,' 4.

48. Gareth Evans, 'From Humanitarian Intervention to the Responsibility to Protect,' *Wisconsin International Law Journal* 3, no. 2 (2006), 710.

49. Scholars have convincingly criticized the notion of (non-Western) state 'fragility' as well as that of 'failed states' as being imbedded in colonial lexicons and attending practices, cf. Baaz and Stern, *Sexual Violence.*

50. UNU-WIDER, *Aid, Governance and Fragility*; Grimm, 'European Union's Ambiguous Concept.'

51. Necla Tschirgi, *Peacebuilding as the Link between Security and Development: Is the Window of Opportunity Closing?* (IPA Policy Report, December 2003); Jos Boonstra and Natalia Shapovalova, *Thinking Security, Doing Development? The Security-Development Nexus in European Policies towards Tajikistan* (Ministry for Foreign Affairs of Finland, EUCAM, 2012).

52. Björn Hettne, 'Peace and Development Contradictions and Compatibilities,' *Journal of Peace Research* 20, no. 4 (1983): 329–42; Björn Hettne, 'Discourses on Peace and Development,' *Progress in Development Studies* 1, no. 1 (2001): 21–36; Björn Hettne, 'Development and Security: Origins and Future,' *Security Dialogue* 41, no. 1 (2010): 31–52; Jon Barnett, 'Peace and Development: Towards a New Synthesis,' *Journal of Peace Research* 45, no. 1 (2008): 75–89; Johan Galtung, 'Violence, Peace, and Peace Research,' *Journal of Peace Research* 6, no. 3 (1969): 167–91; Paul Collier, *Breaking the Conflict Trap: Civil War and Development Policy, A World Bank Policy Research Report* (Washington, DC: World Bank, Oxford University Press, 2003).

53. For an overview see Hans G. Brauch, 'Conceptual Quartet: Security and its Linkages with Peace, Development, and Environment,' in *Globalization and Environmental Challenges: Reconceptualizing Security in the 21st Century*, eds. Hans G. Brauch, Úrsula Spring, Czeslaw Mesjasz, John Grin, Pál Dunay, Navnita Behera, Béchir Chourou, Patricia Kameri-Mbote, and P.H. Liotta (Berlin: Springer, 2008), 65–98.

54. Ole Weaver, 'Peace and Security: Two Evolving Concepts and Their Changing Relationship,' in *Globalization and Environmental Challenges: Reconceptualizing Security in the 21st Century*, eds. Hans G. Brauch, Úrsula Spring, Czeslaw Mesjasz, John Grin, Pál Dunay, Navnita Behera, Béchir Chourou, Patricia Kameri-Mbote, and P.H. Liotta (Berlin: Springer, 2008), 99–113; Faye Donnelly, 'Critical Security Studies and Alternative Dialogues for Peace: Reconstructing "Language Barriers" and "Talking Points",' in *The Palgrave Handbook of Disciplinary and Regional Approaches to Peace*, eds. Oliver P. Richmond, Sandra Pogodda, and Jasmin Ramovic (Palgrave Macmillan, London, 2016), 272–98, for an overview.

55. Stern and Öjendal, 'Mapping the Security-Development Nexus'; Peter Uvin, 'Development and Security: Genealogy and Typology of an Evolving International Policy Area,' in *Globalization and Environmental Challenges Reconceptualizing Security in the 21st Century*, eds. Hans G. Brauch, Ürsula Spring, Czeslaw Mesjasz, John Grin, Pál Dunay, Navnita Behera, Béchir Chourou, Patricia Kameri-Mbote, and P.H. Liotta (Berlin: Springer, 2008), 151–63.

56. Brauch et al., *Globalization and Environmental Challenges*.

57. Human security: in the beginning of the 1990s, a profound critique of state-centric security prompted the development of the concept of 'human security'. Human security, pioneered by the Canadian International Development Agency (CIDA) has since become a central focus for peace and conflict studies and development studies alike, offered a sorely needed venue for highlighting the particular vulnerabilities of peoples who suffer violence from representatives of the state, as well as other forms of violence and injustices. In 1994, the Human Development Report from the United Nations Development Programme (UNDP) officially 'launched' the concept of human security as a viable alternative. Human security provided a sort of 'catch-all' for an approach to security that would address all peoples' security needs, including needs that had previously fallen outside of traditional thinking about security—in the field of development, a 'participatory revolution' that emphasized the significance of 'reconnecting' to the true 'subjects' of development, namely, the poor, the local, the grass roots and the voiceless. To 'put the last first' (Chambers 1983), 'small is beautiful', 'appropriate technology' (Schumacher 1973) and (later) 'empowerment' (Friedman 1992) became common calls. These alternative development approaches looked both 'inwards' and 'backwards' for (true) development. The security-development nexus can be seen as the merging of human development and human security—as intricate and complex ambitions in idealist and normative combinations. See Robert Chambers, *Rural Development: Putting the Last First* (London: Longman, 1983); E.F. Schumacher, *Small Is Beautiful: A Study of Economics as If People Mattered* (London: Blonde & Briggs, 1973); John Friedmann, *Empowerment* (Oxford: Blackwell, 1992).

58. Stern and Öjendal, 'Mapping the Security-Development Nexus.'

59. See Caroline Hughes and Joakim Öjendal, 'Reassessing Tradition in Times of Political Change: Post-War Cambodia Reconsidered,' *Journal of Southeast Asian Studies* 37, no. 3 (2006), 417.

60. Johan Galtung, 'Violence, Peace, and Peace Research,' *Journal of Peace Research* 6, no. 3 (1969): 167–91.

61. Conrad Brunk, 'Shaping a Vision: The Nature of Peace Studies,' in *Peace and Conflict Studies: A Reader* eds. Charles Webel and Jorgen Johansen (Oxfordshire: Routledge, 2012), 13–16; Paul Rogers, 'Peace Studies,' in *Contemporary Security Studies*, ed. Alan Collins (Oxford: Oxford University Press, 2007).

62. Amartya Sen, *Development as Freedom* (New York: Oxford University Press, 1999).

63. Jon Barnett, 'Peace and Development: Towards a New Synthesis,' *Journal of Peace*

Research 45, no. 1 (2008): 75–89; UNDP, *Human Development Report 1994* (New York: UN Development Programme, 1994).

64. Hettne, 'Discourses on Peace and Development.'

65. Hettne, 'Development and Security.'

66. Hettne, 'Peace and Development Contradictions'; cf. Frances Stewart, 'Development and Security,' *Conflict, Security & Development* 4, no 3, (2004): 261–88.

67. Hettne, 'Peace and Development Contradictions,' 329, 340.

68. UN, *Transforming our World: The 2030 Agenda for Sustainable Development*, A/RES/70/1 (New York: United Nations, 2015).

69. B. Hettne, 'Discourses on Peace and Development,' 21. See also Wolfgang Sachs, ed., *The Development Dictionary: A Guide to Knowledge as Power* (London: Zed, 1992).

70. UN, *Transforming Our World*.

71. Paul Collier. *Breaking the Conflict Trap: Civil War and Development Policy. A World Bank Policy Research Report*. (Washington, DC: World Bank, Oxford University Press, 2003).

72. See, for example, Hettne, 'Discourses on Peace and Development'; Georg Sørensen, 'Peace and Development: Looking for the Right Track,' *Journal of Peace Research* 22, no. 1 (1985): 70.

73. See Kamil Zwolski, 'The EU and a Holistic Security Approach after Lisbon: Competing Norms and the Power of the Dominant Discourse,' *Journal of European Public Policy* 19 no. 7 (2012): 988–1005; Stefan Gänzle, 'Coping with the "Security-Development Nexus": The European Community's Instrument for Stability—Rationale and Potential,' *DIE Studies* 47 (Bonn: Deutsches Institut für Entwicklungspolitik, 2009).

74. Boutros Boutros-Ghali, *Report of the UN Secretary-General: 'Agenda for Peace'* (New York: United Nations, 1992); Boutros Boutros-Ghali, *An Agenda for Development* (New York: United Nations, 1995); United Nations, *Brahimi Report* (New York: United Nations, 2000); see also Roland Paris, *At War's End: Building Peace after Civil Conflict* (Cambridge: Cambridge University Press, 2004). The Peacebuilding Commission at the United Nations was established in 2006.

75. Oliver P. Richmond, *The Transformation of Peace* (Basingstoke: Palgrave Macmillan, 2005); Oliver P. Richmond, 'The Problem of Peace: Understanding the "Liberal Peace",' *Conflict, Security & Development* 6, no. 3 (2006) :291–314; Oliver P. Richmond, *Peace in International Relations* (Oxon: Routledge, 2008); Oliver P. Richmond, 'Peace in International Relations Theory,' in *The Palgrave Handbook of Disciplinary and Regional Approaches to Peace*, eds. Oliver P. Richmond, Sandra Pogodda, and Jasmin Ramovic (Palgrave Macmillan, London, 2016); Roger Mac Ginty and Gurchathen Sanghera, 'Hybridity in Peacebuilding and Development: An Introduction,' *Journal of Peacebuilding & Development* 7, no. 2 (2012): 3–8; Jabri, 'Peacebuilding'; John Heathershaw, 'Unpacking the Liberal Peace: The Dividing and Merging of Peacebuilding Discourses,' *Journal of International Studies* 36, no. 3 (2008): 597–621.

76. Roland Paris and Timothy D. Sisk, *Managing Contradictions: The Inherent Dilemmas*

of Postwar Statebuilding (International Peace Academy, 2007); Danielle Breswick and Paul Jackson, *Conflict, Security and Development: An Introduction* (New York: Routledge, 2013).

77. Oliver P. Richmond, ed., *Palgrave Advances in Peacebuilding: Critical Developments and Approaches* (Basingstoke: Palgrave Macmillan, 2010).

78. Thania Paffenholz, 'Unpacking the Local Turn in Peacebuilding: A Critical Assessment Towards an Agenda for Future Research,' *Third World Quarterly* 36, no. 5 (2015): 857–74.

79. Richmond, *Palgrave Advances in Peacebuilding*.

80. John Paul Lederach, *Building Peace: Sustainable Reconciliation in Divided Societies* (Washington: United States Institute of Peace Press, 1997).

81. See Jabri, 'Peacebuilding.'

82. There has also been much critique waged against the notions of 'the local' that emerge in such accounts. See Caroline Hughes, Joakim Öjendal, and Isabell Schierenbeck, 'The Struggle Versus the Song—the Local Turn in Peace Building: An Introduction,' *Third World Quarterly* 36, no. 5 (2015): 817–24.

83. See Russett (this volume) and Gowa and Pratt (this volume).

84. Autesserre, *Peaceland*, 17. In addition, arguably, the faith in the Weberian ideal of the state and a sanitized nostalgic view of Western state formation, whereby violence in many forms and long historical processes, has been written out of the story of the establishment of state sovereignty. As such, state-building emerges as a relatively swift endeavour (consolidated through peacebuilding efforts), the components and processes of which are known (enough) and can be translated into operations that are governed by external actors. See Étienne Balibar, ed., *Politics and the Other Scene* (London: Verso, 2002); David Campbell, *Writing Security: United States Foreign Policy and the Politics of Identity* (Manchester: Manchester University Press, 1998); Dipesh Chakrabarty, *Provincializing Europe Postcolonial Thought and Historical Difference* (Princeton: Princeton University Press, 2007).

85. See David Chandler, *International State-Building: The Rise of Post-Liberal Governance* (London: Taylor & Francis, 2010); Pierre Englebert and Dennis M. Tull, 'Postconflict Reconstruction in Africa: Flawed Ideas about Failed States,' *International Security* 32, no. 4 (2008): 106–39.

86. Jan Bachmann, 'Policing Africa,' *Security Dialogue* 45, no. 2 (2014): 119–36; Paul Jackson, 'Security Sector Reform and State Building,' *Third World Quarterly* 32, no. 10 (2011): 1802–22; Necla Tschirgi, *Peacebuilding as the Link between Security and Development: Is the Window of Opportunity Closing?* (IPA Policy Report, December 2003).

87. B. Boutros-Ghali, *Agenda for Peace*.

88. Recall all of the varying meanings of security and development that become evoked in the questions recalled in the beginning of the chapter, e.g., Stern and Öjendal, 'Mapping the Security-Development Nexus.'

89. See Lisa Denney, 'Reducing Poverty with Teargas and Batons: The Security-Development Nexus in Sierra Leone,' *African Affairs* 110, no. 439 (2011): 275–94;

Ken Menkhaus, 'Vicious Circles and the Security Development Nexus in Somalia,' *Conflict, Security and Development* 4, no. 2 (2004): 149–65; Doug Porter, Deborah Isser and Louis-Alexandre Berg, 'The Justice-Security-Development Nexus: Theory and Practice in Fragile and Conflict-Affected States,' *Hague Journal of the Rule of Law* 5 (2013): 310–28. Furthermore, Höglund and Kovacs note, 'In particular, it has been suggested that contemporary research displays a tendency to assume a causal relationship between negative peace and positive peace: if only the physical and immediate violence can be stopped, a positive peace will follow.' Kristine Höglund and Mimmi Kovacs, 'Beyond the Absence of War: The Diversity of Peace in Post-settlement Societies,' *Review of International Studies* 36 (2010): 367–90, 371

90. Yasmine Shamsie, 'Pro-poor Economic Development Aid to Haiti: Unintended Effects Arising from the Conflict Development Nexus,' *Journal of Peacebuilding and Development* 6, no. 3 (2011): 32–44; Christina Steenkamp, 'In the Shadows of War and Peace: Making Sense of Violence after Peace Accords,' *Conflict, Security & Development* 11, no. 3 (2011): 357–83.

91. Sara E. Davies and Jacqui True, 'Reframing Conflict-Related Sexual and Gender-Based Violence: Bringing Gender Analysis Back In,' *Security Dialogue* 46, no. 6 (2015): 495–512.

92. Ken Menkhaus, *If Mayors Ruled Somalia*, NAI Policy Note 2 (Uppsala: NAI, 2014).

93. See Mark Downes and Robert Muggah, 'Breathing Room: Interim Stabilization and Security Sector Reform in the Post-war Period,' in *The Future of Security Sector Reform*, ed. Mark Sedra (Waterloo, ON: The Center for International Governance Innovation, 2010); Heiner Hänggi, 'Conceptualising Security Sector Reform and Reconstruction,' in *Reform and Reconstruction of the Security Sector*, eds. Alan Bryden and Heiner Hänggi (Geneva: Geneva Centre for Democratic Control of Armed Forces, 2004).

94. See Mark Sedra, *The Future of Security Sector Reform* (Waterloo, ON: Centre for International Governance Innovation, 2010).

95. See Rita Abrahamsen, *Disciplining Democracy* (London: Zed, 2000); Rita Abrahamsen, 'The Power of Partnerships in Global Governance,' *Third World Quarterly* 25, no. 8 (2004): 1453–67; David Chandler, *International State-Building: The Rise of Post-Liberal Governance* (London: Taylor & Francis, 2010); Simon Chesterman, 'Whose Strategy, Whose Peace? The Role of International Institutions in Strategic Peace-building,' in *Strategies of Peace: Transforming Conflict in a Violent World*, eds. Daniel Philpott and Gerard Powers (Oxford: Oxford University Press, 2010), 119–40.

96. Rita Abrahamsen and Michael Williams, *Security Beyond the State* (Cambridge and New York: Cambridge University Press, 2011); Mark Duffield, *Development, Security and Unending War: Governing the World of Peoples* (Cambridge/Malden: Polity, 2007); Chesterman, 'Whose Strategy'; Elke Krahmann, 'Conceptualizing Security Governance,' *Cooperation and Conflict* 38, no. 1 (March 1, 2003): 5–26.

97. Abrahamsen and Williams, *Security Beyond the State*, 66.

98. Oliver P. Richmond and Jason Franks, *Liberal Peace Transitions* (Edinburgh

University Press, 2011); Neil Cooper, Mandy Turner, and Michael Pugh, 'The End of History and the Last Liberal Peacebuilder: A Reply to Roland Paris,' *Review of International Studies* 37, no. 4 (2011): 1995–2007.

99. Paul Collier and Nicholas Sambanis, *Understanding Civil War: Evidence and Analysis.* Vol. 1, *Africa.* (Washington, DC: World Bank, 2005), https://openknowledge .worldbank.org/handle/10986/7437; Oliver P. Richmond, 'Failed Statebuilding versus Peace Formation,' *Cooperation and Conflict* 48, no. 3 (2013): 378–400; Roger Mac Ginty, 'Routine Peace: Technocracy and Peacebuilding,' *Cooperation and Conflict* 47, no. 3 (2012): 287–308; Roger Mac Ginty, 'Against Stabilization,' *Stability: International Journal of Security and Development* 1, no. 1 (2012): 20–30; Hughes, Öjendal, and Schierenbeck, 'The Struggle Versus the Song.'

100. Mac Ginty, 'Routine Peace'; Mac Ginty, 'Against Stabilization'; Cooper, Turner, and Pugh, 'The End of History'; Shahrbanou Tadjbakhsh, ed., *Rethinking the Liberal Peace: External Models and Local Alternatives* (Abingdon: Routledge, 2011).

101. David Chandler, 'The Security-Development Nexus and the Rise of Anti-Foreign Policy,' *Journal of International Relations and Development* 10, no. 4 (2007): 362–86; Mark Duffield, 'The Liberal Way of Development and the Development—Security Impasse: Exploring the Global Life-Chance Divide,' *Security Dialogue* 41, no. 1 (2010): 53–76.

102. Roland Paris, 'Saving Liberal Peacebuilding,' *Review of International Studies* 36 (2010): 337–65.

103. Virginai M. Bouvier, *Colombia: Building Peace in a Time of War* (Washington, DC: United States Institute of Peace, 2009).

104. World Bank, *World Development Report: Conflict, Security, and Development* (Washington, DC: World Bank, 2011); Jan Bachmann, Colleen Bell, and Caroline Holmqvist, eds., *War, Police and Assemblages of Intervention* (London: Routledge, 2015).

105. See Bachmann, Bell and Holmqvist, *War, Police and Assemblages of Intervention.*

106. Bachmann, Bell, and Holmqvist, *War, Police and Assemblages of Intervention*; Chandler, 'The Security-Development Nexus.'

107. See European Parliament, *EU Policy Coherence.*

108. Joanna Spear, and Paul Williams, *Security and Development in Global Politics: A Critical Comparison* (Washington, DC: Georgetown University Press, 2012).

109. Stephan Keukeleire and Kolja Raube, 'The Security-Development Nexus and Securitization in the EU's Policies Towards Developing Countries,' *Cambridge Review of International Affairs* 26, no. 3 (2013): 556–72.

110. Stephen Baranyi, 'Canada and the Security-Development Nexus in Haiti: The "Dark Side" or Changing Shades of Gray?' *Canadian Foreign Policy Journal* 20, no. 2 (2014): 163–75; see Paul Jackson, 'Security Sector Reform and State Building,' *Third World Quarterly* 32, no. 10 (2011): 1802–22; Michael E. Smith, 'The European External Action Service and the Security-Development Nexus: Organizing for Effectiveness or Incoherence,' *Journal of European Public Policy* 20, no. 9 (2013): 1299–1315; Graham Mayeda, 'Legal Aspects of the Security-Development Nexus: International

Administrative Law as a Check on the Use of Development Assistance in the "War on Terror", *Chicago Journal of International Law* 13, no. 1 (2012): 71–121. Also, for a discussion of the developmentalization of security, see Jonathan Pugh, Clive Gabay, and Alison Williams, 'Beyond the Securitisation of Development: The Limits of Intervention, Developmentalisation of Security and Repositioning of Purpose in the UK Coalition Government's Policy Agenda, *Geoforum* 44 (2012): 193–201.

111. Shamsie, 'Pro-poor Economic Development Aid,' 40.

112. Derek McDougall, 'The Security-Development Nexus: Comparing External Interventions and Development Strategies in East Timor and Solomon Islands,' *Asian Security* 6, no. 2 (2010): 170–90, 171.

113. Ibid., 187

114. Erlend G. Krogstad, 'Security, Development, and Force: Revisiting Police Reform in Sierra Leone,' *African Affairs* 111, no. 443 (2012): 261–80, 264.

115. Ibid., 279.

116. Maurizio Carbone, 'An Uneasy Nexus: Development, Security and the EU's African Peace Facility,' *European Foreign Affairs Review* 18, no. 4 (2013): 103–24; Denney, 'Reducing Poverty with Teargas'; see Stern and Öjendal, 'Mapping the Security-Development Nexus,' for an overview.

117. Stern and Öjendal, 'Mapping the Security-Development Nexus'; Chandler, 'The Security-Development Nexus'; Duffield, *Development, Security and Unending War*; Mark Duffield, 'The Liberal Way of Development and the Development—Security Impasse: Exploring the Global Life-Chance Divide,' *Security Dialogue* 41, no. 1 (2010): 53–76.

118. Roger Mac Ginty and Oliver P. Richmond, 'The Local Turn in Peace Building: A Critical Agenda for Peace,' *Third World Quarterly* 34, no. 5 (2013): 763–83; Hughes, Öjendal, and Schierenbeck, 'The Struggle versus the Song.'

119. See Shamsie, 'Pro-poor Economic Development Aid.'

120. Duffield, 'The Liberal Way of Development Security Dialogue'; Chandler, 'The Security-Development Nexus'; Keukeleire and Raube, 'The Security-Development Nexus.'

121. Denney, 'Reducing Poverty with Teargas.'

122. Steffen Jensen, 'The Security and Development Nexus in Cape Town: War on Gangs, Counterinsurgency and Citizenship,' *Security Dialogue* 41, no. 1 (2010): 77–97; Lars Buur, Steffen Jensen, and Finn Stepputat, *The Security-Development Nexus: Expressions of Sovereignty and Securitization in Southern Africa* (Uppsala and Cape Town: Human Sciences Research Council and Nordiska Afrikainstitutet, 2007).

123. See Buur, Jensen, and Stepputat, *The Security-Development Nexus*; Neclâ Tschirgi, Michael S. Lund and Francesco Mancini, *Security and Development: Searching for Critical Connections—International Peace Institute Project* (Boulder, CO: Lynn Rienner, 2010); Adedeji Ebo, 'The Challenges and Lessons of Security Sector Reform in Post-conflict Sierra Leone,' *Conflict, Security and Development* 6, no. 4 (2006): 481–501; Maurizio Carbone, 'An Uneasy Nexus: Development, Security and the EU's African Peace Facility,' *European Foreign Affairs Review* 18, no. 4 (2013): 103–24;

Jensen, 'The Security and Development Nexus in Cape Town'; Anwar Shah, *Local Governance in Developing Countries* (Washington, DC: World Bank, 2006).

124. Collier 2005; Mac Ginty and Richmond, 'The Local Turn in Peace Building.'

125. Paul Collier, *Breaking the Conflict Trap: Civil War and Development Policy. A World Bank Policy Research Report* (Washington, DC: World Bank, Oxford University Press, 2003); Roger Mac Ginty and Gurchathen Sanghera, 'Hybridity in Peacebuilding and Development: An Introduction,' *Journal of Peacebuilding & Development* 7, no. 2, (2012): 3–8; Joakim Öjendal, Isabell Schierenbeck, and Caroline Hughes, 'Special Issue: The "Local" Turn in Peacebuilding,' *Third World Quarterly* 36, no. 5 (2015); Oliver P. Richmond and Jason Franks, 'Liberal Hubris? Virtual Peace in Cambodia,' *Security Dialogue* 38, no. 1 (2007): 27–48.

Deterrence and Disarmament

13.

The Causes of Peace: The Role of Deterrence

Bruno Tertrais

Introduction

'Deterrence' and 'peace' are two words that contrast starkly with each other.[1] At the root of the first is the Latin verb *terrere*, 'to terrorize'. Not an easy match with 'peace'. Whatever impact deterrence has on peace, this mismatch calls for a rather restrictive definition of peace, understood here as the absence of direct, open military conflict between two parties (including when they are still, legally speaking, in a state of war, such as with North and South Korea). It is restrictive in the sense that, just as democracy is not only about elections, peace is not only about the absence of war.

In the contemporary public debate, deterrence is often understood as a process through which a party is prevented, through a rational calculation on its part, from attacking another because such aggression would trigger nuclear reprisals, which would exceed the expected benefits of aggression. Such a restrictive definition is unwarranted in four respects. Deterrence is not a concept limited to the military domain: it operates in many aspects of human life, with some dating it to God's threat to Adam and Eve (to not eat the fruits of the tree of the knowledge of good and evil under penalty of becoming mortals). In the strategic domain—that of state-to-state relations, the focus of this paper—deterrence is not only nuclear: it also exists at the conventional level. It can be exercised through 'denial' (persuading the adversary that achieving its goals would be difficult because of the obstacles it would face) as much as by 'retaliation'.[2] It has never been based *solely* on a rational calculation, even though most Cold War deterrence theory—just like economic analysis—was premised on the rationality of actors. Emphasizing the origins of the word 'deterrence' helps remind analysts that there was always an irrational component to the concept it embodies.

Deterrence before 1945

The idea of military deterrence is almost as old as organized warfare. However, *deterrence as a strategy* is a more recent innovation.[3]

It is probably the meaning of the famed Roman adage *si vis pacem, para bellum* (if you want peace, prepare for war), the idea being that one would hesitate before attacking a well-armed adversary. Such an idea is also to be found in Thucydides's works.[4] 'When there is mutual fear, men think twice before they make aggressions upon one another,' says Hermocrates of Syracuse, as quoted by Thucydides.[5]

Deterrence was a state of fact more than a war-prevention instrument.[6] It did not appear as such in Prussian General Carl von Clausewitz's writings, for instance. Diplomacy and alliances, not deterrence, were essential to prevent war. Classical deterrence as a concept operated—and continues to operate—through denial and not retaliation.[7] The notion of a 'fleet in being' proposed by Lord Torrington in 1690 was an early example. Deterrence through the threat of unacceptable violence is a more recent innovation: it was present in the writings of the early theorists of aerial bombardment such as Douhet in Italy, Trenchard in the UK, and Mitchell in the US.[8] But overall, before 1945 deterrence was at best an 'occasional stratagem'.[9] It was not a *strategy*—the deliberate articulation of particular means towards the achievement of specific goals—and even less a key war-avoiding instrument. What changed after 1945 is that with nuclear weapons, deterrence became an elaborate strategy mostly based on the threat of *retaliation* and designed to *prevent war*.[10] Nuclear weapons, as Kenneth Waltz put it, 'purified deterrent strategies by removing elements of defense and war-fighting'.[11]

In the late 1970s, the expression 'conventional deterrence' appeared by contrast with nuclear deterrence, but it was hardly dissociable from the nuclear context: the idea behind it was that so-called precision guided munitions (PGM) could help raise the nuclear threshold.[12]

Overall, two lessons of history regarding the effectiveness of conventional deterrence appear. Firstly, deterrence depends much less on the overall correlation of forces than on the volume and quality of forces deployed on the theatre, their degree of availability, and the type of military strategy employed.[13] It is likely to fail if one of the parties has the ability to undertake a *blitzkrieg*; conversely, it is likely to succeed if the other party has the ability to embark in prolonged attrition warfare.[14] Secondly, deterrence of weaker states will fail if such states are highly motivated or misperceived some facet of the situation, or if they are able to exploit vulnerabilities of stronger states (in particular through the use of unconventional tactics).[15]

A Nuclear Peace? Examining the Evidence

The case for nuclear deterrence has to be based on two propositions: that there has been an absence of war between countries armed with nuclear weapons and—given that a negative proposition can never be fully demonstrated—that such absence of war cannot be satisfactorily explained by other factors than the existence of deterrence strategies based on nuclear weapons. The statistical evidence rests on the absence, since 1945, of major-power war, major war between nuclear-armed countries, and major military attacks against nuclear-armed or nuclear-protected countries.

Exhibit A in support of nuclear deterrence is the absence of major-power war since 1945.[16] If one defines great powers as the five permanent members of the UN Security Council, which are also the five nuclear weapons states in the sense of the Nuclear Non-Proliferation Treaty (NPT), clearly there was never any open military conflict between them, even less a major war (1,000 battle-related deaths in a single year). A broader definition including Germany and Japan, which are protected by the US nuclear umbrella, also makes the cut.

John Lewis Gaddis forged the expression 'the Long Peace' forty years after the end of WWII; it is now seven decades old. No comparable period of great-power peace has ever existed in the history of modern states (perhaps not even since the Roman Empire). For instance, there were two dozen conflicts among major powers in the equivalent amount of time following the Treaties of Westphalia (1648), and nine between the Vienna Congress (1815) and WWI.[17] Is there not here an exceptional proposition that deserves an explanation?

The idea of a Long Peace has been challenged by two arguments.

The first is that it is *not so exceptional*. Here, coding (i.e., What is a major-power war? What is the relevant duration of the Long Peace?) is the bone of contention. Some would mark its beginning only in 1947 (the Iron Curtain speech), in 1949 (the first Soviet nuclear test), or even in 1953 (the end of the Korean War). Some would end it as early as 1989: the narrowest definition thus leads to a short Long Peace of only . . . thirty-six years. If one simultaneously discounts some past events as being non-major-power wars, then previous periods of non-war become lengthier, thus negating the exceptionality of the Long Peace. For instance, discounting the Franco–Spanish War of 1823 and the first Russian–Turkish War of 1828–1829 leads to a thirty-three-year period of great-power peace (1815–1848); and discounting the second Russian-Prussian War of 1877–1878 and the Russian–Japanese War of 1905 leads to a forty-three-year period of peace (1871–1914). Thus, two authors claim that 'historical periods of major power peace are frequently as long as forty-two years'.[18]

This is a valuable debate, but I am not convinced of the 'banality of the Long Peace'. To begin, I find the coding of the Korean War as a major-power one debatable. It pitted US-led UN forces against North Korea and, a few months later, its Chinese ally. At that time, the People's Republic of China was neither a permanent member of the UN Security Council (its WWII victor's seat was occupied by Taipei) nor an economic giant, a formidable military power, or a nuclear state. Its intervention was mostly defensive: the fear that the US forces would attack China.[19] Next, and more importantly, I find no reason to conclude the Long Peace in 1989 or any posterior year. Even if one uses 1953 as a starting point and demotes several past major-power wars, sixty-three years without a great-power war is an exceptional duration.

The second is that it is *statistically irrelevant*. According to Cirillo and Taleb,[20] the history of large-scale wars shows a fat-tailed distribution in which properties such as the mean are determined by extremes. It has been a homogeneous Poisson (purely random) process in the past 500 years. A seventy-year period without a massively destructive event means nothing from a statistical point of view, given that in the past 2,000-plus years the 'waiting time' between two 10-million-deaths events—an example taken from their results—is, on average, 133 years, and the mean absolute deviation is 136 years (though only 52 and 63 years when rescaled to today's population).[21] Pinker accepts that the distribution of wars may be a Poisson process but writes, 'nothing says that the probability has to be constant over long stretches of time'.[22] The occurrence of major war may be random, but its probability not constant, a 'non-stationery Poisson process with a declining rate parameter'.[23] Pinker accepts the theoretical possibility that the Long Peace could be just a statistical illusion but argues that a combination of historically unprecedented developments that have accompanied the absence of major-power war gives credence to the idea that 'something new' is happening, lowering the chances of such war, without discarding the possibility of a new one, which could be even more destructive than its predecessors.[24] Cirillo and Taleb reply that 'data does not support the idea of a structural change in human belligerence'.[25] They do not, however, limit their analysis to great-power wars, the immediate topic of our analysis, and their paper does not directly address whether or not the absence of any great-power war (be it a 1,000-deaths one or a 10-million-deaths one) in the past sixty-three years is a statistical anomaly.

It is quite possible that the Long Peace is not statistically exceptional and thus does not need an explanation. However, if there is a credible explanation for it, then it may not be just a long period of non-major-powers war (in addition to the fact that each year without a nuclear war makes the Long Peace through nuclear deterrence hypothesis more credible)—especially since two other interesting phenomena have been observed.

A broader dataset includes other dyads of nuclear-armed countries involving India, Israel, North Korea, Pakistan, and South Africa—until the late 1980s. There has never been a major war between two nuclear-armed states.[26] Beyond this mere observation, two recent quantitative studies have shown that the possession of nuclear weapons by two countries significantly reduced—all things being equal—the likelihood of war between them.[27] Events in Asia since 1949 provide an interesting test case. China and India fought a war in 1962 but have refrained from resorting to arms against each other ever since. There were three India–Pakistan wars (1947, 1965, and 1971) before both countries became nuclear, but since the late 1980s (when the two countries acquired a minimum nuclear capability), neither of the two has launched any significant air or land operations against the other. Neither the Ussuri crisis of 1969 nor the Kargil conflict of 1999 qualifies as a major war (neither caused the death of more than 1,000).[28]

The third dataset concerns dyads in which only one party is endowed with, or protected by, nuclear weapons. No nuclear-armed country has ever been invaded or its territory the object of a major military attack.[29] The 1973 Yom Kippur War and the 1982 Falklands War are often suggested as counter-examples. However, these are not persuasive. Israel was invaded in 1948, on the day of its independence. But in 1973, Arab states deliberately limited their operations to disputed territories (the Sinai and the Golan Heights).[30] It is thus incorrect to take the example of the Yom Kippur War as a 'proof' of the failure of nuclear deterrence. Likewise, India refrained from penetrating Pakistani territory at the occasion of the South Asian crises of 1990, 1999, 2001–2002, and 2008, whereas it had done so in 1965, but nothing indicates that it was covered by nuclear deterrence. Furthermore, it would be erroneous to take these two events as evidence that extended deterrence does not make sense, since deterrence is meant to cover interests that are much more important to the protector than non-essential territories; for instance, during the Cold War, Germany was much more 'vital' to the US than, say, Puerto Rico.

No country covered by a nuclear guarantee has ever been the target of a major attack. Here again evidence can be found *a contrario*. The US refrained from invading Cuba in 1962, for instance (the 1961 Bay of Pigs attempted invasion was a proxy operation), but did not hesitate in invading Grenada, Panama, or Iraq. The Soviet Union invaded Hungary, Czechoslovakia, and Afghanistan, but not a single US treaty ally. China has refrained from invading Taiwan, which benefits from a US de facto defence commitment, even if (deliberately) ambiguous. North Korea invaded its southern neighbour in 1950 after Washington had excluded it from its 'defensive perimeter' but has refrained from doing so since Seoul has been covered with a nuclear guarantee. US allies South Vietnam and Kuwait were not covered by a US nuclear protection. Russia could afford to invade Georgia or Ukraine because they were not NATO members.

To sum up, the available statistical evidence seems to make a reasonably good case for the fact that for at least sixty-three years there has not been any major power war, that nuclear-armed countries have not gone to war against each other, and that non-nuclear-armed countries have refrained from going to war against them or their allies. There seems to be correlation. But is there causation?

The Analytical Evidence

The dominant view among political scientists and historians is that nuclear deterrence has been a key, if not *the* key, to peace among great powers since 1945. While the literature on other datasets is less abundant, it also seems to explain the absence of major military attacks against nuclear-protected countries in general.

The role of nuclear deterrence to explain this (possible) anomaly has been highlighted by leading historians and authors such as Lawrence Freedman, John Lewis Gaddis, Raymond L. Garthoff, Sir Michael Howard, Sir Michael Quinlan, Richard Rhodes, Marc Trachtenberg, and Kenneth Waltz. They all point to the restraining power that the bomb had in great powers' strategic calculations.

If nuclear deterrence worked, how did it work? I would argue that it was both 'mostly by fear, to some extent by interest'.

Nuclear weapons, when mated with ballistic missiles (and even more so when powerful thermonuclear weapons appeared), brought a revolution in warfare: the near certainty of fast, massive, large-scale retaliation. Moreover, due to planning; targeting; and command, control, communications, and intelligence (C3I) advances, the ability to retaliate became less and less contingent on who the aggressor would be and more on where he would attack.

The rational actor assumption that underlined most of the Cold War strategic literature has been successfully challenged, even more so since the seminal publication of *Psychology and Deterrence* more than thirty years ago.[31] But nuclear deterrence does not rely solely on cold calculations. The peculiar nature of nuclear weapons—which kill through blast, fire, and radiation—and the memories of Hiroshima have given them a specific aura, which has been made even stronger by the development of thermonuclear weapons, the theory of 'nuclear winter', and various apocalyptic, end-of-the-world scenarios associated with escalation to the extremes. The absence of any precedent for a 'true nuclear war' (Hiroshima and Nagasaki were just the coda of a massive city-bombing campaign) makes it even more unpredictable than conventional war. It is possible that nuclear balances of power, models, and equations of nuclear use were much less relevant to the success of nuclear deterrence than the mere combination of a significant arsenal and of the apparent will to use it. One can go as far as saying that nuclear deterrence may be complex in theory but easy in practice. Or, at least, to use Patrick Morgan's distinction, that 'general deterrence' might have been enough to deter an adversary, as opposed to 'immediate deterrence'.[32]

In concluding his seminal collective study of how the Cold War statesmen 'confronted the Bomb', Gaddis made the most forceful case for nuclear deterrence. Major powers feared nuclear war and took deliberate precautions to reduce the risks of direct conflict.[33] Nuclear weapons were 'supremely relevant' to the Long Peace.[34] They 'did play the determining role in making great power war obsolete, at least during the Cold War'.[35]

Without going that far, it is likely that nuclear deterrence has limited the scope and intensity of possible conflict among the major states. If crises in Europe, as well as wars in Asia and the Middle East, did not turn into global conflicts, it is probably due largely to nuclear weapons. A former Russian official even writes, 'I dare claim and am ready to prove that nuclear weapons were the greatest "civilizing tool" for these elites. They cleansed their ranks of all radicals and ideologues, and they strengthened the pragmatists who saw their main goal in averting a nuclear war or the clashes that had the potential to escalate to a nuclear conflict.'[36] One author goes as far as claiming that nuclear weapons 'tamed' great powers.[37]

Without nuclear weapons, Washington might have hesitated to guarantee the security in Europe ('no nukes, no troops', as was said at the time) and might have returned to isolationism; and without US protection, the temptation for Moscow to grab territory in Western Europe would have been stronger.[38] Prominent anti-nuclear activist Gareth Evans claims that there is 'no evidence that at any stage during the Cold War years either the Soviet Union or the United States ever wanted to cold-bloodedly initiate war'.[39] However, in order to assert that nuclear deterrence was key in the preservation of major-power peace, one does not need to postulate a Soviet desire for war: as Michael Quinlan put it, it is enough to argue that 'had armed conflict not been so manifestly intolerable the ebb and flow of friction might have managed with less caution, and a slide sooner or later into major war, on the pattern of 1914 or 1939, might have been less unlikely'.[40]

It might be imprudent to state boldly, as Kenneth Waltz once did, that 'the probability of major war among states having nuclear weapons approaches zero'.[41] But if the 'nuclear deterrence hypothesis' is correct, then the statistical debate incarnated by the Pinker/Taleb controversy may be largely irrelevant given that we have probable causation in addition to correlation.

Are Alternative Theories Convincing?[42]
To make the case for nuclear deterrence as cause of the Long Peace, one has to discard alternative explanations. Those supporting them generally do not completely rule out a role for nuclear weapons but argue that they played at best a marginal—and non-necessary—role in the preservation of peace.[43]

The *realist explanation* suggests that the overall stability of the Cold War bipolar system was the dominant factor. However, that might be a reversal of cause and effect. Nuclear weapons were a central element of the US commitment to European security.[44] They did as much to consolidate alliances as to break them: the US nuclear guarantee (and access to nuclear sharing) was a non-trivial dimension of the attraction and staying power of NATO, and France stayed in the Atlantic Alliance after developing its own nuclear force. Regarding the post-Cold War period, US hegemony might very well be a key cause of the absence of major war, but it remains underwritten by US nuclear primacy.

The *liberal explanation* involves institutions, interdependence, and democracy. The construction of a new global institutional order based on collective security and a global organization is insufficient as an explanation: the order based on the League of Nations did nothing to prevent WWII.[45] Economic interdependence is not a satisfying explanation regarding the Cold War: there was no such interdependence between the Western and Communist blocs. Neither is the progress of democratization around the world an explanation: the risk of major power war was, and remains, between democracies and authoritarian regimes.[46] Perhaps the creation of the European Communities became a powerful barrier against the return of war on the continent (through political and economic integration)? The argument confuses cause and effect: the integration process that began in 1957 would have been much more difficult without the US and NATO umbrella.[47]

The *constructivist explanation* rests on the evolution of norms and social constructs.

'War fatigue' is a key argument. The case has been made by John Mueller, notably, that the 'obsolescence of major war' is largely due to the cultural impact of the twin shocks of the two world wars.[48] The argument carries weight among anti-nuclear activists. For instance, Gareth Evans claimed recently that 'what has stopped—and will continue to stop—the major powers from deliberately starting wars against each other has been, more than anything else, a realization, after the experience of World War II and in the light of all the rapid technological advances that followed it, that the damage that would be inflicted by *any* war would be unbelievably horrific, and far outweigh, in today's economically interdependent world, any conceivable benefit to be derived'.[49]

A broader argument is the delegitimization of armed violence. It rests on the observation that the number of wars (and the proportion of war-related deaths in the total number of deaths) has been steadfastly declining since 1945. If true, then one does not need the hypothesis of nuclear deterrence.[50] A related argument is the gradual consolidation of a norm against territorial conquest and annexation of territory by force.[51] In the three decades that followed the end of WWII, there were still many instances of territorial conquests and post-conflict (or post-decolonization) annexations, but much less so in the past four decades.[52] The Organization of African Unity Charter of 1963 adopted the principle of the immutability of borders. The Helsinki Act of 1975 consecrated the territorial status quo in Europe. The International Court of Justice (ICJ), in its seminal 1986 *Burkina Faso v. Mali* decision, upheld the *uti possidetis* principle (as you have, so you shall possess), creating an important precedent that was followed in many border settlements. In addition, some of the most significant attempts to conquer territory by force have failed, such as the Iran–Iraq War (1980–1988), the Falklands War (1982), and the Iraq War (1991); this may have contributed to 'dissuasion' of forceful territorial aggrandizement. It has also helped that decolonization and the creation of several dozens of new countries have reduced the number of pro-independence and secession movements. Perhaps the behaviour of Russia in Ukraine, and of China in its maritime environment, will put an end to this era; but generally speaking, it seems, indeed, that wars of territorial conquest are no longer considered a normal instrument of external policies.

However, cultural arguments have limitations. If war fatigue existed, one would have to argue that it did not exist in Europe after 1870, or after 1918. (It did: pacifism and disgust for war were widely shared in the 1920s.) Thus, one would have to posit the existence of a 'threshold effect' in 1945. Gaddis notes, 'Prior to the development of thermonuclear weapons, it seems fair to say that war was indeed regarded as a remote prospect because the costs of the recent war were still so evident. But war was not at that time seen as an irrational act, in which there could be no correspondence between expected costs and intended benefits'.[53] One would also have to assume that war fatigue was transmitted from one generation to another, given that the statesmen of WWII are now gone. One would finally also have to discard the many minor wars and military interventions of the post-1945 era deliberately initiated by former parties to the 1939–1945 conflict.

The claim that 'war is on the decline' has been challenged on statistical and analytical grounds. It is argued, in particular, that the usual metric of battle-related deaths may be misleading, either because the downward trend reflects improvement in preventive care, battlefield medicine, and military and soldier protection, or because it does not represent the true overall costs of collective armed violence.[54]

US expert Elbridge Colby holds that the cultural argumentation 'markedly overestimates the durability of historically contingent value systems while seriously downplaying the enduring centrality of competition, fear, uncertainty and power'.[55] Likewise, Kenneth Waltz writes that 'in a conventional world even forceful and tragic lessons have proved to be exceedingly difficult for states to learn'.[56]

Additionally, the realist, liberal, and constructivist explanations can hardly account for the absence of major war involving Israel and its neighbours since 1973 (excluding Israeli interventions in Lebanon in 1982 and 2006) or between India and Pakistan since these countries became full-fledged nuclear-armed countries in the late 1990s.[57]

As Lawrence Freedman puts it, 'Given the undoubted existence of deep antagonism between East and West, it seemed grudging not to attribute at least part of the credit for avoiding yet another total war to the dread of global confrontation involving nuclear exchanges and to the policies adopted, at times by both sides, to reinforce this dread by means of deliberate deterrence.'[58] In this sense, explaining the Long Peace mostly by nuclear deterrence might be an implementation of Occam's razor: sometimes the simplest answer is the best one.[59]

There remains, of course, the possibility that 'divine providence' intervened to refrain major powers from going to war against each other. Such is the explanation given by the late Pope John Paul II. However, we venture here outside the bounds of political analysis.[60]

The Future: Escaping Nuclear Deterrence?

Assuming that nuclear deterrence was—and is—largely, though perhaps not solely, responsible for the Long Peace does not exempt it from criticism. Two broad strands of arguments are presented. The first arguments concern the costs-and-benefits equation of nuclear deterrence. Do its benefits really outweigh its potential risks? Nuclear deterrence may be a fragile construct. Among nuclear-armed adversaries, there have been slow learning curves tainted with dangerous events: Cuba (1962), the Ussuri River (China/Soviet Union, 1969), Twin Peaks (India/Pakistan, 2001–2002).

The deterrent effect of nuclear weapons may change over time as the memories of Hiroshima and images of surface tests fade away, or if the so-called tradition of non-use is broken one day (although the detonation of a single nuclear weapon in anger might actually restore the deterrent power of nuclear weapons, not push the whole concept into oblivion). Among nuclear powers, even a very small probability of deterrence failure—and of subsequent major nuclear war, with possible global (climate-related) repercussions—might be enough to negate its alleged benefits.[61] In sum, even if nuclear weapons prolonged the expected duration between two world wars—say, from thirty to one hundred years instead—would they not make the possible 'next' conflict even more deadly than it would have been?[62]

Also, might there not be hidden costs of nuclear deterrence? NATO nuclear strategy may have worked 'too well': archives show that the Soviet Union did believe that NATO would use nuclear weapons in a major war—and thus planned for massive pre-emptive nuclear operations against its forces. If war had broken out despite nuclear deterrence, then the risk of early escalation might have been greater than thought at the time. The same phenomenon could be at work today in South Asia despite the apparent success of nuclear deterrence so far.

The stability/instability paradox conceptualized by Glenn Snyder in 1965 seems to have been a reality: perhaps nuclear weapons did prevent major armed conflict between nuclear-armed adversaries, but this came at the price of the multiplication of bloody indirect wars and sub-conventional conflicts, from the East–West context (the Berlin crises) to the India–Pakistan theatre.[63] Fear of war may have moderated superpower behaviour and restrained Washington and Moscow during major crises, but at the same time encouraged them to take dangerous initiatives, as Lebow and Janice Gross Stein suggest (including through public posturing, which 'convinced their adversaries that they were aggressive, risk-prone, and even irrational').[64] They may have, as suggested by the work of Jervis, incited fear, hubris, and misperceptions, making them inherently destabilizing.[65]

A broader question relates with the impact of nuclear weapons on great-power cooperation. How much was it the fear of nuclear war that led the two superpowers to create a mesh of cooperative security arrangements, including the establishment of 'hotlines', the Strategic Arms Limitations Talks (SALT) process, the drafting of the Nuclear Non-Proliferation Treaty (NPT), and the conclusion of the Helsinki Final Act? Patrick Morgan suggests that nuclear weapons may have hastened the end of the Cold War by giving confidence to Soviet leaders that the country's survival would be assured even after the loss of the Eastern European *glacis*.[66] On the contrary, Lebow and Janice Gross Stein, as well as Gaddis, argue that they may have perpetuated the Cold War.[67] So maybe nuclear weapons made détente and peaceful coexistence *easier*, but real peace *more difficult*, in addition to extending the life of communism.

Conclusion: The Legitimacy of Nuclear Weapons

The second strand of arguments is about the legitimacy of nuclear weapons.

Is nuclear deterrence legitimate or even legal? Legitimacy of nuclear weapons possession is seemingly ensured by the NPT, but nearly half of nuclear-armed countries are not parties to it (including North Korea, which announced its withdrawal in 2003). Furthermore, the ICJ, in its advisory opinion of July 1996, stated that the 'threat or use' of nuclear weapons is illegal in most circumstances (without, however, condemning what it called the 'policy of deterrence') and that Article VI of the NPT did include an obligation to disarm. And since the end of the Cold War, the Vatican has repeatedly called for nuclear disarmament.

Is it even morally acceptable, as a matter of principle, to rely on the threat of mass destruction to ensure peace? This argument is well known and as old as nuclear weapons themselves.

There are possible rebuttals for each of these arguments.[68] In addition, the relationship between nuclear disarmament and peace is a complex one—that is, even if one questions the net benefits of nuclear deterrence, it is by no means certain that going to zero would result in more security.

However, taken together, they constitute at least an incitement to look beyond nuclear deterrence to prevent major war. For these reasons, nuclear deterrence should be seen only as a temporary fix or second-best solution to ensure peace among major powers and nuclear-armed adversaries. The good news is that strategic deterrence—aimed at avoiding major war—may, in the future, increasingly rely on other instruments.

Could deterrence with modern conventional assets be a substitute to the threat of nuclear retaliation? Two weaknesses of conventional deterrence would remain. Massive and assured damage on the adversary's centres of power would still require several weeks of bombardment, which would give it time and ability to adjust and adapt; moreover, in an era where images of warfare are broadcasted 24/7 all over the world, the adversary could bank on the fact that the attacker would have to cede to international pressure and public outcry. Another weakness is that modern conventional weapons—increasingly accurate and more deadly—will hardly be as scary as nuclear ones. Could conventional deterrence at least credibly threaten enemy leaders with decapitation strikes? Technically, yes, but on the condition that proper intelligence would be available. (The initial US strikes targeting Saddam Hussein in March 2003 failed for lack of timely intelligence.) However, for a few advanced countries, the ability to combine numerous swift, accurate long-range conventional strikes against centres of power, coupled with targeted cyber-attacks, might be enough to make an aggressor think twice before attacking the vital interests of his adversary.

In addition, territorial missile defence has now become a reality despite inherent technical limitations (and dubious cost-effectiveness); it protects partly and to varying degrees the territories of the US and of some of its friends and allies in Europe, the Middle East, and East Asia and thus can now represent a complement, or partial substitute, to nuclear deterrence.[69]

Other non-military instruments could gain importance in the future in preventing direct military aggression, such as the threat of personal prosecutions by the International Criminal Court (ICC) and special tribunals, which have multiplied since the end of the Cold War, or economic and financial sanctions, which have become a more efficient tool (e.g., vis-à-vis Iran, Russia).

This brings us to economic and financial interdependence. Does it, can it prevent major war? To this time-old question, new answers have been given. First, in an era of globalization, the classic mercantilist argument that war does not 'pay' may be truer than in the past; from a strictly rational point of view, deliberate major war would be a 'Great Illusion'. Second, major war would 'cost' even more today. Third, the classic counterargument that 'economic interdependence did not prevent World War I' has been challenged: it may not have been a failure of economic interdependence after all.[70]

The idea that interdependence reduces the chances of war has found new empirical support.[71] In an increasingly interconnected and interdependent world, the risk of major war may be dampened in several ways: by raising the direct and indirect (impact on global markets) costs of conflict; by increasing the information available to parties; and by reducing the incentives for economic war given the globalization of resource markets and the rise of foreign direct investment (FDI). International relations theory tends to see situations when a rising power threatens to displace a ruling power as a dangerous one—resulting in war, according to a recent study, three-quarters of the time.[72] But the most worrying major powers dyad presents a unique case, not least because of the amount of US Treasury bonds held by China.[73] Many scholars suggest that the combination of deterrence and interdependence can dampen the bilateral rivalry.[74] In sum, economic and financial interdependence could play a stronger role in preventing major war than it did in the past.

It is not an intellectual stretch to claim that nuclear deterrence is a form of global common good, notwithstanding its possible negative side effects. All non-nuclear-weapons states benefitted from it during the past seventy years. Without the nuclear peace, would Asia have known the peace and stability that allowed for its massive transformation and development, leading to hundreds of millions of human beings being lifted out of poverty? At the same time, the argument could be reversed: a nuclear war could set back Asia's progress by a decade, without mentioning its indirect impact on the global economy. Nuclear deterrence is an imperfect and fragile instrument, which has significant downsides (a 'powerful but very dangerous medicine').[75] It should thus be seen at least as a provisional, imperfect measure or as an insurance against the failure of the liberal order.

A few years ago, US analyst Michael O'Hanlon gave the following advice: 'Perhaps nuclear deterrence has been only a minor factor in preserving peace in the past; the issue is arguable. But policymakers need to be careful, and gradual, about how they run the experiment to test that proposition.'[76] Or, as Winston Churchill put it at a time when the nuclear age was just a few years old, 'Be careful above all things not to let go of the atomic weapon until you are sure and more than sure that other means of preserving peace are in your hands.'[77]

Notes

1. The author is grateful to Alice Pannier and Elbridge Colby for their thoughtful comments on an earlier draft. This version also takes into account a discussion held at the Nobel Symposium held in Bergen, Norway, in June 2016.
2. Glenn H. Snyder, *Deterrence and Defense: Toward a Theory of National Security* (Princeton, NJ: Princeton University Press, 1961), 15.
3. It differs, for instance, from mere 'self-deterrence', in which a party would renounce attacking another based on the observed correlation of forces and opponent's behaviour.
4. Richard N. Lebow, 'Thucydides and Deterrence,' *Security Studies* 16, no. 2 (April–June 2007).
5. Thucydides, *History of the Peloponnesian War*, Book IV.
6. Raoul Naroll, Vern L. Bullough, and Frada Naroll, eds., *Military Deterrence in History: A Pilot Cross-Historical Survey* (Albany: University of New York Press, 1974).
7. Robert Jervis, *The Meaning of the Nuclear Revolution: Statecraft and the Prospect of Armageddon* (Ithaca, NY: Cornell University Press, 1989).

8. George Quester, *Deterrence before Hiroshima: The Airpower Background of Modern Strategy* (Piscataway, NJ: Transaction, 1986).

9. Lawrence Freedman, *Does Deterrence Have a Future?* (Sandia National Laboratories, 1996), 1.

10. Patrick M. Morgan, 'Elaborate Strategy' in *Deterrence Now* (Cambridge: Cambridge University Press, 2003), 3.

11. Kenneth N. Waltz, 'Nuclear Myths and Political Realities,' *The American Political Science Review* 84, no. 3 (September 1990): 732.

12. John J. Mearsheimer, 'Precision-Guided Munitions and Conventional Deterrence,' *Survival* 21, no. 2 (March–April 1979).

13. Richard J. Harknett, 'The Logic of Conventional Deterrence and the End of the Cold War,' *Security Studies* 4, no. 1 (Fall 1994).

14. John J. Mearsheimer, *Conventional Deterrence* (Ithaca, NY: Cornell University Press, 1983); Edward Rhodes, 'Conventional Deterrence,' *Comparative Strategy* 19, no. 3 (2000); Michael Gerson, 'Conventional Deterrence in the Second Nuclear Age,' *Parameters* (Fall 2009).

15. Barry Wolf, *When the Weak Attack the Strong: Failures of Deterrence*, N-3261-A (The Rand Corporation, 1991); Ivan Arreguin-Toft, 'Unconventional Deterrence: How the Weak Deters the Strong,' in *Complex Deterrence: Strategy in the Global Age*, eds. T.V. Paul, Patrick Morgan, and James Wirtz (Chicago: University of Chicago Press, 2009); Mindaugas Rekasius, 'Unconventional Deterrence Strategy' (PhD dissertation, Monterey, Naval Postgraduate School, 2005).

16. John Lewis Gaddis, *The Long Peace* (New York: Oxford University Press 1987).

17. Franco–Spanish War (1823), First Russian–Turkish War (1828–1829), War of Crimea (1853–1856), Austro–Prussian War (1856), War of Italian Succession (1859), Austro–Prussian War (1865–1866), French–Prussian War (1870–1871), Second Russian–Prussian War (1877–1878), First Russian-Japanese War (1903–1905).

18. Randolph M. Siverson and Michael D. Ward, 'The Long Peace: A Reconsideration,' *International Organization* 56, no. 3 (Summer 2002).

19. Hao Yufan and Zhai Zhihai, 'China's Decision to Enter the Korean War: History Revisited,' *The China Quarterly* 121 (March 1990).

20. Pasquale Cirillo and Nassim N. Taleb, 'On the statistical properties and tail risk of violent conflicts,' *Physica A: Statistical Mechanics and its Applications*, Vol. 452 (2016):29-45.

21. Pasquale Cirillo and Nassim Nicholas Taleb, *What Are the Chances of a Third World War?* (undated) Available at www.fooledbyrandomness.com; and Pasquale Cirillo and Nassim Nicholas Taleb 'On the Statistical Properties and Tail Risk of Violent Conflict,' Tail Risk Working Papers, 19 October 2015. Note that the first paper mistakenly reports the findings of the second as 136 (which is the reported mean absolute deviation in the second).

22. Steven Pinker, *The Better Angels of Our Nature* (Penguin, 2012), 206.

23. Ibid., 207.

24. Steven Pinker, *Fooled by Belligerence: Comments on Nassim Taleb's 'The Long Peace Is a Statistical Illusion,'* (undated) available at www.stevenpinker.com.

25. Cirillo and Taleb, 'What Are the Chances of a Third World War?' *Significance* 13, Vol. 2 (2016): 44–45.

26. The only instance when US and Soviet forces clashed directly was the 1950–1953 Korean War, but Soviet pilots were flying under North Korean or Chinese colours.

27. James F. Pasley, 'Chicken Pax Atomica: The Cold War Stability of Nuclear Deterrence,' *Journal of International and Area Studies* 15, no. 2 (December 2008); Robert Rauchhaus, 'Evaluating the Nuclear Peace Hypothesis: A Quantitative Approach,' *Journal of Conflict Resolution* 53, no. 2 (April 2009).

28. Although the COW dataset lists Kargil as a major war, the sum of the official tally of battle-related deaths is under 1,000.

29. I implicitly note here that the forces abroad of several nuclear states were attacked at several occasions (e.g., China in 1950 during the Korean War); but nuclear deterrence covers only the most vital interests of countries endowed with or protected by nuclear weapons and is never understood as covering any attack on expeditionary forces. An exception is the Iraqi Scud campaign against Israel (1991), though nuclear deterrence can probably explain the absence of chemical or biological munitions (see Bruno Tertrais, *In Defense of Deterrence: The Relevance, Morality and Cost-Effectiveness of Nuclear Weapons* [Institut français des relations internationales, 2011].). Other exceptions are the attempted Libyan missile launch against the Italian island of Lampedusa (1986) and the North Korean shelling of Yeonpyeong island (2010); but the very limited character of the attacks and their location (regarding the second one, a maritime area not recognized by Pyongyang as being part of South Korean territory) make them hard to count it as failures of extended deterrence.

30. See for instance T.V. Paul, *The Tradition of Non-use of Nuclear Weapons* (Stanford: Stanford University Press, 2009), 147–48.

31. Robert Jervis, Richard Ned Lebow, and Janice Gross Stein, *Psychology and Deterrence* (Baltimore: Johns Hopkins University Press, 1985); Bradley A. Thayer, 'Thinking about Nuclear Deterrence Theory: Why Evolutionary Psychology Undermines Its Rational Actor Assumptions,' *Comparative Strategy* 26 (2007).

32. Morgan, *Deterrence Now,* 9.

33. John Gaddis, Philip Gordon, Ernest May, and Jonathan Rosenberg, eds., *Cold War Statesmen Confront the Bomb: Nuclear Diplomacy since 1945* (New York: Oxford University Press, 1999). See also John G. Hines, Ellis M. Mishulovich, and John F. Shull, *Soviet Intentions 1965–1985* (The BDM Corporation, 1995).

34. Gaddis et al., *Cold War Statesmen Confront the Bomb,* 267.

35. Ibid., 270.

36. Sergei Karaganov, 'Nuclear Weapons in the Modern World,' in Harold Brown, Graham Allison, Gilles Andreani, King Sung-han, Sergei Karaganov, Ariel E. Levite, Masashi Nishihara, and Rajiv Sikri, *Nuclear Disarmament and Nonproliferation* (report to the Trilateral Commission, no. 64, 2010), 65.

37. Godfried van Benthem van den Bergh, *The Taming of the Great Powers* (policy outlook, Carnegie Endowment for International Peace, 2009).

38. See James Schlesinger, 'The Impact of Nuclear Weapons on History,' *The Washington Quarterly* 16, no. 4 (Autumn 1993).

39. Gareth Evans, 'Restoring Reason to the Nuclear Debate,' *Bulletin of Atomic Scientists*, November 16, 2015.

40. Michael Quinlan, *Thinking about Nuclear Weapons: Principles, Problems, Prospects* (Oxford: Oxford University Press, 2009), 28.

41. Waltz, 'Nuclear Myths and Political Realities,' 740.

42. A school of thought argues that 'it cannot be nuclear deterrence' on the grounds that, *inter alia*, the 1945 nuclear bombings were not the cause of the Japanese surrender, and more generally, that massive destruction and city-bombing have historically proven poor ways to win major wars. Ward Wilson, *Five Myths about Nuclear Weapons* (Boston: Houghton Mifflin Harcourt, 2013). For a rebuttal, see Bruno Tertrais, *In Defense of Deterrence*, Proliferation Papers no. 39 (2011); Bruno Tertrais, 'The Four Straw Men of the Apocalypse,' *Survival* 55, no. 6 (December 2013–January 2014).

43. Underlying the need for other, non-nuclear related explanations is the argument according to which the frequency of major war has been reduced for centuries: Jack S. Levy, *War in the Modern Great Power System, 1495–1975* (Lexington: University Press of Kentucky, 1983).

44. James Schlesinger, 'The Impact of Nuclear Weapons on History,' *The Washington Quarterly* 16, no. 4 (Autumn 1993).

45. Some claim that WWII offered a proof of failure of mutual deterrence, because the major contenders on the European theatre possessed chemical weapons. But nobody ever pretended—nor is there any reason to believe—that chemical weapons could preserve peace. Incidentally, this case can be partly brought to the credit of the logic of mutual deterrence. *A contrario*, Japan used them against China, which did not possess them. For a demonstration that 'World War II serves as a case study of deterrence in action' (the non-use of chemical and biological weapons), see Stephen L. McFarland, 'Preparing for What Never Came: Chemical and Biological Warfare in World War II,' *Defense Analysis* 2, no. 2 (June 1986).

46. To understand why Germany and Japan, for instance, went from being war-prone countries to being pacifist ones, one does not need to refer to nuclear deterrence. It is highly unlikely that Germany could have attacked France, or Japan attacked China, if Paris or Beijing did not have nuclear weapons.

47. Elbridge A. Colby, 'Why Nuclear Deterrence Is Still Relevant,' in *Deterrence in the 21st Century: Enduring Questions in a Time of Rising Powers, Rogue Regimes, and Terrorism*, ed. Adam Lowther (New York: Palgrave McMillan, 2012).

48. John Mueller, *Retreat from Doomsday: The Obsolescence of Major War* (New York: Basic Books, 1989).

49. Evans, 'Restoring Reason to the Nuclear Debate.'

50. See in particular Human Security Project, Human Security Report 2009–2010: 'The

Causes of Peace and the Shrinking Costs of War, 2010'; and Pinker, *The Better Angels*. If true, this hypothesis almost certainly requires, in turn, a combination of realist and liberal explanations: the end of empires (which reduces the risk of wars of expansion and wars of self-determination) in the 1960s; the rise of UN operations (which reduce the occurrence and length of some conflicts) as well as occasional 'global peace operations' (Korea in 1950, Kuwait in 1991, Kosovo in 1999); the rapid expansion of international trade since the early 1990s (which lowers the incentives for resources grabs at the international level); economic development (which reduces the risk of civil war); and the growing proportion of democracies (which tend to avoid fighting against each other). The 'norm against warfare' may then be a product as much as a cause, notwithstanding other explanations such as a higher price put on human life (which may have deeper roots), etc.

51. See Mark W. Sacher, 'The Territorial Integrity Norm: International Boundaries and the Use of Force,' *International Organization* 55, no. 2 (Spring 2001).

52. Examples include: Western Sahara, Goa, the Tomb and Abu Mussa Islands, Sikkim, the Golan.

53. Gaddis, *The Long Peace,* 269.

54. Tanisha M. Fazal, 'Dead Wrong? Battle Deaths, Military Medicine, and Exaggerated Reports of War's Demise,' *International Security* 39, no. 1 (Summer 2014); John Gray, 'Steven Pinker Is Wrong about Violence and War,' *Guardian*, March 13, 2015.

55. Colby, 'Why Nuclear Deterrence is Still Relevant,' 56.

56. Waltz, 'Nuclear Myths and Political Realities,' 743.

57. One possible alternative explanation for India and Pakistan is the role of US diplomacy in helping to defuse the crises of 1990, 1999, and 2001–2002—not necessarily a key factor, but probably a significant one. However, the US involvement would not have been as strong in the absence of nuclear weapons.

58. Lawrence Freedman, *Deterrence* (Cambridge: Polity, 2004), 13–14.

59. 'Mostly' is understood here as 'at least 51 percent'. An in-between explanation is suggested by Patrick Morgan: the nuclear revolution may have been the icing on the cake, that is, the culmination of a delegitimization process that had begun earlier on, in particular by annihilating strategies based on the prospect of cheap victory. Morgan, *Deterrence Now*, 38.

60. 'May Divine Providence be praised for this, that the period known as the "Cold War" ended without violent nuclear conflict' (Testament of John-Paul II). The point has been suggested by François Heisbourg.

61. Critics also point to the risk of nuclear terrorism stemming from the buildup of military nuclear complexes around the world.

62. This also raises moral questions related with the 'utility' of the number lives saved for seventy years versus that of the lives lost during the 'next world war'.

63. Robert Rauchhaus, 'Evaluating the Nuclear Peace Hypothesis: A Quantitative Approach,' *Journal of Conflict Resolution* 53, no. 2 (April 2009).

64. Richard Ned Lebow and Janice Gross Stein, 'Deterrence and the Cold War,' *Political Science Quarterly* 10, no. 2 (Summer 1995): 180.

65. Robert Jervis, *The Meaning of the Nuclear Revolution: Statecraft and the Prospect for Armageddon* (Ithaca, NY: Cornell University Press, 1989).

66. Morgan, *Deterrence Now*, 27.

67. John Lewis Gaddis, *We Now Know: Rethinking Cold War History* (New York: Oxford University Press, 1997); Richard Ned Lebow and Janice Gross Stein, *We All Lost the Cold War* (Princeton, NJ: Princeton University Press, 1994).

68. See for instance Tertrais, *In Defense of Deterrence.*

69. In addition to the nuclear-tipped interceptors that have protected the region of Moscow since the 1970s.

70. Erik Gartzke and Yonatan Lupu, 'Trading on Misconceptions: Why World War I Was Not a Failure of Economic Interdependence,' *International Security* 36, no. 4 (Spring 2012).

71. See sources quoted in Gartzke and Lupu, 'Trading on Misconceptions.'

72. See Graham Allison, 'The Thucydides Trap: Are the US and China Headed for War?' *Atlantic*, September 2015.

73. The US-China interdependence involves other components, such as the importance of US sources and technologies for the continuation of Chinese economic development, or the presence of many children of Chinese leaders in US schools and universities.

74. See Stein Tønnesson, 'Deterrence, Interdependence and Sino-US Peace,' review essay, *International Area Studies Review* 18, no. 3 (2015).

75. Lebow and Stein, 'Deterrence and the Cold War,' 180.

76. Michael E. O'Hanlon, *A Skeptic's Case for Nuclear Disarmament* (Washington, DC: The Brookings Institution, 2010), 74.

77. Winston Churchill, *Address to the US Congress*, January 17 1952.

14.

Disarmament: Cause, Consequence, or Early Warning Indicator of Peace?

Paul F. Diehl

Introduction

States build up their militaries and acquire more weapons not only to be more effective when they fight wars, but in the hope that such actions will give them greater security and prevent the need for war by deterring enemies. The latter was the stated objective of the North Korean government in developing nuclear weapons; that state views the US and South Korea as aggressors who threaten its existence. Nevertheless, acquiring more weapons makes the targets of such actions less secure and more inclined to build up military capacity themselves. This has led some analysts to worry about arms races causing war and, accordingly, to promote arms control and disarmament efforts.

Disarmament has long been a goal of activists and some global leaders, believing that it was an essential element of a peaceful world. Yet does disarmament actually promote peace, or does it occur primarily as a consequence of increasingly peaceful relations between actors? That is, does reducing armaments make war less likely and peace more likely, or does arms reduction occur as a result of a reduction in the threat of war and an increase in peaceful interactions? Might it also be a signal, neither fully causal nor consequential, in the development of peace? This chapter explores these concerns with the goal of understanding disarmament's role in the process of building peace. Accordingly, disarmament represents a possible alternative to deterrence strategies discussed in the chapter by Bruno Tertrais in the 'Deterrence and Disarmament' section of this work.

A necessary first step is providing some clarity to the two concepts central to the analysis: disarmament and peace, respectively. 'Disarmament' has often been used synonymously with 'arms control'. Technically, this is incorrect. All disarmament involves arms control, but the reverse is not the case. Traditionally, disarmament signifies the elimination of all military capabilities, at the extreme, and more commonly the elimination of certain classes of weaponry, such as chemical weapons. The term has evolved over time to represent any reduction in weapons, even as they have not been completely eliminated. In contrast, arms control denotes limitations placed on armament possession or acquisition. When this involves the *reduction* of armaments, then disarmament has occurred. Nevertheless, some arms control actually specifies limits *above* current stockpiles and therefore doesn't constitute disarmament in any conventional sense of the word. For the purposes of this analysis, however, the terms 'disarmament' and 'arms control' will be used interchangeably but, in either case, only to signify the reduction or elimination of military capabilities and weapons.

'Peace' is a term that has involved a considerably wider range of connotations. Scholarly studies usually define peace as the absence of war, what has been called 'negative peace'.[1] Prominent works on the decline of war[2] argue that the world is more peaceful largely because of declining violent behaviour—particularly that resulting in battle deaths. An extensive scholarly literature explores the 'democratic peace',[3] which depends entirely on the absence of a bona fide war between two democracies, not the absence of armed conflict or the presence of peaceful interactions, per se. Similarly, as we have seen in earlier chapters, some call the post-WWII period the Long Peace,[4] defined as the longest period of history without a war between major-power states. Nevertheless, the Cold War was a period of superpower competition characterized by the development of extensive nuclear arsenals, unprecedented military spending, and a variety of interstate and civil proxy wars.[5]

In order to study peace, one needs a conceptualization that is not a mirror image or 'symmetric' to war.[6] Negative peace is an important concept, and it is more nuanced than merely stating that actors are not at war. Nevertheless, it does not get at the positive peace elements that characterize many friendly relationships. In those interactions, war is absent, but many other conditions operate. These include extensive cooperation and integration between actors. Non-traditional aspects of security, such as human security, development, and human rights, characterize the relationship between states and constituent groups. Some conceptions also include key values embedded in the relationship; these include equity and justice. In the analyses below, I focus on both negative and positive peace between states. Disarmament's role in promoting peace (or not) should be assessed in terms of both kinds of peace. That is, its goals are more than preventing war, but also promoting conditions under which war is 'unthinkable'.

The analysis of disarmament and peace begins with reference to the awarding of the Nobel Peace Prize for achievements related to disarmament and arms control. Special attention is given to the frequency of this occurrence and whether such elements were for accomplishments that furthered peace or were aspirational in the pursuit of peace. The following sections examine the theoretical arguments and empirical research on armaments and war for insights into the causal relationship and its direction between disarmament and peace. Following this is an empirical analysis of the effect of disarmament efforts and arms control agreements on state relationships and whether they facilitate peace, both in its negative and positive variations.

Disarmament and the Nobel Peace Prize

The Norwegian Nobel Committee has awarded 96 Peace Prizes to 131 laureates (some prizes are shared) over the 1901–2017 period. Diehl coded these to determine the prevalence of recognition for positive versus negative peace activities.[7] Awards for disarmament fall squarely within the negative peace category, as the reduction of armaments was believed to be an important step in lessening the prospects for war, both following WWI and in the nuclear age. Awards for arms control and disarmament activities were much more prevalent after WWII, even as the incidence of recognition in Nobel Prizes for negative peace declined. Early on, a number of Nobel recipients were active in peace movements and organizations, many of which advocated disarmament. Nevertheless, arguably only four awards (out of forty-five, or just under 9 percent from 1901 to 1958) were directly or indirectly for arms control efforts. As an example of the former, Arthur Henderson was recognized in 1934 primarily for his work in disarmament efforts for the League of Nations. Sir Norman Angell was the award recipient the year before, indirectly for arms control causes, as his classic work *The Great Illusion* included criticism of arms races as dangerous (and thereby implicitly favouring a reduction of weaponry).

After WWII, disarmament concerns are an important part of Nobel Peace Prizes, even as a wider range of positive peace concerns such as human rights, the status of women, economic development, and the environment are reflected in award decisions. Beginning with Philip Noel-Baker's award in 1959, disarmament and arms control efforts are recognized in eleven different years (or just over 25 percent of the time) and among fifteen individuals or organizations. Nuclear issues seem to be the central concern, with awards to individual disarmament activists (e.g., Linus Pauling in 1962) and organizations (e.g., International Physicians for the Prevention of Nuclear War in 1985), diplomats (Alva Myrdal in 1982), national leaders (Eisaku Sato in 1974), and international organizations (e.g., International Atomic Energy Agency in 2005) working on reducing or eliminating nuclear weapons. The last twenty years have expanded the scope of weaponry that has received attention to include landmines (1997) and chemical weapons (2005), respectively.

Krebs examined all Nobel Prizes through 2009 to examine whether they were based on accomplishment or merely aspirational.[8] Those based on accomplishment involved 'past actions [that] have led relatively directly to tangible easing of human suffering or the cessation of violence'.[9] In contrast, aspirational awards are to those individuals 'whose causes, at the time of the award, remain far from having been achieved'.[10] Using his coding,[11] a slight majority of the prizes for disarmament and arms control were aspirational, such as that given to Carl von Ossietzky in 1935 for exposing German rearmament. Actual accomplishments are slightly fewer, the difficulty signified most recently by the 2017 award to the International Campaign to Abolish Nuclear Weapons (ICAN), which supports banning nuclear weapons.

Several elements are evident in trying to understand the role of disarmament and arms control in peace. First, whether rooted in aspirations or accomplishments, the emphasis is on negative peace or the prevention of war. There is an implicit or explicit assumption that reducing or eliminating weapons lessens the dangers of escalation or war, as opposed to promoting deterrence, for example. That is, there is an expectation about the causal direction and effect of disarmament, but not necessarily evidence that this has been achieved. None of the awards suggests that reducing weapons will produce cooperative behaviour or other aspects of positive peace, although this is not precluded. It could be the disarmament is a precursor or prerequisite for positive peace initiatives, but this is not specified in the award statements.

Second, even among accomplishments, it is not clear that achievements have produced negative peace. Krebs focuses on the impact of the awards themselves and concludes that awards for disarmament have had little impact. He argues that the awards have not heightened public awareness of disarmament issues or otherwise had much impact. Krebs does acknowledge some agenda-setting success in less well-known classes of weapons. He offers the 1997 award to Jody Williams and the International Campaign to Ban Landmines as illustrative—the Ottawa Convention or the Mine Ban Treaty was open for signature shortly after the Peace Prize was awarded and the agreement came into force in early 1999.[12]

It is one thing to say that the Nobel Prizes themselves had little impact and another to claim that the efforts for which the prize was given had no effect on peace. Almost by definition, the aspirational efforts did not promote peace, positive or negative; most goals, if not all, were unfulfilled—especially those with respect to nuclear concerns. Any accomplishments for which the awards were given are more ambiguous. The Japanese signature on the Non-Proliferation Treaty (1974 award to Sato) is considered a milestone, but has it decreased the chances that Japan will become involved in rivalry or remilitarize? Was this act equally important to or more important than military restrictions in the post-war constitution or security guarantees from the US? This is difficult to ascertain. The Organisation for the Prohibition of Chemical Weapons (OPCW; 2013 winner) perhaps influenced the *conduct* of war but has not likely made war less likely, much less promoted positive interactions between states; subsequent revelations about Syria's use of chemical weapons even calls into questions whether OPCW activities are effective.

What can be concluded from disarmament, peace, and Nobel Peace Prizes? First, the impact of disarmament on peace is squarely thought to be negative peace; that is, disarmament is purportedly associated with reducing the likelihood of war rather than promoting greater cooperation, characteristic of positive peace. Second, the Peace Prizes, especially those given for aspiration, are indicative of the Nobel Institute's belief that disarmament promotes peace; the causal direction is clear in thought, if not necessarily reflected in practice. Third, the accomplishments that received recognition don't necessarily represent instances in which more peaceful outcomes resulted, or at least they are difficult to measure given other factors that affect state relationships.

If the Nobel Prizes offer some hints at the disarmament, existing scholarly work provides further insights about the relationship and causal direction. In the next section, I discuss the logic behind the relationship between disarmament and peace as well as looking to empirical studies for whether such logic is validated or not.

Disarmament and Peace: Theoretical Rationales

At the outset of the chapter, I outlined three possible causal connections for disarmament and peace: cause, consequence, and early warning indicator. Each has a different theoretical logic. Disarmament as a causal agent for peace is largely based on a rationale that arms build-ups or capabilities are dangerous and therefore, with reverse logic, reducing or eliminating those lessens the chances for war;[13] again, negative peace is the outcome, not necessarily more positive interactions. Most notable in scholarly circles is the 'security dilemma'[14] and the associated spiral model of arms races.[15] This idea holds that states acquire arms, often for defensive purposes, in order to enhance their own security, but this creates fear and distrust in the eyes of their enemies who see such acquisition as being designed for offensive purposes. The enemy state then begins its own weapons acquisition in response, setting off a cycle of action and reaction. How this leads to war is not fully clear in many formulations, but the assumption is that the resulting tension, mistrust, misperception, and hostility undermine the ability of states to solve disagreements and confrontations peacefully when they arise.

Disarmament and arms control come into play in that agreements for these are designed to stop or slow the spiral, and therefore war is purportedly less likely. Goertz and Diehl contend that security treaties, of which arms control agreements are a significant part, are able to alter the dynamics of enduring rivalries, promoting conflict *management* if not *resolution*.[16] Arms control can do more than eliminate the sources of tension and hostility; according to some, it can also improve relations. Barash and Webel argue that with arms control agreements, 'contending parties can progressively gain greater confidence in each other, as they become more familiar with their counterparts, comfortable with their motivations, and thus more willing to engage in serious agreements in the future'.[17] This is suggestive of positive peace effects from disarmament.

Other connections between arms and war stem from postulated effects of having a substantial military capacity for war. One of the arguments is based on 'simple opportunity':[18] more weapons increase the likelihood that they will be used for conflict. The reasoning here relies on a causal chain in which leaders choose the military force option because of weapons availability, and the accompanying increase in likely success because of that availability. For this to occur, however, there must be a step in which pure opportunity influences willingness. This can come from the purported increase in influence that military leaders have in government when states are highly armed; for this to operate, however, a second assumption—that military leaders prefer use of offensive military force to diplomacy or other alternatives—is needed.[19]

A variation of the opportunity argument is that accidents and so-called accidental wars are more likely with more weapons; this is based on the logic that there is always a positive probability that any weapons system has an unintended usage and that increasing the number of weapons or systems increases that additive probability that an accident involving one or more of them will occur. This argument tends to ignore that the baseline probability is extremely low and assumes linearity in effects. This rationale has also been applied primarily to nuclear weapons, and it is unclear how well it translates to other weapons types. The bottom line then is that any reduction in arms necessarily lowers the likelihood of an accident.

One of the problems with this theoretical formulation is that arms (and, by extension, the reduction of such arms) are postulated to have a mono-causal relationship with the outbreak of war. Yet we know that there are a variety of conditions that increase or depress the likelihood of war, and arms levels might be only one of them. The steps-to-war model is one of the few that incorporates arms increases as one of the dangerous inputs in relationships—other such inputs include territorial disputes, alliances, and the rise of hard-line leaders. Individually and collectively, these are independent factors that contribute to raising the risk of war.[20]

In the above formulations, reducing arms is always desirable as a pathway to peace, or at least in reducing the chances of war (negative peace). An alternative view, based in deterrence theory, is that the increase or decrease of armaments can have multiple effects, some of which promote peace and others that have the opposite effect. Deterrence—clearly something designed for negative peace, not positive peace—is based on some distribution of capabilities depending on the formulation (e.g., equal, mutually assured destruction, second-strike capability) between enemy states. To the extent that disarmament influences that balance in ways that promote deterrence, such reductions can lessen the chance for war. Nevertheless, arms control that locks in or precipitates an unfavourable capability distribution might actually promote conflict and escalation to war (it does beg the question, however, of why a disadvantaged state would agree to such an arrangement). Increases in armaments could have the same sets of effects.

Among the possible flaws in the arguments that disarmament leads to peace is the assumption of causal symmetry.[21] It is assumed that if increases in arms are dangerous, then reductions must have positive effects. This is not necessarily the case. Arms races might be dangerous, but the absence of arms races only leaves states with the baseline probabilities of going to war (that is, the effects of arms racing are relative to a null baseline). Reducing arms (which might or might not involve stopping extant arms races) doesn't necessarily further reduce the likelihood of war.

The notion that arms reductions are a consequence of more peaceful relations also relies on a connection between conflict and arms increases, although the causal order is reversed. A simple argument that arms increase occurs during extended wars and then arms reduction occurs when the war is over is superfluous from a theoretical standpoint. Rather, a more sophisticated view first sees increases in arms as symptoms or consequences of long-term hostile relationships, conventionally described as rivalries.[22] Accordingly, arms control and reductions occur when that hostility dissipates. Thus, the causal direction has rivalry or conflict as the independent variable and disarmament as the result.

Rider, Findley, and Diehl contend that arms increases occur exclusively or primarily in the context of rivalries.[23] Outside of this setting, two states are only coincidentally arming and not necessarily even targeting one another. Building up weapons involves a long-term acquisition and deployment process, and this only makes sense in protracted geopolitical competitions as opposed to sudden and single-shot crises. By implication, when the threat dissipates and the rivalry ends, so too should the arms race. It is less clear, however, whether disarmament is a consequence of rivalry termination. A state might have multiple rivalries (both old and new) and therefore the need to continue to maintain and even enhance military capabilities to address those other threats. In addition, there is a tendency for a 'ratchet effect' in military spending[24] in which some of the increases in military expenditures from war and other military threats become permanent features of defence budgets, even after the precipitating processes end. That is, military spending might decline after war or rivalry, but never return fully to pre-war or pre-rivalry levels. Thus, the disarmament-as-consequence perspective does not regard disarmament as a cause of peace, but a result of more peaceful relations between former enemies. Nevertheless, the end of an arms race does not necessarily produce arms reductions. Starting from the logic that rivalries produce arms races does not necessarily lead to the inference that the end of rivalry produces disarmament—only the end of arms increases. A variation of the two main perspectives above is that arms control efforts are early warning indicators of better relationships on the road to peace. The causal relationship between disarmament and peace is recursive. Improving relations between enemies produces an agreement to control weapons systems, and thus disarmament is a result. Then such agreements also lower tension and provide the basis for further cooperation in other areas; that is, the initial disarmament might be consequential, but produces a spill over effect promoting deeper peace thereafter.[25]

Disarmament and Peace: Empirical Evidence

To what extent do empirical studies support (or not) any or all of the theoretical relationships outlined above? Unfortunately, there have been few studies that specifically look at the reduction of arms in relation to peace. The predominant mode is to investigate the impact of an arms race on the outbreak of war. One difficulty in discovering empirical connections between disarmament and negative peace is that the baseline probability of war is low; that is, war is a rare event and any factor will need to have a profound effect to reduce that likelihood even further in a meaningful way. Although there are insights about disarmament and arms control that can be gained from these studies, there are important inferential limitations, as noted above.

Most directly, Koubi looks at the impact of arms control agreements on hostility in the US–USSR rivalry. She finds that they did not reduce tension in the relationship[26] or even result in reduced military spending.[27] This might be because such agreements do nothing more than codify the abandonment of old technology and do not manage the kinds of competition that will occur in the future. Nevertheless, arms control pacts did reduce the subsequent incidence of militarized disputes.[28] Therefore, this is suggestive that arms control might lessen confrontations that could escalate to war but has no other moderating influence in promoting peace among rivals.

Some other studies consider arms reductions as one factor among many in promoting peace. Gibler and Tir report that military spending and militarization decline *following* border settlement between neighbours.[29] As border settlement, in their view, is the key element reducing the chances for war, disarmament (implied by lower military spending) is a consequence of better relations rather than a precursor for it. This is consistent with Owsiak, Diehl, and Goertz, who find that border settlement leads to negative peace,[30] and therefore it is not surprising that military capability is reduced in the face of diminished threat. In partial contrast, Fortna finds that arms control agreements among recent belligerents reduce the chance of another war.[31] This suggests support for a modified version of the early warning framework. It might take the end of a war and a (negative) peace agreement for arms control to occur, but once the latter does, it reinforces negative peace in the longer term. In sum, the direct tests of the impact of disarmament on peace are few and, at best, provide only some hint at what happens when states reduce arms.

I turn now to the empirical work on arms races and war, which has a long pedigree. There are other reviews of that literature[32] and there is little reason to repeat the history of the various debates and early studies of the connection between these two phenomena. Most relevant to the concerns here are two attempts to integrate all the past findings and to address two of the main theoretical approaches outlined above. Rider and colleagues demonstrate that rivalries are the context for most arms races, giving credence to the 'arms as consequence' causal relationship.[33] Nevertheless, they also find that arms races that occur in the late stages of enduring rivalries do increase (a 'modest' relationship) the likelihood that military confrontations escalate to war; this is suggestive of arms as causal agents in the process to war. Their findings are consistent with the steps to war logic of Senese and Vasquez that arms acquisition is one of the actions that move enemy states closer to war.[34]

Susan Sample also attempts to sort out the different causal paths for arms and war and finds some results quite similar to those noted immediately above.[35] Operating in the 'steps to war' framework, she finds that arms races have a consistently positive association with war outbreaks. Within the rivalry context, this means that the increase in the probability of war is approximately 8 percent, again a modest impact. As with most of the arms race war literature, this study examines the impact of war on dispute escalation, either immediately or within a subsequent five-year time frame. That the states involved already experience a militarized dispute is indicative of a precarious negative peace relationship. Thus, eliminating arms races doesn't necessarily prevent further confrontations, but rather merely lowers the likelihood, in a limited fashion, that there will be escalation to war. Indeed, hostile relations are likely to continue.

All these formulations and associated studies dance around the relationship(s) between disarmament and peace. What we lack is a direct test of how disarmament changes (or not) ongoing relationships between states. Does disarmament facilitate negative peace? Transform state relations into positive peace? In the next section, I offer one of the few attempts at understanding when disarmament occurs in the conflict process and what effect it has on subsequent state interactions.

Understanding the Impact of Disarmament on Peace: Some New Analyses

In this section, I present some original analyses on disarmament and how it affects (or is affected by) the level of peace and hostility in interstate relationships. Specifically, I look longitudinally at the 'peace scale' level of those relationships and whether disarmament can precipitate a shift to more peaceful relations; conversely, I also explore whether transitions to more peaceful relations are followed by arms control agreements.

Rather than focus on a single event—militarized disputes or war—the study of peace requires broader and longer-term perspectives on the impact of disarmament. Goertz, Diehl, and Balas first define a population of interstate relationships and then classify them along a five-point continuum, from very hostile to very friendly and integrated.[36] Placement along this continuum depends broadly on the number and salience of disputed issues, as well as how states handle the issues over which they disagree and a series of other conditions.

At one end of the continuum are severe rivalries (e.g., India–Pakistan since

1947), which involve states that see one another as enemies and competitors. Unresolved salient issues often drive such sentiments, which encourage rivals to handle their contested issues via frequent and intense uses of violence. As a result, rivals plan their foreign policy around their counterparts, particularly as past negative interactions lead them to expect such interactions to continue or repeat in the foreseeable future. This is the context for most wars, although war is the exception rather than the norm for most of the rivalry period. Nonetheless, severe rivalry relationships can transition into those in which violence abates or ends altogether.

The next category constitutes what Goertz and colleagues label lesser rivalries.[37] Lesser rivalries (e.g., Colombia–Venezuela during the period 1841–1982) are not as hostile as severe rivalries. Within these relationships, both the frequency and severity of violent interactions are lower. The sentiments of threat, enmity, and competition that remain, however—along with the persistence of unresolved issues—mean that lesser rivalries still experience isolated violent episodes, diplomatic hostility, and nonviolent crises.

Violent, hostile episodes almost disappear entirely when we move into the middle of the continuum: negative peace. Pairs of states at negative peace (e.g., Egypt and Israel after 1989) possess a number of characteristics: they maintain war plans; rarely or never fight or threaten one another militarily; make statements suggesting that conflict remains possible but have resolved or mitigated their major issues; only possess unresolved issues of low salience; recognize one another diplomatically; and communicate officially with one another. At negative peace, states are therefore neither close friends nor bitter enemies.

Beyond negative peace lie two additional, more peaceful relationship types (positive peace): warm peace (e.g., the US and UK since 1941)—defined by increasing integration and the removal of military options for managing disagreements—and security communities (e.g., many EU relationships)—which involve compatible values, expectations of mutual reward, institutionalized conflict-management processes, and mutual responsiveness.[38] Although conceptually a security community could include a formal merger of two political entities, in practice states retain their sovereign independence to a substantial degree. War is not only unthinkable between members, but extensive communication links and transaction flows also bind the parties together. Security communities might also involve shared identities, values, and meanings as well as interactions at several levels (private as well as governmental) and common long-term interests.

Of interest here among these five types is whether and how they transition from one point on the peace scale to another, particularly if it is in a more peaceful direction—for example, from severe rivalry to negative peace or from negative peace to warm peace. Goertz and colleagues code all state relationships from 1900 to 2015 along the peace scale and, thus, one is able to detect the exact timing (down to the day, according to the coding) when state relationships move (or not) from one category to another. The question here is the timing of any arms control agreements or disarmament actions vis-à-vis shifts along the peace scale. If they occur, are they before or after relations improve? That is, when do they become more peaceful? I am also concerned about whether disarmament is associated in these ways with negative peace or with more positive varieties.

Ideal Cases

The analysis begins with what are essentially two ideal cases: South Africa and Costa Rica. The former involves a state that possessed nuclear weapons and subsequently decided to relinquish them.[39] Thus, this presents an opportunity to ascertain how the decision to disarm affected South Africa's relations with its neighbours (or vice versa). The latter is a country that lacks a standing army,[40] and therefore one can determine how peaceful (or not) its relations are with relevant states.[41]

South Africa developed a nuclear weapons capability in the late 1960s, although most of those efforts were covert and there was significant ambiguity about its possession and any testing that occurred. The white apartheid regime had a series of rivalries (both lesser and severe) with its neighbours after 1945. South Africa began to dismantle its nuclear weapons capacity in 1989 and signed the NPT in 1991. How does this map with any changes in its relationships with states in the region? South Africa ended its rivalry with Angola in 1988,[42] when both sides agreed to stop assisting rebel groups in the other's territory. Temporally, disarmament follows this rapprochement, but there is little historical evidence to suggest a causal connection.

In South Africa's other rivalries (e.g., with Mozambique and Zambia, respectively), 1990 marked the outset of a four-year transition period in relationships as they moved from different levels of rivalry to negative peace (the middle of the peace scale). This transition ended in 1994 with open elections and assumption of power of the African National Congress and its leader, Nelson Mandela.[43] Disarmament actions occurred just before and during the transition, suggesting that it is both cause and effect in the peace process. More peaceful relations and relinquishing nuclear capability took place with the dramatic policy shifts of the de Klerk government in South Africa on the path to majority rule in that country. Disarmament certainly assisted in improving relations with regional neighbours, but it was one of many actions that did so, and arguably other internal changes were more significant.

None of the South African relationships that was at negative peace prior to the nuclear disarmament (e.g., with Lesotho and Swaziland, respectively) were affected.[44] Even the rivalries that were terminated did not transform relationships into positive peace ones; all transitioned to negative peace and moved no further.[45] Thus, at best, disarmament in the South African case has had a limited causal effect in improving relationships and more likely follows a series of other policy changes that transform rivalries. In no cases, however, does positive peace result.

Costa Rica has had thirty relationships with other countries since 1900. All but one began and ended in the negative peace category.[46] Given that Costa Rica gave up its military in 1949, this has had little effect—for better or worse—on its general foreign relations. Costa Rica had had a rivalry, or rivalries,[47] with Nicaragua in the post-WWII period. The rivalry began in 1948 when the Somoza regime supported anti-democratic forces in Costa Rica. Costa Rica's decision to disarm a year later was not a logical consequence of the rivalry. Neither did eliminating the military influence the dynamics of the rivalry thereafter. This case illustrates several things. It might suggest that complete disarmament lessens the chance for rivalry, although, as the relationship with Nicaragua indicates, rivalry is not completely foreclosed. As with the South African case, disarmament is consistent with negative peace, but there is no evidence that it can produce positive peace. Finally, there is no support from the Costa Rican case for any of the causal connections discussed in the previous sections.

The Impact of Arms Control Agreements on State Relationships

Trade, environmental, and other international agreements number in the thousands.[48] In contrast, arms control agreements are relatively rare. The Congressional Research Service lists only forty-five such treaties, at least in the last one hundred or so years.[49] That small number alone means that arms control cannot be a necessary condition for the numerous transitions that occur toward more peaceful relationships. That does not mean that such agreements do not have an impact in selective cases. Barash and Webel argue that the Rush-Bagot Treaty of 1817, between the US and UK, demilitarized the border between the US and Canada and 'helped set the stage for good relations' in the years to come.[50] This followed the War of 1812, and indeed the two states would not fight another war on opposite sides and certainly not with respect to North American claims. Nevertheless, a rivalry between the two states occurred from 1837 to 1861, despite the previous treaty. It might be correct that limiting naval armaments and installations along the Great Lakes prevented an escalation of the militarized disputes that took place, but then, at best, the arms control agreement reinforced negative peace; closer and more peaceful relations between the US and UK would be a century away.[51]

To look more systematically at the effect of arms control agreements requires a narrower focus than even the forty-five agreements noted above. Many on the list involve no actual reduction of armaments. Some are designed to influence the conduct of war (*jus in bello*) through restrictions in the kinds of weapons that might be employed; the Geneva Protocol of 1925, which banned the use of poison gas in war, is illustrative. Others demilitarize uninhabited and as yet not militarized parts of the world—the Antarctic, outer space, and the seabed, respectively. Still other so-called arms control agreements are designed to limit accidents or misunderstandings rather than restrict the acquisition or use of weaponry; the Hot Line Agreement of 1963 and the Treaty on Open Skies of 1992 are examples. Finally, some deal with monitoring and confidence building measures rather than weapons control per se. These and a series of other agreements do not constitute disarmament per se and do not provide a test of its effects on peace, even as they might be desirable and prompt better relations.

Excluding the agreements not involving reduction of weaponry and those whose restrictions involve use in warfare from the list leaves us with even fewer agreements. That is, arms reduction agreements are the exceptions to internationally negotiated treaties and to the general pattern of military spending increases by states. Below, I look at selected major agreements designed to limit, reduce, or eliminate weapons since 1900; these are listed in table 14.1.[52]

The list is heavily weighted toward nuclear weapons issues; the Conventional Forces in Europe agreement is an exception. For each of the agreements, I look at the relationships between pairs of treaty parties in the ten years prior and the ten years after agreement entered into force.[53] I consider whether the agreement was preceded by a shift in the relationship along the five-point peace scale and whether a change in the relationship occurred following the agreement; the former is suggestive of disarmament as a consequence and the latter a cause of peace.[54]

Many of these agreements are directional; that is, they are designed to affect relationships between the parties whose militaries might be used against one another (e.g., US–USSR) rather than between allied co-signatories (e.g., NATO members). Accordingly, I only examine the effects of a treaty on the adversarial relationships.[55] With respect to nuclear-free zones and agreements between major powers, all relationships are considered, as the behaviour of all states in the agreement potentially affects all others. In addition, removing the spectre of a nuclear threat (from one's own acquisition or from allies) might be the context for improving relations generally among those in the region. Overall, there are 549 different state-state relationships

Table 14.1. Selected Arms Control Agreements, 1900–2011

Agreement	Entry into Force Year	Number of Parties
New START	2011	2
African Nuclear-Weapon-Free Zone Treaty	2009	40
Central Asian Nuclear-Weapon-Free Zone	2009	5
SORT Agreement	2003	2
Southeast Asian Nuclear-Weapon-Free Zone Treaty	1997	10
START I	1994	2
US-Kazakhstan Nuclear Agreement	1994	2
US-Ukraine Nuclear Agreement	1993	2
Treaty on Conventional Armed Forces in Europe	1990	30
INF Treaty	1987	2
South Pacific Nuclear-Weapon-Free Zone	1985	13
SALT I Interim Agreement ABM Treaty	1972	2
Latin America Nuclear Weapons Free Zone	1969	24
Washington Naval Treaty	1924 (1930; 1936)	5

among the parties to the agreements analysed. In some instances, there was no relationship in the ten years prior to the agreement, but the relationship was established sometime in the ten years after the agreement;[56] the data are coded as missing (n = 26) for the analysis of the ten years before the agreement. The relationship data are available only through 2015,[57] and therefore the effect of agreements on relationships in the decade after cannot be determined for more recent agreements, especially two instances of nuclear-weapon-free zones (Africa and Central Asia); accordingly, the data are coded as missing (n = 5) for the analysis of the ten years after the agreement in those cases.[58] Thus, the missing data cases (n = 26 + 5 = 31) are not factored into the 'no effect' category.

Table 14.2 reports the results of the analysis on the timing of arms control agreements vis-à-vis changes in state relationships. Most treaties occur among pairs of parties that are in the middle of the peace scale, at negative peace. We tend to think of arms agreements as only being necessary among enemies, but broad agreements encompass mostly states that are neither friends nor enemies. Nevertheless, states that enjoy strong peaceful relationships (e.g., European Union) have no need to sign arms control agreements with one another. From a different vantage point, this is perhaps not surprising, in that negative peace relationships regularly constitute 75 to 80 percent of all relationships in the last one hundred years.[59] As the findings indicate, becoming part of a treaty to restrict weapons does not change the foundations of these relationships; more than 94 percent of relationships are unaffected by an arms agreement and most of these are negative peace ones.

The evidence for arms control agreements fundamentally changing state relationships is limited; as early signals of change, the results are also not encouraging. Only 5 percent of cases involve a relationship shift in the ten-year period after the two states become parties to the agreement. Even this small number is misleading in favour of the cause-of-peace perspective. More than a third of the post-agreement shifts were actually in the *wrong* direction, with relations deteriorating following the treaty; UK

Table 14.2. Arms Control Agreements and State Relationships

Causal Relationship	Percentage (n)
Consequence (relationship shift within ten years before agreement)	3.3% (523)
Cause (relationship shift within ten years after agreement)	5.0% (544)
No Effect (same relationship before and after agreement)	94.8% (518)

relationships with Japan and Italy several years after the Washington Naval Treaty and a decade before WWII are illustrative. A number those cases that shift to positive peace are coterminous with the establishment of regional economic integration schemes among minor states that arguably owe little or no credit to nuclear-free zones; the East Caribbean Common Market is an example. Admittedly, I only considered changes in the ten-year period following the agreement, but any longer temporal window brings in a host of other confounding factors, and a perusal of individual cases suggests that the results herein are robust to such changes in the research design.

The results are even less encouraging for the disarmament-as-consequence perspective; barely 3 percent of paired relationships saw a shift in the decade prior to joining an arms control agreement. The START I agreement between the US and Russia is perhaps the most prominent instance, as that treaty was concluded several years after the end of the Cold War and a shift from severe rivalry to lesser competition. Almost all of these are shifts in the correct direction, but they are very few in number. In terms of placement on the peace scale, not many of the changes involve positive peace relationships; none occur when states become part of security communities.

Notably absent from table 14.1 and the resulting analyses are global agreements with many parties, such as the Nuclear Non-Proliferation Treaty and the Chemical Weapons Convention. These were excluded for a number of reasons. First, positive peace is more likely, theoretically and empirically, to come from regional initiatives and not global efforts at promoting better relations.[60] Second, there are significant statistical problems associated with their inclusion. The massive state relationship combinations encompassed by agreements with almost 200 parties would swamp the reported effects from all of the smaller treaties. Even so, many of those relationships are already reflected in the analyses of regional agreements. Thus, including a few global agreements would lead to duplication because of the spatial and temporal overlap of cases. In any case, there is no reason to believe that the results above would be altered by a more expansive consideration of agreements.

Conclusion

The assumption has been that disarmament, or the reduction or limitation of weapons stockpiles, promotes peace. This is reflected in public discourse and in the selection of Nobel Peace Prize winners. The underlying logic is that arms control reduces tension between actors, lessens the chances for accidents, limits the influence of the military on decision makers, and promotes cooperation during confrontations and more generally at other times. One alternative perspective is that disarmament follows peace rather than precipitating it. A third view is a combination of the first two: disarmament is an early warning indicator of better relations, an initial consequence that subsequently takes on a causal role on the path to peace.

What have we learned about these viewpoints and, therefore, about disarmament's role in peace? There are several conclusions from the analysis here. There are few empirical studies about disarmament and peace per se. Most scholarly analyses are devoted to the intersection of arms races and conflict, but disarmament is not synonymous with stopping arms races. Even when insightful, those studies offer modest results, at best, in linking arms races to conflict escalation.

Disarmament, at least in terms of international agreements, is relatively rare, especially compared to treaties in other substantive areas. Furthermore, arms control agreements often do not involve reductions in extant weapons stockpiles, but deal with conditions of use, deployment location, verification, and other matters. Agreements have also concentrated disproportionately on nuclear weapons as opposed to conventional ones. In an analysis of state relationships along a peace scale, arms control agreements had no apparent impact on improving relationships in their aftermath. Neither did they follow movements toward greater peace among states. Any promotion of peace that occurred from disarmament did so in terms of lessening the likelihood of war, rather than in lessening hostility and promoting cooperation. Disarmament as a source of peace is based more on wishful thinking than on empirical evidence that it works and under specified conditions. Nevertheless, this is an under-researched area, and a number of fruitful avenues remain for consideration.

Do mutual reductions in military spending have different effects than arms control agreements on state relationships? Heretofore, there has been exclusive emphasis on halting arms races or controls on weapons stockpiles, but military expenditures encompass a wider range of activities and their limitation might have a broader and deeper effect. What role do unilateral reductions in weapons and military spending have in promoting peaceful relations? Such actions are often regarded as signs of weakness, but do they promote reciprocity and peace? Some game-theoretic formulations are suggestive of this, provided certain conditions are met.[61] This and the previous point have substantial implications for Europe, as it has reduced its weaponry and spending in the post-Cold War era (even in the face of Russian rearmament). Is there a peace dividend that comes from disarmament? Such a dividend (the conversion of defence resources to other sectors of the economy) might provide another causal, albeit indirect, path from disarmament to (positive) peace. Indeed, early twentieth-century disarmament efforts also had an underlying economic logic. Nevertheless, what was once a popular focus for scholarly inquiry,[62] has largely fallen out of favour.

Calls for disarmament largely reflect the hopes and dreams of policymakers, scholars, activists, and the general public that war can be made impossible or at least less likely. Unfortunately, there is little evidence that the infrequent efforts at arms control produce the desired effects of lessening conflict, much less promoting cooperation in other issue areas. This is not to suggest that disarmament lacks some positive consequences, and indeed, except for some claims about complete and unilateral disarmament in the face of an aggressor, there appear to be few dangers to limiting weapons. Nevertheless, the simple aphorism that 'weapons cause war' and thereby limiting them leads to peace has little or no empirical evidence behind it.

Notes

1.   Johan Galtung, 'Violence, Peace, and Peace Research,' *Journal of Peace Research* 6, no. 3 (1969): 167–91.

2.   Joshua Goldstein, *Winning the War on War: The Decline of Armed Conflict Worldwide* (New York: Dutton, 2011); Pinker, *The Better Angels of Our Nature*.

3.   For example, Bruce Russett and John Oneal, *Triangulating Peace: Democracy, Interdependence, and International Organizations* (New York: Norton, 2001).

4. Gaddis, *The Long Peace.*

5. For the limitations of the negative peace concept, see Paul F. Diehl, 'Exploring Peace: Looking Beyond War and Negative Peace,' *International Studies Quarterly* 60, no. 1 (2016): 1–10; Gary Goertz, Paul F. Diehl, and Alexandru Balas, *The Puzzle of Peace: The Evolution of Peace in the International System* (New York: Oxford University Press, 2016).

6. For a definition of symmetry in this context, see Gary Goertz and James Mahoney, *A Tale of Two Cultures: Qualitative and Quantitative Research in the Social Sciences* (Princeton, NJ: Princeton University Press, 2012).

7. Diehl, 'Exploring Peace.'

8. Ronald Krebs, 'The False Promise of the Nobel Peace Prize,' *Political Science Quarterly* 124, no. 4 (2009–2010): 593–625.

9. Ibid., 597, note 13

10. Ibid.

11. His data go through 2009, and I have extended these through 2017.

12. Krebs, 'False Promise.'

13. For a timeless discussion of this position, a critique, and some guidelines, see Inis Claude, *Swords into Plowshares*, 4th ed. (New York: Random House, 1971).

14. Shiping Tang, 'The Security Dilemma: A Conceptual Analysis,' *Security Studies* 18, no. 3 (2009): 587–623.

15. Robert Jervis, *Perception and Misperception in International Politics* (Princeton, NJ: Princeton University Press, 1976). See also Charles Glaser, 'The Security Dilemma Revisited,' *World Politics* 50, no. 1 (1997): 171–201.

16. Gary Goertz and Paul F. Diehl, 'Treaties and Conflict Management in Enduring Rivalries,' *International Negotiation* 7, no. 3 (2002): 379–98.

17. David Barash and Charles Webel, *Peace and Conflict Studies*, 2nd ed. (Los Angeles: Sage, 2009), 271.

18. Harvey Starr and Benjamin Most, *Inquiry, Logic, and International Politics* (Columbia, SC: University of South Carolina Press, 1989).

19. Jack Snyder, 'Civil-Military Relations and the Cult of the Offensive, 1914 and 1984,' *International Security* 9, no. 1 (1984): 108–46.

20. John Vasquez, *The War Puzzle* (Cambridge: Cambridge University Press, 1993); Paul Senese and John Vasquez, *The Steps to War: An Empirical Study* (Princeton, NJ: Princeton University Press, 2008).

21. Goertz and Mahoney, *Tale of Two Cultures.*

22. Michael Colaresi, Karen Rasler, and William Thompson, *Strategic Rivalries in World Politics Position, Space and Conflict Escalation* (Cambridge: Cambridge University Press, 2008).

23. Toby Rider, Michael Findley, and Paul F. Diehl, 'Just Part of the Game? Arms Races, Rivalry, and War,' *Journal of Peace Research* 48, no. 1 (2011): 85–100.

24. Diehl and Gary Goertz, 'Trends in Military Allocation Since 1816: What Goes Up Does Not Always Come Down,' *Armed Forces and Society* 12, no. 1 (1985): 134–44.

25. The above theoretical frameworks are designed for interstate conflicts, the focus of the analysis here. Few works have addressed disarmament in an intrastate context, and previous formulations have limited, at best, applicability with respect to governments and rebel groups. There has been an increasing tendency, however, to incorporate disarmament, demobilization, and reintegration (DDR) provisions in agreements that end civil wars; peacekeeping operations are often charged with implementing these mandates. These call for former combatants to lay down their arms, militias and other groups to disband, and combatants to return to civilian society. These might lessen the chances for war renewal (negative peace), but also are designed to permit longer term integration and cooperation between warring parties.

26. Vally Koubi, 'International Tensions and Arms Control Agreements,' *American Journal of Political Science* 37, no. 1 (1993): 148–64.

27. Vally Koubi, 'Military Buildups and Arms Control Agreements,' *International Studies Quarterly* 38, no. 4 (1994): 605–20.

28. Ibid.

29. Douglas Gibler and Jaroslav Tir, 'Settled Borders and Regime Type: Democratic Transitions as Consequences of Peaceful Territorial Transfers,' *American Journal of Political Science* 54, no. 4 (2010): 951–68.

30. Andrew Owsiak, Paul F. Diehl, and Gary Goertz, 'Border Settlement and the Movement Toward Negative Peace,' *Conflict Management and Peace Science* 34, no. 2 (2017): 176–93.

31. V. Page Fortna, *Peace Time: Cease-Fire Agreements and the Durability of Peace* (Princeton, NJ: Princeton University Press, 2004).

32. Most recently, Susan Sample, 'Arms Races: A Cause or a Symptom?' in *What Do We Know about War?* ed. John Vasquez (Lanham, MD: Rowman and Littlefield, 2012), 111–38.

33. Rider et al., 'Just Part.'

34. Sense and Vasquez, *Steps to War.*

35. Sample, 'Arms Races.'

36. Goertz et al., *The Puzzle of Peace.*

37. Ibid.

38. Ibid.

39. Following the dissolution of the Soviet Union, three new states—Ukraine, Belarus, and Kazakhstan—had nuclear weapons on their territories and subsequently relinquished them after a short time. Nevertheless, none ever had operational control over them during that interlude nor could any of those states afford to maintain the weapons, and all received aid in return for giving up the weapons.

40. It does have a police force that performs some internal security and border patrol functions.

41. There are other countries without military forces, but most are micro-states (e.g., Nauru or the Marshall Islands) that are not good tests of the effects of disarmament either because of their sizes or because their security is delegated to another state.

See 'List of Countries without Armed Forces,' *Wikipedia*, accessed on June 11, 2018, https://en.wikipedia.org/wiki/List_of_countries_without_armed_forces.

42. David Dreyer and William Thompson, *Handbook of International Rivalries* (Washington, DC: CQ Press, 2012).

43. Goertz et al., *The Puzzle of Peace.*

44. Ibid.

45. Ibid.

46. Ibid. This is not necessarily unusual as approximately 75 to 80 percent of state relationships are consistently in this category, with the pair of states neither friends nor enemies.

47. Dreyer and Thompson, *Handbook*, has it as one continuous rivalry from 1948 to 1990, whereas Goertz et al., *The Puzzle of Peace*, code two separate rivalry periods, 1948 to 1957 and 1977 to 1998.

48. For just the multilateral agreements, see the *United Nations Treaty Collection*, accessed on June 11, 2018, https://treaties.un.org/.

49. The temporal scope is unclear, with the earliest one listed in 1925 and the most recent 2011. It is also the case that the list might have a bias toward agreements that focus on US interests and therefore might miss some bilateral agreements that reduce weapons or troops. Amy Woolf, Paul Kerr, and Mary Beth Nikitin, *Arms Control and Nonproliferation: A Catalog of Treaties and Agreements, 7-5700* (Washington, DC: Congressional Research Service, 2014). This list is similar to ones in other sources, including 'Treaties & Agreements' *Arms Control Association*, accessed on June 11, 2018, https://www.armscontrol.org/treaties and 'Arms Control Treaties,' *Wikipedia*, accessed on June 11, 2018, https://en.wikipedia.org/wiki/Category:Arms_control _treaties.

50. Barash and Webel, 'Peace and Conflict Studies,' 267.

51. See Charles Kupchan, *How Enemies Become Friends: The Sources of Stable Peace* (Princeton, NJ: Princeton University Press, 2012).

52. I draw these from Woolf et al., 'Arms Control' and add the Washington Naval Treaty of 1922.

53. Mere signature does not legally bind states; they must be 'parties', which occurs only after ratification. Also note that the entry into force date usually occurs after certain states (number or specific identities) become parties and then the entry into force might vary by dyad as some states join the treaty after it is already in force between other parties.

54. If a relationship is formed after an arms control agreement and the relationship begins with 'warm peace' or 'security community'—a positive peace relationship—then I code that a shift in relationships has occurred in the period; empirically, however, there are only 'warm peace' cases. Otherwise, I do not code a shift as occurring; only negative peace cases—no rivalries—occur empirically.

55. Note that only pairs of states with relationships (and only those years in which the relationship is present) are included, as defined by Goertz et al., *Puzzle of Peace*.

Especially in multilateral agreements, some parties have little direct connection with one another and therefore no relationship.

56. As long as there was at least one day of a relationship in the ten years before or after the agreement, there was a code for whether a relationship change occurred or not in that period.

57. Updated from Goertz et al., *Puzzle of Peace.*

58. One exception is the 2011 New START agreement, in which I assume that the coding of lesser rivalry between the US and Russia continues after the agreement.

59. Goertz et al., *Puzzle of Peace.*

60. Ibid.

61. Robert Axelrod, *The Evolution of Cooperation*, revised ed. (New York: Basic Books, 2006).

62. For example, see Stephen Chan, 'Grasping the Peace Dividend: Some Propositions on the Conversion of Swords into Plowshares,' *Mershon International Studies Review* 39, no. 1 (1995): 53–95.

The Causes of Peace: The Statistical Evidence

15.

The Causes of Peace and the Future of Peace

Kristian Skrede Gleditsch

Introduction

The claims that warfare and political violence have declined have generated a great deal of interest and controversy. The book-length treatments by Goldstein and Pinker review a wealth of data on trends in conflict and have helped disseminate the idea that political violence has declined.[1] Whereas Goldstein's focus is largely on conventional war and the post-1945 era, Pinker sees the decline of warfare as part of a more general decline of violence, reflecting processes that play out over a much longer time span.

In this chapter, I consider the evidence for a decline in political violence, with an emphasis on the plausible causes for such a decline, based on what we know about historical data, and their implications for the future of peace. The conventional wisdom is fickle and has a poor track record as a source of insight on trends in warfare. Thus, even if documenting political violence and the factors that may affect trends can be difficult, close attention to empirical data and explicit methods of assessment is our only hope for a structured debate and inferences about conflict trends. Moreover, I will argue that the lack of attention to possible causes for the decline of political violence makes it more difficult to evaluate the implications for peace and what would make the decline in violence more or less likely to be sustained in the future.

I will discuss the future of peace based on what we know about how active political accommodation can decrease domestic violent conflict through reducing grievances, focusing especially on evidence from civil war and domestic terrorism. I do not claim that grievances and accommodation are the only forces affecting the prospects for peace. However, focusing on these helps identify specific influences that are also, to some extent, open to intervention and reform as well as to evaluate central challenges. Although it is difficult to predict—especially about the future—I offer a relatively optimistic future outlook.

Learning about Conflict from the Past: The Decline of Conventional War

One remarkable feature of the current debate on the decline of war is how recent these claims are, even though data sources on conflict have been available for a long time. Sorokin and Richardson started pioneering efforts to collect data on wars before WWII.[2] Still before the end of the Cold War, Jack Levy noted a declining trend in the frequency of war between major powers, extending prior analyses by Richardson.[3] However, prior to the recent wave of research, warfare was often perceived as inescapable or even increasingly frequent. Much of the traditional research on conflict and peace has emphasized the inevitability of conflict and posited war as a natural state. For example, Waltz simply asserts that 'war occurs because there is nothing to prevent it', suggesting instead that it is periods of peace that call for an explanation.[4] Only recently have scholars started to engage with the so-called puzzle of war, or the need to account for why parties cannot simply settle on the expected outcome of a war in advance, without fighting and incurring the actual costs of war.[5] Moreover, even though the Cold War entailed a risk that the tension between the superpowers could escalate to a devastating nuclear war, it was also widely believed that the superpower competition had a stabilizing effect in deterring conflict and that the end of the Cold War thus would lead to an inexorable increase in armed conflict. Mueller provides an excellent review of the extreme pessimism that prevailed at the end of the Cold War, where scholars and policymakers competed to offer dire warnings about the rise of future conflict.[6]

Given the wealth of data on conflict available, it is remarkable how few tried to look at whether these sources actually supported the pessimistic claims that rose to prominence after the Cold War. A number of early contributions that tried to do so turned out to find evidence suggesting a declining trend rather than increasing warfare. For example, an early analysis by Wallensteen and Sollenberg of the armed conflict data collected at the Department of Peace and Conflict Research at Uppsala University found a lower incidence of conflict after the Cold War.[7]

However, the analysis was limited to a six-year period (1989–1994), and the authors themselves downplayed the significance of their finding in emphasizing how it was premature to dismiss interstate war as obsolete in a follow-up article the subsequent year.[8] Ted Gurr, drawing on the data from the Minorities at Risk project on ethno-political conflict, was perhaps the first to make a strong claim about clear evidence of a waning in warfare and insisted that the decline involved something more than just a temporary deviation.[9] However, this prior research failed to generate the same attention as the Goldstein and Pinker volumes.

In retrospect, the prevalent focus on identifying factors leading to conflict within individual states or dyadic relations between states probably overshadowed any attention paid to global trends in conflict. The two concerns, however, are obviously related in the sense that changes in the distribution of relevant state or dyadic characteristics believed to influence conflict should entail implications for future conflict trends. Again, beyond noting the decline in conflict, Gurr was one of the first to highlight specific causal mechanisms. In brief, Gurr argued that ethnic warfare had started to decline throughout the world due to changes toward greater accommodation of ethnic groups, greater political democracy, and opportunities for nonviolent mobilization, as well as greater international conflict management efforts. Gurr further predicted that these trends would continue and that future changes toward greater accommodation would lead to further decreases in ethnic warfare. I will return to the evidence for the specific mechanisms highlighted by Gurr after first reviewing the evidence for a decline in conflict in a bit more detail.

In the panel on the left, figure 15.1 displays the distribution of conventional

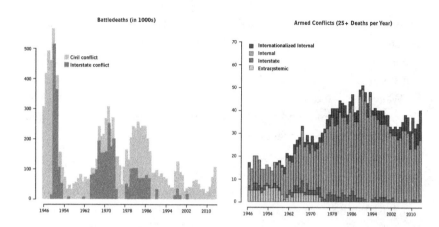

FIGURE 15.1. *Left panel: distribution of ongoing armed conflicts by type.[10]*
Right panel: deaths from ongoing conflicts by type.[11]

armed conflicts involving more than twenty-five deaths per calendar year over the period 1946–2015, by type. As can be seen, interstate conflict has been a relatively rare phenomenon, and even less common since the end of the Cold War.[12] Domestic conflict is by far the dominant contemporary form of armed conflict. Although the number of ongoing civil wars increases with decolonialization in the late 1960s, there has been a clear decline since the mid-1990s. The data on conflict severity in terms of battle deaths in the panel on the right of figure 15.1 display an even more dramatic decline.

Interstate conflicts have been the most severe in terms of historical perspective, but the increase in the number of intrastate conflicts did not lead to more severe conflicts in terms of producing high casualties. Of course, some vehemently dispute that warfare is declining,[13] but many of these criticisms show little interest in engaging with data or empirical research. Others raise more productive questions about how issues such as the quality of the data may affect our analyses and ability to infer trends in conflict,[14] and these questions have generated a dialogue and led to valuable new research and findings. It may be premature to say that a consensus has emerged, but my view is that observed data on conventional conflict are relatively clear and robust to the main criticisms.[15]

The Rise of New and Uncivil Violence?

One prominent empirical challenge to claims about the decline of conflict is that the nature of political violence has changed from conventional war to unconventional forms of violence.[16] The many forms of this claim are difficult to evaluate due to the lack of specificity. Moreover, the available measures and data sources for political violence beyond conventional civil war are less clear.[17] However, terrorism is one important alternative form of political violence where, arguably, the available data suggest an increasing trend.[18]

Although terrorism is a contested concept,[19] a useful possible definition distinguishes terrorism from conventional warfare through the use of indirect targeting, where the specific targets in an attack are not the main intended audience.[20] Put differently, non-state actors in conventional conflicts try to coerce a government through direct attacks or confrontation with government forces, whereas in indirect terrorist attacks the identity of the specific victims (often civilians) may be entirely arbitrary or irrelevant, and subordinate to the overarching aim of coercing the government through the broader consequences of the attack.

Although not as extensive as data on conventional war, the Global Terrorism Database (GTD) records individual attacks from 1970 to 2013.[21] Figure 15.2 indicates an increasing trend in both the number of terrorist attacks and the number of people killed as a result up to the end of the Cold War, followed by a subsequent decline. Engene finds a similar decline in domestic terrorism in Western Europe, taken over a longer time series, after peaks in the 1970s and 1980s, while Valentino finds that violence against civilians in general has declined.[22] However, unlike conventional conflict, the GTD data indicate an increase in terrorism from the mid-2000s, especially in the current decade.

The increase in terrorism in figure 15.2 at first glance seems consistent with the idea of a transformation of political violence over the decline of conventional wars in figure 15.1. However, there is little evidence for direct substitution, or that we see terrorism instead of conventional political conflict. The shading in figure 15.2 indicates that the vast majority of terrorist attacks

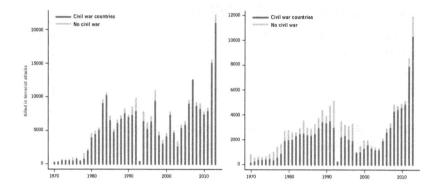

FIGURE 15.2. *Left panel: number of terrorist attacks, from Global Terrorism Database.*[23] *Right panel: deaths from attacks. The share of terrorist incidents in civil war countries is shown in black, based on PRIO/Uppsala data.*[24]

take place in countries already experiencing civil war, with Afghanistan, Iraq, and Syria as prominent current examples. This suggests complementarity rather than substitution, or that terrorism has become a more common tactic in ongoing conventional civil war.

There are a number of factors that may account for why terrorism is increasingly common in civil war.[25] For example, many current civil wars are strongly asymmetric, and terrorist attacks can be tactically advantageous for relatively weak rebels. For rebels in conflicts that follow ethnic or religious cleavages, attacks on civilians associated with the government may be acceptable to a group's core audience. Terrorist attacks may spread through diffusion or become popular if perceived as effective elsewhere. Some argue that the increase in terrorism reflects a new tendency to classify any attacks on civilians as 'terrorism' after 9/11, or possibly better reporting of incidents.[26] However, better media reporting may itself increase incentives for terrorist attacks, as 'terrorists want a lot of people watching and a lot of people listening'.[27]

The strong overlap between terrorism and civil war suggests more generally that similar motives and causes are likely to be relevant for both and raises the question of whether the changes leading to a decline in civil war may also help contain terrorism. I will argue in the next section that there is considerable support for this.

Learning about Causes of the Decline in Violence

Even if the empirical claim that conflict is declining is relatively well supported and gaining acceptance, there is less consensus on specific causes for the decline. Some suggested explanations invoke very broad phenomena, in particular the idea that violence declines as part of a more general civilizing process,[28] with little delineation of clear mechanisms. In this sense, the current macro-level research takes a step back from earlier efforts to explain variation in conflict risk for state or pairs of actors, which typically emphasize particular classes of conflict, with specific motivating, facilitating, or inhibiting factors.

I will focus primarily on the causes of domestic conflict. The causes for the decline of interstate conflict are, in my view, generally better understood and documented elsewhere, thus providing a better basis for predicting future conflict risks. Territory is widely regarded as a main motive for interstate conflict. Although contested territory remains common, Goertz, Diehl, and Balas argue that the emergence of international norms and conflict management institutions have made territorial conquest less likely to succeed and they have suppressed escalation to military conflict.[29] Doctrines of humanitarian intervention or the responsibility to protect and prevent human rights could conceivably be invoked to justify more efforts to change the government in other states through force.[30] However, there is no evidence that increases in interventions of these type outweigh the decline in violent territorial conflict. Beyond international institutions, the research on the liberal peace in representative political systems emphasizes how potential higher economic disruption has made interstate conflict more costly and increased the likelihood that the public would oppose and thus constrain any leader's inclination to resort to aggressive actions.[31]

Many see domestic political violence as essentially a Hobbesian problem of weak states and emphasize how stronger states can create stable orders and deter violent challenges.[32] The finding that civil wars are more common in poorer countries is sometimes seen as supporting the importance of state strength. Few would deny that greater coercive capacity can make military challenges by non-state actors more difficult. However, coercive capacity is arguably only one component of state capacity, which also includes other features such as public goods provision, bureaucratic and administrative capacity, as well as integrative capacity.[33]

Beyond a failure of military deterrence or insufficient coercive capacity, states may 'fail' in the sense of either generating or not addressing political or social grievances that motivate dissident mobilization and a willingness to resort to violence. They key political motives for civil war are aspirations for independence through territorial separation/ethnic autonomy or changing control over the government to overcome political and economic exclusion. The most common operational measure for state capacity, per capita income, could also reflect a number of other characteristics, such as widespread poverty, that could induce grievances and motivate political revolt, and the empirical findings are thus more ambiguous.

The new wave of research on civil war that emerged after the Cold War was very critical of the earlier research on grievances as a motive for rebellion, notably the work of Gurr.[34] The criticisms hinged on a number of theoretical and empirical points. The older grievance literature emphasized actions based largely on psychological individual factors in ways that did not sit easily with rational-actor approaches to political mobilization. It also largely overlooked the problem of collective action when any benefits of mobilization for political change are collective and non-excludable while, at the same time, the cost to individual participation is great.[35] Critics argued that grievances were ubiquitous while rebellion was not. Early influential analyses of civil war also claimed that the grievance motivation could be dismissed as irrelevant on empirical grounds, since common factors such as income inequality and political democracy did not seem to provide strong predictors to identify countries prone to civil war.[36]

A number of subsequent studies challenge this dismissal of grievances as premature and argue that stronger attention to theories and better measures provide much stronger evidence in support of political and economic inequalities as a core motivation for conflict by disadvantaged groups. Cederman, Gleditsch, and Buhaug, for example, argue that political and economic grievances have clear, identifiable influences on the willingness to resort to violence when they overlap with ethnic group cleavages, where groups have established collective identities and networks that facilitate collective action.[37] Using new disaggregated data on ethnic groups and conflict involvement, they demonstrate a systematically higher risk of civil war for ethnic groups that are either politically excluded or economically marginalized relative to the national average. Although opportunities clearly are not irrelevant, as larger excluded ethnic groups are more likely to become involved in civil war, civil wars do not break out simply when groups are large in the absence of plausible grievances and exclusion, as the simple state-strength argument would suggest.

Beyond groups or interests that are ethnically defined, we can think of general political exclusion through authoritarian rule as a motivating factor. Democratic political institutions allow aggrieved groups to utilize nonviolent political means to bring about change rather than resorting to violent challenges.[38] This does not mean that the underlying conflict between actors disappears, but alternative tactics become more attractive than the use of violence. Indeed, few new civil wars have broken out in democratic states. Democracy and ethnic cleavages can have a complicated relationship, however, and some civil wars involve peripheral ethnic communities that see themselves as under colonialization or marginalized from national political institutions, even if we have transitions to competitive elections. Prominent examples include Basques in Spain or Catholics in Northern Ireland. Beyond conventional civil war, domestic terrorism has often been motivated by similar concerns. Engene notes that the bulk of terrorist events in Western Europe since 1945 were carried out by ethnically based terrorist organizations and sees the failure to successfully integrate ethnic minorities in nation-states as the main cause.[39] For example, the most active group in his data is the Corsican separatist group *Front de la Libération Nationale de la Corse* (FLNC), advocating independence from France.

In sum, there is a growing recognition that political and economic grievances are important motives for domestic political violence. Thus, changes

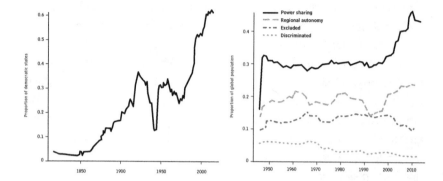

FIGURE 15.3. *Left panel: share of democratic states, based on Polity data.*[42] *Right panel: share of global population by political ethnic status, based on Ethnic Power Relations data.*[43]

towards greater accommodation and addressing grievances over in recent times provide a plausible candidate for the observed decline of violence. By the logic above, the major wave of transitions to democracy since the 1970s should provide more opportunities for substitution to nonviolent political methods,[40] even if the underlying incompatibilities do not cease to be relevant. As first shown by Gurr,[41] ethnic discrimination has declined since the end of the Cold War, and active ethnic inclusion through arrangements such as power-sharing or regional autonomy have become increasingly frequent. The left-hand panel in figure 15.3 documents the pronounced increase in democracy, while the right-hand panel indicates a decrease in active ethnic exclusion and discrimination and an increase in ethnic power-sharing and regional autonomy arrangements since the end of the Cold War.

It is tempting to conclude that if political exclusion and marginalization can increase the risk of conflict, then by implication active inclusion and reform should also help promote conflict termination and reduce the likelihood of civil war and political violence. However, the latter turns out to be a more contentious claim than the former, in part because political violence can be path-dependent and difficult to eradicate once violent organizations have become established.

Indeed, the perceived inexorable rise of civil war was accompanied by a widespread belief that weakening authoritarian rule would tend to exacerbate conflict and instability.[44] A more common contemporary scepticism points to how most conflicts are not new outbreaks per se, but rather recurrences of previous armed conflicts. Power-sharing or regional autonomy arrangements may be characteristic of peaceful societies, but sceptics question whether government reform will bring peace to societies that have experienced conflict, as violent organizations can have incentives to continue to use violence to increase their own influence further rather than accept an agreement that limits their influence.[45] Others point to how agreements can give rise to spoilers and extremists who try to undermine proposed settlements through violence.[46] Efforts to provide accommodation can be highly contentious and are often rejected by hard-liners on the government side who feel that concessions go too far, while factions on the rebel or dissident side may feel that concessions do not go far enough.

All attempts to provide settlements will create winners and losers, but I believe that existing research has been overly pessimistic about the ability to induce peace through accommodation. There is accumulating evidence that accommodation lowers the motivation and incentives for political violence and hence the expected frequency of conflict. Going beyond the observed data, Buhaug, Cederman, and Gleditsch use their model estimates to predict conflict out-of-sample and show that adding information on ethnic exclusion and inequality provides more accurate forecasts of where we see conflict than a model limited to standard country characteristics reflecting state strength or development.[47]

Moreover, beyond an association in levels, there is also evidence that the actual changes that we have observed away from ethnic discrimination and toward ethnic inclusion and democratization precede a lower risk of ethnic conflict. Cederman, Gleditsch, and Wucherpfennig revisit Gurr's 2000 prediction that the decline in ethnic warfare would continue, by asking whether one could anticipate a decline of conflict from the mid-1990s, based on a model using only the data available at the time and the changes observed in the world towards greater ethnic accommodation.[48] Their results show that, taking into account the changes toward greater group accommodation, the analysis successfully predicts a lower incidence of conflict that tracks the observed decline in ethnic conflict quite well. By contrast, a purely trend-based projection of ethnic conflict, ignoring any positive changes toward accommodation, vastly over-predicts conflict in the forecast period.

This largely positive assessment at first seems at odds with the more cautious conclusions of the literature on power-sharing and conflict institutions. These seemingly divergent findings can be reconciled by looking beyond binary conceptions of violence and how accommodation affects the incentives of specific actors. Gleditsch and Polo show that group-specific accommodation leads to lower frequency of terrorist attacks associated with the ethnic group, even if terrorism may not be fully eradicated.[49]

One simple way to think about these results is to consider how accommodation will affect active support and recruitment to an organization.[50] All groups need to recruit personnel and acquire resources to carry out sustained terrorist campaigns. If the group constituency includes a mix of individuals ranging from moderate to more extreme in terms of the settlements with the government that they will accept, then any settlement that improves on the status quo for the group should satisfy at least some and reduce recruitment or funding. Thus, even if the leadership of an organization reject reforms as inadequate or splinter groups emerge in opposition to an agreement, the ability of actors to sustain a large number of attacks will be reduced. For example, the 1998 Good Friday Agreement did not completely eradicate terrorism in Northern Ireland, but the number of attacks by dissident republicans was clearly much lower afterwards than during the peak of the activities of the Irish Republican Army.

Gleditsch and Polo find evidence that these experiences generalize beyond Western Europe and the frequency of ethnic terrorist attacks declines notably following accommodation.[51] This is consistent with the view that it is possible to bring about the move from terrorist attacks to conventional political engagement through accommodation. Gleditsch and Polo estimate 60 percent additional terrorist attacks in the absence of the changes, away from discrimination against ethnic groups that we have observed since 1970. Residual groups and splinter groups may step up activities, but their overall activity will be lower. This is not in line with the pessimistic claims about the transformation of political violence. Rather, terrorism often seems to be driven by motives that are at least conceptually similar to the societal incompatibilities seen in civil wars, and the factors that have plausibly reduced conventional conflict also appear to exert similar effects on terrorist activity.

Figure 15.1 also suggest similar results for the magnitude of civil wars, as the number of deaths in civil wars has declined more than the number of conflicts that are in progress, reflecting generally that the active armed conflicts are smaller in scale but a large number of splinter groups are involved in recurrent conflicts, with the notable exception of the Syrian civil war.

Beyond domestic political accommodation as a form of conflict management, there is also likely to be an important international component in the decline of civil war through international conflict-management efforts. The end of the Cold War and the rivalry between the superpowers greatly expanded the opportunities for the UN to try to assist parties in settling violent domestic conflict. Doyle and Sambanis highlight how the UN can help compensate for lack of governance and state capacity at the local level and show that civil wars are less likely to recur when we see comprehensive peacekeeping missions.[52] Others emphasize how the UN and other external parties can help the antagonists overcome practical challenges in peace processes, such as commitment problems that may arise under pervasive mistrust between the parties involved.[53]

A proposed peace agreement may in principle be acceptable to all the parties involved, yet specific terms such as demobilization or elections may be difficult to implement if one side fears exploitation by the other. Consistent with such an interpretation, peacekeeping missions make ongoing civil conflicts more likely to terminate,[54] and there is also evidence the deployment of peacekeeping to specific places helps decrease future conflict events in that location and confine the geographical spread of conflict.[55]

Moreover, although there is often a gap between demand and supply of conflict management efforts, the organization of peacekeeping has evolved to make greater use of relatively less expensive troops from developing countries, and the pool of contributing countries has increased from only 46 in 1990 to 120 in 2010.[56]

Conclusion: The Future of Peace

There is a renewed interest in the possibilities for predicting conflict. This is spurred both by a negative recognition that many studies of conflict are prone to over-fitting to the observed data and do not have good predictive power out-of-sample, as well as a growing positive recognition of possibilities for improving predictive modelling and its benefits for theory evaluation.[57] We have seen that considering group-specific grievances helps improve on predictions of the locations and places that are likely to see conflict out-of-sample, at least when looking ahead over short time periods. Can this type of knowledge also help us evaluate the prospects for long-term and stable peace through accommodation?

Long-range forecasting is a rather different proposition than the short-term, out-of-sample forecasts that are typically considered. Short-term forecasts of conflict risks usually assume that the relevant factors influencing political violence stay constant or change in simple, pre-specified ways—for example, a simple intervention in one location.[58] For long-term forecasts, we need to forecast the factors affecting political conflict into the future. Some researchers have developed elaborate models to try to project some of the core factors believed to affect conflict and forecast the incidence of conflict over the next fifty years.[59] These models usually do not seek to make point predictions about specific likely future conflicts, but rather try to provide forecasts of the likely overall amount of conflict and how this differs under different specific scenarios. From this perspective, such models can provide structured ways to consider the future of conflict and peace under more or less difficult or benign scenarios, the likelihood of each of these scenarios coming about, and the effects of possible interventions. I will not attempt to fully review formal prediction models here but instead comment on likely development in the key factors relevant to peace discussed above, based on our current knowledge. Plausible scenarios should take into account both past trends as well as our theoretical knowledge on limiting factors and our confidence that the relationship will be stable. Nordhaus provides an insightful critique of global modelling efforts based on resource-use availability that ignore existing data and economic theory.[60]

In terms of political accommodation, I believe that there are considerable grounds for optimism that current changes will remain stable and that further advances are likely. Both political democracy and group-specific accommodation show positive historical trends, and simply projecting past trends thus suggests future improvements. Moreover, we have not seen the dramatic reversals proposed by sceptics after the end of the Cold War. There was a clear and important reversal of democracy during the interwar period, but the apparent second wave of democratic reversals in figure 15.3 is primarily due to the emergence of new independent autocracies with decolonialization.[61] Many countries and regions retain significant forms of political exclusion.

The Arab Spring may have failed to bring about democratic transitions, and many regimes have shown their willingness to resort to extreme measures to retain political power when challenged. However, future challenges tend to inspire new efforts, and it is also clear that many autocratic regimes face long-term challenges. At the time of writing, for example, declining income is likely to increase popular dissatisfaction and create incentives for elite opportunism and defection in oil-rich autocracies. External pressures have also increased; even if other countries do not follow fully consistent policies on demands for human rights and democracy, repressive autocracies have fewer opportunities for aid and military support than during the Cold War. Moreover, we see increased learning, organization, and innovation in dissident movements seeking to bring down dictators.[62] As such, I believe that future demands for political liberalization and group accommodation are likely to continue and to result in political changes that ultimately reduce the motives and incentives for violence. In the economic realm, the projected future trends also generally seem positive, suggesting decreasing global poverty and that globalization generally will increase welfare for the poorest.[63] Although these features alone may not lead to transitions to democracy, they are at least likely to support further improvements in governance.

With regards to international conflict management, the current outlook perhaps looks less rosy. There is some evidence of a deteriorating relationship between the major powers, thus decreasing the opportunities for UN involvement. We clearly do not have the same kind of overarching conflict of interest as during the Cold War. Yet some states, and notably the permanent Security Council members China and Russia, display concerns over US and Western dominance in international affairs. They are often reluctant to endorse international involvement in domestic conflicts and more likely to express concerns for the need to respect state sovereignty. Fears of Western dominance and exploitation were further fuelled by the NATO operation in Libya, which originally started with the limited objective to protect civilians during the civil war but eventually appeared to become extended to provide active support for efforts to bring down the Gaddafi regime. Tensions between the major powers have thwarted previous peacekeeping missions. For example, China vetoed the extension of the United Nations Preventive Deployment Force (UNPREDEP) in Macedonia in 1999, after the country recognized Taiwan,[64] thereby plausibly failing to prevent the subsequent 2001 Albanian revolt after the conflict in Kosovo.

A declining consensus between the superpowers does not necessarily mean that all proposed peacekeeping efforts will be opposed, but it may be more difficult to get consent for a mandate for UN involvement in major conflicts. Paradoxically, if the relatively easy conflicts have already been settled or benefitted from peacekeeping, we may be left with a set of conflicts that are particularly poorly suited to be addressed through international peacekeeping efforts. The UN's experiences with 'peace-making' have been largely negative, and observers generally conclude that peacekeeping is unlikely to work without broad support for a peace agreement framework among the conflict parties.[65]

Sceptics have pointed to a number of challenges that could undermine the positive trends highlighted. For example, some postulate that global warming will have direct effects that increase the risk of conflict as well as indirect social and economic effects that exacerbate conflict.[66] Others point to the lack of consensus on the consequences of conflict for climate change.[67] Ultimately, the consequences of climate change will also depend on the human capacity for adaptation, including our ability to convert to alternative energy sources and the costs of such alternatives. Many have expressed concerns over the consequences of unchecked population growth in the past—Ehrlich predicted that mass starvation would begin in the 1970s, as population growth would outpace food production.[68]

However, there is now increasing concern over the security implications of a declining and ageing population and the likely decline of the West relative to other parts of the world.[69] Huntington's predicted claims about future increases in 'clashes of civilizations' have not materialized twenty years later.[70] The relative persistence of conflict in Muslim countries, counter to the general decline of conflict,[71] combined with high popular resentment against the West over perceived interventions or support for unpopular governments, has the potential to fuel future terrorist attacks and conflict expansion.

Many interstate conflicts have emerged out of domestic conflicts,[72] with the Peloponnesian War and WWI as prominent examples. However, despite the many transnational links, the ongoing conflict in Syria has not escalated to a larger regional or interstate conflict, and it appears, if anything, as if risks of escalation have induced caution among other states. In sum, the above challenges are plausible sources of concern, but in the absence of stronger evidence for divergences from past trends, we still, in my view, lack a strong justification for assigning these pessimistic scenarios a higher probability than a more optimistic scenario where the past positive trends either continue or at least do not deteriorate.

In a previous millennium, I wrote a doctoral dissertation on the diffusion of democracy, conflict, and peace.[73] I noted that interstate conflict had declined after the end of the Cold War but did not systematically discuss the possibility of a long-term decline in civil war, even though my main argument implied that both conflict and peace were affected by transnational factors and diffusion processes. In this sense, a main force for the future of civil peace is how peace itself has substantial benefits that can help further strengthen the prospects for peace. We know that conflict is contagious in time and space. Most domestic conflict outbreaks tend to be related to previous violence. Moreover, conflict has spill over effects that can increase the risk of conflict in other countries.

Conversely, longer spells of peace make conflict recurrence substantially less likely. Beyond the direct effects of peace, stable peace is likely to contribute to other factors that affect the risk of conflict, such as accommodation, governance, and prosperity. Regional peace can foster prosperity and encourage reform, and the positive experiences of peace in other countries and examples of conflict settlement can diffuse to other states through learning and emulation. Although Milton's poem 'To the Lord General Cromwell, May 1652' first praised the puritan leader for his willingness to use force, 'through . . . a cloud of war', his subsequent claim that 'peace has its victories too, no less renowned than war' alerts us to how peace itself can be an important force for change.

Notes

1. Joshua Goldstein, *Winning the War on War* (Plume, 2012); Pinker, *The Better Angels of our Nature*.
2. Pitirim A. Sorokin, *Social and Cultural Dynamics* (London: Owen, 1957[1937]); Lewis F. Richardson, *Statistics of Deadly Quarrels* (Pittsburgh, PA: Quadrangle/Boxwood, 1960).
3. Jack Levy, *War in the Modern Great Power System, 1495–1975* (Lexington, KY: University of Kentucky Press, 1983), 114–36.
4. Kenneth Waltz, *Man, the State and War: A Theoretical Analysis* (New York: Columbia University Press, 1959), 188.
5. James D. Fearon, 'Rationalist Explanations for War,' *International Organization* 49, no. 3 (2015): 379–414. Fearon stresses information asymmetries and commitment problems as possible explanations for war within a unitary rational actor framework. However, one can also imagine 'irrational' factors such as honour and aggression as alternatives, or domestic politics or private incentives undermining the unitary actor assumptions.
6. John Mueller, 'The Catastrophe Quota: Trouble after the Cold War,' *Journal of Conflict Resolution* 38, no. 3 (1994): 355–75.
7. Peter Wallensteen and Margareta Sollenberg, 'After the Cold War: Emerging Patterns of Armed Conflict 1989–94,' *Journal of Peace Research* 32, no. 3 (1995): 345–60. These data were later extended back to 1945 in Nils Petter Gleditsch, Peter Wallenstein, Mikael Eriksson, Margareta Sollenberg, and Havard Strand, 'Armed Conflict 1946–2001: A New Dataset,' *Journal of Peace Research* 39, no. 5 (2002): 615–37.

8. Peter Wallensteen and Margareta Sollenberg, 'The End of International War? Armed Conflict 1989–95,' *Journal of Peace Research* 33, no. 3 (1996): 353–70.

9. Ted R. Gurr, 'Ethnic Warfare on the Wane,' *Foreign Affairs* 79, no. 3 (2000), 52–64; see also Ernest J. Wilson and Ted R. Gurr, 'Fewer Nations are Making War, *Los Angeles Times*, 22 August 1999.

10. Gleditsch et al., 'Armed Conflict'.

11. Bethany Lacina and Nils Petter Gleditsch, 'Monitoring Trends in Global Combat: A New Dataset of Battle Deaths,' *European Journal of Population Studies* 21, nos. 2–3 (2005): 145–66.

12. Some analyses focusing on more encompassing measures of interstate tensions such as the militarized interstate disputes (MIDs) claim to find an increasing frequency of interstate conflict, see e.g., Mark Harrison and Nikolaus Wolf, 'The Frequency of Wars,' *Economic History Review* 65, no. 3 (2012): 1055–76. However, there is no increase in the frequency of MIDs with casualties, which in turn calls for an explanation of why MIDs escalate less frequently to violence, see Kristian Skrede Gleditsch and Steve Pickering, 'Wars Are Becoming Less Frequent: A Reply to Harrison and Wolf,' *Economic History Review* 67, no. 1 (2014): 214–30. There are also strong reasons to believe that the apparent increase in non-fatal MIDs may reflect better reporting over time of lower-level conflict. There most recent version of the MID data also show a decreasing trend in new onsets, and the coding criteria have been applied more strictly than in previous versions, see Glenn Palmer, Vito D'Orazio, Michael Kenwick, and Matthew Lane, 'The MID4 Dataset, 2002–2010: Procedures, Coding Rules and Description,' *Conflict Management and Peace Science* 32, no. 2 (2015): 215.

13. E.g., John Gray, 'Steven Pinker Is Wrong about Violence and War'; Slavo Žižek, *Violence* (London: Verso, 2008).

14. Anita Gohdes and Megan Price, 'First Things First: Assessing Data Quality Before Model Quality,' *Journal of Conflict Resolution* 57, no. 6 (2012), 1090–108.

15. A separate concern is whether the observed data suffice for inferences about changes in the underlying distribution of conflict. Cirillo and Taleb extend research by Richardson on the heavy-tailed frequency and severity distribution of war and the apparent random timing of war outbreaks. Their analysis shows how we would need much longer periods without severe wars to reject the null hypothesis of no fundamental change in their likelihood. This result is not controversial per se, but their interpretation that this undermines any claim of a decline in conflict is. Pinker and others argue that supporting evidence from other types of violence can strengthen confidence in that violence has declined, and advocate looking at alternative outcomes beyond just the severe wars, as well as factors believed to affect the risk of conflict to gain information about the likelihood of shifts in underlying distributions and the risk of future wars. Both Cederman et al. and Braumoeller provide evidence for structural shifts in conflict frequency rates after the Cold War, but Braumoeller expresses concerns about the lack of tests for the significance of the absence of major power wars after 1945. Braumoeller (this volume); Lars-Erik Cederman, Kristian

Skrede Gleditsch, and Julian Wucherpfennig, 'Predicting the Decline of Ethnic Civil War: Was Gurr Right and for the Right Reasons?' *Journal of Peace Research* 54, no. 2 (2017): 262–74; Cirillo and Taleb, 'On the Statistical Properties and Tail Risk of Violent Conflicts,' *Physica A: Statistical Mechanics and Its Applications* 452, no. 15, (2016): 29–45, and this volume; Lewis F. Richardson, 'The Distribution of Wars in Time,' *Journal of the Royal Statistical Society* 57, nos. 3/4 (1944): 242–50; Lewis F. Richardson, 'Variation of the Frequency of Fatal Quarrels with Magnitude,' *Journal of the American Statistical Association* 43, no. 244, (1948): 523–46; Michael Spagat and Steven Pinker, 'Warfare,' *Significance* 14, no. 3 (2016): 44.

16.   Konstantin Ash, 'Representative Democracy and Fighting Domestic Terrorism,' *Terrorism and Political Violence* 28, no. 1 (2016):114–34; Gray, 'Steven Pinker Is Wrong'; Mary Kaldor, *New Wars and Old Wars: Organised Violence in a Global Era* (Cambridge: Polity, 2013[1999]); Žižek, *Violence*.

17.   Civil war can be defined as armed conflict involving organized actors (of which at least one is a state) with a specific political incompatibility (i.e., territory or government), that generates battle deaths beyond some minimum threshold (i.e., twenty-five in the case of the Uppsala/PRIO data; see Gleditsch et al., 'Armed Conflict').

18.   *2015 Global Terrorism Index 2015*, 7 (accessed on 28 October 2018), http:// economicsandpeace.org/wp-content/uploads/2015/11/Global-Terrorism-Index-2015 .pdf.

19.   A content analysis uncovered more than 260 distinct definitions of terrorism in the academic literature. See Alex P. Schmid and Albert J. Jongman, *Political Terrorism: A New Guide to Actors, Authors, Concepts, Data Bases, Theories, and Literature* (New Brunswick, NJ: Transaction, 1988).

20.   Todd Sandler, 'The Analytical Study of Terrorism: Taking Stock,' *Journal of Peace Research* 50, no. 2 (2014): 257–71.

21.   Gary LaFree and Laura Dugan, 'Introducing the Global Terrorism Database,' *Terrorism and Political Violence* 19, no. 2 (2007): 181–204. Note that the GTD has no data for the year 1993.

22.   Jan Oskar Engene, *Terrorism in Western Europe: Explaining the Trends since 1950* (Cheltenham, UK: Edward Elgar, 2005); Benjamin Valentino, 'Why We Kill: The Political Science of Political Violence against Civilians,' *Annual Review of Political Science* 17 (2014): 89–103.

23.   LaFree and Dugan, 'Introducing the Global Terrorism Database.'

24.   Gleditsch et al., 'Armed Conflict.'

25.   Sara M.T. Polo and Kristian Skrede Gleditsch, 'Twisting Arms to Send a Message: Terrorism in Civil War,' *Journal of Peace Research* 169, no. 3 (2016): 207–29.

26.   'Dying to Lose: Explaining the Decline in Global Terrorism,' *Human Security Brief 2007* (Vancouver: Simon Fraser University), accessed on 28 October 2018, https:// www.files.ethz.ch/isn/55856/HSRP_Brief_2007.pdf.

27.   Brian M. Jenkins, 'International Terrorism: A New Mode of Conflict,' in *International*

Terrorism and World Security, eds, D. Carlton and C. Schaerf (London: Croom Helm, 1975), 15.

28. Norbert Elias, *The Civilizing Process*. (Oxford: Blackwell, 2000[1939]).

29. Goertz, *The Puzzle of Peace*.

30. Ryan Goodman, 'Humanitarian Intervention and Pretexts for War,' *American Journal of International Law* 100, no. 1 (2006): 107–41; Bruce M. Russett, 'Bushwhacking the Democratic Peace,' *International Studies Perspectives* 6, no. 4 (2005): 395–408.

31. John R. Oneal and Bruce M. Russett, *Triangulating Peace: Democracy, Interdependence, and International Organizations* (New York: Norton, 2001). Ray and Russett argue that the end of the Cold War could have been anticipated from the pacifying effects of democracy and globalization, although they focus on tension between the superpowers rather than a decline of interstate conflict in general. James Lee Ray and Bruce M. Russett, 'The Future as Arbiter of Theoretical Controversies: Predictions, Explanations and the End of the Cold War,' *British Journal of Political Science* 26, no. 4 (2016): 441–70.

32. James D. Fearon and David D. Laitin, 'Ethnicity, Insurgency, and Civil War,' *American Political Science Review* 97 (2003): 75–90; Samuel P. Huntington. *Political Order in Changing Societies* (New Haven: Yale University Press, 1968); Steven Pinker, *The Blank Slate* (New York: Penguin, 2002).

33. Kenneth E. Boulding, *The Three Faces of Power* (Newbury Park, CA: Sage, 1992); Cullen S. Hendrix, 'Measuring State Capacity: Theoretical and Empirical Implications for the Study of Civil Conflict,' *Journal of Peace Research* 47, no. 3 (2010): 273–85.

34. Ted R. Gurr, *Why Men Rebel* (Princeton, NJ: Princeton University Press, 1970).

35. Mark I. Lichbach, *The Rebel's Dilemma* (Ann Arbor, MI: Michigan University Press, 2015).

36. Paul Collier and Anke Hoeffler, 'Greed and Grievance in Civil War,' *Oxford Economic Papers* 56, no. 4 (2004): 563–95; Fearon and Laitin, 'Ethnicity, Insurgency, and Civil War.'

37. Lars-Erik Cederman, Kristian Skrede Gleditsch, and Halvard Buhaug, *Grievances and Inequality in Civil Wars* (Cambridge and New York: Cambridge University Press, 2013).

38. Kristian Skrede Gleditsch and Håvard Hegre, 'Regime Type and Political Transition in Civil War,' in *Routledge Handbook of Civil War*, eds. Karl DeRouen and Edward Newman (London: Routledge, 2014), 145–56.

39. Engene, *Terrorism in Western Europe*; Jan Engene, 'Five Decades of Terrorism in Europe: The TWEED Dataset,' *Journal of Peace Research* 44, no. 1 (2007): 109–21.

40. Kristian Skrede Gleditsch and Michael D. Ward, 'The Diffusion of Democracy and the International Context of Democratization,' *International Organization* 60, no. 4 (2016): 911–33.

41. Gurr, 'Ethnic Warfare on the Wane.'

42. Keith Jaggers and Ted R. Gurr, 'Tracking Democracy's Third Wave with the Polity III Data,' *Journal of Peace Research* 32 (1995): 469–82.

43. Lars-Erik Cederman, Andreas Wimmer, and Brian Min, 'Why Do Ethnic Groups Rebel? New Data and Analysis,' *World Politics* 62, no. 1 (2010): 87–119.

44. Jack Snyder, *From Voting to Violence: Democratization and Nationalist Conflict* (New York: Norton, 2000).

45. Donald L. Horowitz, 'Ethnic Power Sharing: Three Big Problems,' *Journal of Democracy* 25, no. 2 (2014): 5–20; Phillip G. Roeder and Donald Rothchild, *Sustainable Peace: Democracy and Power after Civil Wars* (Ithaca, NY: Cornell University Press, 2005).

46. Michael G. Findley and Joseph K. Young, 'Terrorism, Spoiling, and the Resolution of Civil Wars,' *Journal of Politics* 77, no. 2 (2015): 1115–28; Stephen J. Stedman, 'Spoiler Problems in Peace Processes,' *International Security* 22 (1997): 5–53.

47. Halvard Buhaug, Lars-Erik Cederman, and Kristian Skrede Gleditsch, 'Square Pegs in Round Holes: Inequalities, Grievances, and Civil War,' *International Studies Quarterly* 58, no. 2 (2014): 418–31.

48. Cederman et al., 'Predicting the Decline of Ethnic Civil War.'

49. Kristian Skrede Gleditsch and Sara M.T. Polo, 'Ethnic Inclusion, Democracy, and Terrorism,' *Public Choice* (2016).

50. Aaron Clauset and Kristian Skrede Gleditsch, 'The Developmental Dynamics of Terrorist Organizations,' *PLoS One* 7 (2012): e48633.

51. Gleditsch and Polo, 'Ethnic Inclusion.'

52. Michael W. Doyle and Nicholas Sambanis, *Making War and Building Peace: United Nations Peace Operations* (Princeton, NJ: Princeton University Press, 2006).

53. Barbara F. Walter, 'The Critical Barrier to Civil War Settlement,' *International Organization* 51, no. 3 (1997): 335–64.

54. Cederman et al., 'Predicting the Decline of Ethnic Civil War.'

55. Kyle Beardsley and Kristian Skrede Gleditsch, 'Peacekeeping as Conflict Containment,' *International Studies Review* 17, no. 1 (2015): 67–89; Theodora-Ismene Gizelis, Andrea Ruggeri, and Han Dorussen, 'Winning the Peace Locally: UN Peacekeeping and Local Conflict,' *International Organization* 71, no. 1 (2017): 163–85.

56. Vincenzo Bove and Andrea Ruggeri, 'Kinds of Blue: Diversity in UN Peacekeeping Missions and Civilian Protection,' *British Journal of Political Science* 46, no. 3 (2016): 681–700.

57. Phillip E. Tetlock, *Expert Political Judgment: How Good is it? How Can we Know?* (Princeton, NJ: Princeton University Press, 2005); Michael D. Ward, Brian D Greenhill, and Kristin M Bakke, 'The Perils of Policy by P-value: Predicting Civil Conflicts,' *Journal of Peace Research* 47, no. 5, (2010): 63–75.

58. In addition to the time horizon, there is an important distinction between classifying the overall distribution of conflict and predicting where and when individual events will occur. Forecasting a range of the likely number of events over a period is normally easier than to predict precisely when and where these events will occur.

59. Håvard Hegre, Joakim Karlsen, Håvard Mokleiv Nygård, Håvard Strand, and Henrik Urdal, 'Predicting Armed Conflict, 2010–2050,' *International Studies Quarterly* 57,

no. 2 (2013): 250–70; Barry B. Hughes, Devin K. Joshi, Jonathan D. Moyer, Jose Roberto Solorzano, and Timothy D. Sisk, *Strengthening Governance Globally* (Boulder, CO: Paradigm, 2014).

60. William D. Nordhaus, 'World Dynamics: Measurement without Data,' *The Economic Journal* 83, no. 332 (1973): 1156–83.

61. Gleditsch and Ward, 'The Diffusion of Democracy.'

62. Srdja Popovic and Mathew Miller, *Blueprint for Revolution: How to Use Rice Pudding, Lego Men and other Non-violent Techniques to Galvanize Communities, Overthrow Dictators or Simply Change the World* (New York: Spigel and Grau, 2015).

63. Hughes et al., *Strengthening Governance.*

64. Paul Lewis, 'Continuation of U.N. Force in Macedonia Faces a Chinese Veto,' *New York Times*, 24 February 1999, http://www.nytimes.com/1999/02/25/world/continuation-of -un-force-in-macedonia-faces-a-chinese-veto.html.

65. Doyle and Sambanis, *Making War and Building Peace.*

66. Solomon M. Hsiang, Marshall Burke, and Edward Miguel, 'Quantifying the Influence of Climate on Human Conflict,' *Science* 341 (2013): 10.1126/science.1235367.

67. Nils Petter Gleditsch and Ragnhild Nordås, 'Conflicting Messages? The IPCC on Conflict and Human Security,' *Political Geography* 43, no. 1 (2014): 82–90.

68. Paul Ehrlich, *The Population Bomb* (New York: Ballantine, 1968).

69. Jack A. Goldstone, 'The New Population Bomb: The Four Megatrends That Will Change the World,' *Foreign Affairs* 89, no. 1 (2010): 31–43.

70. Samuel P. Huntington, 'The Clash of Civilizations,' *Foreign Affairs* 72, no. 1 (1993): 22–49.

71. Nils Petter Gleditsch and Ida Rudolfsen, 'Are Muslim Countries More Prone to Violence?' *Research & Politics* (2016): 10.1177/2053168016646392

72. Kristian Skrede Gleditsch, Idean Salehyan, and Kenneth Schultz, 'Fighting at Home, Fighting Abroad: How Civil Wars Lead to Interstate Disputes,' *Journal of Conflict Resolution* 52, no. 4 (2008): 479–506.

73. Later published as Kristian Skrede Gleditsch, *All International Politics Is Local: The Diffusion of Conflict, Integration, and Democratization* (Ann Arbor, MI: University of Michigan Press, 2002).

CPSIA information can be obtained
at www.ICGtesting.com
Printed in the USA
BVHW030736081219
565983BV00003BA/7/P

9 781544 505053